Accession no.
36074373

KU-005-966

International Human Resource Management

2nd Edition

WITHDRAWN

Chris Brewster
Paul Sparrow
Guy Vernon

WITHDRAWN

Chris Brewster is Professor of International HRM at Henley Management College and the University of Reading.

Paul Sparrow is Director of the Centre for Performance-Led HR and Professor of International HRM at Lancaster University Management School.

Guy Vernon is Lecturer in Human Resource Management at Southampton University.

The CIPD would like to thank the following members of the CIPD Publishing editorial board for their help and advice:

- Pauline Dibben, Sheffield University
- Edwina Hollings, Staffordshire University Business School
- Caroline Hook, Huddersfield University Business School
- Vincenza Priola, Keele University
- John Sinclair, Napier University Business School

The Chartered Institute of Personnel and Development is the leading publisher of books and reports for personnel and training professionals, students, and all those concerned with the effective management and development of people at work. For details of all our titles, please contact the publishing department:
Tel: 020–8612 6200
Email publish@cipd.co.uk
The catalogue of all CIPD titles can be viewed on the CIPD website:
www.cipd.co.uk/bookstore

International Human Resource Management

2nd Edition

Chris Brewster
Paul Sparrow
Guy Vernon

LIS - LIBRARY

Date	Fund
13/7/09	bs

Order No.

2042678

University of Chester

Chartered Institute of Personnel and Development

Published by the Chartered Institute of Personnel and Development, CIPD House,
151, The Broadway, London, SW19 1JQ

This edition first published 2007
Reprinted 2008

© Chartered Institute of Personnel and Development, 2003, 2007

All rights reserved. No part of this publication may be reproduced, stored in a
retrieval system, or transmitted, in any form or by any means, electronic, mechanical,
photocopying, recording, or otherwise, without the prior written permission of the
publisher.

This publication may not be sold, lent, hired out or otherwise dealt with in the course
of trade or supplied in any form of binding or cover other than that in which it is
published without the prior written permission of the publisher.

No responsibility for loss occasioned to any person acting or refraining from action as
a result of any material in this publication can be accepted by the editor, authors or
publisher.

Designed and typeset by Kerrypress Ltd, Luton, Bedfordshire

Printed in Great Britain by The Cromwell Press, Trowbridge, Wiltshire

British Library Cataloguing in Publication Data
A catalogue of this publication is available from the British Library

ISBN 978 1 84398 159 6

The views expressed in this publication are the authors' own and may not necessarily
reflect those of the CIPD.

The CIPD has made every effort to trace and acknowledge copyright holders. If any
source has been overlooked, CIPD Enterprises would be pleased to redress this in
future editions.

Chartered Institute of Personnel and Development, CIPD House, 151, The Broadway, London, SW19 1JQ
Tel: 020 8612 6200
E-mail: cipd@cipd.co.uk   Website: www.cipd.co.uk
Incorporated by Royal Charter.   Registered Charity No. 1079797

Contents

LIST OF TABLES

LIST OF FIGURES

Acknowledgements

We are grateful to the United Kingdom's Chartered Institute for Personnel and Development and particularly to the past and present International Vice Presidents – Bob Morton, Peter Squire, John Campbell and Martin Ferber – and especially to Fran Wilson in the CIPD international office, for their support for the original research. We are grateful too to Mick Brookes from Middlesex Business School for his work on some of the tables. Finally, we would like to thank Ruth Lake and Jenna Steventon for their help throughout the production of the first and second editions of this book.

Chris Brewster, Paul Sparrow and Guy Vernon

International human resource management: an introduction

CHAPTER 1

CHAPTER OBJECTIVES

When they have read this chapter, students will:

- appreciate the growing internationalisation of the world in which HRM is conducted
- understand the additional complexity of HRM in an international context
- be able to describe the key features of the three main approaches to IHRM
- be able to identify some of the key HR challenges facing organisations working internationally
- know the format of the rest of the book.

INTRODUCTION

This chapter starts with a general introduction to the text – it outlines the dual objectives of the text:

- to give readers a better understanding of international HRM in a way that will help them as practitioners
- and, for those who are concerned, to help them get through the International Personnel and Development element of the CIPD Standards.

The first section explains what is new about this latest edition of the book. The next section (*Key trends*) considers the background of the growth of international business and the implications for HRM. The third section (*International HRM*) outlines the importance of countries and presents the three main approaches to IHRM: cultural, comparative and international. In so doing it explores the differences between domestic and international HRM for practitioners. The final section of this chapter (*An outline of the book*) provides a guide to the other chapters in the book.

LEARNING ACTIVITY

- From your experience and study of the subject, what do you consider to be the key elements of 'best practice' in HRM?
- To what extent can these be applied on a global level?

(Identify the reasons underlying your arguments.)

WHAT IS NEW ABOUT THIS EDITION?

The aim of this text remains the same: to help you explore the meaning and implications of the concepts of international and comparative human resource management. We do not assume that there is only one way of defining or understanding the nature of HRM. On the contrary, we believe that HRM varies according to the cultural and institutional environment in which it is conducted. A crucial aspect of this environment is the country in which HRM is conducted. This text addresses directly the issues raised by the fact that HRM is different from country to country. One effect that this must have is on people like you, who are trying to gain an understanding of the full range of meanings of HRM. Another effect is on those, like some of you, trying to manage HRM in organisations whose reach crosses national boundaries. These issues are covered in this text.

A key task for organisations which operate across international boundaries is to manage the different stresses of the drive for integration (being coherent across the world) and differentiation (being adaptive to local environments). Reading this text will give you some flavour of the way that HRM – and particularly what is seen as 'good' HRM – is defined differently in different national cultures, and is presented and operates differently in different national institutional environments; some flavour, too, of the ways in which international organisations attempt to deal with the issues these differences create.

We believe that the text will be of value to anyone involved in, or interested in, comparative and international human resource management. However, in writing it we have kept a close eye on the CIPD's International Personnel and Development Standards. If you are teaching a course, or studying for the CIPD qualification, this book will form a comprehensive course text.

ACTIVITY

- Why would adopting a global approach to managing people be beneficial to an organisation?
- Why might it be harmful?

Provide examples for each perspective.

For many of you, these first paragraphs will already be raising some key questions. What is the culture of Spain, with its Castilians, Catalans, Andalucians, Basques, etc? What is the culture of Singapore, with its Malay, Indian and Chinese populations? What is the institutional and labour market position of the European Union, where many laws apply across national boundaries and there are few institutional limitations to cross-border labour markets? And, of course, basing the text on national differences inevitably blurs some of these important 'within-nation' and 'beyond-country' issues. These are critical matters – but outside the scope of this text. We have chosen here to concentrate upon the national differences partly because they are so powerful (employment laws, labour markets, trade unions, etc, tend to operate at national level), and partly as an introduction to an often-neglected element of human resource management – the fact that it does vary considerably around the world. Our consideration of these issues is focused on Europe, but we will take the opportunity to draw on examples from other continents whenever that is appropriate.

We are using this new edition not just to bring our coverage of this rapidly changing subject even more up to date (see Sparrow, Brewster and Harris, 2004) but also to extend both the number of chapters and the material covered within the chapters. It has been fascinating to note that the number of books and articles on international and comparative human resource management has expanded almost exponentially even in the short time since the first edition of this text. Whereas in many organisations IHRM used to be the concern of a rather separate department arranging terms and conditions for expatriate employees, it is increasingly becoming a more and more significant part of organisations' attempts to manage their entire workforce across the world in the most cost-effective manner possible. As such, it is becoming a key contributor to organisational success. Little wonder, then, that it is beginning to attract the attention of more and more researchers, publishers and consultancies.

We note in the *Outline* of the book the details of the new topics that we have addressed chapter by chapter. Here it suffices to say that we have responded to the book's users by adding specific chapters detailing comparative aspects of training and development and reward, and have used the latest research to extend the material on the way that international organisations manage their workforces internationally.

KEY TRENDS

It is a truism to point out that the world is becoming more international. This applies to our technology, our travel, our economies and our communications – if not always obviously to our understanding. The growth of global enterprises leads to increased permeability in the traditional business boundaries, which in turn leads to high rates of economic change, a growing number and diversity of participants, rising complexity and uncertainty. Key indicators of this trend include:

- Multinationals are economically dominant – 63,000 transnational companies dominate world trade, accounting for two thirds of all of it. And the top 100 corporations account for 14% of worldwide sales, 12% of assets and 13% of employment (UNCTAD, 2004). The ten biggest of those industrial multinationals each have annual sales larger than the Australian government's tax revenues (*Economist*, 2000a). Around 60% of international trade involves transactions between two related parts of multinationals (*Economist*, 2000b).

- The physical location of economic value creation is difficult to ascertain. Multinational companies increasingly operate as seamless global organisations, with teams of workers based all over the world, passing projects backwards and forwards via the Internet or the companies' private in-house intranets. This makes it difficult for tax authorities to demand that economic activity and value creation be attributed to a particular physical location (*Economist*, 2000b).

- Economic consolidation through mergers and acquisitions remains a potent force for globalisation. The *Economist* Intelligence Unit analysed foreign direct investment (FDI) flows for 60 countries for the years 2001 to 2005 (*Trends International*, 2001) using econometric and competitiveness data. Despite the recent slump, overall investment rose from $6,500 billion in 2000 to $10,000 billion by 2005. The USA received 26.6% of global investment in this period, followed by the UK (9.3%), Germany (7.8%) and China (6.5%).

We are also witnessing the global transfer of work – either in terms of the creation of new jobs or through the global sourcing of certain parts of an individual's or unit's work. This is having a major impact on the type of organisations and nature of work that remain viable in different parts of the world. In the first wave of globalisation two decades ago, low-level manufacturing work began to transfer to low-cost locations. In the second wave, simple service work such as credit card processing began to relocate. In the third wave, higher-skill white-collar work is being transferred. By 2015 it is estimated that 3.3 million US white-collar jobs and $136 billion of wages will shift to low-cost countries (Engardio, Bernstein and Kripalani, 2003).

A few brief examples capture the issues. Bank of America is outsourcing up to 1,100 US jobs to Indian companies where work can be done at 20% of US labour cost; Philips has shifted research and development on most TVs, cell phones and audio products to Shanghai; and Boeing has faced industrial action after it opened its Moscow Design Centre, initially employing 700 Russian engineers.

INTERNATIONAL HUMAN RESOURCE MANAGEMENT

In all these international organisations or multinational enterprises (MNEs) human resource management (HRM) is a key to success. For the vast majority of organisations, the cost of the people who do the work is the largest single item of operating costs. Increasingly, in the modern world, the capabilities and the knowledge incorporated in an organisation's human resources are the key to success. So on both the cost and benefit sides of the equation, human resource management is crucial to the survival, performance and success of the enterprise. For international organisations, the additional complications of dealing with multicultural assumptions about the way people should be managed and differing institutional constraints become important contributors to the chances of that success.

The need for human resource specialists to adopt an increasingly international orientation in their functional activities is widely acknowledged and becoming ever clearer. It is important not just to people working in the giant MNEs but also to many in small to medium-sized enterprises (SMEs). The freer economic environment of the twenty-first century, the reduction of restrictions on labour movement in areas such as the European Community, and the advent of new technology have combined to mean that many fledgling enterprises operate internationally almost as soon as they are established. It is also worth reminding ourselves that international organisations do not have to be in the private sector. Many international organisations such as those in the UN family, the OECD, the regional trade bodies, etc, have employees who work across national borders. So do many charities and religious groups (Brewster and Lee, 2006).

Any review of world events over the last few years will emphasise the essentially unpredictable and rapidly changing nature of political, economic and social upheavals. Vaill (1989; p.2) used the metaphor of 'permanent white water' to describe the nature of doing business in the latter part of the twentieth century:

> **'Most managers are taught to think of themselves as paddling their canoes on calm, still lakes ... Sure, there will be temporary disruptions during changes of various sorts – periods when they will have to shoot the rapids in their canoes – but the disruptions will be temporary, and when things settle back down, they'll be back in a calm, still lake mode. But it has been my experience that you never get out of the rapids!'**

Managers working in an international environment are obviously more subject to the impact of multi-country, regional and global change and dynamism than managers in a single-country operation. And this applies to HR managers as much as any others (Stiles, 2006). Hardly surprisingly, choices in this context become complex and ambiguous.

LEARNING ACTIVITY

- Imagine that you are a human resource manager in a domestically based company that has decided to operate internationally. You have been charged with sorting out the HR effects of the decision.

What questions should you be asking?

HR professionals who contemplate internationalisation typically need to address the following:

- Do we have a strategy for becoming an international firm?

- What type of managers will we need to be successful? And how do we find or develop them?

- How can I find out about the way that HRM is conducted in other countries: the laws, trade unions, labour market, expectations ...?
- What will be the impact of local cultural norms on our home-based ways of working? Can we use all or any of them in other countries?
- How will we choose whether to send expatriates or use local employees?
- How do we manage international moves if we choose to send some people out from home?
- How do we manage knowledge across geographical and cultural distance?

The additional complexities of managing an international workforce in any of these organisations call for a different mindset and different skills for practitioners. A publication for the Chartered Institute for Personnel and Development (CIPD, 2002) argued that individuals working in an international context need to be competent in:

- interpersonal skills (especially cultural empathy)
- influencing and negotiating skills
- analytical and conceptual abilities
- strategic thinking

and that they will also need a broader base of knowledge in such areas as:

- international business
- international finance
- international labour legislation
- local labour markets
- cultural differences
- international compensation and benefits.

Furthermore, and to complete for a moment the list of complexities that internationalisation adds to the role of HR managers, they will have to manage a wider set of multiple relationships. HR managers in the European context, for instance, might find themselves having to deal with such groups as:

- headquarters, regional and subsidiary line managers
- headquarters and subsidiary employees
- national, European-level and international trade union bodies
- national and European-level legislative bodies
- local and regional communities.

How are we to start the process of understanding all this complexity? The first step is to be clear about different kinds of analysis. These are not always defined in the literature – partly perhaps because of a confusion in the United States of America, where 'international' is often applied to anything outside the USA. However, generally, the subject matter of IHRM is covered under three headings:

- cross-cultural management
- comparative human resource management

■ international human resource management.

In broad terms, authors in the *cross-cultural* tradition argue that every nation has its own unique sets of deep-lying values and beliefs, and that these are reflected in the ways that societies operate, and in the ways that the economy operates and people work and are managed at work. The *comparative* HRM tradition focuses more specifically on the way that people work and explores the differences between nations in the way that they manage this process. In general, the comparative tradition makes more of the institutional differences than the cultural differences. *International* HRM (and its more recent 'strategic' derivative, SIHRM) examines the way organisations manage their human resources across these different national contexts.

Cross-cultural management

A key factor in the increasing internationalisation of employment is that there are cultural differences between nations – differences in national values and attitudes. Many of us have stereotypes of taciturn Finns, ebullient Spaniards, work-obsessed Americans, polite Japanese, modest Malays, etc. These are stereotypes: even though the next Finn we meet may be loud and confident, the next Spaniard quiet and reserved, and so on, they indicate real, general, truths. There is now plenty of research evidence (see Chapter 2) that different nationalities do have different values and that these affect the way people organise, conduct and manage work.

An awareness of cultural differences is therefore an essential part of an international HR manager's brief. The normal HR activities such as recruitment and selection, training and development, reward and performance appraisal, may all be affected by cultural values and practices in the respective host countries. As a result, great care must be taken when deciding whether or not to adopt standardised HR policies and practices throughout the world.

Comparative human resource management

The distinction between comparative human resource management and international human resource management has been clearly made by Boxall (1995). Comparative human resource management explores the extent to which HRM differs between different countries – or occasionally between different areas within a country or different regions of the world, such as North America, the Pacific Rim states or Europe (Brewster and Larsen, 2000). We know that countries may be small or large, have more or fewer regional differences, include one or many language groups, and be more or less economically developed. More immediately, we know that they may have different labour markets and education systems, different employment laws and trade unions, and the different cultural expectations that we have already noted. It should be no surprise, therefore, to find that employment systems differ noticeably between countries and that managing human resources has to vary from country to country.

International human resource management

International HRM examines the way in which international organisations manage their human resources across these different national contexts. The international context adds extra complexity to the management of people beyond that found in a purely national setting.

The organisation that manages people in different institutional, legal, and cultural circumstances has to be aware not only of what is allowed and not allowed in the different nations and regions of the world, but also of what makes for cost-effective management practices. To take one often-quoted example: a performance appraisal system which depends upon US-style openness between manager and subordinate, each explaining plainly how they feel the other has done well or badly in their job, may work in some European countries. However, it is unlikely to fit with the greater hierarchical assumptions and 'loss-of-face' fears of some of the Pacific countries. It may even be unlawful in some states. The literature is replete with examples of such home-country practices that may be allowed in other countries but which depress rather than improve productivity and effectiveness.

Organisations that address IHRM, therefore, have to deal not just with a variety of practices but also with a range of policy and even strategy issues. IHRM explores how MNEs manage the demands of ensuring that the organisation has an international coherence in and cost-effective approach to the way it manages its people in all the countries it covers, while at the same time ensuring that it is responsive to the differences in assumptions and in what works from one location to another. This includes, in particular, the management of those people who have to work internationally.

AN OUTLINE OF THE BOOK

Following this introductory chapter, the text is divided into the three areas of theory we have already identified, and a section examining new developments and the role of HRM.

Part One deals with national cultures.

- *Chapter 2 The impact of national culture* on managing people defines the meaning of culture, outlines the literature on cultural differences, and explores the extent to which aspects of work practices are nationally or locally based. It uses some previously developed frameworks and applies these to the world of work.

- *Chapter 3 Culture and organisational life* continues this exploration, looking at the implications of operating across national cultures for concepts of business, management and human resource management. It first examines concepts of leadership – a key influence on the shape of HR policies and practices. The extent to which national cultures have different styles of leadership are discussed, and whether organisations can create global leaders. It also examines what makes for successful international/multinational teams (real and virtual). Finally, it considers the debates over the nature of cultural intelligence.

Part Two addresses the issue of comparative HRM. There is an overall theory chapter and then a series of chapters exploring the way that different aspects of HRM practices vary across national boundaries. It is important for readers to understand that in teaching these topics there is no longer a simple divide between Comparative and International HRM modules. Many of the topics and issues covered under a Comparative theme would find relevance on a course on International HRM. To provide an example: in the chapter on recruitment and selection (Chapter 6), the discussion of the impact of culture on practices is used to show how an in-country business partner of an MNE has to understand the local complexities of practice – a topic easily taught under an IHRM banner. Similarly, the coverage of new developments in global mobility and resourcing in that chapter could well be taught alongside traditional IHRM topics of expatriation. We have adopted this structure to best organise the material, but would emphasise that the conceptual divide between Parts Two and Three – and the relative number of chapters in each Part – should not be seen as indicative of the best way to either teach or learn about these topics. In the world of actual HR practice, the two perspectives are increasingly blended together. Part Two therefore concentrates principally on key HR functions.

- *Chapter 4 Comparative HRM: theory and practice* identifies the differences between the universalist and the contextualist paradigm and explores the contextual determinants for differences in country-level HR practices. Attention is paid to the different employment law and institutional contexts within which HRM specialists have to operate. This chapter also explores the attempts that have been made to group countries in relation to similarities of HR practices, explores whether

HRM in different countries is converging as a result of globalisation, and, given the origin of the notion of HRM in the USA, explores how far HRM prescriptions from the United States might apply in the rest of the world.

■ *Chapter 5 Comparative HRM: the role of the HR department* looks at similarities and differences at country level in relation to the meaning of HRM, the role of the national institutes, and the role of the HR department in terms of issues such as strategic integration and devolvement. The changing nature of HRM is briefly considered, but particular attention is given to the role of line management in HRM.

■ *Chapter 6 Comparative HRM: recruitment and selection* explores and compares some of the ways in which organisations across different countries act in order to obtain and retain the kinds of human resources they need. The chapter examines the resourcing process: making sure that the organisation has people of the right quality. It therefore looks first at recruitment and selection and considers the ways in which culture can be seen to influence such local HR practices. However, a good deal of international recruitment today is carried out in the context of global resourcing strategies and increasingly global labour markets. The chapter accordingly also looks at global skill supply strategies and the role of recruitment in the internationalisation of the organisation. Finally, it introduces some of the questions that these developments raise about the recruitment of international employees.

■ *Chapter 7 Comparative HRM: rewarding* explores the nature of rewards and the different bases of pay. It considers a number of theoretical perspectives important for the study of rewards, such as agency theory, socially healthy pay and distributive justice. The links between national culture and rewards practice are examined and attention is given to the international differences in the incidence of pay for performance and comparative evidence on best practice.

■ *Chapter 8 Comparative HRM: training and development* identifies key trends, similarities and differences at country level in relation to vocational education and training systems. It also explores workplace and on-the-job training. Finally, attention is given to development through participation and competence profiles.

■ *Chapter 9 Comparative HRM: flexibility and work–life balance* explores trends in the issue of flexible working practices and patterns. Flexible working practices include the development of such approaches as part-time employment, short-term employment and a host of other non-standard working forms. It explores the similarities and differences in the use and meaning of such practices across national boundaries and considers the impact of these practices at national, employer and individual levels, as well as the implications for HRM specialists. Finally, it looks at developments concerning work–life balance in an international context.

■ *Chapter 10 Comparative HRM: employee relations and communications* outlines the issues raised by individual and collective communications around the world. It identifies the range of employee relations systems around the world and examines the ways in which employers relate to trade unions in different countries.

Part Three of the book deals with international HRM, the way that different organisations respond to, deal with and exploit the different cultural and national institutional contexts within which they have to operate.

■ *Chapter 11 International HRM: theory and practice* begins by examining the different levels of analysis across which globalisation might be studied. It covers some of the main models that have influenced the field of IHRM such as life cycle, organisation design and contingency models. It then reviews theoretical perspectives in the field of strategic IHRM (SIHRM).

- *Chapter 12 Managing international working* considers the most widely discussed aspect of international HRM activities – managing people on international assignments. We start with an area that often gets less attention: analysing the function of and need for expatriates in the first place, or setting expatriation policies in a strategic context. We note trends in expatriation. Then we identify the critical components of the human resource management of the expatriation cycle.

- *Chapter 13 Managing diversity in international working* addresses issues of diversity in international organisations. These include new forms of international working, the nature of international working and its impact on individuals and on traditional career management processes in organisations, and the implications of international working on work–life balance for individuals. We also look at the ways in which the positive benefits of diversity can be harnessed.

Part Four of the book deals with new developments and the role of the HR function.

- *Chapter 14 New developments in international HRM.* In the last two chapters we make a distinction between those developments that are affecting the overall nature of international HRM inside organisations and the actual role of international HR professionals. In exploring the first of these issues, this chapter looks at some new developments, such as organisational capability, the impact of technology, models of shared service delivery and centres of excellence, and issues associated with levels of outsourcing, and global offshoring of HR activities.

- *Chapter 15 Managing international HRM* assesses the critical components of effectiveness for HR on a global scale. This involves understanding how the function can help develop global competitiveness and manage talent, the employee value proposition and employment brand on a global basis. The chapter evaluates the need to reconfigure the nature of HR in an international context.

SUMMARY

This chapter has introduced you to the overall aims and objectives of the book. In particular, it has examined the growing internationalisation of the world economy and detailed the additional complexity of human resource management in an international context. It has also introduced the three key approaches to the study of international human resource management. A central theme throughout the book is the need to balance integration and differentiation in human resource policy and practice.

REFERENCES

Boxall, P. (1995) 'Building the theory of comparative HRM', *Human Resource Management Journal*, 5 (5): 5–17

Brewster, C. J. and Larsen, H. H. (2000) *Human Resource Management in Northern Europe.* Oxford, Blackwell

Brewster, C. and Lee, S. (2006) 'HRM in not-for-profit international organisations: different, but also alike', in H. H. Larsen and W. Mayrhofer (eds) *European Human Resource Management.* London, Routledge

CIPD (2002) *Globalising HR.* London, Chartered Institute of Personnel and Development

Economist (2000a) 'Special report: A survey of globalisation and tax', *The Economist*, 354 (8155), 29 January: 1–18

Economist (2000b) 'The world's view of multinationals', *The Economist*, 354 (8155), 29 January: 21–2

Engardio, P., Bernstein, A. and Kripalani, M. (2003) 'The new global job shift', *Business Week*, 3 February

Harris, H., Brewster, C. and Sparrow, P. (2001) *Globalisation and HR: A literature review*. London, CIPD

Sparrow, P., Brewster, C. and Harris, H. (2004) *Globalising Human Resource Management*. London, Routledge

Stiles, P. (2006) 'The human resource department: roles, coordination and influence', in G. Stahl and I. Björkman (eds) *Handbook of Research in International HRM*. London, Edward Elgar

Trends International (2001) 'Foreign investment: Belgium favourite', *Trends International*, Belgium, April, 3: 42

UNCTAD (2004) Research Note: World Investment Report 2004 – the shift towards services. *Transnational Corporations* 13 (3): 87–124

Vaill, P. (1989) *Managing as a Performing Art: New ideas for a world of chaotic change*. San Francisco, Jossey-Bass

National cultures

The impact of national culture

When they have read this chapter, students will:

■ understand what culture is

■ appreciate how national cultures differ

■ be able to interpret the major cultural frameworks

■ know how to use culture to define attitudes and behaviours at work

■ understand the link between individual personality and culture

■ be aware of the limitations of over-generalising about culture.

INTRODUCTION

Case study

Individualism v accidents

In December 1999 a Korean Air Boeing 747 cargo plane crashed just after taking off from Stansted Airport. All four crewmen were killed. Eyewitnesses reported that the Boeing 747 appeared to explode in a 'huge fireball'. A far greater disaster was avoided only because the plane crashed in Hatfield Forest, rather than on a residential area, scattering debris over a wide area. The pilots did not have time to issue a mayday call.

This tragedy followed a series of safety-related incidents and accidents involving KAL, South Korea's national airline, whose rapid expansion had matched that of the South-East Asian economies. The company has one of the worst aviation safety records in the world. An estimated 700 people have died in crashes involving its planes over the past 20 years (World Socialist Web Site: www.wsws.org). Reports in the press pointed to problems with 'an insular cockpit culture' as a major factor in the tragedy. A Dow-Jones report (1999) cited Korea's authoritarian culture, reflected in a hiring and promotion policy favouring former military flyers over civilians. Too often the effect has been friction that hampers the pilot teamwork needed to fly Western-built jets. A rigid training programme and poor English were also perceived to make it harder for some Korean Air pilots to deal with air controllers and cope with emergencies.

Six years before this tragedy, Phillips (1994) had reported a study by the Boeing Commercial Airplane Group showing that countries with high individualism ratings had low aeroplane accident rates. Countries with a combination of high individualism and less hierarchical structures at work had accident rates 2.6 times lower than those with low individualism and strong hierarchical structures, such as Korea. A possible explanation put forward for this was the fact that highly individualistic pilots try to avert accidents by responding rapidly to perceived problems, whereas those from collectivist countries were more likely to confer with others before taking action, thus losing time to avoid accidents (Parker, 1998). The Korean Airlines tragedy eerily played out these earlier predictions and demonstrated the power of cultural conditioning on collective behaviours.

Differences in national cultures are apparent to any of us, even if we never step outside our own countries. The impact of information technology and global media has brought the world into our living-rooms. We can experience many of the manifestations of different cultures through the films, soaps and documentaries that abound on our screens. Travelling to another country heightens this sense of difference; food, customs, language, transport, housing, entertainment – all these everyday things may have to be reconsidered and seen through other eyes.

At the same time as we are gaining more knowledge about different cultures, the increasing globalisation of markets, competition and organisations has led many people to believe that cultures are converging. Advances in telecommunications, information technology and global consumer products are thought of as leading to a 'global village' in which everyone will be wearing the same brand-name jeans and trainers while watching MTV on Japanese digital televisions and texting their friends with the latest mobile phone technology. The rush to adopt 'world-class' manufacturing, logistics and marketing processes brings with it a belief in the convergence of management practice and the creation of a global corporate village. Under the convergence argument, management is management, consisting of a set of principles and techniques that can be universally applied.

In contrast, world events reflect a move towards divergence in cultures. For example, the tensions in world politics since 11 September 2001 vividly illustrated the deep and enduring nature of differences between the values and beliefs of the Western (capitalist) world and those of many Muslim societies. Ethnic conflicts in Central Europe and Africa in the last years of the twentieth century revealed a desire to protect and reinforce cultural differences between groups.

In the management context, the need to take cultural differences into account is demonstrated in the growing field of worldwide mergers and acquisitions. One recent survey of mergers and acquisitions involving large US firms reported that seven out of ten did not live up to their financial promise, and three-quarters of participants cited cultural incompatibility between the partners as the largest reason for failure (Grossmann, 1999).

WHAT IS CULTURE?

These opening paragraphs have indicated the all-pervading influence of culture on our actions and values, and also the ongoing tensions between the forces of convergence of cultures and those of divergence. The concept of culture is deeply rooted in human history and its scope extends far beyond the boundaries of organisational activity. However, organisations are the product of the societies and times in which they exist, and as such are important manifestations of prevailing values and belief sets. But what is culture exactly?

ACTIVITY

Think about the difference between countries – and try to write a definition of 'culture'.

Attempting a definition of culture is difficult. At present there are estimated to be over 200 different definitions. The concept of culture is often seen as being vague and hard to grasp.

One of the core elements of culture is that it is a shaping process. For a culture to exist, members of a group or society share a distinct way of life with common values, attitudes and behaviours that are transmitted over time in a gradual, yet dynamic, process. Schein (1985; p.9) defined culture as:

'a pattern of basic assumptions – invented, discovered, or developed by a given group as it learns to cope with its problems of external

adaptation and internal integration – that has worked well enough to be considered valid and, therefore, to be taught to new members as the correct way to perceive, think, and feel in relation to those problems.'

Although the problems that all human societies face are universal ('etic'), different groups will resolve them in different ways ('emic'). The resolutions are internalised and become taken for granted, but shape the way in which groups of people live and think. They represent the *why* – *why* people behave the way they do, and *why* they hold the beliefs and values they espouse (Schneider and Barsoux, 1997).

Schein's (1985) model of organisational culture can also be applied to the broader concept of culture (see Figure 1). This model sees culture in terms of three levels, each distinguished by its visibility and accessibility to individuals.

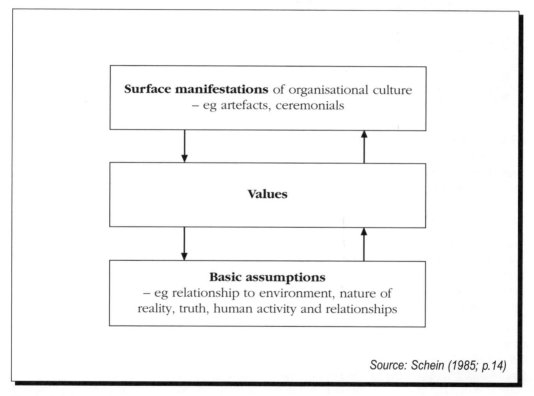

Source: Schein (1985; p.14)

Figure 1 *Schein's three levels of culture*

The *first level* consists of easily observed artefacts, rituals and behaviour. At this level culture is manifested in objects, customs, language and architecture. Within an organisational context we can observe many examples, such as differences in office space – ie preference for open or closed offices. In Japan, a highly collectivist country, large, open offices are the norm, whereas in Germany, a society where privacy is valued, separate offices are more likely. Where management fads impose practices that do not fit the culture of the society, we see adaptations such as the use of partition walls in open-plan offices by US and British workers, immortalised in the Dilbert cartoons. Dress codes, greetings rituals, the level of formality in addressing people – all these things and more make up the easily perceivable culture of the organisation (and likewise the nation).

The *second level* concerns values and beliefs. These are located below the surface manifestations and underpin them. Management scholars such as Hofstede, Trompenaars and Laurent (see below) have shown that employees and managers around the world differ widely in their values regarding work practices. Indeed, most work on national culture has concentrated on this level of analysis. Values, defined by Schwartz (1994) as cross-situational principles, lend themselves to easier measurement and can be linked to a lot of other work on individual psychology.

Finally, at the *third level* basic assumptions are the core of the culture. They include assumptions that individuals hold about societies and organisations and how they function. They relate to aspects of human behaviour, the nature of reality and the community's relationship to its environment. They are invisible, preconscious and 'taken for granted', and are therefore difficult to access.

Across these levels, cultural differences can be seen to lead to strongly contrasting ideas about what constitutes good management. In countries such as France, a leader must stand apart and be the expert. In contrast, Scandinavian countries prefer a more democratic and participative style of leadership. These issues are explored in more detail later in this chapter and the following one.

QUESTIONS

- What is the predominant style of leadership within your organisation?
- How does this reflect cultural influences?

Approaches to the study of culture

It is important to realise that people who study culture – anthropologists, sociologists, psychologists or management specialists – have to make a number of tacit assumptions, and each of these carries potential biases (Sackmann and Phillips, 2004). The way in which we conceptualise culture tends to make it or more or less legitimate to ask certain questions and identify different effects of culture. There have been three streams of research:

Cross-national comparisons, driven by a logic and assumption that 'culture equals nation'. This kind of research has been guided by a quest to determine universally applicable dimensions of national culture to help managers 'navigate' in different countries while doing their work. These dimensions of culture have generally been identified in large-scale quantitative studies. In this chapter we outline the best-known of these models.

Study of intercultural interactions – generally initiated once the competitive success of non-US management models was being questioned (such as the success of Japanese-transplant factories in the USA and the growth of European and Asian multinational corporations). National culture is still seen as a fundamental source of individual identification, but within an organisational setting culture is considered to emerge as a result of a 'hidden negotiation' between interaction partners. More attention in this type of study is given to how people interact across cultures and the characteristics and processes through which new cultures are formed.

The multiple cultures perspective, based on more recent conceptions of organisations operating in a multicultural context. Organisations are considered to be home to and carriers of several cultures at levels that include function, organisation and business unit, profession and occupational group, ethnic group, project-based network, regional institution, geographical and economic region, ideology and religion. Developments in information technology have enabled and accelerated the process of globalisation, and new communication media have brought a wealth of real-time information from remote cultures, thereby changing patterns of problem-solving at work. This approach argues that individuals may identify with and hold simultaneous membership in several cultural groups.

Elements of culture

The basic elements making up national-level cultures were seen by anthropologists Kluckhohn and Strodtbeck (1961) to lie in the responses that nations make in relation to six fundamental questions:

Who are we? How does a society conceive of people's qualities as individuals? If societies believe that people are basically good, they will try to exercise social control through praise and encouragement. If people are seen as fundamentally bad, control will be exercised via rules, laws and policing. If societies see people as capable of being changed, they will prefer reform to punishment. In management, this assumption can be seen in McGregor's (1960) Theory X and Theory Y. Under Theory X, workers are perceived to be lazy and therefore to require as much direction and control as necessary. In contrast, under Theory Y, workers are regarded as self-directed and responsible and requiring very little direct management.

How do we relate to the world? How important is nature and the environment in our thinking? And how do we conceive of nature? Some societies feel that it is important to fit in with the world and accept it, as expressed in the Arabic '*insh'allah*' or 'God willing'. In contrast, countries like the USA expect to overcome the constraints imposed by the environment. The American belief, continually voiced by celebrities such as Oprah Winfrey, that 'Anyone can be whatever they want' is exemplified in the Nike slogan 'Just do it!' This belief in individuals' ability to change strong environmental constraints is viewed by many in Europe and the East as naïve, where the influence of context in terms of societal norms and history is acknowledged.

What do we do? How do we think of ourselves and our situation? If you ask Britons 'What do you do?', they will tell you what profession they are in. If you ask the Japanese the same question, they will tell you who they work for. Are the most important things those you have done for yourself, or are they connected to your background and your group? Basically, status can be based either on what someone does, or on what someone is. In an ascriptive society, such as China or Venezuela, status is usually attributed to those who 'naturally' evoke admiration – for example, males and older people, or members of high-ranking families. In an achievement-based society, in contrast, a person gains status as a result of his or her own efforts and the climb up the organisational hierarchy.

How do we relate to each other? Do we think of ourselves as individuals or as members of a group? In many Western cultures we are happy to live far from members of our family and to have non-emotional links with the organisations we work for. In contrast, members of collectivist societies expect support from and loyalty to the extended family. In the business world, this aspect of culture affects the extent to which countries are happy with individual leadership and individual responsibility and target-setting, or the extent to which they prefer group working and shared responsibility instead.

How do we think about time? In a cultural sense, time has two elements, locus and speed. In Western societies time moves in one direction, with the locus of attention on the future. In other societies – in much of the Asia-Pacific region, for example – all parts of time are connected. The past is as important as the present, with the future regarded as less important. In a business context, Western societies see time as a commodity to be managed and used well. Other societies have a more relaxed approach to the timing of things, causing problems with perceptions of correct business conduct.

How do we think about space? The amount of space we feel we need varies around the world. In the northern hemisphere, the further west you go, the larger the rooms and offices tend to be. Physical space between people is also culturally determined. In Arab societies it is common to stand close to the person one is talking to; the British prefer to stand at about an arm's length away. The use of space in organisations gives clues as to the status of the person occupying the area, but these have to be interpreted from a cultural perspective.

These dimensions are amongst the most commonly used by management scholars, as shown in Figure 2.

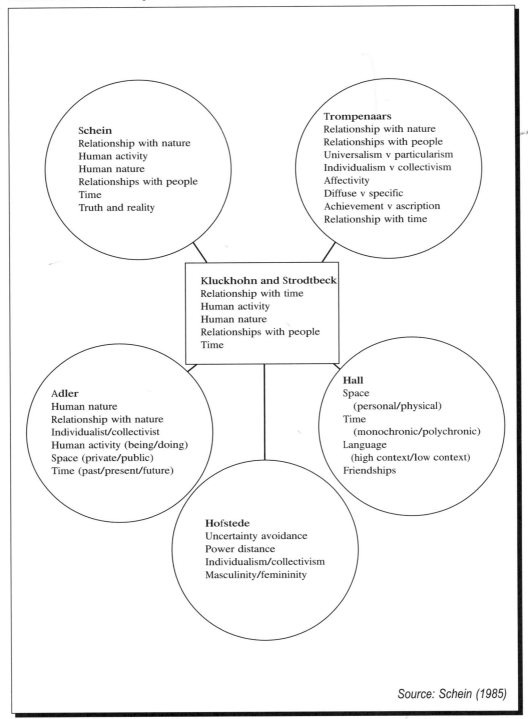

Figure 2 *Key dimensions of culture*

The increasing internationalisation of business has made the concept of culture and its impact for good or bad on organisations' operations a critical topic for study. An extensive literature has emerged in respect of both organisational culture and national cultural differences as they relate to work.

NATIONAL CULTURES AND ORGANISATION

Early research on the influence of cultural conditioning on collective human behaviours challenged the assumption of the universalism of management practices emanating from the USA (and, indeed, from other countries such as Japan). In an increasingly borderless world, managers need to know how national cultural differences might affect organisation structure and processes, notions of leadership, HR practices, etc. Management scholars have consequently been inspired to translate the work of social anthropologists to the world of work. Three European researchers – André Laurent, Geert Hofstede and Fons Trompenaars – and a US anthropologist – Edward Hall – have been particularly influential in this respect.

Hall's research

Hall (1959, 1976, 2000) made a distinction between what he described as 'high-context' and 'low-context' cultures. This is a multifaceted concept, but at its heart is the understanding that all cultures can be situated in relation to one another through the styles in which they communicate. In high-context cultures information is pre-programmed within the individual receiver of the message and the setting. Only minimal information is transmitted in the message. In a low-context culture the reverse is true. Context therefore refers to the framework, background and surrounding circumstances in which any communication or event takes place. Individuals from high- or low-context cultures have different ways of experiencing the world.

Examples of high-context societies include Japan, China, and Asian cultures in general, as well as native societies such as that of the Maoris in New Zealand. African, Middle Eastern, Latin American, Latin, Central and Slavic European cultures also fall in this category. In high-context cultures there is a tendency to cater towards in-groups – groups that have similar expectations and experiences – and these groups can rely on their common background and on the context of the situation to explain what is really meant, rather than words. A great deal of information is already internalised within groups. Discussions within in-groups can be wide-ranging and mutual expectations are generally accurate. Group members have their own private networks for information, which they keep to themselves. Many things can be left unsaid – the culture explains the meaning. Messages include other clues that enable you to understand the communication, such as body language and the use of silence. Understanding the role played by family status, age differences and social setting also helps the receiver decode the real message. Messages can be implied and not uttered. The focus on in-groups means that relationships and group processes are important. High-context cultures are often more traditional and unchanging, such that the context can remain stable over generations. Because of the importance of relationships, they tend to be deep and longer-lasting.

Examples of low-context societies include most of the English-speaking (interestingly, Britain is an exception to this rule) and Germanic-speaking countries, such as the USA, Canada, Australia, northern European countries such as Germany, Sweden and Switzerland. In low-context cultures the situation has to be explained more explicitly because there are not common backgrounds. The boundaries between in-groups are much more fluid. Low-context cultures tend to be more changeable so that the context for one generation is very different from that for another. Mutual expectations are less accurate and communication is therefore more verbal, explicit, direct, linear and task-focused. Channels of communication are generally clear. Information is easy to obtain and is shared more overtly. Communication has an informational function and is a neutral tool to convey thoughts. Accuracy, directness and clarity in speech are therefore valued. Communications are more transactional and can end once completed. Familiarising yourself with the people before you communicate or conduct business is unnecessary.

Hall also argued that time is not socially absolute and is similarly culturally programmed. He talked of low-context societies' generally also being 'monochronic', by which he meant that time is sequential and highly scheduled – an endless ribbon of appointments and obligations such that time can be 'wasted', 'killed', or 'saved'. Many high-context cultures are 'polychronic' (Japan is actually an exception). They have a more indulgent view of lateness. Time is like a balloon that swells and deflates depending upon what is going on. The more people present, the larger the social network, the more useful the moment is. Meetings are just for giving general guidelines and may be cancelled or postponed if they are outside this moment.

QUESTIONS

- Would you say that Britain is high- or low-context? Why?

- What aspects of international management might be more susceptible to differences between high and low context?

The UK is actually considered to be a relatively high-context culture. Consider the following amusing examples in Table 1 that have been used to demonstrate to foreign managers the role that context can play in understanding what a British manager might really mean. The examples show that the individual must know what is meant at the covert or unexpressed level, and this knowledge enables him or her to react appropriately.

What the British say	What they really mean
Not bad	Good, or Very good
Quite good	A bit disappointing
Interesting	That *is* interesting, or It is interesting that you think it is interesting – it seems rather boring to me!
Oh, by the way, …	I am about to get to the primary purpose of our discussion
I was a bit disappointed that you …	I am most upset and cross
I hear what you say	I disagree and do not wish to discuss it any further
With the greatest respect, …	I think that you are wrong (or a fool)
Perhaps we could consider some other options	I don't like your ideas

Table 1 *Interpreting high-context communications*

The potential for miscommunication and misinterpretation of actions between high- and low-context cultures is clear from the examples in Table 1. In general, differences in communication context have been shown to be important in relation to issues such as cross-cultural negotiations, mergers and acquisitions and, one could infer, performance management discussions.

There is some correlation between high-context cultures and cultures that value the group over the individual (collectivist societies) – but the correlation is limited. Similarly, not all high-context cultures are necessarily polychronic. Within a low-context culture, individuals can find themselves in high-context situations, and vice versa. So, for example, within a low-context American culture, communications among family members are generally high-context because of the high level of shared experience.

Laurent's research

Laurent (1983) studied different conceptions of what an organisation is. He argued that the best way to understand the role of culture is to ask managers questions and see how they solve the problem. Their solution will show how they think about the role of managers, hierarchies and power (as an example, see

Figure 3). Analysis of the results showed that nationality had three times more influence on the shaping of managerial assumptions than any of the respondent's other characteristics such as age, education, function, type of company, etc.

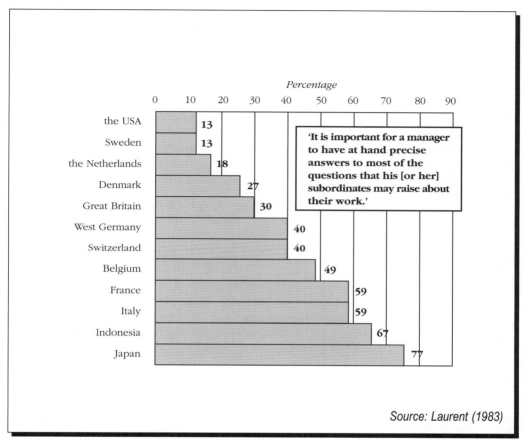

Figure 3 *The role of managers*

Whereas only a minority of North American and northern European managers agreed with this statement, a majority of southern Europeans and South-East Asians did. Laurent classified the nationalities concerned according to separate theories of organisations. Political systems epitomise organisations in which managers are seen to play a political role and negotiate. Obtaining power is seen as more important than achieving specific objectives. Latin European managers were more likely to adhere to this view than their Nordic and Anglo counterparts. Role-formalisation systems describe organisations where managers prefer detailed job descriptions and well-defined roles and functions. Germanic managers felt at ease in this type of system, whereas Nordic and Anglo managers felt that the world was too complex to be able clearly to define roles and functions. Finally, hierarchical systems reflect the differences in opinion mentioned above, where the boss is expected to be respected through the possession of expert knowledge.

Hofstede's research

One of the most influential pieces of research in relation to national cultures is the work of Hofstede (1980; 2001). Hofstede's framework is widely used by researchers and practitioners in the field of intercultural management. Hofstede found that the differences in responses could be explained by four main factors:

- power distance

- uncertainty avoidance

- individualism

- masculinity.

Power distance

Power distance relates to the extent to which societies accept that power in institutions and organisations is and should be distributed unequally. In organisational terms, this relates to the centralisation of authority and the degree of autocratic leadership. Societies with 'high power distance' scores are reflected in hierarchical organisations where it is felt to be right that the superior is seen to be more powerful than subordinates. Examples of countries with high power distance scores are the Philippines, Singapore, France and Greece. In contrast, countries with low power distance scores such as Britain, Sweden and New Zealand favour a more democratic style of management and flatter organisational structures (see Table 2).

Score rank	Country	Score rank	Country	Score rank	Country
1	Malaysia	18/19	Turkey	37	Jamaica
2/3	Guatemala	20	Belgium	38	the USA
2/3	Panama	21/23	East Africa	39	Canada
4	the Philippines	21/23	Peru	40	the Netherlands
5/6	Mexico	21/23	Thailand	41	Australia
5/6	Venezuela	24/25	Chile	42/44	Costa Rica
7	Arab countries	24/25	Portugal	42/44	West Germany
8/9	Ecuador	26	Uruguay	42/44	Great Britain
8/9	Indonesia	27/28	Greece	45	Switzerland
10/11	India	27/28	South Korea	46	Finland
10/11	West Africa	29/30	Iran	47/48	Norway
12	Yugoslavia	29/30	Taiwan	47/48	Sweden
13	Singapore	31	Spain	49	Republic of Ireland
14	Brazil	32	Pakistan	50	New Zealand
15/16	France	33	Japan	51	Denmark
15/16	Hong Kong	34	Italy	52	Israel
17	Colombia	35/36	Argentina	53	Austria
18/19	El Salvador	35/36	South Africa		

Source: Hofstede (1991)

Table 2 *Power distance index (PDI) rankings for Hofstede indices*

Uncertainty avoidance

Uncertainty avoidance refers to the degree to which societies feel threatened by ambiguous situations and the extent to which they try to avoid uncertain situations. In countries with high uncertainty avoidance, such as France, organisations adopt strong bureaucracies and career stability and generally discourage risk-taking activities. Countries such as Sweden, Britain and Norway which exhibit low uncertainty avoidance will adopt more flexible structures and encourage more diverse views (see Table 3).

Score rank	Country	Score rank	Country	Score rank	Country
1	Greece	19	Israel	37	Australia
2	Portugal	20	Colombia	38	Norway
3	Guatemala	21/22	Venezuela	39/40	South Africa
4	Uruguay	21/22	Brazil	39/40	New Zealand
5/6	Belgium	23	Italy	41/41	Indonesia
5/6	El Salvador	24/25	Pakistan	41/42	Canada
7	Japan	24/25	Austria	43	the USA
8	Yugoslavia	26	Taiwan	44	the Philippines
9	Peru	27	Arab countries	45	India
10/15	France	28	Ecuador	46	Malaysia
10/15	Chile	29	West Germany	47/48	Great Britain
10/15	Spain	30	Thailand	47/48	Republic of Ireland
10/15	Costa Rica	31/32	Iran	49/50	Hong Kong
10/15	Panama	31/32	Finland	49/50	Sweden
10/15	Argentina	33	Switzerland	51	Denmark
16/17	Turkey	34	West Africa	52	Jamaica
16/17	South Korea	35	the Netherlands	53	Singapore
18	Mexico	36	East Africa		

Source: Hofstede (1991)

Table 3 *Uncertainty avoidance index (UAI) rankings for Hofstede indices*

Individualism

Individualism reflects the extent to which individuals are integrated into groups. Where individualism is high – for example, in the USA – people are expected to take care of themselves and their immediate family only. In collectivist societies such as Japan, however, people are integrated into strong, cohesive groups which throughout people's lifetimes continue to protect them in exchange for unquestioning loyalty (see Table 4). Whereas in individualist societies the emphasis for individuals within organisations is to gain self-respect and personal achievement, in collectivist societies the focus is on fitting in harmoniously and face-saving.

Hofstede (1991) found a strong correlation between high power distance and collectivism and vice versa in the countries within his IBM sample. He explains this by stating that in cultures in which people are dependent on groups, the people are usually also dependent on power figures. The converse is true in individualist countries. Exceptions to this are countries such as France and Belgium, which combine high power distances with strong individualism. Crozier (1964) argues that a belief in an absolutist authority can be reconciled within a bureaucratic system where impersonal rules avoid the need for direct dependence relationships, a characteristic of collectivist societies.

Masculinity

Masculinity measures the extent to which the dominant values are (in Hofstede's terms) 'male' – values such as assertiveness, the acquisition of money and goods, and not caring for others. Gender roles are more rigidly defined in masculine societies than in 'feminine' societies. The most masculine countries in Hofstede's framework are Japan and Austria; the USA falls into this category. In contrast, the Scandinavian countries fall into the feminine category, with more emphasis on work–life balance. (See Table 5.)

Score rank	Country	Score rank	Country	Score rank	Country
1	the USA	19	Israel	37	Hong Kong
2	Australia	20	Spain	38	Chile
3	Great Britain	21	India	39/41	West Africa
4/5	Canada	22/23	Japan	39/41	Singapore
4/5	the Netherlands	22/23	Argentina	39/41	Thailand
6	New Zealand	24	Iran	42	El Salvador
7	Italy	25	Jamaica	43	South Korea
8	Belgium	26/27	Brazil	44	Taiwan
9	Denmark	26/27	Arab countries	45	Peru
10/11	Sweden	28	Turkey	46	Costa Rica
10/11	France	29	Uruguay	47/48	Pakistan
12	Republic of Ireland	30	Greece	47/48	Indonesia
13	Norway	31	the Philippines	49	Colombia
14	Switzerland	32	Mexico	50	Venezuela
15	West Germany	33/35	East Africa	51	Panama
16	South Africa	33/35	Yugoslavia	52	Ecuador
17	Finland	33/35	Portugal	53	Guatemala
18	Austria	36	Malaysia		

Source: Hofstede (1991)

Table 4 *Individualism index (IDV) rankings for Hofstede indices*

Score rank	Country	Score rank	Country	Score rank	Country
1	Japan	18/19	Hong Kong	37/38	Spain
2	Austria	20/21	Argentina	37/38	Peru
3	Venezuela	20/21	India	39	East Africa
4/5	Italy	22	Belgium	40	El Salvador
4/5	Switzerland	23	Arab countries	41	South Korea
6	Mexico	24	Canada	42	Uruguay
7/8	Republic of Ireland	25/26	Malaysia	43	Guatemala
7/8	Jamaica	25/26	Pakistan	44	Thailand
9/10	Great Britain	27	Brazil	45	Portugal
9/10	West Germany	28	Singapore	46	Chile
11/12	the Philippines	29	Israel	47	Finland
11/12	Colombia	30/31	Indonesia	48/49	Yugoslavia
13/14	South Africa	30/31	West Africa	48/49	Costa Rica
13/14	Ecuador	32/33	Turkey	50	Denmark
15	the USA	32/33	Taiwan	51	the Netherlands
16	Australia	34	Panama	52	Norway
17	New Zealand	35/36	Iran	53	Sweden
18/19	Greece	35/36	France		

Source: Hofstede (1991)

Table 5 *Masculinity index (MAS) rankings for Hofstede indices*

The Chinese values survey

Concerned about the Western bias amongst cross-cultural researchers, Bond – a Canadian who lives and works in Hong Kong – and a group of Chinese colleagues developed a questionnaire reflecting Chinese cultural values. Twenty of the countries were also in Hofstede's study. The results from the study revealed four dimensions of culture, three of which reflected Hofstede's dimensions of power distance, individualism/collectivism and masculinity/femininity. The fourth represented Chinese values related to Confucianism. Bond and his colleagues called this dimension 'Confucian work dynamism'. Hofstede relabelled it 'long-term versus short-term orientation'. In countries exhibiting a high Confucian work dynamism, or which are long-term-oriented, there is a focus on the future, and thrift (ie saving) and persistence are valued. Companies in Japan, which is an example of a long-term-oriented society, have traditionally taken a longer-term view of investments. In contrast to companies in Western economies, it is not necessary to show profits year by year, but rather progress towards a longer-term goal. Japan's continuing economic crisis may well force a fundamental change in perspective for its organisations. In contrast, countries low in Confucian work dynamism, or short-term-oriented, value the past and present. There is respect for tradition and fulfilling social obligations, but the present is the most important.

Management implications of power distance and uncertainty avoidance

These dimensions can inform our understanding. For example, taking these two dimensions together reveals differences in the implicit model that people from different cultures may have about organisational structure and functioning (see Figure 4).

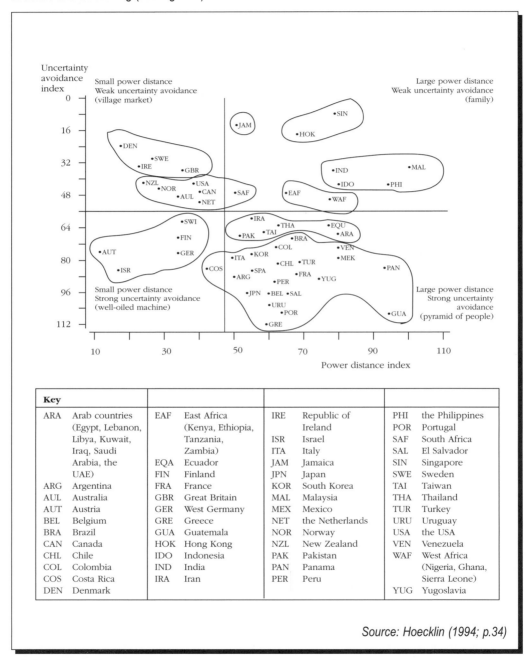

Key							
ARA	Arab countries (Egypt, Lebanon, Libya, Kuwait, Iraq, Saudi Arabia, the UAE)	EAF	East Africa (Kenya, Ethiopia, Tanzania, Zambia)	IRE	Republic of Ireland	PHI	the Philippines
				ISR	Israel	POR	Portugal
				ITA	Italy	SAF	South Africa
		EQA	Ecuador	JAM	Jamaica	SAL	El Salvador
		FIN	Finland	JPN	Japan	SIN	Singapore
ARG	Argentina	FRA	France	KOR	South Korea	SWE	Sweden
AUL	Australia	GBR	Great Britain	MAL	Malaysia	TAI	Taiwan
AUT	Austria	GER	West Germany	MEX	Mexico	THA	Thailand
BEL	Belgium	GRE	Greece	NET	the Netherlands	TUR	Turkey
BRA	Brazil	GUA	Guatemala	NOR	Norway	URU	Uruguay
CAN	Canada	HOK	Hong Kong	NZL	New Zealand	USA	the USA
CHL	Chile	IDO	Indonesia	PAK	Pakistan	VEN	Venezuela
COL	Colombia	IND	India	PAN	Panama	WAF	West Africa (Nigeria, Ghana, Sierra Leone)
COS	Costa Rica	IRA	Iran	PER	Peru	YUG	Yugoslavia
DEN	Denmark						

Source: Hoecklin (1994; p.34)

Figure 4 *Power distance and uncertainty avoidance index comparison*

Employees in high power distance and low uncertainty avoidance societies such as Singapore, Hong Kong and Indonesia tend to think of their organisations as traditional families. The head of the family is expected to protect family members physically and economically in exchange for continued loyalty from family members. A key control and co-ordination mechanism for the family is a standardisation of work processes by specifying the contents of the work.

In societies where both power distance and uncertainty avoidance are high – such as France, Brazil and Mexico – organisations are viewed as pyramids. Reporting lines are clear. Management provides co-ordination and control by emphasising who has authority over whom, and in what way this authority can be exercised.

A combination of medium uncertainty avoidance and low power distance gives rise to organisations which are perceived as well-oiled machines. Roles and procedures are well defined and co-ordination and control are achieved through standardisation and certification of skills. Examples of countries in this quadrant are Israel, Austria, Germany and Switzerland.

Finally, in countries where there is low uncertainty avoidance and low power distance, a 'village market' model is apparent. This model includes countries such as the UK, the USA, Denmark and Ireland. Here, control and co-ordination tends to take place through mutual adjustment of people through informal communication, and by specifying desired results.

QUESTION

Using the Hofstede dimensions,

■ What would be the key people management considerations for a UK-based organisation that wished to expand into France, Germany and Japan?

Trompenaars' research

Trompenaars (1993) found seven dimensions of difference, three of which are detailed below (the others – concerned with what people do, individualism, time and environment – have already been discussed).

Universalism versus particularism

This measures the extent to which people believe that general principles are more, or less, important than unique circumstances and relationships. The distribution of scores across countries shows a separation between East and West and between North and South, with Western and Northern states believing more in universalist principles.

Trompenaars and Hampden-Turner (1997) identify four main implications of this for international business, relating to:

■ contracts
■ the timing of business trips
■ the role of head office
■ job evaluations and rewards.

In respect of contracts, universalist cultures believe that a weighty contract summarising all aspects of the deal is essential in international transactions. In particularist cultures, where strength of relationships is paramount, drawing up a contract may be perceived as a lack of trust or respect and can lead to the breakdown of the deal. As for the timing of business trips, business people from universalist cultures need to take time to create a sound relational and trustworthy basis that equates the quality of the product with the quality of the personal relationship. This dimension also plays out in the third implication, the role of head office. In universalist cultures, head office tends to control global functions. In more particularist cultures, head office often fails to shape local ways of operating. The fourth implication, relating to job evaluations and rewards, indicates that organisations from universalist cultures are more likely to apply standardised systems of evaluation and measurement. Particularist societies are more likely to allow individual supervisors to determine promotion and rewards. The main business areas affected by this dimension are summarised in Table 6.

Universalism	Particularism
• Focus is more on rules than relationships • Legal contracts are readily drawn up • A trustworthy person is the one who honours his/her 'word' or contract • There is only one truth or reality – that which has been agreed to • A deal is a deal	• Focus is more on relationships than on rules • Legal contracts are readily modified • A trustworthy person is the one who honours changing circumstances • There are several perspectives on reality relative to each participant • Relationships evolve

Source: Hoecklin (1994; p.41)

Table 6 *Business areas affected by universalism versus particularism*

Specific versus diffuse relationships

This dimension deals with the degree of involvement individuals are comfortable with in dealing with other people. Individuals will have various levels to their personalities, from a more public level to the inner, more private level. In more specific cultures, such as those of the USA and the UK, people tend to have a large public area and a smaller private area. This private life is kept very separate and guarded closely. In diffuse cultures, such as in Germany, the 'private' space is usually larger while the public area is smaller and more guarded. Specific and diffuse cultures are sometimes also called low-context and high-context.

High-context cultures such as those of Japan and Venezuela are rich and subtle, but require considerable interpretation by foreigners before they can be assimilated. Britain's is also a high-context culture. Low-context cultures such as those of the USA or the Netherlands have more explicit rules and ways of doing things and tend to be more adaptable and flexible.

Specific	Diffuse
• More 'open' public space; more 'closed' private space • Appears direct, open and extrovert • Is to the point and often abrasive • Is highly mobile • Separates work and private life • Varies approach to fit circumstances, especially with use of titles (eg 'Herr Doktor Müller' at work is 'Hans' in social and some business environments)	• More 'closed' public space – but once in, more 'open' private space • Appears indirect, closed and introvert • Often evades issues and beats about the bush • Is not very mobile • Work and private life are closely linked • Consistent in approach, especially with use of titles (eg 'Herr Doktor Müller' is 'Herr Doktor Müller' in any setting)

Source: Hoecklin (1994; p.41)

Table 7 *Business areas affected by specific and diffuse relationships*

Neutral versus affective relationships

This dimension relates to the different ways in which cultures choose to express relationships. In affective cultures it is natural to express emotions openly, whereas in more neutral cultures emotions have to be held in check in order not to confuse work situations. This dimension is particularly apparent in intercultural communication issues. For instance, both styles of verbal communication and tone of voice differ widely between different countries. For example, people in 'Anglo-Saxon' countries tend not to interrupt each other, but to commence a response immediately after the other person has finished talking. In Latin countries, there is an overlap between speakers, whereas in Oriental cultures, gaps in conversation are frequent.

Affective	Neutral
• Shows immediate reactions either verbally or non-verbally • Expressive face and body signals • Is at ease with physical contact • Raises voice readily	• Opaque emotional state – does not readily express what he/she thinks or feels • Is embarrassed or awkward at public displays of emotion • Is uncomfortable with physical contact outside 'private' circle • Is subtle in verbal and non-verbal expressions

Source: Hoecklin (1994; p.44)

Table 8 *Business areas affected by affective and neutral relationships*

We return to the views of Trompenaars in relation to the topic of cultural intelligence in the next chapter.

The Spony Profiling Model

As an example of a cross-cultural profiling model, we outline a framework developed by Spony (2001; 2003). This model enables assessment of individual values and behaviours as well as of their position within cultures. Spony's model (the Spony Profiling Model, or SPM) extends Schwartz's (1992; 1994; 1999) work into individual and cultural differences in value systems. Schwartz found that two fundamental axes – self-enhancement versus self-transcendence, and conservatism versus openness to change – were effective at eliciting both individual differences in value systems within countries and cultural differences between countries. Based on his empirical findings, Schwartz developed a new motivational theory of human values highlighting the fundamental dilemmas of human nature. In the SPM, Schwartz's two fundamental axes were renamed 'self-enhancement versus consideration for others' and 'group dynamics versus individual dynamics'.

Individuals are able to move along the two axes. For instance, we have all learned to be able both to be assertive and to also take others into consideration in our daily social behaviours. However, our positioning on the axes reflects our underlying motivational preferences. These are influenced by both our personality and the impact of our culture.

At a more in-depth level of analysis, each fundamental pole of the SPM encompasses three attitudinal orientations that reflect the main components of human experience:

- thinking
- action
- relationships.

Figure 5 shows that each attitudinal orientation on a particular pole is symmetrically opposed to the same orientation on the opposing pole. From this circular structure six fundamental dilemmas emerge in human decisions at work which closely relate to Schwartz's cross-cultural theory about human motivations. The core novelty of the model is to enable French and British managers, for example, to visualise their personal work-value system on a cross-cultural map and to develop awareness about the cumulative effect that these individual and cultural differences may trigger (see Figure 6).

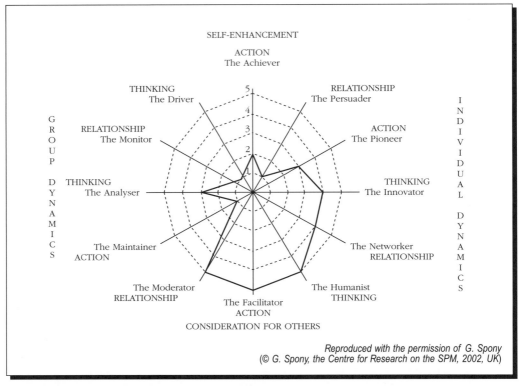

Figure 5 *Six fundamental dilemmas and twelve styles of the Spony Profiling Model*

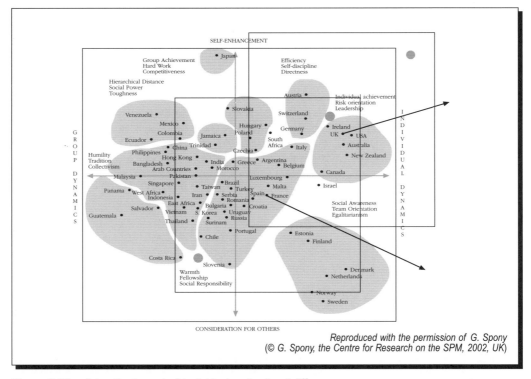

Figure 6 *Visualising the impact of individual and cultural differences*

Figure 6 shows the spread of results for British and French managers using the SPM. The large spread of results around the country highlights the impact of individual differences:

- The smaller square fully enclosed by the main square covers the results of 95% of the French managerial population.

- The smaller square overlapping at top and right of the main square represents the spread of 95% of the British managerial population.

- The larger spots at top right and bottom left of each smaller square identify individual managers.

The SPM can therefore be used to help managers and organisations to overcome the trap of damaging stereotypes while taking into consideration the determinant impact of culture on management and social behaviours. Further validation of the model's results is currently ongoing in some other countries (Canada, Mexico, India and Taiwan). Similarly, the extension of Schwartz's dilemma theory to the domain of soft competencies and organisational cultures is also the subject of ongoing research projects.

CULTURE AND THE INDIVIDUAL

Objections to the validity of studying national cultural differences are sometimes put forward by those who resist the notion that culture is a significant influence on behaviour. They argue that individual differences, not cultural ones, explain why people act the way they do. Addressing this question of the interaction between culturally determined behaviours and individual personality differences, Hofstede (1991) explains that culture lies between human nature on the one side and individual personality on the other.

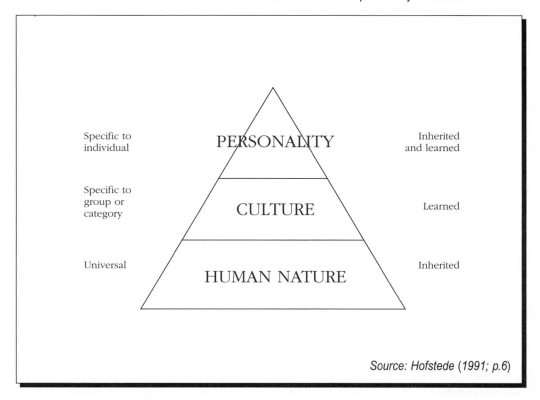

Figure 7 *Three levels of uniqueness in human mental programming*

Hofstede (1991; pp.5–6) describes the differences in the levels as follows:

'Human nature is what all human beings ... have in common: it represents the universal level in a person's mental software. The human
ability to feel fear, anger, love, joy, sadness, the need to associate with
others, to talk about it with other humans all belong to this level of
mental programming. However, what one does with these feelings, how
one expresses fear, joy, observations, and so on, is modified by culture.
The personality of an individual, on the other hand, is his/her unique
personal set of mental programs which he/she does not share with any
other human being. It is based upon traits which are partly inherited
with the individual's unique set of genes and partly learned.'

A key problem that can occur when working in intercultural situations is therefore the tendency to confuse personality and culture. Culture is, by definition, a group-based concept, whereas personality is an individual-based concept.

However, some psychologists have started to find ways of looking at how important cultural values might be reflected at the individual level. It has become known as the *new cultural paradigm research tradition*. They have used scales that can treat cultural dimensions as quasi-individual difference characteristics. Earley and Mosakowski (2002) argued that whereas people from a particular culture can on average share or endorse a given cultural value or belief, and it is only the level of the country that is the single most important determinant of these scores, when values are measured at the individual level there is still enough distribution of scores across a cultural scale between members from within any single country for their scores on the value-orientation to be treated as an important individual difference. Where such measurement of culture is also based on values that are known to operate at the individual level (rather than, for example, just using scales that were designed to reflect nationally derived cultural dimensions) this approach can be helpful to global HR practitioners.

One question that has been pursued by these researchers has been to investigate individual preferences for HR practices and then find out which preferences are values-free, and which can be predicted at the individual level by knowing that person's value-orientations (Sparrow, 2006). Put practically, this question concerns the room for manoeuvre that there might be for international HR directors in transferring practices abroad. If the *values* of an organisation's workforce significantly predict their preference for the nature of HR practices, the organisation will have a harder job in transferring them successfully. The organisation can change employee attitudes and mindsets to specific practices by communication and educational processes, but employee values tend to be more resistant to change. Preliminary evidence suggests that the answer to this question might be sobering for international HR directors. In a study of over 400 Taiwanese employees at firms such as Tatung, Mitac and Acer, Sparrow and Wu (1998) found that 75% of the 'menu' of various HR practices – for example, choices like whether a performance appraisal scheme should measure what you achieve (objectives) or how you achieve it (competencies) – could be predicted by individual-level cultural values. A similar impact was also found in a later study of Kenyan employees (Nyambegera, Sparrow and Daniels, 2000).

Clearly, in some countries cultural values, as reflected at the individual level, will help explain whether people find the HR practices they are subjected to desirable, sensible, appropriate or not. An HR professional might, however, also ask how important the cultural values are, especially in relation to other factors that might explain how desirable an individual finds any particular HR practice. There are lots of other individual factors that might shape the extent to which employees find a specific HR practice desirable or not. Together with a background of various demographic factors such as age, service, gender, and grade, an individual's cultural values by themselves explain from 10 to 16% of the attractiveness (or not) of various HR practices to him or her (Sparrow, 2006). Cultural values are important and worth knowing about, but they are of course just one of many factors that explain differences in work behaviour across countries. Attention is also being given to other factors and a broader set of explanations of cultural behaviour at the individual level is being explored. As Earley and Mosakowski (2002; p.316) noted: 'Now is an opportune time for researchers to move away from the tried and true friends of cultural values as the sole indicators of cultural differences.'

Their work is examined in the next chapter, but in the final sections of this chapter we note some of the important limitations in current work on national culture.

LIMITATIONS OF CULTURAL GENERALISATIONS

So although these cultural frameworks are useful in explaining some of the key ways in which societies (within a work context) might differ, it is important to note some of their limitations. There has been a growing critique of work on national culture in the international management field. In attempting to categorise cultural groups, a lot of models have produced dichotomies – such as individualistic versus collectivistic cultures – that rely on what might be erroneous assumptions. By categorising cultures we might be tempted to view culture as being immutable, monolithic and definable with coordinates on a limited set of cultural dimensions. A number of points of criticism must be remembered (Sparrow, 2006).

The majority of the work undertaken in this area still has been carried out by Western – and in particular, European – researchers. Bond's work on Chinese values is an example of a move to address this problem. A study of global values carried out by the Dentsu Institute of Human Studies, based in Japan, between 1996 and 2000 called into question several conventional Western perceptions of Asian cultural values and showed more similarities between Western and Asian respondents than is usually the case.

It is dangerous to over-generalise or stereotype on the basis of these descriptions of generalised characteristics of cultural values. Hofstede himself makes the point that these generalisations are valid only as statistical statements about large numbers of people. Value contrasts are not either/or dichotomies but rather descriptions of two cultures' overall tendencies to be nearer to or farther from a particular value-orientation. For instance, when comparing two countries across the same value, it is important to note that the strength of the value in each country will have its own bell-shaped distribution curve. However, the norms between the two may be quite different. Understanding the relative distance between the norms allows people to generalise about the relative difficulty members of one culture may have in relating to members of the other culture along that dimension (see Figure 8). In addition, an awareness of the exceptions to the norms at the end of the curves and the possible overlap between the curves helps to avoid stereotyping (see Wederspahn, 2000).

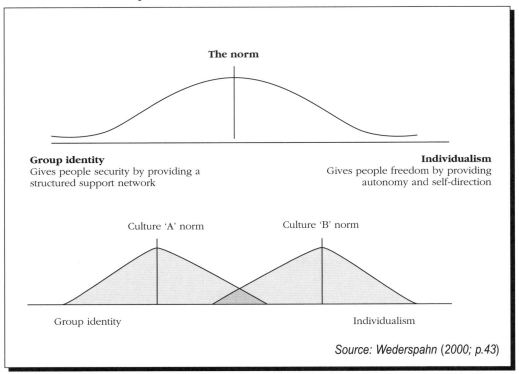

Figure 8 *Value contrast curves*

Approaches that create categories of cultures have, then, been criticised for making a *homogeneity assumption*. This criticism argues that there are significant differences on most of these sorts of measures across groups within any single country (Koslowsky, Sagie and Stashevsky, 2002). Not only huge countries – such as Russia, China, Indonesia and India – but also small countries – like Belgium and Switzerland – may contain distinctive multiple cultures within their national borders. For example, the individualistic cultures of the USA, Italy, Germany, France and Britain can still be differentiated, and even within any one of them multiple brands of individualism exist across ethnic groups. Regional differences have an impact. In the USA, for example, distinctive Northeast, Midwest, West and Deep South brands of individualism can be identified. Similarly, the collectivistic systems of Confucianism, Buddhism and Marxism differ significantly from each other in particular values, meanings and customs. The homogeneity assumption rests on the ability to infer that there are commonalities of core beliefs and assumptions that cut across ethnic, linguistic and religious differences within any single country, and that these shared commonalities can still explain important work behaviours, despite the variety of espoused values and observed behaviours that evidently differ within a country (Menon, 2004).

Closely associated with this argument about within-societal variation, Gelfand, Nishii and Raver (2007) have re-drawn attention to the idea of 'cultural *tightness* or *looseness*', and developed a series of explanations for how this impacts on life in organisations. 'Tightness' reflects the strength of social norms (how clear or pervasive the norms are within any society) and the degree of sanctions (how much tolerance there is for deviation), both of which vary from one society to another. Loose and tight societies also differ in terms of the amount of accountability (Tetlock, 2002) and the degree to which there is 'felt accountability' amongst individuals (Frink and Klimoski, 1998). It is only where individuals have this felt sense of accountability that external societal constraints get internalised into their own behaviour. It is a separate construct from individualism/collectivism. Anthropologists argue that countries such as Japan, Germany or Singapore, or certain ethnic groups such as Pueblo Indians, are tight societies, whereas for example in the USA, New Zealand, northern Finland or Thailand, society is much looser (Pelto, 1968). The degree of tightness depends on things like the degree of population density, the economic system and the role of kinship. Individuals in 'tight' societies have a lower sense of separation of their own self from others' selves (called psychological differentiation). This idea has been discussed only sporadically by people studying national culture – in the work, for example, of Berry (1966), Triandis (1989) and Carpenter (2000). Gelfand, Nishii and Raver (2007) point out that tightness/looseness varies within societies as well – between, for example, different domains of life, regions, and ethnic and religious groups.

QUESTIONS

- To what extent would someone from the southern states of the USA share his or her values and beliefs with those of all North Americans?
- Would a person from Delhi share the values and beliefs of someone from Chennai?

Finally, some important points have been made about how individuals vary in the way they exhibit a culturally related behaviour *depending on the situation*. Members of a collectivistic culture may be highly communal with in-group members, but that does not mean they are communal with out-group members. Members of individualistic cultures may actually be more communal with out-group members than collectivists! Consider the hospitality that individualist Americans can show to strangers. The reference group is therefore very important (Freeman and Bordia, 2001). Single-dimension cultural factors rarely capture the complexity of such individual behaviour.

It is important to be aware, then, that the more popular culture has become as a means of explaining the way people behave at work across countries, the more careful the global HR practitioner has to be at taking findings at face value. There are good and bad studies of national culture, and there are good and bad measures of cultural values. Even when culture has been assessed in some direct way, or where cross-country differences are used as a proxy for culture, it is important to be aware of some of the main criticisms that have been made about cultural research.

A common feature of many studies has been to test the way that national contextual variables – such as individualism and collectivism – moderate the behaviour of individual workers. This is sometimes done by taking a country-level measure (like the ones outlined in this chapter devised by people like Hofstede or Trompenaars) and then assigning each individual a score on the basis of the average score for the nation he or she comes from. Or the individual might be scored using instruments that were really designed to assess national-level constructs. The first approach falls foul of the *ecological fallacy* observed by Hofstede (1980), whereby national-level data is used to predict individual-level behaviour, which leads to incorrect estimations of the real effects of the contextual variables. This manifests itself in two ways. Firstly, cultural values which are known to be held by a group are projected onto an individual who is a member of the group. This is known as stereotyping. Stereotyping of itself is not necessarily a negative process but rather a way for us to try to make sense of the world by categorising things and individuals. However, it can become problematic when it is inaccurate – if, for example, we assume that all Japanese are group-oriented and do not show emotion, or that all Swedish managers favour consensus-based, participative work practices. Stereotyping becomes dangerous when group-level data is used to categorise individuals, particularly in a negative and prejudicial manner. Secondly, an ecological fallacy can occur by projecting from individuals to groups.

QUESTIONS

Following the above examination of recent criticisms of research into cultural differences,

- Can we safely assume the existence of single national cultures?

- Is the existence of culture as an explanatory variable decreasing in the wake of continued globalisation?

Are there conditions that evoke universal responses from employees regardless of culture?

SUMMARY

This chapter has explored the notion of national culture and its impact on the values and behaviours of individuals. Despite claims that 'culture' is irrelevant in our 'global village' world, evidence from both research and world and business events repeatedly emphasises the enormous impact of different cultural orientations (for good or bad) on our everyday lives. At present, our understanding of cultural differences relies mainly on cross-cultural frameworks, working at a national level and derived from quantitative sampling techniques. Whether this is a valid method for capturing the true nature (and level) of cultural differences is the subject of vigorous ongoing academic debate. Such frameworks, however, provide practising managers with an initial map of the types of issues they may need to take into account when working in an intercultural context. There is also some reflection of national culture at the individual level in terms of value-orientations that people hold. By keeping these as helpful indicators, and understanding the limitations of some of our evidence and the assumptions that we make when we try to study culture, managers can avoid the tendency to stereotype and can experiment with appropriate behaviours and processes that will hopefully lead to better intercultural ability. Although the impact of cultural differences is important at an individual level, it is even more critical to understand what effect they can have at the team and organisational level. The next chapter addresses the impact of national culture on key organisational processes including HRM practices, leadership, and international management teams.

LEARNING QUESTIONS

1 How well do the indices and measures here reflect your own country? Give reasons for your answer.

2 Are national cultural differences likely to be more, or less, strong than organisational or gender differences in culture? Explain your views.

3 How might cultural differences make it difficult for a UK visitor to Japan to do business?

4 Choose an aspect of human resource management such as selection, appraisals, training or industrial relations, and explain how cultural differences might affect it.

5 Argue that an organisation should have clear rules about the management of people that cover operations in all its different countries. Argue that such rules should be varied for the different national cultures represented within the organisation. Can the two views be reconciled?

REFERENCES

Berry, J. W. (1966) 'Temne and Eskimo perceptual skills', *Journal of Personality and Social Psychology*, 7: 415–18

Carpenter, S. (2000) 'Effects of cultural tightness and collectivism on self-concept and causal attributions', *Cross-Cultural Research*, 34: 38–56

Crozier, M. (1964) *The Bureaucratic Phenomenon*. London, Tavistock

Dentsu Institute (2001) *Value Changes with Globalization: The fifth 'Comparative Analysis of Global Values'*. Dentsu Institute for Human Studies, www.dci.dentsu.co

Earley, P. C. and Mosakowski, E. (2002) 'Linking cultures and behaviour in organisations: suggestions for theory development and research methodology', in F. Dansereau and F. J. Yammarino (eds) *Research in Multi-level Issues. Volume 1: The Many Faces of Multi-level Issues*. San Francisco, Elsevier Science

Freeman, M. A. and Bordia, P. (2001) 'Assessing alternative models of individualism and collectivism: a confirmatory factor analysis', *European Journal of Personality*, 15: 105–21

Frink, D. D. and Klimoski, R. J. (1998) 'Toward a theory of accountability in organisations and human resource management', *Research in Personnel and Human Resources Management*, 16: 1–51

Gelfand, M. J., Nishii, L. H. and Raver, J. L. (2007) 'On the nature and importance of cultural tightness/looseness', *Journal of Applied Psychology*, in press

Grossmann, R. (1999) 'Corporate courtship: irreconcilable differences', *HR Magazine*, April: 2

Hall, E. T. (1959) *The Silent Language*. New York, Anchor Books

Hall, E. T. (1976) *Beyond Culture*. New York, Doubleday

Hall, E. T. (2000) 'Context and meaning', in L. A. Samovar and R. E. Porter (eds) *Intercultural Communication: A Reader*, 9th edition. Belmont, CA, Wadsworth Publishing

Hoecklin, L. (1994) *Managing Cultural Differences*. Harlow, Addison-Wesley Longman

Hofstede, G. (1980) *Culture's Consequences: International differences in work-related values*. London, Sage

Hofstede, G. (1991) *Cultures and Organizations: Software of the mind*. London, McGraw-Hill

Hofstede, G. (2001) *Culture's Consequences*, 2nd edition. London/Thousand Oaks, CA, Sage

Kluckhohn F. F. and Strodtbeck F. L. (1961) *Variations in Value Orientations*. New York, Row, Peterson & Co

Koslowsky, M., Sagie, A. and Stashevsky, S. (2002) 'Introduction: Cultural relativism and universalism in organisational behaviours', *International Journal of Cross-Cultural Management*, 2 (2): 131–5

Laurent, A. (1983) 'The cultural diversity of Western conceptions of management', *International Studies of Management and Organization*, 13 (1, 2): 75–96

McGregor, D. (1960) *The Nature of Human Enterprise*. New York, McGraw-Hill

Menon. S. T. (2004) 'Culture's consequences for twenty-first-century research and practice', *International Journal of Cross-Cultural Management*, 4 (2): 135–40

Nyambegera, S., Sparrow, P. R. and Daniels, K. (2000) 'The impact of cultural value orientations on individual HRM preferences in developing countries: lessons from Kenyan organisations', *International Journal of Human Resource Management*, 11 (4): 639–63

Parker, B. (1998) *Globalization and Business Practice: Managing across boundaries*. London, Sage

Pelto, P. (1968) 'The difference between "tight" and "loose" societies', *Transaction*, 5: 37–40

Phillips, D. (1994) 'Culture may play role in flight safety', *Seattle Times*, 22 August; pp.E1, E3

Sackmann, S. A. and Phillips, M. E. (2004) 'Contextual influences on culture research: shifting assumptions for new workplace realities', *International Journal of Cross-Cultural Management*, 4 (3): 370–90

Schein, E. H. (1985) *Organisational Culture and Leadership*. San Francisco, Jossey-Bass

Schneider, S. and Barsoux, J.-L. (1997) 'The multicultural team', in *Managing Across Cultures*. Hemel Hempstead, Prentice Hall

Schwartz, S. H. (1992) 'Universals in the content and structure of values: theoretical advances and empirical tests in 20 countries', in M. P. Zanna (ed.) *Advances in Experimental Social Psychology*, 25, New York, Academic Press

Schwartz, S. H. (1994) 'Beyond individualism/collectivism: new cultural dimensions of values', in U. Kim, H. C. Triandis, C. Kagitcibasi, S. C. Choi and G. Yoon (eds) *Individualism and Collectivism*. London, Sage

Schwartz, S. H. (1999) 'A theory of cultural values and some implications for work', *Applied Psychology: an International Review*, 48 (1): 23–47

Sparrow, P. R. (2006) 'International management: some key challenges for industrial and organisational psychology', in G. Hodgkinson and J. K. Ford (eds) *International Review of Industrial and Organizational Psychology. Volume 21*. Chichester, Wiley

Sparrow, P. R. and Wu, P. C. (1998) 'How much do national value-orientations really matter? Predicting HRM preferences of Taiwanese employees', *Employee Relations: the International Journal*, 20 (1): 26–56

Spony, G. (2001) *The Development of a Work-Value Model Assessing the Cumulative Impact of Individual and Cultural Differences on Managers' Work-Value Systems: Empirical evidence from French and British managers*. Cranfield, Bedfordshire, Cranfield School of Management

Spony, G. (2003) 'The development of a work-value model assessing the cumulative impact of individual and cultural differences on managers' work-value systems: empirical evidence from French and British managers', *International Journal of Human Resource Management*, 14 (4): 658–79

Tetlock, P. E. (2002) 'Social functionalist frameworks for judgement and choice: intuitive politicians, theologians, and prosecutors', *Psychological Review*, 109: 451–71

Triandis, H. C. (1989) *Culture and Social Behavior*. New York, McGraw-Hill

Trompenaars, F. (1993) *Riding the Waves of Culture: Understanding cultural diversity in business*. London, Economist Books

Trompenaars, F. and Hampden-Turner, C. (1997) *Riding the Waves of Culture: Understanding cultural diversity In business*, 2nd edition. London, Nicholas Brealey Publishing

Wederspahn, G. M. (2000) *Intercultural Services: A worldwide buyer's guide and sourcebook*. Houston, Gulf Publishing

Culture and organisational life

CHAPTER OBJECTIVES

When they have read this chapter, students will:

- understand the ways in which cultural assumptions influence organisational life
- appreciate the impact of culture on leadership styles
- be aware of the impact of culture on HRM practices
- be able to describe the nature of global leadership competencies
- be able to advise on the strategies used to manage multicultural teams.

INTRODUCTION

De Vries and Florent-Treacy (2002; p.301) recount the case of Groupe Danone's acquisition of a company in Moscow.

Case study

Entente cordiale

The authors noted that the Russian and French employees of the factory managed to overcome the mindset still often found in Russia based on the Soviet legacy of a centrally planned, production-oriented economy.

The new CEO, sent in by Danone to lead the transformation process, had gone about his task in an unexpected way. By virtue of his own French-Russian bicultural background, he understood that the Russian employees were not yet ready for empowerment or participatory management as practised in Western countries. Accustomed to job security at any cost, their primary concern was for stability, and they looked to strong leadership to protect them from the turbulence in Russia. Thus, the CEO's first actions were designed to reassure his subordinates. Very significantly, he assured workers that Danone headquarters had a long-term vision for the factory and would support it through temporary market downturns. He directed the factory's human resources department to do everything possible to help employees who had been laid off to find new jobs, a policy nearly unheard of in Russia. At the same time, he kept relatively tight control over decision-making and information flow, knowing that paternalistic, autocratic leadership is still seen by Russians as a guarantee against anarchy.

The authors commented that although employees at Danone were in no way 'empowered' according to Western standards, the CEO's actions helped establish a reassuring sense of community. Even at the shopfloor level, employees said that their new leader was a man they respected and trusted, and that they were proud to be a part of a French global organisation. They were also motivated and positive about the future, a state of mind still rare in Russia.

The experience of this manager illustrates how important it is to understand the way differences in national cultures can affect attitudes and behaviours in the work environment. These attitudes and behaviours in turn become embedded in organisational cultures and systems. The need to study the impact of national cultures on organisational life should therefore be a given in this global world. However, many management texts (primarily US and Western) still adopt a universalist approach, focusing on 'best practice', often without any acknowledgment of how transferable these practices might be in different societal contexts. This chapter looks at the ways in which national culture impinges on organisational life, in particular with respect to HR policies and practices, managerial values, leadership styles, teams and the development of cultural intelligence.

ACTIVITY

■ Identify some of the ways in which we might examine how culture influences organisational life.

How might you try to design such a study, and what sort of things should you look at?

THE IMPORTANCE OF DIFFERENT NATIONAL VALUES

Cultural assumptions answer questions for group members. They suggest the types of interactions and behaviours which should lead to effectiveness. They determine the information that managers will notice, interpret and retain. They lead to different ways of seeing the same event and therefore different problem resolution strategies. A vast body of literature exists (see Chapter 2) which reports empirical evidence suggesting that employees and managers from different cultures are different from each other in the processes, behaviours and values that come into play in a decision-making situation. Cultural assumptions are therefore linked to a wide range of organisational behaviours. These include power and authority relationships, coping with uncertainty and risk-taking, interpersonal trust, loyalty and commitment, motivation, control and discipline, co-ordination and integration, communication, consultation and partici-pation (Tayeb, 1996). These value-orientations are determined by an individual's psychology (itself a product of various cultural, social, political and personal influences), his or her lifestage and his or her generational sub-culture.

One way in which academics attempt to show the impact of national culture is to compare managers who work in similar organisations across societies. For example, Tayeb (1988) found that matched-pair Indian and English organisations were similar on such universal dimensions as specialisation and centralisation but were considerably different from one another on the amount of consultation and delegation of authority that took place. English managers consulted their subordinates more widely before they made a decision and delegated authority farther down the hierarchy than did their Indian counterparts. Also, English employees communicated with each other to a far greater extent than did the Indian employees. The differences between the two samples were consistent with the cultural differences between Indian and English peoples as a whole (Tayeb 1988; p.91).

Similarly, a comparative study of Chinese and British manufacturing firms showed that decisions which were broadly within the competence of supervisors in the British organisations were within the gift only of senior managers in China (Easterby-Smith, Malina and Yuan, 1995). Observational studies also showed that whereas party and ideological work only took up 1% of a Chinese manager's time now, the manager spent nearly a quarter of the time servicing a series of 'father- and mother-in-law' relationships. Chinese managers spent the same amount of time looking down the pyramid as their Western counterparts, but four times as much looking up, and half the time looking outward (Boisot and Xing, 1991).

Organisation dimensions	Examples of the underlying process	Examples of relevant cultural traits
Centralisation	Power relationship	Attitudes to power and authority; trust and confidence in others; respect for other people's views
Specialisation and formalisation	Clear-cut job specifications, job territory	Ability to cope with uncertainty; attitude to privacy and autonomy
Formalisation and standardisation	Control and discipline	Attitude to control and discipline
Direction of communication	Information-sharing	Attitude to information-sharing; respect for other people's views
Span of control	Power relationship	Attitude to power and authority

Source: Tayeb (1988; p.92)

Table 9 *Culture-specific aspects of an organisation*

Table 9 identifies examples of the kinds of processes that underlie organisational life and the cultural traits which could be argued to be linked to them. These dimensions form part of our everyday life at work and are often so familiar that we only realise they are culturally determined when we travel to a foreign subsidiary, or if our organisation merges, or enters into a joint venture, with a company from another country. Perhaps the most obvious embodiment of cultural differences for individuals within organisations is perceived differences in leadership/management styles (the terms are themselves culturally significant).

THE IMPACT OF NATIONAL CULTURE ON HRM PRACTICES

This section explores the impact of national culture, reinforced by the leadership processes outlined later in this chapter, on HR policies and practices in international organisations. The work of cross-cultural researchers such as Hofstede and Trompenaars discussed in the previous chapter clearly demonstrates that organisations are 'culture-bound' and that management practices are heavily influenced by collectively shared values and belief systems. Rosenzweig and Nohria (1994) argued that HR is the area of management most likely to be subject to national differences. Laurent (1986; p.97) warned against assuming that management approaches developed in one particular culture can be deemed to be valid for any other culture:

'If we accept the view that HRM approaches are cultural artefacts reflecting the basic assumptions and values of the national culture in which organisations are embedded, international HRM becomes one of the most challenging corporate tasks in multinational organisations.'

He observed that in order to build, maintain and develop their corporate identity, multinational organisations need to strive for consistency in their ways of managing people on a worldwide basis. At the same time, in order to be effective locally, they also need to adapt those ways to the specific cultural requirements of different societies. Laurent inserts a note of caution into attempts by international organisations to create a 'supra-national' corporate culture. He argues that the concept of organisational culture should be restricted to the more superficial layers of implicit and explicit systems of norms, expectations and historically based preferences, constantly reinforced by their behavioural manifestations and assigned meanings. Using this reasoning, organisations could expect their employees to display appropriate behaviours to match the corporate culture, but could not demand any further immersion in corporate ideology.

We explore some of these specific HRM practices in later chapters – recruitment and selection in Chapter 6, rewarding in Chapter 7, training and development in Chapter 8, flexible working practices in Chapter 9, and communications and consultation in Chapter 10. These chapters demonstrate the potential impact of culture on the design and acceptance of individual HR policies and practices. They do not, however, resolve the question of whether certain HR practices are applicable universally or which are context-specific. In addition, they do not address the degree to which culture can be seen to influence bundles of HR practice.

Sparrow *et al* (1994) used the results of a worldwide survey by Towers Perrin (1992) to explore how different cultural groupings of countries might affect the usage of a range of HRM variables. Based on the work of Moss-Kanter (1991) and Hofstede (1993), two hypotheses were developed.

- The first was that some countries – such as a few EU states, the major English-speaking countries (the USA, Canada, Australia and the UK), and a number of Latin American states – will group together (have cultural allies in terms of their HR practice), and some – such as Korea and Japan – will be idiosyncratic (have unique practices and be seen as cultural islands in this regard).

- The second hypothesis was more tentative and exploratory, and argued that there will be differences in the ways in which human resource policies and practices are seen as important for gaining competitive advantage across nations.

They thus discerned an 'Anglo-Saxon' grouping composed of Australia, Canada, the United Kingdom and the United States, three cultural islands (France, Korea and Japan), and a further grouping of cultural allies comprising the South American or Latin countries of Brazil, Mexico and Argentina. The authors highlighted the impact of historical factors on the present configuration of HR policies and practices in individual nation states. Other research studies addressing the same issue of 'emic' versus 'etic' HRM practices include the Best International Human Resource Management Practices Project led by Von Glinow (Teagarden *et al*, 1995) and the Cranet Project (Brewster and Hegewisch, 1994; Brewster *et al*, 2000; 2004). We draw upon these datasets in some of the subsequent chapters.

MOVING TOWARDS A MORE GLOBAL MINDSET IN HR?

While recognising the power of national culture, Pucik (1997) has challenged the HR function to develop a more global mindset by pointing out that the currently distinctly national HR systems that exist around the world are parochial and ethnocentric. A more global mindset and role for HR in helping to champion the best aspects of globalisation means that HR functions have to 'do' international HRM differently. In particular they have to:

- recognise the ways in which cultural values influence HR systems

- understand the different values that are placed on people around the world.

ACTIVITY

Read Jackson, T. (2002) 'The management of people across cultures: valuing people differently', *Human Resource Management*, 41 (4): 455–75.

It was Jackson (2002; p.458) who wrote:

> **'The importance of cultural values to the conduct of organisational life is well-established in the literature. Yet the way cultural differences influence how people are valued in organisations has not been sufficiently discussed.'**

The literature indicates that cultural values shape the conduct of HRM through the following mechanisms (Sparrow and Hiltrop, 1997):

- attitudes held about, and definitions of, what makes an effective manager, and their implications for the qualities recruited, trained and developed

- the giving of face-to-face feedback, levels of power distance and uncertainty avoidance, and their implications for recruitment interview, communication, negotiation and participation processes

- expectations of the manager–subordinate relationship, and their implications for performance management and motivational processes

- differential concepts of distributive justice, socially healthy pay and the individualisation of rewards, and their implications for the design of pay systems

- the mindsets used to think about organisational structuring or strategic dynamics.

ACTIVITY

Thinking back to specific cultural values outlined in the previous chapter, how would you expect the following HR activities to be influenced by them?

- recruitment and selection
- performance management
- communication.

Jackson (2002) has provided a theoretical framework to help capture such links between culture and HRM practice. He does this by developing the concept of the 'locus of human value'. The cross-cultural literature shows two contrasting management perceptions of the value of people in organisations: instrumental and humanistic. These perceptions are manifested in specific policy orientations, and in turn a series of HRM practices naturally flow from these policy orientations.

The two loci of human value therefore lie at the heart of international HRM, and each approach – instrumental or humanistic – is a product of cultural factors. These are shown in Figure 9.

Global cultural interaction brings these two loci of human value into conflict or contradiction. Through the process of 'crossvergence', management systems from each country are borrowed and adapted. Managing globally, however, 'goes further than simply adapting practices effectively from one culture to another' (Jackson, 2002; p.470). It needs managers to incorporate the learning points experienced along the way into their thought processes. This moves us on to a discussion of the impact of culture on leadership and management styles.

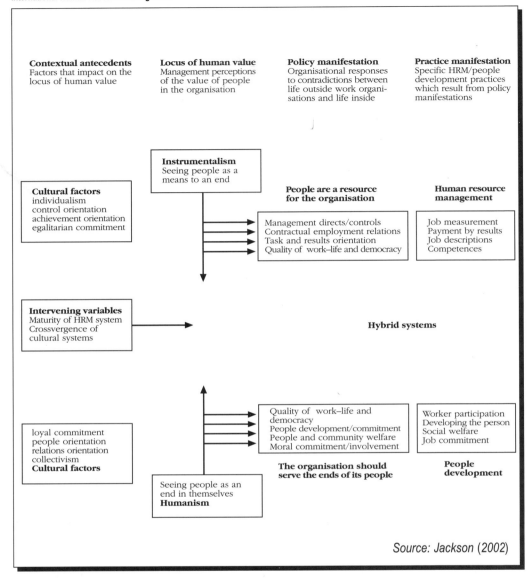

Contextual antecedents
Factors that impact on the locus of human value

Locus of human value
Management perceptions of the value of people in the organisation

Policy manifestation
Organisational responses to contradictions between life outside work organisations and life inside

Practice manifestation
Specific HRM/people development practices which result from policy manifestations

Instrumentalism
Seeing people as a means to an end

Cultural factors
individualism
control orientation
achievement orientation
egalitarian commitment

People are a resource for the organisation

Human resource management

Management directs/controls
Contractual employment relations
Task and results orientation
Quality of work–life and democracy

Job measurement
Payment by results
Job descriptions
Competences

Intervening variables
Maturity of HRM system
Crossvergence of cultural systems

Hybrid systems

Quality of work–life and democracy
People development/commitment
People and community welfare
Moral commitment/involvement

Worker participation
Developing the person
Social welfare
Job commitment

loyal commitment
people orientation
relations orientation
collectivism
Cultural factors

The organisation should serve the ends of its people

People development

Seeing people as an end in themselves
Humanism

Source: Jackson (2002)

Figure 9 *Conceptual framework for the locus of human value*

LEADERSHIP AND MANAGEMENT STYLES

Leadership styles are a key determinant of the organisational context in which HR policies and practices must be developed. Another way of understanding how culture shapes organisations, therefore, is to examine the way that people *lead* in different countries. Leadership involves being able to set a vision, communicate it, and motivate people to follow. In essence, every manager should be a leader ... but that does not always come to pass.

However, is being a good leader the same thing in China as it is in the USA? We have already seen the different levels of decision-making discretion and the different ways in which managers prioritise their time. One look at the shelves of leadership texts written by management gurus in airport bookshops might well lead us to believe that there is one recipe for successful leadership and that this emanates from the United States. Nearly twenty years ago, Bass (1990) reported that there had been more than 3,500 studies of leadership conducted by social scientists working in the United States. These included some of the most influential in shaping managerial behaviour and development:

- trait theory
- Theory X and Theory Y
- the Ohio State and University of Michigan behavioural theories
- Managerial Grid theory
- situational and/or contingency theory/theories
- Path-Goal theory.

Despite this proliferation of US-based theories, little or inconclusive support has been found for them in research with data collected in the United States (Yukl, 1994). With little empirical evidence supporting these theories in their country of origin, their applicability to other countries must also be questioned.

Some attempts have been made to develop a global leadership model including the studies by Adler and Bartholomew (1992), which link different types of global strategy with different types of leader competencies. A key study in this area was carried out by Black, Morrison and Gregersen (1999). An important finding from their research was that about two-thirds of the characteristics of effective global leaders are generalisable, whereas the other one-third are idiosyncratic or context-specific. Four major context-specific factors were perceived to affect idiosyncratic characteristics: company affiliation, managerial position, country affiliation, and functional responsibility.

For instance, US lawyers need some skills that are different from those of Chinese engineers. All leaders have to develop their own set of idiosyncratic skills that suit their work context. Three core characteristics were identified from the research, labelled 'demonstrating savvy', 'exhibiting character' and 'embracing duality'.

Demonstrating savvy comprises two facets: global business savvy and global organisational savvy. Global business savvy is understood as the ability to make money for the organisation on a worldwide basis from identifying opportunities for cheaper production, for new markets, and through economies of scale and standardisation.

Exhibiting character comes through emotionally connecting with people and demonstrating high personal integrity.

Embracing duality consists of two competencies: the ability to manage uncertainty and the ability to balance the often powerful tensions between globalisation and localisation pressures. Black *et al* (1999) found that global leaders actually seek out environments in which uncertainty and tension are at their highest. The authors identified a fourth dimension, inquisitiveness, which holds the model together and gives it life. They do not see this as a competency that can be developed but more a state of mind. Possession of inquisitiveness fosters learning, which is regarded as essential for keeping savvy, character and perspective fresh.

Cross-cultural studies generally indicate a strong connection between culture and leadership styles. Specific cultural traditions, values, ideologies and norms are 'bound to differentiate as much or even more than structural factors between societies' (Lammers and Hickson, 1979; p.10). The cross-cultural frameworks presented in the last chapter provide evidence of distinct national differences in working values and behaviours, and Laurent's (1986) work suggests significant differences in managerial values across nations.

This work has been carried on in more recent projects. A key example is the GLOBE Project (House *et al*, 2002). The GLOBE project findings on leadership show a picture of subtle, but meaningful, variations in

LIBRARY, UNIVERSITY OF CHESTER

scores around leadership dimensions, but also demonstrate that charismatic, team-oriented and participative styles are the most effective leadership styles. House *et al* (2002) stress that although the dimension 'charismatic' (which consists of such attributes as visionary, inspirational, self-sacrificial, of notable integrity, decisiveness, and performance-oriented) appears to be universally rated as the most important leadership style, the interpretation of 'charisma' in different societal settings may differ. Likewise, the dimension 'team-oriented' has to be interpreted differently in individualistic cultures as opposed to family- or group-oriented cultures. The GLOBE project introduces a new cross-cultural framework and positioning of societies in clusters which provides a link between cultural background and preferred leadership styles. Overall, the research supports the argument that leadership is culturally contingent, although the key dimensions of effective leadership are consistent across societal clusters.

Case study

The GLOBE Project

The GLOBE (Global Leadership and Organisational Behaviour Effectiveness) Project is a multi-phase, multi-method project in which investigators spanning the world are examining the inter-relationships between societal culture, organisational culture and organisational leadership. The project involves 150 social scientists and management scholars from 61 cultures (the findings are detailed by Ashkanasy, Trevor-Roberts and Earnshaw, 2002; House, Javidan, Hanges and Dorfman, 2002; and House *et al*, 2004). The meta-goal of GLOBE is to develop an empirically based theory to describe, understand and predict the impact of specific cultural variables on leadership and organisational processes, and the effectiveness of these processes. Four of the fundamental questions the project is trying to address are:

■ Are there leader behaviours, attributes and organisational practices that are accepted and effective across cultures?

■ Are there leader behaviours, attributes and organisational practices that are accepted and effective only in some cultures?

■ How do attributes of societal and organisational cultures affect the kinds of leader behaviours and organisational practices that are accepted and effective?

■ Can the universal and culture-specific aspects of leader behaviours, attributes and organisational practices be explained in terms of an underlying theory that accounts for systematic differences across cultures?

Questionnaires were distributed to middle managers in 62 national cultures. These measured aspired values (in terms of 'what should be') but asked what values were reflected in behaviours and practices (in terms of 'what is'). Ten distinct national clusters emerged within the overall sample in respect of preferred leadership styles, based on nine dimensions of national culture. Many of the nine cultural dimensions are already in the literature and were discussed in the previous chapter, such as Hofstede's uncertainty avoidance and power distance. His masculinity dimension was also reflected in what the GLOBE Project called 'gender egalitarianism and assertiveness', and long-termism was reflected in a 'future-orientation'. However, because data was analysed at the organisational level, two additional dimensions of 'performance-orientation' (the extent to which an organisation or society encouraged and rewarded group members for performance improvement and excellence), and 'humane orientation' (the degree to which individuals in organisations or societies encouraged and rewarded individuals for being fair, altruistic, friendly, generous, caring and kind to others) were identified. The findings also differentiated between societal collectivism, which reflected the degree to which organisational and societal institutional practices encouraged and rewarded collective distribution of resources and collective action, and in-group collectivism, which reflected the degree to which individuals expressed pride, loyalty and cohesiveness in their organisations or families.

A total of 23 different leadership styles were deemed to be effective in one or more of the different societal cultures of the world (each leadership style was considered to represent a *culturally endorsed implicit leadership theory* or CELT). There were six underlying dimensions or styles of an effective global leadership style. The results showed a picture of subtle but meaningful variations in scores around leadership dimensions, but also demonstrated that the charismatic, team-oriented and participative styles were the most effective leadership styles across cultures. The charismatic dimension (which consisted of such attributes as visionary, inspirational, self-sacrificial, integrity, decisiveness, and performance-orientation) appeared to be universally rated as the most important leadership style, but the interpretation of charisma in different societal settings was considered to vary. There was high within-culture agreement with respect to leader attributes and behaviours, and two out of six leader behaviour dimensions were viewed universally as contributors to effective leadership. One was viewed nearly universally as an impediment to leadership, and one as nearly universally a contributor. The endorsement of the remaining two varied by culture. In short, there were 21 specific behaviours that were universal, 8 impediment behaviours, and 35 behaviours that depended upon the cultural context. Overall, the research supported the argument that leadership is culturally contingent, although the key dimensions of effective leadership are consistent across societal clusters.

In the first part of this chapter we have looked at the way that culture shapes HRM practices and pointed out that a key challenge is for managers to understand the role of culture and then incorporate this learning from the globalisation process into their solutions. We have also shown that fundamental managerial behaviours such as values, decision-making latitude, use of time, and leadership style are all affected by national culture. In the final three sections of this chapter we take a brief look at different sets of competencies that can assist individuals and organisations in coping with these cultural differences.

Researchers have learned about these competencies by attempting to understand three important aspects of organisational life:

- how managers demonstrate global leadership behaviours
- what being a successful member of a multicultural team involves
- what it takes to demonstrate 'cultural intelligence'.

DEVELOPING GLOBAL LEADERSHIP COMPETENCIES

Confirmation of differing leadership styles around the world poses a critical question for all organisations operating across borders: is there such a thing as a global leadership model?

> **'As companies rely more and more on global strategies, they require more and more global leaders. This tie between strategy and leadership is essentially a two-way street: the more companies pursue global strategies, the more global leaders they need; and the more global leaders companies have, the more they pursue global strategies.'**
>
> *Morrison (2000; p.119)*

In thinking about this issue, a distinction is typically made between:

- the expatriate (or international) manager – an executive in a leadership position that involves international assignments across countries and cultures, with skills defined by the location of the assignment
- the global (or transnational) manager – an executive assigned to positions with cross-border responsibilities, who has a hands-on understanding of international business, with competencies defined more by their frame of mind.

We deal with the knowledge, skills and abilities that become important for international managers and expatriates in Chapter 12 on *Managing international working*. However, we concentrate here on the issue of global leadership, which involves a different set of capabilities. Pucik (1998; p.41) points out that:

> **'Some global managers may be expatriates; many, if not most, have been expatriates at some point in their career, but probably only few expatriates are global managers.'**

The earliest debates on international management strategy argued that strategic capability is ultimately dependent on the 'cognitive processes' of global managers and the ability of firms to create a 'matrix in the minds of managers' or a 'transnational mentality' (Bartlett and Ghoshal, 1989; p.195). There have only been a few studies that have looked at global leaders in detail and the evidence still tends to be more anecdotal. For example, from a practitioner perspective, the chief executives of HSBC, Schering-Plough, General Electric, Flextronics and Egon Zehnder have given their response to the pioneering work of Bartlett and Ghoshal to explain their view of what global leadership involves (*Harvard Business Review*, 2003).

Academics have focused more on how organisations can help 'build' global leadership skills in managers. They have looked at the role played by both the social networks and effective global leaders. Rather than just focusing on a particular set of skills or range of competencies that are important for effective international management (we look at these in Chapter 7), we maintain that there are two important additional aspects or components to this global 'mentality':

- attitudes and values
- mindset (cognitive structures).

The first aspect – attitudes and values – has been called an *international orientation*. This factor is assumed to correlate with both the extent and the quality of international experience. Researchers have attempted to develop measures that correspond to the core dimensions of a manager's thinking about international strategy and international organisation, and have then shown how this mindset changes over time. For example, Murtha *et al* (1998) looked at the type of cognitive change towards a more global mindset in managers over a three-year period within a single multinational organisation, identifying a core value-set or logic that is associated with global operations.

Global managers must also have a good mental model of *how knowledge and information is shared* across the people with whom they need to interact if they are to help their organisation deliver an important global business process, product or service. Recent work has looked at the role of international managers as important brokers of knowledge, arguing that they help to diffuse practices across borders. Global managers also have to understand how tacit knowledge spreads within top management teams. What are the 'advice networks' that exist inside the organisation? International managers often build up a lot of 'social capital' because they have 'boundary-spanning roles' and this puts them in touch with many different networks inside the organisation. They also develop important insights into the organisation through their interpersonal cross-border relationships. All of these factors help global managers build superior mental models of the organisation, and enable them to become more effective (Sparrow, 2006).

Organisations like Shell International argue that global leadership in a mature multinational organisation depends on creating face-to-face cross-cultural leadership at all levels (Steel, 1997). Graen and Hui (1999), coming from an industrial and organisational psychology perspective, argue that in order for cross-national differences to be managed effectively, organisations need to develop global leadership by enhancing the level of 'transcultural skills' and using these to help resolve the complexity of cross-cultural management (see Table 10).

Progressive stage	Characteristics distinguishing transculturals from non-transculturals
Adventurer	Stereotypes held from an ethnocentric perspective: development of an adventurer's mentality towards cultures other than one's own
Sensitiser	An outsider's view of norms: attunement of behaviours and attitudes to a culture other than one's own; has learned to read and conform to new cultural norms
Insider	Knows what one doesn't know: has developed a knowledge-base rich enough to behave and display feelings inside another culture vastly different from one's own; has sufficient insight to understand the value of what is not known
Judge	Makes valid generalisations about attributes: in the eyes of observers is considered to be able to conceptualise useful differences and similarities between cultures for the purpose of comparison; has developed behaviours, feelings and knowledge to conduct cross-cultural negotiations
Synthesiser	Can discover functional equivalences: has been socialised into the culture of interest and can synthesise both the home and host culture; can identify constructs of functional equivalence between cultures or develop a third culture of relevance to both cultures

Source: after Graen and Hui (1999)

Table 10 *Progressive stages of transcultural competence*

DEBATE

■ Graen and his colleagues argue that even the most adept global leader has only learned how to operate through insight into approaches that can serve an equivalent function in a new culture, rather than truly being of that culture.

Do you agree with this, and if you do, what are the implications for multinational organisations?

THE MULTICULTURAL TEAM

Looking at the different assumptions that we make about the skills and competencies that are needed by global leaders, one could be forgiven for saying 'But surely this is only important for large organisations that employ a small cadre of internationally mobile managers and expatriates? What about organisations that might simply source international employees from and in different parts of the world? Do they need to recruit for the sorts of competencies discussed here?' If we look at what we know about the use of international employees, then the answer is probably 'Yes.' Organisations rely upon cross-cultural skills and at surprisingly low levels in the hierarchy.

The use of teams, even within highly individualist countries such as the United States, has become accepted as a key means of coping with the highly complex and dynamic nature of work in the twenty-first century. Why do internationalisation strategies require managers increasingly to work through multinational team networks? There are three main reasons:

■ Organisations are pursuing strategies of localisation, attempting to reduce their reliance on expatriates in their traditional co-ordination and control role.

■ Strategies that rely on rapid internationalisation through international joint-venturing, strategic partnership arrangements and global start-ups place international managers in team and work contexts in which they may have less position-power but a heightened need to ensure that their organisation learns from the partnership.

■ As organisations globalise their operations, the requirement for international working is pushed lower down the hierarchy.

It is essential for HR professionals to develop policies and practices that support the use of teams. This includes selecting team players, rewarding on the basis of teamwork, and developing mentoring and coaching behaviours for potential leaders.

For international organisations, there are a number of benefits of working in transnational teams (Schneider and Barsoux, 1997). They can encourage cohesiveness amongst national and functional units. They are very useful in creating lateral networks to improve communication and information flow between subsidiaries and HQ, and among subsidiaries (Ghoshal *et al*, 1994). They provide opportunities for team members to understand international issues better and to note the interdependencies between units. They also provide opportunities for team members to learn how to function more effectively within different cultures with suppliers, customers or employees. Finally, they can help foster knowledge transfer and organisational learning.

Evans *et al* (2002) view cross-boundary teams as the basic unit of the global economy and argue that strategic decisions in global organisations are complex. They say that the best way to achieve sound decisions is often through a transnational team of managers and specialists whose talents have been carefully blended. Transnational teams therefore contribute to what they term 'glue technology'. This describes the underlying process technology used in co-ordinating mechanisms within international organisations. Under this perspective, the foundation of most mechanisms of co-ordination is relationships between people.

Cross-boundary teams can take many shapes and forms – they may (for example) be part of an international supply chain in a major pharmaceutical company, or a cross-national team of consultants put together to deliver a business solution for a global services company, or an international relief team working for a not-for-profit organisation.

QUESTIONS

From our earlier discussions of cross-cultural differences,

- What would you see to be the pros and cons of forming a team with individuals from the USA, Germany, Japan and Brazil?
- What process recommendations would you make to ensure effective functioning of the team?

Research suggests that multicultural teams tend to be either very high-performing or very low-performing (Shapiro *et al*, 2002). Figure 10 shows the relative productivity of a series of four- to six-member problem-solving teams. Culturally diverse teams tend to become either the most or the least effective, whereas single-culture teams tend to be average.

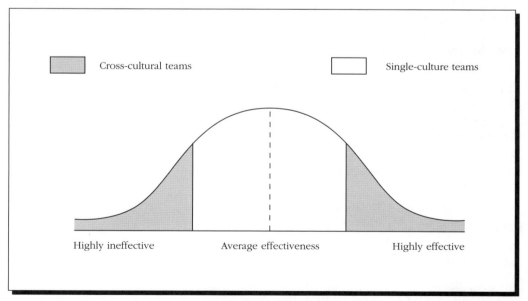

Figure 10 *Relative productivity of cross-cultural and single-culture teams*

Adler (1997) argues that the difference between highly productive and less productive teams lies in how they manage their diversity, not in the fact that they include diversity. According to Adler, a multicultural team's productivity depends on its task, stage of development and the ways in which its diversity is managed (see Table 11).

	Effective	Ineffective
Task	Innovative Divergence (earlier)	Routine Convergence (later)
Stage	Differences recognised Members selected for task-related abilities	Differences ignored Members selected on basis of ethnicity
Conditions	Mutual respect Equal power Superordinate goal External feedback	Ethnocentrism Culturalism dominance Individual goals No feedback (complete autonomy)

Source: Adler (1997; p.139)

Table 11 *Managing diversity effectively*

In terms of task, multicultural or diverse teams are seen to perform better than homogeneous teams in situations where innovative ideas/solutions are required. Most of the major consulting companies will form international and cross-functional teams to deliver competitive, leading-edge solutions for multinational clients. In contrast, a team working on the standardised assembly of electronic components will require individuals with the same standard of manual dexterity. A team will also progress through various stages, defined by Adler as:

- entry
- work
- action.

At the *entry* stage a team needs to develop cohesiveness. This involves members beginning to know and to trust each other. Creativity is essential at the *work* stage when the team has to create ways of defining its objectives, gathering and analysing information and assessing alternative plans of action. Convergence is needed at the final *action* stage when agreement on a final solution is required. Diversity can be seen to hinder both the first and final stages, but be extremely beneficial at the middle stage (see Table 12).

Stage	Process	Diversity makes the process	Process based on
Entry: initial team formation	Trust-building (developing cohesion)	More difficult	Using similarities and understanding differences
Work: problem description and analysis	Ideation (creating ideas)	Easier	Using differences
Action: decision-making and implementation	Consensus-building (agreeing and acting)	More difficult	Recognising and creating similarities

Source: Adler (1997; p.140)

Table 12 *Managing diversity, based on the team's stage of development*

Key competencies for multicultural teams

There are a number of things that members of international teams have to understand (Sparrow, 2006). What is the desired behaviour? Why is the behaviour considered desirable? At whom is the behaviour aimed? Where is the behaviour most often seen? How is the behaviour delivered? Although individuals with cultural intelligence are important, it is also the quality of cross-cultural communication at team level that determines the effectiveness of multicultural teams (Kealey and Protheroe, 1996; Gudykunst, 1998;

Matveev and Nelson, 2004). Table 13 shows the specification of cross-cultural communication competence that can be applied to individual and also to team interactions.

Interpersonal skills	Team effectiveness	Cultural uncertainty	Cultural empathy
Ability to acknowledge differences in communication and interaction styles Ability to deal with misunderstandings Ease when communicating with foreign nationals Awareness of own cultural conditioning Basic knowledge about the country, the culture, and the language of team members	Ability to understand and define team goals, roles and norms Ability to give and receive constructive feedback Ability to discuss and solve problems Ability to deal with conflict situations Ability to display respect for other team members Participatory leadership style Ability to work co-operatively with others	Ability to deal with cultural uncertainty Ability to display patience Tolerance of ambiguity and uncertainty due to cultural differences Openness to cultural differences Ability to exercise flexibility	Ability to see and understand the world from others' cultural perspectives Ability to exhibit a spirit of inquiry about other cultures, values, beliefs and communication patterns Ability to appreciate dissimilar working styles Ability to accept different ways of doing things Non-judgemental stance towards the ways things are done in other situations

Source: Matveev and Nelson (2004)

Table 13 *Cross-cultural communication competence*

Strategies for managing multicultural teams

Multicultural teams do not differ from mono-cultural teams in terms of basic team dynamics – they go through stages of development (the 'forming, storming, norming and performing' aspect). They also need to consider composition issues such as the resources allocated to the team, membership profile, numbers, etc. And they need to address how to run the team. Core team dynamics studies would identify both task and process issues relating to effective team performance. The same is true for multicultural groups, but given the complexity of different cultural perspectives, assumptions about the nature of task and process issues ought to be questioned by all team members in order to achieve a 'common reality' and from there to establish common ground rules for the development of the team.

A comprehensive list of the issues to be addressed in both task and process aspects of managing multicultural teams is presented by Schneider and Barsoux (1997; p.186) – see below.

Task strategies

- What is the purpose, process, and timing of meetings?
- To what extent does the mission need to be made clear and explicit?
- Is it more important to achieve cost targets, or are cost overruns OK given time/quality targets?
- What does 'on time' mean?
- What is the priority of time?

- What is the importance and priority of deadlines?
- Is it more important to achieve time deadlines, or to delay for higher quality?
- What do we do about missed commitments?
- To what extent does the agenda need to be clearly structured and followed?
- To what extent do the rules of the game need to be spelled out?
- To what extent do roles and responsibilities need to be formalised and written?
- Who should attend, and when?
- What is the role of the leader? Of team members?
- How will the tasks be divided up and then integrated?
- What work can be done together or apart?
- What technologies can be used (video-conferencing, email)?
- What is an effective presentation?
- What is needed to be convincing – facts and figures, philosophy, feelings?
- How will information be passed? To whom? When? Formally or informally? Within the team or outside?
- How, where and when do we make decisions? Consensus, majority rule, compromise?

Process strategies

- How will we manage relationships – dive right into business, or take time to socialise?
- To what extent will we socialise together, and when?
- What is trust, and how is it earned?
- How will we address people? First or last name? Titles?
- How formal or informal will we be?
- What language(s) will we use?
- How will differences in language fluency be managed?
- To what extent does participation reflect potential contributions?
- Who dominates?
- Who listens to whom?
- Who talks to whom?
- How are interruptions managed?
- How is conflict managed? Forcing, accommodating, avoiding, collaborating, compromising?
- How is negotiation viewed? Win/lose, or win/win?
- How is feedback provided? Face to face, third-party, direct?

The checklist above illustrates the potential for conflict on even the most basic team management issues. Teams incorporating diverse nationalities tend to ignore differences at the start-up stages of the teams and to focus on similarities (ie young, well-educated, professional). With depressing regularity, team dynamic problems surface later, when the pressure of work kicks in. Complaints of non-inclusion from those from high-context, neutral cultures are greeted with shocked surprise by UK and US members who view their time- and task-focused approach, combined with an assertive manner, as the 'right' approach to teamwork.

The introduction of intercultural awareness sessions, combined with discussion around team-building issues for multicultural teams (perhaps using selected questions from Schneider and Barsoux's task and process strategy checklist), leads to a significant decrease in complaints and more effective teams.

DEVELOPING CULTURAL INTELLIGENCE

In the final section of this chapter we pull together much of the material covered in the book so far by asking the question 'Can organisations develop cultural intelligence amongst their employees?' We have seen that this is an important part of global leadership skills and that it also is important for the effective functioning of international management teams. A book by Earley and Ang (2003) and a subsequent article by Earley and Mosakowski (2004) have moved the debate on and sparked off an important exchange of views between cross-cultural researchers. In the article, the authors introduced a concept that they termed 'cultural intelligence' (CQ). This is an attitude and skill that enables individuals to adapt effectively across cultures. In practical terms, it enables an individual to interpret unfamiliar and ambiguous gestures in ways as accurately as a home national could. Understanding the nature of CQ has important applications for individuals, teams and organisational functioning. Earley and Mosakowski (2004; p.140) argue that managers with global responsibilities can be socially intelligent in their own settings, but ineffective in novel cultures, yet:

> **'A person with high cultural intelligence can somehow tease out of a person's or group's behaviour those features that would be true of all people and all groups, those peculiar to this person or this group, and those that are neither universal or idiosyncratic. The vast realm that lies between those two poles is culture.'**

As we have seen, research on intercultural competence has a long tradition and it shows that a range of factors can predict effectiveness in this area, including previous experience, personality factors, cross-cultural attitudes and communication behaviours, and situational factors such as cultural training or the 'distance' between two cultures. Cultural intelligence is an individual difference, but unlike personality, which is relatively enduring, it is considered to be something that can be developed and enhanced through interventions that organisations can make. It has four components:

1   Mind (meta-cognitions): learning strategies, whereby people can acquire and develop coping strategies. We need to identify a 'point of entry' into a foreign culture – for example, a form of behaviour or a context that can be used to subsequently interpret different patterns of behaviour

2   Knowledge about different cultures (cognition)

3   Heart (emotional/motivational): people must have the desire to persevere in the face of challenge when adapting to a new culture, and a belief in their own ability to master a situation (called self-efficacy)

4   Body (physical behaviour): people must develop a repertoire of culturally appropriate behaviours. This centres on the ability to mirror customs and gestures, and adopt habits and mannerisms, in order to enter the world of a foreign culture and enable the development of trust.

Rather than the progressive stages of transcultural competence suggested by Graen and Hui (1999), which were discussed earlier in relation to the debate about global leadership, for Earley and Ang (2003) an individual may be strong in some of these areas, weaker in others. Based on survey data from 2000 relating to managers from 60 cultures, six typical combinations were identified (such as provincial, analyst, mimic, natural, ambassador), with the ultimate being a chameleon, who has strengths in all areas.

They argued that CQ shares some common features with another 'brand' of intelligence – emotional intelligence – but also has unique features. It shares the propensity to suspend judgement and to think before acting, because in order to avoid the hazards of stereotyping, managers have to gather information about all of the personalities that are interacting before them and discern how they are different from those in the home culture yet similar to each other. However, emotional intelligence is developed within the confines of a single culture, whereas cultural intelligence requires that people develop understanding across cultures. Although some aspects of cultural intelligence are considered to be innate, Earley and Mosakowski (2004; p.140) argue that 'anyone reasonably alert, motivated and poised can attain an acceptable level of cultural intelligence'.

There are commonplace training strategies that can be designed to build capability in each of the four elements noted above.

DEBATE

Hampden-Turner and Trompenaars (2006) point out that supporters of the concept of cultural intelligence have to contend with and come up with convincing answers to three critical views. Critics argue that:

- Cultures are entirely relative in their values. There is no 'best way' of understanding culture as an issue in organisational life, or understanding other cultures (called the cultural relativism argument). We cannot judge values or use values – we can merely ask questions that help us understand how values fit the environment that any particular society finds itself in.

- Cultural studies are a backward step, leading to grand theories. We need to have multiple theories and perspectives, all of which can be partially legitimate. Given that everything just represents a point of view, there cannot be an objective thing known as cultural intelligence (called the post-modernist argument).

- All attempts to categorise cultures are crude stereotypes inferred from superficial features of culture, and they miss deeper and subtle realities and meanings (called the latent argument). All that cross-cultural research does is tell us what we already know – for example, that the Japanese are impassive and the French excitable. It all depends really on circumstances.

Do you think that the evidence for cultural intelligence can answer these criticisms or not?

The case study below helps to bring together the discussion of different taxonomies of culture that were covered in Chapter 2 with the range of work on transcultural competence that has been covered in this chapter. The latest thinking shows increasing consensus amongst experts. It is important that global HR practitioners understand these viewpoints because they guide most of the currently available cultural awareness and training products and processes.

Case study

Is cultural intelligence just another trendy concept, or has it got substance? What the experts say

Three years after the publication by Earley and Ang (2003), a special issue of *Group and Organisation Management* in 2006 was used to bring together the views of a number of leading researchers in the areas of culture and intelligence (Ng and Earley, 2006). This case is based on the premise of the special issue – that cross-cultural experts can no longer ignore the evidence on intelligence in the workplace and vice versa. Understanding the impact of culture on organisational life requires us to think about both issues. The outcome of the debate has very important implications for organisations that attempt to build cultural intelligence amongst their employees. The key views expressed included the following:

There is pervasive evidence that people in different cultures think and act differently, and that what is considered intelligent differs from one place to the next (Sternberg and Grigorenko, 2006). People's implicit theories of social intelligence go beyond what is typically measured in psychometric instruments, which concentrate on cognitive intelligence. Successful intelligence (understanding how to adapt, shape or select out, and achieve goals) requires a combination of analytical, creative and practical abilities, and these tend to apply within a single culture. It is the tacit knowledge that these abilities assess that is the most predictive of managerial performance and certainly leadership effectiveness. This tacit knowledge does not correlate with more traditional cognitive measures of intelligence. Cultural intelligence, as articulated by Earley and Ang (2003), is a form of social intelligence that is relevant across cultures and helps us understand intelligence in a broader way.

Cross-cultural experts such as Brislin, Trompenaars, Hampden-Turner, Thomas and Triandis have all helped explain the sorts of learning strategies and 'meta-cognitions' that become important. The term 'meta-cognition' is used by psychologists to refer to an individual's ability to understand his or her own thought processes and behaviour when he/she plans and performs. These are some of the most important ways in which these work.

- Cultural intelligence revolves around the ability to suspend judgement until further relevant information has been understood. The culturally intelligent person looks for current behaviour in different situations to identify the impact that personality might have on another's behaviour. Such a person has the ability to identify what is important information on which to base an assessment. To make a person culturally intelligent requires extensive training. Cognitive, emotional and behavioural training are all necessary to help people integrate a lot of information, learn how to use multiple cues, and suspend judgements. Only then can we limit our natural tendency to assume that 'normal' is what happens in our own culture. This is the view taken by Triandis (2006).

- A culturally intelligent person has to possess three capabilities in order to see beyond differences in values across cultures: the ability to see the synergies that exist between the contrasting values in any culture and understand how people reconcile them; the ability to treat these opposing values as complementary rather than contradictory and understand how people move between each value; and the ability to understand how dominant and more hidden values interact with each other and how people express the less dominant values in any culture. This is the view taken by Hampden-Turner and Trompenaars (2006).

- Culturally intelligent people are skilful at recognising behaviours that are influenced by culture and do this in four ways: observing behaviours in different cultures; developing reasons that explain these differences; considering the emotional implications and associations that arise from these behaviours; and then transferring this new knowledge into novel situations. In order to do this, people have to be able to anticipate and to accept confusion, but also to make a distinction between competitive encounters, where their cultural exploration might be exploited, and collaborative encounters, where it will be accepted. This is the view taken by Brislin *et al* (2006).

- Cultural intelligence has three components: knowledge of culture and fundamental principles of cross-cultural interactions; a heightened awareness of, and enhanced attention to, current experience, such as a new cultural environment (this is called 'mindfulness'); and behavioural ability to become competent across a wide range of cultural situations. Of these three, it is the mental skill of 'mindfulness' that is perhaps the most important. People make the link between having knowledge about other cultures and developing the ability to behave appropriately through this 'mindfulness'. It allows us to concentrate on new strategies rather than falling back upon tried and tested ways of behaving, which is what we all do unless we focus our minds. This is the view taken by Thomas (2006).

SUMMARY

This chapter clearly demonstrates the powerful impact of culture on organisational practices. A consistent theme is that despite movements towards global convergence, there are still consistent national cultural differences that affect approaches to broad organisational and HR policies and practices and leadership. The implications of this for global HR practitioners are a need for sensitivity to differences and an ability to blend the best of the many different approaches societies adopt in the management and motivation of workforces. This sensitivity becomes particularly evident when managers exercise global leadership or when they work as members of international management teams. Moreover, recent work suggests that there is a form of intelligence that reflects individual effectiveness in being able to work and adapt across cultures.

LEARNING QUESTIONS

What does the study of how managers actually spend their time and their decision-making powers in like-for-like organisations really tell us? What are the messages for key areas of HRM policy?

Can HR managers rise to Pucik's challenge of not standing in the way of globalisation while also remaining the guardians of national culture in an organisation?

Can leadership be considered more than just a product of national culture? What do leaders have to do to transcend national borders?

Is global leadership something that can be readily developed in managers, or do you think that it would be better to recruit a handful of ready-made international managers?

In what ways are the skills needed by international management teams any different from the traditional team-building skills needed to cope with heterogeneous groups from within a single culture?

Is there such a thing as cultural intelligence, and if there is, can we now specify what it involves? What, then, does it involve?

REFERENCES

Adler, N. J. (1997) *International Dimensions of Organisational Behavior*, 3rd edition. Cincinnati, South Western Publishing

Adler, N. and Bartholomew S. (1992) 'Managing globally competent people', *Academy of Management Executive*, 6 (3): 52–65

Ashkanasy, N. M., Trevor-Roberts, E. and Earnshaw, L. (2002) 'The Anglo cluster: legacy of the British Empire', *Journal of World Business*, 37: 28–39

Bartlett, C. A. and Ghoshal, S. (1989) *Managing Across Borders: The transnational solution.* Boston, MA, Harvard Business School Press

Bass, B. M. (1990) *Leadership and Performance beyond Expectations*. New York, Free Press

Black, S., Morrison A. and Gregersen H. (1999) *Global Explorers: The next generation of leaders.* New York, Routledge

Boisot, M. and Xing, G. L. (1991) 'The nature of managerial work in China', in N. Campbell, S. R. F. Plasschaert and D. H. Brown (eds) *Advances in Chinese Industrial Studies: Volume 2, The changing nature of management in China.* London, JAI Press

Brewster, C. and Hegewisch, A. (1994) (eds) *Policy and Practice in European Human Resource Management: The Price Waterhouse Cranfield Survey.* London, Routledge

Brewster, C., Mayrhofer, W. and Morley, M. (2000) (eds) *New Challenges for European Human Resource Management.* London, Macmillan

Brewster, C., Mayrhofer, W. and Morley, M. (eds) (2004) *Trends in Human Resource Management in Europe: Convergence or divergence.* London, Butterworth-Heinemann

Brislin, R., Worthley, R. and Macnab, B. (2006) 'Cultural intelligence: understanding behaviours that serve people's goals', *Group and Organisation Management*, 31 (1): 40–55

De Vries, M. F. R. and Florent-Treacy, E. (2002) 'Global leadership from A to Z: creating high-commitment organisations', *Organizational Dynamics*, 30 (4): 295–309

Earley, P. C. and Ang, S. (2003) *Cultural Intelligence: Individual interactions across cultures.* Stanford, CA, Stanford University Press

Earley, P. C. and Mosakowski, E. (2004) 'Cultural intelligence', *Harvard Business Review*, October: 139–46

Easterby-Smith, M., Malina, D. and Yuan, L. (1995) 'How culture-sensitive is HRM? A comparative analysis of practice in Chinese and UK companies', *International Journal of Human Resource Management*, 6 (1): 31–59

Evans, P., Pucik, V. and Barsoux, J.-L. (2002) *The Global Challenge: Frameworks for international human resource management.* Boston, MA, McGraw-Hill Irwin

Ghoshal, S., Korine, H. and Szulanski, G. (1994) 'Interunit communications in multinational corporations', *Management Science*, 40 (1): 96–110

Graen, G. B. and Hui, C. (1999) 'Transcultural global leadership in the 21st century: challenges and implications for development', in W. Mobley, M. J. Gessner and V. Arnold (eds) *Advances in Global Leadership.* Stamford, CT, JAI Press

Gudykunst, W. B. (1998) 'Applying anxiety/uncertainty management theory to inter-cultural adjustment training', *International Journal of Intercultural Relations*, 22: 227–50

Hampden-Turner, C. and Trompenaars, F. (2006) 'Cultural intelligence: is such a capacity credible?', *Group and Organisation Management*, 31 (1): 56–63

Harvard Business Review (2003) 'Perspectives: in search of global leaders', *Harvard Business Review*, August: 38–45

Hofstede, G. (1993) 'Cultural constraints in management theories', *Academy of Management Executive*, 7 (1): 81–93

House, R., Javidan, M., Hanges, P. and Dorfman, P. (2002) 'Understanding cultures and implicit leadership theories across the globe: an introduction to Project GLOBE', *Journal of World Business*, 37: 3–10

House, R. J., Hanges, P. J., Javidan, M., Dorfman, P. W. and Gupta, V. (2004) *Culture, Leadership and Organisation: A GLOBE study of 62 societies*. Thousand Oaks, CA, Sage

Jackson, T. (2002) 'The management of people across cultures: valuing people differently', *Human Resource Management*, 41 (4): 455–75

Kealey, D. J. and Protheroe, D. R. (1996) 'The effectiveness of cross-cultural training for expatriates: an assessment of the literature on the issue', *International Journal of Intercultural Relations*, 20 (2): 141–65

Lammers, C. J. and Hickson, D. (eds) (1979) *Organisations Alike and Unlike*. London, Routledge & Kegan Paul

Laurent, A. (1983) 'The cultural diversity of Western conceptions of management', *International Studies of Management and Organisation*, 13 (1, 2): 75–96

Laurent, A. (1986) 'The cross-cultural puzzle of international human resource management', *Human Resource Management*, 25 (1): 91–102

Matveev, A. V. and Nelson, P. E. (2004) 'Cross-cultural communication competence and multicultural team performance: perceptions of American and Russian managers', *International Journal of Cross-Cultural Management*, 4 (2): 253–70

Morrison, A. J. (2000) 'Developing a global leadership model', *Human Resource Management*, Summer/Fall, 39 (2, 3): 117–31

Moss-Kanter, R. (1991) 'Transcending business boundaries: 12,000 world managers view change', *Harvard Business Review*, 69 (3): 151–64

Murtha, T. P., Lenway, S. A. and Bagozzi, R. P. (1998) 'Global mind-sets and cognitive shift in a complex multinational corporation', *Strategic Management Journal*, 19: 97–114

Ng, K.-Y. and Earley, P. C. (2006) 'Old constructs, new frontiers', *Group and Organisation Management*, 31 (1): 4–19

Pucik, V. (1997) 'Human resources in the future: an obstacle or a champion of globalisation?', *Human Resource Management*, 36 (1): 163–7

Pucik, V. (1998) 'Selecting and developing the global versus the expatriate manager: a review of the state of the art', *Human Resource Planning*, 21 (4): 40–54

Rosenzweig, P. M. and Nohria, N. (1994) 'Influences on human resource management in multinational corporations', *Journal of International Business Studies*, Second Quarter: 229–51

Schneider, S. C. and Barsoux, J.-L. (1997) 'The multicultural team', in *Managing Across Cultures*. Hemel Hempstead, Prentice Hall

Shapiro, D. L., Furst, S. A., Spreitzer, G. M. and Von Glinow, M. A. (2002) 'Transnational teams in the electronic age: are team identity and high performance at risk?', *Journal of Organizational Behavior*, 23: 455–67

Sparrow, P. R. (2006) *A Guide to International Recruitment, Selection and Assessment*. Wimbledon, Chartered Institute of Personnel and Development

Sparrow, P. R. and Hiltrop, J. M. (1997) 'Redefining the field of European human resource management: a battle between national mindsets and forces of business transition', *Human Resource Management*, 36 (2): 1–19

Sparrow, P. R., Schuler, R. S. and Jackson, S. (1994) 'Convergence or divergence: human resource practices and policies for competitive advantage worldwide', *International Journal of Human Resource Management*, 5 (2): 267–99

Steel, G. (1997) *Global Leadership in a Mature Multinational Enterprise: Academy of Management symposium on global leadership in the 21st century*. Boston, MA

Sternberg, R. J. and Grigorenko, E. L. (2006) 'Cultural intelligence and successful intelligence', *Group and Organisation Management*, 31 (1): 27–39

Tayeb, M. H. (1988) *Organisations and National Culture*. London, Sage

Tayeb, M. H. (1996) *The Management of a Multicultural Workforce*. Chichester, John Wiley & Sons

Teagarden, M. B, Von Glinow, M. A., Bowen, D. E., Frayne, C. A., Nason, S., Huo, Y. P., Milliman, J., Arias, M. E., Butler, M. C., Geringer, J. M., Kim, N. H., Scullion, H., Lowe, K. B. and Drost, E. A. (1995) 'Toward a theory of comparative management research: an idiographic case study of the best international human resources management project', *Academy of Management Journal*, 38 (5): 1261–87

Thomas, D. C. (2006) 'Domain and development of cultural intelligence', *Group and Organisation Management*, 31 (1): 78–99

Towers Perrin (1992) *Priorities for Gaining Competitive Advantage: A worldwide human resource study*. London, Towers Perrin

Triandis, H. C. (2006) 'Cultural intelligence in organizations', *Group and Organisation Management*, 31 (1): 20–6

Yukl, G. A. (1994) *Leadership in Organisations*, 3rd edition. Englewood Cliffs, NJ, Prentice Hall

Comparative HRM

PART 2

Comparative HRM: theory and practice

CHAPTER 4

CHAPTER OBJECTIVES

When they have read this chapter, students will:

- be able to describe the strengths and weaknesses of the universalist and contextualist paradigms
- appreciate the arguments concerning convergence and divergence
- understand the differences between the US and other models of HRM
- be able to identify some key areas of similarity and difference in HR practice between countries.

INTRODUCTION

This chapter explores why we should be considering the comparative dimensions of HRM. After all, every organisation has to recruit workers, deploy them, pay them, motivate them and eventually arrange for their departure. Indeed, many texts are written as if their messages are universal. However, there is little doubt that things are done differently in different countries: not only do they have different cultures (as discussed in Chapters 2 and 3), but they also operate with differently educated and skilled workforces, in different economic situations, with different labour laws, trade union arrangements, government support or control, and so on. It is hardly surprising therefore that research shows that HRM not only varies between countries in the way that it is conducted, but that how it is defined and what is regarded as constituting good practice are also very distinct.

ACTIVITY

Examine your existing HR practices.

- Which of them are the product of your country's legal, economic, political or social institutions?

Provide explanations for your answer.

The issue of whether HR practices can be transferred is reflected in a fundamental division between two approaches to research and thinking in the field of HRM: the universalist and the contextual – or, in the terms of this chapter, the comparative (Brewster, 1999). These two approaches are also reflected in the debate between the two schools of thought that contest the notion of convergence. Some argue that even where there are differences, they are diminishing as the notion of globalisation becomes more entrenched and societies move towards each other in the way they do things – including the way they manage their human resources (see below and, for example, Lammers and Hickson, 1979; Child, 1981; Miles and Snow, 1986). Others argue that there is little evidence of such a moving together and that, in fact, societies remain steadfastly different and even unique (see below and, for example, Maurice, Sellier and Sivestre, 1986; Poole, 1986).

This chapter explores these conceptual differences as an introduction to the subsequent chapters in Part Two, which attempt to examine evidence about comparative human resource management policies and practices. It outlines the notions of universalism and contextual HRM; it explores the the concept of convergence and divergence and then, within that, explores the impact and relevance of US versions of HRM.

UNIVERSALIST VERSUS CONTEXTUAL HRM

Universalist HRM

The universalist paradigm is dominant in the United States of America but is widely used elsewhere. This paradigm assumes that the purpose of the study of HRM, and in particular strategic human resource management (SHRM – see, for example, Tichy, Fombrun and Devanna, 1982; Ulrich, 1987; Wright and Snell, 1991; Wright and McMahan, 1992), is to improve the way that human resources are managed strategically within organisations. The ultimate aim of this work is to improve organisational performance, as judged by its impact on the organisation's declared corporate strategy (Tichy, Fombrun and Devanna, 1982; Huselid, 1995), the customers (Ulrich, 1989) or shareholders (Huselid, 1995; Becker and Gerhart, 1996; Becker *et al*, 1997). It is implicit in these writings that this objective will apply in all cases. Thus the widely cited definition by Wright and McMahan (1992; p.298) states that SHRM is:

> **'the pattern of planned human resource deployments and activities intended to enable a firm to achieve its goals.'**

Arguably, there is a degree of coherence in the USA around what constitutes 'good' HRM, and views tend to coalesce around the concept of 'high-performance work systems'. These have been characterised by the US Department of Labor (1993) as having certain characteristics:

- careful and extensive systems for recruitment, selection and training
- formal systems for sharing information with the individuals who work in the organisation
- clear job design
- local-level participation procedures
- monitoring of attitudes
- performance appraisals
- properly functioning grievance procedures
- promotion and compensation schemes that provide for the recognition and financial rewarding of high-performing members of the workforce.

It would appear that, although there have been many other attempts to develop such lists (see, for example, from the UK, Storey 1992; 1995), and they all differ to some degree, the Department of Labor list can be taken as an exemplar of *the universalist paradigm*. Few US researchers in HRM would find very much to argue with in this list, although they are likely to label their studies as SHRM. Both researchers and practitioners in other countries, however, find such a list contrary to experience and even to what they would conceive of as good practice. So they might argue for sharing information with representative bodies such as trade unions or works councils, for flexible work boundaries, for group reward systems. And they might argue that attitude monitoring, appraisal systems, etc, are culturally inappropriate.

Writings by the universalists are usually produced in one country and base their work on a small number of by now well-known cases. As long as they are read by specialists in the relevant country, with interests in these kinds of organisations, this may not be too much of a problem. But the world, and especially the academic world in HRM, is becoming ever more international. This is a major problem in relation to the US literature. The cultural hegemony of US teaching, publishing, websites and the US journals means that these texts are often utilised by other readers. US-based literature searches – now all done on computer, of course – generally fail to note any writing outside the universalist tradition. For analysts and practitioners elsewhere, and with interests in different countries, many of these descriptions and prescriptions fail to meet their reality.

Contextual HRM

In contrast, the contextual or comparative paradigm searches for an overall understanding of what is contextually unique and why. In our topic area, it is focused on understanding what is different between and within HRM in various contexts, and what the antecedents of those differences are. The policies and practices of the 'leading-edge' companies (something of a value-laden term in itself), which are the focus of considerable HRM research and literature in the USA, are of less interest to contextualists than identifying the way labour markets work and what the more typical organisations are doing.

Among most researchers working in this paradigm, it is the explanations that matter – any link to firm performance is secondary. It is assumed that HRM can apply to societies, governments or regions as well as to firms. At the level of the organisation (not just the 'firm', for public-sector and not-for-profit organisations are also included) the organisation's objectives and strategy are not necessarily assumed to be 'good' either for the organisation or for society. There are plenty of examples where this is clearly not the case. Nor, in this paradigm, is there any assumption that the interests of everyone in the organisation will be the same; or any expectation that an organisation will have a strategy that people within the organisation will support.

The assumption is that not only will the employees and the unions have a different perspective from that of the management team (Kochan et al, 1986; Barbash, 1987; Keenoy, 1990; Storey, 1992; Purcell and Ahlstrand, 1994; Turner and Morley, 1995), and different groups of employees within the organisation will have different needs and requirements (Lepak and Snell, 1999), but that even within the management team there may be different interests and views (Kochan et al, 1986; Koch and McGrath, 1996; Hyman, 1987). These, and the resultant impact on HRM, are issues for empirical study. Contextualist researchers explore the importance of such factors as culture, ownership structures, labour markets, the role of the state and trade union organisation as aspects of the subject rather than as external influences upon it. The scope of HRM goes beyond the organisation to reflect the reality of the role of many HR departments – for example, in lobbying about and adjusting to government actions, in dealing with such issues as equal opportunities legislation or with trade unions and tripartite institutions.

THE VALUE OF THE DIFFERENT PARADIGMS

Many management researchers find that the universalist paradigm, ironically, excludes much of the work of HR specialists in such areas as compliance, equal opportunities, trade union relationships and dealing with local government and the environment. In addition, the universalist paradigm only operates at the level of the organisation, ignoring policy at the national or international level. This is not helpful in regions like Europe, where a good deal of employment contract bargaining is still above the organisational level and significant HR legislation and policy is enacted at European Union level (eg freedom of movement, employment and remuneration, equal treatment) as well as those of particular countries or sectors (Sparrow and Hiltrop, 1994; Brewster, Mayrhofer and Morley, 2004; Brewster, 2004). The contextual paradigm provides better insights into these issues.

Nevertheless, the universalist paradigm exists because it has strengths – a simple, clear focus, a rigorous methodology, and clear relationships with the needs of industry. Neither paradigm is right or wrong. Both these approaches, and the others that exist in other parts of the world, have a contribution to make. The difficulty comes when writers are unaware of the paradigm within which they are working.

It is to some degree the difference between these paradigms, lack of awareness of them, and the tendency for commentators to drift from one to another that has led to the confusion about the very nature of HRM as a field of study pointed out by many of its leading figures (eg Conrad and Pieper, 1990; Guest, 1992; Singh, 1992; Storey, 1992, 1995; Boxall, 1993; Dyer and Kochan, 1995). In practice, these are often debates between the different paradigms used to understand the nature of HRM.

CONVERGENCE AND DIVERGENCE IN HRM

Convergence in HRM

A second, and linked, significant debate is between those who believe that the world is getting more globalised and therefore all aspects of management, including human resource management, are becoming more alike, and those who believe that each country continues to have its own approach to management in general and human resource management in particular.

There is more than one version of the convergence concept. Some see it as a market-based issue. They argue that the logic of technology and its increasing diffusion mean that eventually, in order to compete, everyone will have to move to adopt the most efficient management and HR practices (Kidger, 1991). The underlying assumption here is that the predominant model will be the US universalist model (Smith and Meiksins, 1995). Comparative HRM researchers have analysed changes in the adoption of a range of specific tools and practices across countries. In examining changes over time in HR practice between European countries and attempting to link the pattern of these changes to competing theoretical explanations of what is happening, Mayrhofer, Morley and Brewster (2004; p.421) noted that 'It is by no means clear what is meant by convergence. Although the general meaning, intuitively, is clear, it becomes more complex at a closer look.' We therefore need a 'more nuanced picture of convergence' (p.434).

What is meant by HR practice convergence or divergence?

Mayrhofer, Morley and Brewster (2004) differentiated between a number of forms of change:

- *Directional convergence* – In comparing changes in HR practices between two countries, directional convergence exists when the trend (developmental tendency) goes in the same direction. Each country might start with a different proportion of organisations using a specific practice, and over time the difference in the proportion of organisations using that particular practice in the two countries might actually have grown larger. However, in both cases, a greater proportion of organisations now use the practice, so the practice has converged in direction – in this case going up. Similarly, the opposite might apply, with change in a negative direction.

- *Final convergence* – When changes in the use of an HR practice in two different countries point towards a common end point (the differences in the use of the practice between the countries are decreasing in magnitude over time), then there is convergence to some final point. However, the direction of the change can vary. The final convergence might be toward a point in which in both countries more organisations use the HR practice, or to a point in which fewer organisations in both countries end up using the practice, or to a point in between where the proportion of organisations using the practice ends up higher in one country but lower in the other. All three are, however, examples of final convergence.

- *Stasis* – When there is no change over time in the proportion of organisations using an HR practice, a state of stability (stasis) exists.

> ■ *Divergence* – Divergence occurs when the changes in use of an HR practice in two different countries are progressing in truly different directions, one increasing and the other decreasing.

Just as in comparing the direction of change in the use of a single HR practice between two countries we can see that the reality might correspond to subtle changes taking place. More to the point, if we study a single country and observe, for example, that there now appear to be a greater proportion of organisations using a specific HR practice, to claim that this is evidence of convergence might be highly misleading. If we only study changes of HR practice in a single country, we might mistakenly think that the increase in the use of this practice by organisations in this country represents some form of convergence with other countries, but in reality they are on a path of directional convergence and so going in the same direction but may actually be growing further apart. For this reason, when we try to make sense of change in several HR practices across numerous countries, the chances of confirming simple patterns of HR practice convergence or divergence must be minimal.

There is also an institutional perspective which argues that although institutional differences (such as differences in legal, trade union and labour market conditions) can create differences in HRM, where, as in the European Union (EU), similar legislation is covering a number of countries, this might lead to a diminution in the differences between the ways in which countries handle their HRM. The EU is passing legislation for all the member states, including social and employment legislation. There is a free labour market in the EU and some companies now try to operate as if the EU was one country. A developing European model of HRM would reinforce the idea of a move toward convergence – but not in the form of regional convergence: rather, global convergence.

Divergence in HRM

Opposed to the idea of convergence there is the concept of cultural differences outlined in Chapters 2 and 3. There is now also a stream of research findings that highlight the existence of different systems of business and, indeed, models of capitalism, and arguing that the development and success of specific managerial structures and practices can only be explained by reference to the various institutional contexts.

Comparative characteristics of business

The nature of the firm

- the degree to which private managerial hierarchies co-ordinate economic activities
- the degree of managerial discretion from owners
- specialisation of managerial capabilities and activities within authority hierarchies
- the degree to which growth is discontinuous and involves radical changes in skills and activities
- the extent to which risks are managed through mutual dependence with business patterns and employees

Market organisation

- the extent of long-term co-operative relations between firms within and between sectors
- the significance of intermediaries in the co-ordination of market transactions
- stability, integration and scope of business groups
- dependence of co-operative relations on personal ties and trust

Authoritative co-ordination and control systems

- integration and interdependence of economic activities

- impersonality of authority and subordination relations

- task, skill and role specialisation and individualisation

- differentiation of authority roles and expertise

- decentralisation of operational control and level of work group autonomy

- distance and superiority of managers

- extent of employer–employee commitment and organisation-based employment system.

Source: Whitley (1992)

These institutional arguments runs broadly as follows. There are a number of different and equally successful ways of organising economic activities (and management) in a market economy (Whitley, 1992). Such different patterns of economic organisation tend to be a product of the particular institutional environments within the various nation states (see box). There is continuing evidence of substantial variations in the type of capitalist business systems (Whitley, 2000). From a pragmatic perspective, this means that the types of firms that are dominant, the shape of customer–supplier relationships, the work systems and employment practices are still divergent despite the pressures for convergence and effects of globalisation.

Case study

Organisation and management in an Anglo-French consortium: Transmanche link

The Channel Tunnel proved to be an adventurous project, technologically unique and built under enormous pressure and conflict between partners. It was also the subject of international comparative organisational and cultural research to explore the behaviour of British and French managers under a common structure (Winch, Clifton and Millar, 2000). A series of organisational and behavioural variables was measured across more than 200 managers. The French managers reported higher unit cohesion based on competition between units. They had significantly more work and decision-making autonomy and were less procedurally oriented than the British, but provided less feedback and opportunity for mutual adjustment. Although both nationalities had high personal accountability and followed the procedures that existed, the French had more control of their work by knowing more about it in advance. Power emanated more from the personal responsibility of the senior managers than from the position and control systems. The French were more action-oriented (*fonceur*) and the British more procedural. There were no differences between the two in terms of job satisfaction or motivation from pay and promotion. However, the British were far more motivated through the use of feedback (praise and encouragement from others). This was unimportant to French managers. The British were also more directly job-involved, in that they expressed unhappiness when performing badly on the job. The boundary between work and home life was more porous for the British, and reported stress was lower. The French managers were by contrast more distant from colleagues and shouldered more personal responsibility, and therefore carried more stress.

Source: Winch, Clifton and Millar (2000)

What does this mean for international HR practitioners? It means that – despite the work outlined in Chapter 2 – they cannot just simply measure cultural values across their operations and predict the behaviours that are related to such values. Instead, the development and success of any specific managerial structures and practice (such as HRM) can only be explained by giving due cognisance to the various institutional contexts. Not all management methods are transferable, even when employee values have converged. The effectiveness therefore of any universal or pan-European conceptualisation of HRM will very probably be constrained by the different institutional contexts. This is a powerful argument in favour of the need for local responsiveness.

THE USA AND THE REST OF THE WORLD

So if there are these differences, what does that imply for our understanding of HRM? The concept of HRM was developed first in the United States of America, although other countries have developed their own, sometimes critical, approaches to the topic, and it is still the American specialists and the US-based journals that drive the subject. Our critique of the universalist paradigm, however, indicates that US conceptions of HRM may not apply around the world. Although there is much to be learned from the USA, and the policies and practices of US multinational corporations and the academic conferences and journals remain the touchstone for thinking about HRM, it is also important to understand what and why things are done differently elsewhere.

Brewster (1994) has pointed out that a core assumption of North American HRM is that the employing organisation has a considerable degree of latitude in regard to taking decisions on the management of personnel, including *inter alia* the freedom to operate contingent pay policies, the option of an absence of or at least a minimal influence from trade unions, and an assumption that the organisation has sole responsibility for training and development.

In other words, central to the notion of North American HRM is an assumption of considerable organisational independence and autonomy. This assumption is reasonable for US companies, given the weakness of the trade union movement in the USA, where membership is currently probably less than one tenth of the working population and union activities are predominantly site-based, coupled with the comparatively low levels of state subsidy, support and control. It also fits comfortably with the notion that the state should interfere in business as little as possible and that it is the right of individuals to do the best for themselves that they can without external interference (Guest, 1990). The question is: how viable are such critical assumptions elsewhere in the world?

In this section, we look critically at a number of issues that make the USA, as one authority put it, 'quite untypical of the world as a whole' (Trompenaars, 1993). Many of our examples are taken from the European context, but we apply elsewhere around the world. We examine:

- the role of the state
- the role of legislation
- the role of the unions
- the role of ownership patterns.

The role of the state

The legislation that determines the firm–employee relationship is a product of a wider, normative conception of what role the state should play within the economic arena. In his book *Capitalisme contre capitalisme* (1991), Michel Albert – a former director of the French Planning Agency – distinguished on the one hand between an 'Anglo-Saxon' capitalism (principally the USA, but also the UK) and a continental, West European type of capitalism which he labelled the 'Rhineland' model. The former is a 'shareholder economy' under which private enterprise is about maximising short-term profits for investors rather than any broader harmony of interests. In contrast, the 'Rhineland model may be seen as a regulated market economy with a comprehensive system of social security. Government, employers' organisations and labour unions consult each other about economic goals [in order to] try to achieve a harmony of interests' (Bolkestein, 1999). In short, the Rhineland model is a 'stakeholder economy' in which competition and confrontation are avoided in the belief that they undermine sustainable, stable economic growth. Patrolling this economy is the state, which variously acts as a referee, guarantor, employer and owner. This contrast between the two systems has been supported by other writers (see, for example, Hall and Soskice, 2001).

In Europe it is typical for governments to be major employers in their own right, since the public sector forms a substantial proportion of the total economy (as much as half, in Sweden, for example). In addition, these governments subsidise jobs extensively. At the end of the twentieth century nearly a quarter of the French labour force relied on government support, whether in the form of unemployment benefit or subsidised jobs (Pedder, 1999; p.11). In other countries – particularly for example, in Africa – these figures may be much higher.

On becoming unemployed, workers in the USA initially receive a level of benefit of about two-thirds their income – not far below levels in much of Europe. But those benefit levels tail off sharply quite quickly. In many European countries, in contrast, benefits are either not time-limited or actually increase the longer that people are out of work. In Sweden and Finland the income replacement rate of 89 per cent actually rises to 99 per cent. It has been argued that this virtual absence of a margin between benefits and wages for the low-skilled unemployed represents a serious disincentive to seek new jobs in many European countries. A French study reported by Pedder (1999) showed that the unemployed in France take five times as long to find a new job as the unemployed in the USA, yet those in work are five times less likely to lose their jobs.

The role of legislation

We can distinguish three aspects to this concept of human resource management:

- the degree of employment protection
- the legislative requirements on pay and hours of work
- legislation on forms of employment contract.

The degree of employment protection

With regard to the first of these, Blanchard (1999) has attempted to quantify differences in employment protection within both Europe and the USA. The argument is that employment protection has three main dimensions:

- the length of the notice period to be given to workers
- the amount of severance pay to be paid according to the nature of the separation
- the nature and complexity of the legal process involved in laying off workers.

Blanchard finds that the USA is significantly different from Europe in general, and from Italy, Spain and Portugal in particular. There is less protection in the USA.

The legislative requirements on pay and hours of work

In relation to the legislative requirements on pay and work there are also marked differences. For example, whereas in Europe legislative developments have ensured that the average hours worked have fallen over the last two decades, in the USA they have risen. Thus in the United States, almost 80% of male workers and 65% of working women now work more than 40 hours in a typical week (International Labour

Organisation). By contrast, in France the working week is by law limited to 35 hours, with overtime limited to 130 hours a year. This policy even extends to making unpaid overtime by senior employees a penal offence. Indeed, in June 1999 a director of a defence company, Thompson Radars and Countermeasures, was fined after the government's jobs inspectorate had monitored executives, researchers and engineers and uncovered substantial unrecorded overtime. In the USA such a scenario would be inconceivable.

Legislation on forms of employment contract

Finally, legislation on employment contracts exists everywhere, but the legislation varies country by country. In Europe, again, employment contracts are the subject of European-level legislation. Legislation in Europe goes beyond anything found in the USA, limiting the ways people can be recruited, the documentation necessary when they start work, how much they can be paid, how management must consult with them, and a host of other matters. One German authority (Pieper, 1990; p.82) pointed out that:

> **'The major difference between HRM in the USA and in Western Europe is the degree to which [HRM] is influenced and determined by state regulations. Companies have a narrower scope of choice in regard to personnel management than in the USA.'**

This statement could be applied to many other countries outside Europe as well.

The role of the unions

Another core feature of the USA is the limited role for trade unions. Most workplaces in the USA are not unionised. In many other countries the situation is the opposite. In European states, for example, legislative status and influence is accorded to unions. Most European countries are more heavily unionised in terms of union membership than the USA (see Chapter 10). However, in reality trade union influence cannot be gauged sufficiently by focusing on union density rates. A more important issue is that of trade union recognition – that is, whether the employer deals with a trade union in a collective bargaining relationship which sets terms and conditions for all or most of the employees (Morley *et al*, 2000). It is in this respect that Europe diverges to a considerable degree from the USA. In most European countries there is legislation in place requiring employers over a certain size to recognise unions for consultative purposes.

Closely related to the issue of trade union recognition is the European practice of employee involvement. Typically, the law requires the establishment of 'works councils' (employee representative bodies) with which managements must communicate whenever the workforce request one. Recent EU legislation is extending these rights to all EU member states. Legislation in countries such as the Netherlands, Denmark and, most famously, Germany requires organisations to have two-tier management boards such that employees have the right to be represented on the more senior Supervisory Board. These arrangements give considerable (legally backed) power to the employee representatives and, unlike consultation in the USA, for example, they tend to supplement rather than supplant the union position. In relatively highly unionised countries it is unsurprising that many of the representatives of the workforce are, in practice, trade union officials. In Germany, as one instance, four-fifths of them are union representatives.

A central theme of HRM is the requirement to generate significant workforce commitment through developing channels of communication. In Europe the use of these formalised employee representation or trade union channels is mandatory. And when upward communication is examined, the two most common means in Europe – by a considerable margin – are through immediate line management *and* through the trade union or works council channel (Mayrhofer *et al*, 2000).

The role of ownership patterns

Patterns of ownership also differ in different countries. Public ownership has decreased to some extent in many countries in recent years – but it is still far more widespread elsewhere than it is in the United States. In some African states and in China, for example, most employment is in the public sector. And private-sector ownership may not mean the same thing. In many countries, ownership of even major companies remains in the hands of single families rather than in the hands of shareholders. By contrast, in Germany a tight network of a small number of substantial banks owns a disproportionate number of companies. Their interlocking shareholdings and close involvement in the management of these corporations mean less pressure to produce short-term profits and a positive disincentive to drive competitors out of the marketplace (Randlesome, 1993).

ACTIVITY

Take a few minutes to think about the options.

Is the way organisations have to go through the processes of recruiting, inducting, developing, paying and working with staff so similar in every country that general points about how human resources are managed (or perhaps should be managed) are valid?

Or is it the case that things are done so differently in different countries that we have to be very aware of the location in which human resources are being managed before we can understand them?

SUMMARY

What can we conclude from the discussion presented in this chapter? Part of the answer lies in the need to be clear about our level of analysis. There will be some aspects of HRM which may be applicable in any country and any circumstances: every organisation in every country has to conduct basic HR practices such as recruitment, payment, etc. There will also be many aspects of HRM which cannot be understood at that level and which must be explored at different levels: workplace, sector, national or regional. A focus on any one of these areas will, like focusing a camera, clarify some areas but blur others. It does not make either true or false – they are merely different perspectives. In this chapter we have argued that the national level of analysis is particularly informative, and that it is often given less priority than it should be. We provide evidence on these issues in the following chapters.

There is less empirical data on the issue of convergence versus divergence, and that is largely the result of the difficulties of researching the issue. Obviously, researching convergence would require a series of longitudinal comparative research programmes – but these are expensive and rare. Even this would not resolve the problem. Which issues are we researching? Are we to research institutional arrangements or how they operate? Are we to research at a national level, an organisational level, or a workplace level? Whose opinions are we to canvass?

ACTIVITY

Fortunately, perhaps, the field is still open. We can each have our views and our different interests. Before going further it may be worth asking yourself:

- Where do I stand on the universalist/contextual axis?

- What are my views about the dominance of the US approaches to HRM?

- And what are the implications of my views for my interests in and study of HRM?

LEARNING QUESTIONS

- Argue for or against the statement that we are seeing an increasing convergence of HRM practice within Europe.

- In the light of the arguments produced in this chapter, is the concept of 'best practice' not applicable in the context of HRM?

- Do you see the state as having any role in determining HR policy and practice in an increasingly global world?

REFERENCES

Albert, M. (1991) *Capitalisme contre capitalisme*. Paris, Seuil

Barbash, J. (1987) 'Like nature, industrial relations abhors a vacuum: the case of the union-free strategy', *Industrial Relations*, 42 (1): 168–78

Becker, B. and Gerhart, B. (1996) 'The impact of human resource practices on organisational performance: progress and prospects', *Academy of Management Journal*, 39: 779–801

Becker, B., Huselid, M., Pickus, P. and Spratt, M. (1997) 'HR as a source of shareholder value: research and recommendations', *Human Resource Management*, 36 (1): 39–47

Blanchard, O. (1999) 'Employment protection and labour market performance', *Employment Outlook*, Paris, OECD

Bolkestein, F. (1999) 'The Dutch model: the high road that leads out of the Low Countries', *The Economist*, 22 May: 75–6

Boxall, P. (1993) 'The significance of human resource management: a reconsideration of the evidence', *International Journal of Human Resource Management*, 3: 645–64

Brewster, C. (1994) 'Human resource management in Europe: reflection of, or challenge to, the American concept', in P. Kirkbride (ed.) *Human Resource Management in Europe: Perspectives for the 1990s*. London, Routledge

Brewster, C. (1999) 'Different paradigms in strategic HRM: questions raised by comparative research', in P. M. Wright, L. D. Dyer, J. W. Bourdreau and G. T. Milkovich (eds) *Research in Personnel and Human Resource Management*. Stamford, CT, JAI Press

Brewster, C. (2004) 'European perspectives on human resource management', *Human Resource Management Review*, 14 (4): 365–82

Brewster, C., Mayrfhofer, W. and Morley, M. (2004) *European Human Resource Management: Evidence of convergence?* London, Elsevier

Child, J. (1981) 'Culture, contingency and capitalism in the cross-national study of organisations', in B. M. Staw and L. L. Cummings (eds) *Research in Organizational Behavior*, 3: 303–56

Conrad, P. and Pieper, R. (1990) 'HRM in the Federal Republic of Germany', in R. Pieper (ed.) *Human Resource Management: An international comparison*. Berlin, Walter de Gruyter

Dyer, L. and Kochan, T. (1995) 'Is there a new HRM? Contemporary evidence and future directions', in B. Downie, P. Kumar and M. L. Coates (eds) *Managing Human Resources in the 1990s and Beyond: Is the workplace being transformed?* Kingston, ON, Industrial Relations Centre Press, Queen's University

Guest, D. (1990) 'Human resource management and the American dream', *Journal of Management Studies*, 27 (4): 377–97

Guest, D. (1992) 'Right enough to be dangerously wrong: an analysis of *In Search of Excellence*', in G. Salaman (ed.) *Human Resource Strategies*. London, Sage

Hall, P. and Soskice, D. (eds) (2001) *Varieties of Capitalism: The institutional foundations of competitive advantage*. Oxford, Oxford University Press

Huselid, M. (1995) 'The impact of human resource management practices on turnover, productivity and corporate financial performance', *Academy of Management Journal*, 38: 635–72

Hyman, R. (1987) 'Strategy or structure? Capital, labour and control', *Work, Employment and Society*, 1 (1): 25–55

Keenoy, T. (1990) 'HRM: a case of the wolf in sheep's clothing', *Personnel Review*, 19 (2): 3–9

Kidger, P. J. (1991) 'The emergence of international human resource management', *International Human Resource Management*, 2 (2): 149–63

Koch, M. J. and McGrath, R. G. (1996) 'Improving labor productivity: human resource management policies do matter', *Strategic Management Journal*, 17: 335–54

Kochan, T., Katz, H. and McKersie, R. (1986) *The Transformation of American Industrial Relations*. New York, Basic Books

Lammers, C. J. and Hickson, D. (eds) (1979) *Organisations Alike and Unlike*. London, Routledge & Kegan Paul

Lepak, D. and Snell, S. (1999) 'The human resource architecture: towards a theory of human capital allocation and development', *Academy of Management Executive*, 24: 1–31

Maurice, M., Sellier, F. and Sivestre, J. (1986) *The Social Foundations of Industrial Power*. Cambridge, MA, MIT Press

Mayrhofer, W., Brewster, C. and Morley, M. (2000) 'Communication, consultation and the HRM debate', in C. Brewster, W. Mayrhofer and M. Morley (eds) *New Challenges for European Human Resource Management*. London, Macmillan

Mayrhofer, W., Morley, M. and Brewster, C. (2004) HRM in Europe: Evidence of Convergence. London, Butterworth Heinemann.

Miles R. and Snow C. (1986) 'Designing strategic human resource systems', *Organizational Dynamics*, 12 (2): 36–52

Morley, M., Brewster, C., Gunnigle, P. and Mayrhofer, W. (2000) 'Evaluating change in European industrial relations: research evidence on trends at organisational level', in C. J. Brewster, W. Mayrhofer and M. Morley (eds) *New Challenges for European Human Resource Management*. London, Macmillan

Pedder, S. (1999) 'A survey of France: for fear of McJobs', *Economist*, 5 June

Pieper, R. (ed.) (1990) *Human Resource Management: An international comparison*. Berlin, Walter de Gruyter

Poole, M. (1986) *Industrial Relations: Origins and patterns of national diversity*. London, Routledge & Kegan Paul

Purcell, J. and Ahlstrand, B. (1994) *Human Resource Management in the Multi-Divisional Firm*. Oxford, Oxford University Press

Randlesome, C. (1993) *Business Cultures in Europe*. Oxford, Butterworth-Heinemann

Rigby, M., Smith, R. and Brewster, C. (2004) 'The changing impact and strength of the labour movement in Europe', in M. Harcourt and G. Wood (eds) *Trade Unions and Democracy: Strategies and perspectives*. Manchester, Manchester University Press

Singh, R. (1992) 'Human resource management: a sceptical look', in B. Towers (ed.) *Handbook of Human Resource Management*. Oxford, Blackwell

Smith, C. and Meiksins, P. (1995) 'System, society and dominance effects in cross-national organisational analysis', *Work, Employment and Society*, 9: 241–68

Sparrow, P. and Hiltrop, J. M. (1994) *European Human Resource Management in Transition*. Hemel Hempstead, Prentice Hall

Storey, J. (1992) *Developments in the Management of Human Resources*. London, Routledge

Storey, J. (1995) *Human Resource Management: A critical text*. London, Routledge

Tichy, N., Fombrun, C. J. and Devanna, M. A. (1982) 'Strategic human resource management', *Sloan Management Review*, 23 (2): 47–60

Trompenaars, F. (1993) *Riding the Waves of Culture*. London, Economist Books

Turner, T. and Morley, M. (1995) *Industrial Relations and the New Order: Case studies in conflict and co-operation*. Dublin, Oak Tree Press

Ulrich, D. (1987) 'Organisational capability as competitive advantage: human resource professionals as strategic partners', *Human Resource Planning*, 10: 169–84

Ulrich, D. (1989) 'Tie the corporate knot: gaining complete customer commitment', *Sloan Management Review*, Summer: 19–28

US Department of Labor (1993) *High Performance Work Practices and Firm Performance*. Washington, DC, US Government Printing Office

Whitley, R. D. (ed.) (1992) *European Business Systems: Firms and markets in their national contexts*. London, Sage

Whitley, R. D. (2000) *Divergent Capitalisms: The social structuring and change of business systems*. Oxford, Oxford University Press

Winch, G. M., Clifton, N. and Millar, C. (2000) 'Organisation and management in an Anglo-French consortium: the case of the Transmanche-link', *Journal of Management Studies*, 37 (5): 663–85

Wright, P. M. and McMahan, G. C. (1992) 'Theoretical perspectives for strategic human resource management', *Journal of Management*, 18 (2): 295–320

Wright, P. M. and Snell, S. A. (1991) 'Toward an integrative view of strategic human resource management', *Human Resource Management Review*, 1: 203–25

Comparative HRM: the role of the HR department

CHAPTER OBJECTIVES

This chapter explores similarities and differences between countries in the role and function of their human resource departments. When they have read this chapter, students will:

- understand that the term 'HRM' has different meanings in different countries

- know – and be able to discuss examples of – the differences between countries in the way that the role of HRM is understood and conducted

- be able to outline the differences between countries in the way that HR tasks are typically allocated to line managers

- understand the potential effects of outsourcing, shared services and e-HRM on the role of the HRM function

- be able to analyse the differences in the role of HR departments throughout the world.

This chapter covers three main topics that show some clear differences around the world:

- the very meaning of 'human resource management' (and similar terms, such as 'personnel management')

- the role that HR departments undertake within organisations

- the role that line managers, non-specialists, and now new organisational forms and new technology, play in the delivery of HRM.

THE MEANING OF HRM

As should already be clear by now, HRM is a term with widely disputed definitions: many books and articles have attempted to pinpoint its meaning. One less often explored source of variation arises from national differences. The concept of HRM itself originates in and builds on a particular view of the world, a view initially from the United States of America. As Legge (1995; p.xiv) put it in her typically trenchant way:

> **'Why the appeal of HRM's particular rhetoric? Because its language ... celebrates a range of very WASP [White Anglo-Saxon Protestant] values (individualism, work ethic, those of the American Dream) while at the same time mediating the contradictions of capitalism ...'**

Other countries have been more resistant to the notion of HRM, either taking it up as a concept much later or staying with the 'personnel management' label. It is notable, for example, that the European and the world professional bodies still call themselves, respectively, the European Association of Personnel

Management and the World Federation of Personnel Management Associations. This is not a question of backwardness: the New Zealand association is one of the most modern, but still uses the 'personnel management' title. In many cases, the 1990s and the first decade of the twenty-first century saw academics and consultants in a country taking up the term while practitioners in the same country remained stubbornly attached to 'personnel' as the title of their area of work.

We noted in the previous chapter that there is a tendency on the part of some commentators to look for universal issues, whereas others are more concerned about understanding their local contingencies. Researchers in the USA typically assume that the focus of HRM is on the well-being of the organisation. On the other hand, in many other countries, commentators tend to be more critical and to take account of a number of stakeholders whose interests do not always overlap – and they are less than committed to the idea that the shareholders' interests are always paramount. This is summed up in a quotation (Hart, 1993; p.29 – here from Storey, 1995; p.23) about the way HRM is presented in the US texts:

> **'I believe HRM to be amoral and anti-social, unprofessional, reactive, uneconomic and ecologically destructive.'**

Even when the terminology has been adopted, we should not assume that the subject matter is uniform across the world. When the multinational team involved in running the Cranet surveys on HR policy and practice (Tregaskis *et al*, 2003) met to decide on the areas their survey would cover, there was far from total unanimity in understanding the nature of the topic. 'Where', the Swedish colleagues wanted to know, 'are the questions about the relationship of the organisation to the natural environment?' They saw this as an element of the HR role. German colleagues wanted more on the role of works councils, French colleagues more on the social environment. When the Japanese joined the network, they felt that despite the importance of national comparisons they could not use all of the questions, some of which would be perceived as too intrusive.

THE NATIONAL INSTITUTES

These issues raise some questions about the role of national HRM and personnel management institutes and associations. Of course they vary considerably (Farndale and Brewster, 2005). Thus, the Chartered Institute of Personnel and Development (CIPD) in the UK seeks to be an all-encompassing organisation, with well over 100,000 members, all of whom have gone through a qualification process. On the other hand, the ANDCP in France is a resolutely elitist organisation covering the heads of HR in the major organisations only. Most of the members of the DGFP in Germany are corporates. Spain has very strong regional associations, with a relatively weak centre. Sweden has a well-resourced central organisation. When these potential variations are extended to the rest of the world, with over 70 different national associations ranging from the giant, long-established Society of Human Resource Management in the USA to tiny, new associations in some of the developing countries of Africa and Asia or the transforming countries of central and eastern Europe, the range becomes huge. Levels of entry qualifications, restrictions on membership, levels of education and the extent of training provided by the associations vary enormously (Farndale and Brewster, 1999, 2005).

The target group for membership of personnel management associations tends to expand, increasing the risk of competition with other professional associations. At the same time, more specialist organisations are established (for people management issues in the public sector, or for coaching specialists, for example). The role of these organisations is going to be increasingly important, and controversial, as the profession expands.

QUESTIONS

■ How important is the professional HR association in your country (or in one you know)?

■ What might it do to achieve more influence?

THE ROLE OF THE HR DEPARTMENT

If the meaning of HRM is disputed, so too is the role of the department charged with managing human resources. Ulrich and Brockbank (2005) updated Ulrich's earlier work (1997) and identified five main roles for the HR department (see Figure 11):

■ employee advocate

■ human capital developer

■ functional expert

■ strategic partner

■ HR leader.

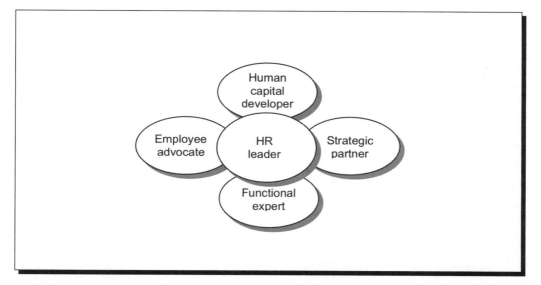

Figure 11 *Ulrich's model of HR roles*

Ulrich's former categorisation of 'employee champion' has been split into two:

■ employee advocate, focused on the needs of today's employee, and

■ human capital developer, focused on the developer preparing employees to be successful in the future.

The model also has:

■ functional expert – administrative practices are central to HR value, and this may be a more attractive title than 'administration'! Some HR practices are delivered through administrative efficiency (such as technology or process redesign), and others through policies, menus and interventions

■   a strategic partner, which has multiple dimensions – business expert, change agent, strategic HR planner, knowledge manager, and consultant

And Ulrich and Brockbank have developed a new category:

■   HR leader, who is required to function in each of these four roles. However, being an HR leader also has implications for leading the HR function, collaborating with other functions, setting and enhancing the standards for strategic thinking, and ensuring corporate governance.

Ulrich himself argues that HR departments have to be good at all these things. For many countries, especially perhaps in what is often called the South – the less developed countries of the world – the department with responsibility for these areas is still most accurately entitled 'Personnel administration'. That is what they do – and it is all that they do. The argument of the HR gurus is that this misses the important and positive roles that Ulrich's other categories represent: HRM departments should be more strategic and create value within organisations (Beatty and Schneider, 1997; Bennett *et al*, 1998; Pfeffer, 1994). Further, many would go on to assert that most of these administrative tasks can now be done more effectively through the use of information technology or through outsourcing.

The diminution of the administrative roles will free up the department to concentrate upon the strategic partner and HR leader roles. Studies in Sweden (Hedlund, 1990; Frank *et al*, 1990) nearly twenty years ago identified a trend away from administrative, system-oriented HRM roles towards more strategy and consultancy work for the HRM professionals as the day-to-day HRM work became more integrated in line operations. Södergren (1992) defined changes in terms of the 'hardware' (formal structures) and the 'software' (working roles, competence, priorities and attitudes) of the decentralisation process. Her research convinced her that the software changes may be the more important. There is other evidence that HR departments in some countries are moving from their traditional servicing and administrative role to a more developmental and strategic one. In Denmark, for example, personnel departments aim to contribute to the formation of corporate strategy by conducting opinion surveys and work environment surveys, and participating in industrial negotiations in close co-operation with the executive committee (Brewster and Mayne, 1994). And there does seem to be evidence in the UK, from the Workplace Employee Relations survey, to show that HR departments are becoming more strategic (Sisson, 2001).

Personnel or HR specialists only rarely reach the very highest positions in employing organisations (Coulson Thomas and Wakeham, 1991). An informed HR input to top-level debates is most likely only where the head of the HR function is a member of the key policy-making forum (Purcell, 1995; p.78):

'There is clear, unambiguous evidence ... that the presence of a personnel director on the main board makes a considerable difference to the role played in corporate strategy.'

Arguably, there are many organisations where the HR people do not have the credibility to play a strategic role. There are others where the organisation's human resources will be taken into account anyway. Thus the position of employee representative required by law in many larger German organisations will do just that – even if the head of the HR function is not on the board. Little evidence is available about what we might call 'psychological' issues – whether the atmosphere and culture of the organisation means that people issues are intrinsically taken into account in all decisions. It is clearly possible to have an organisation with explicit policies and an HR specialist on the board, nominally involved in the development of corporate strategy, and yet still to find, in Purcell's words (1995; p.78), a 'relatively modest role for corporate personnel'.

Arguably, too, there could be a cultural or institutional issue here, making formalisation more likely because, for example, the organisation operates in a country with comparatively low hierarchical structures, so that written policies that everyone can refer to may be more common. In other countries the senior specialists may prefer to leave themselves free to take decisions unencumbered by paperwork, knowing that their hierarchical position will give them the credibility they need for implementation. Or the extensive legal and trade union constraints mean that there is inevitably more formalisation and a greater involvement of HR in corporate strategy in order to make sure that the organisation does not fall foul of its obligations, with consequent disruption and cost.

Integration of HR heads into the board of directors

Figure 12 is taken from the Cranet data and shows the proportion of companies with an HR presence at the level of the board (or equivalent – the data covers different countries with different legal governance arrangements and different sectors). There are significant differences. In around half of the organisations in the UK, the personnel manager is a member of top management. In Sweden, on the other hand, and even more so in France and Spain, at least three-quarters of their organisations have an HR representation on the main board.

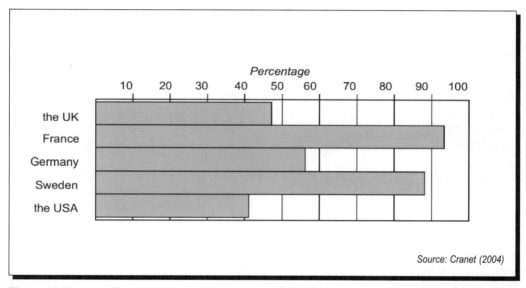

Figure 12 *Head of HR on the board (selected countries)*

Other data in the research indicates that where there is no specialist presence at this level, the responsibility for HRM rests most frequently with the managing director or an administration manager. Of course, in such circumstances this could mean either that the topic is taken very seriously, being allocated specifically to the top person, or that it is not taken seriously at all, being dumped into the 'and everything else that goes on in the organisation' category and hence swept under the CEO's general responsibilities. In either case, it is not clear that the specialist input to decisions from the HR angle is always going to be available.

Involvement of HR in strategic decision processes

Membership of the board certainly gives the head of the HR function an opportunity to influence corporate strategy – but is it taken, and is it the only way to ensure that HR is taken seriously in such decisions? Storey (1992) claimed that personnel directors were rarely involved in strategic policies as 'strategic changemakers', and Purcell (1995; p.77) argues that both finance and personnel people believe that:

'It is in the implementation of decisions that the personnel function is most likely to be involved.'

This too, however, seems to vary considerably by country.

Other evidence from the Cranet study examined at what point the personnel function is involved in the development of corporate strategy. It showed that on this key issue – using data collected, remember, from the senior HR specialist in the organisation – that somewhere between a half and two-thirds of all organisations claim to be involved from the outset. In the UK, HR influence from the outset of the development of corporate strategy approximately mirrors board-level involvement. In Sweden there are considerable numbers of HR specialists with a place on the board who, nevertheless, by their own admission, are not involved in the development of corporate strategy until a later stage. However, the data shows that in Germany human resource issues are taken into account from the outset in the development of corporate strategy by significantly more organisations than the number who have board-level representation for the HR function: companies apparently consult with non-board HR specialists at the earliest stage of formulating corporate strategy – a result we need to explain.

Implications for the concept of SHRM

In fact, the evidence is not only that the strategy process varies by country (Brewster and Larsen, 2000). It may involve different objectives (Brewster, 2006). In practice it may work in different ways and through different systems involving different people. Thus, the strategic implications of a management decision in the Netherlands or Germany will be subject to the involvement or scrutiny of powerful works council representatives or the worker representatives on the supervisory board of the company. Indeed, in most of these companies the knowledge that their decisions are subject to scrutiny – and can be reversed or varied – at that level means that managers tend to operate with HR issues in mind. Inevitably, this means that the assumptions in the universalist paradigm that HRM strategies are 'downstream' of corporate strategies cannot be made: there is a more interactive process in which both sets of strategy potentially influence each other simultaneously. And assumptions that strategies are the preserve of senior managers (or even just managers) cannot be sustained either. Hence our finding (see Figure 13) that HR is involved in the development of corporate strategy in these countries in more organisations than have allocated the HR department head a place on the board.

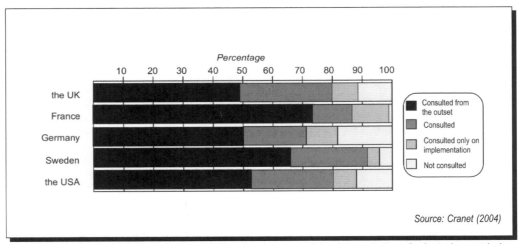

Source: Cranet (2004)

Figure 13 *Stage at which HR is involved in the development of business strategy (selected countries)*

ACTIVITY

■ Describe the effect that worker directors on the board might have on the role of the HR department in the Netherlands or Germany.

THE CHANGING NATURE OF THE HRM FUNCTION

There is ever greater pressure on the personnel or HR department to prove its value. The evidence shows wide variations in the extent and kind of evaluation of the department used in European organisations. Evaluation of the effectiveness of HR departments is not common – although the question is perhaps even less often asked of other support functions. Elsewhere, studies have found that 20% of firms in Quebec evaluate their HR department (Dolan and Harbottle, 1989) and similar proportions in the USA (Cashman and McElroy, 1991).

The role of the HRM department in any country is ambiguous and dynamic (Stiles, 2006). Like other functional specialists, HR professionals are constantly challenged to meet three competing aims: to make themselves more cost-effective through reducing the costs of services and headcount (the operational driver), to improve their services to meet the increasing demands of line managers and employees (the relational driver), and to address the strategic objectives of organisations (the transformational driver) (Gueutal and Stone, 2005; Snell, Stueber and Lepak, 2001).

To meet these challenges, HRM departments, it was argued, needed to turn to changes in supply chain management and organisational restructuring policies, including (Cooke, 2006; CIPD, 2005a; Reddington *et al*, 2005):

■ allocating more responsibility to line managers

■ outsourcing transactional activities

■ developing shared service models

■ greater use of electronic HRM

■ downsizing the function.

In each case, it is worth pointing out that the rhetorical pressures may be greater than the extent of change in practice – and that these pressures vary from country to country. The rest of this chapter addresses these issues in turn.

LINE MANAGEMENT IN INTERNATIONAL HRM

This section of the chapter is based on work carried out by one of the authors, with colleagues (Brewster and Larsen, 1992; 1994; 2000; Hoogendoorn and Brewster, 1992; Brewster and Soderstrom, 1994; Larsen and Brewster, 1996; 2003; Brewster, Larsen and Mayrhofer, 1997; 2000).

One key issue in human resource management – one that is said to differentiate it from 'personnel administration' – is the responsibility placed on line managers for the management of their people. This varies considerably around the world. What is the balance of responsibilities for the management of people between the specialists in the human resources department and the line managers who have day-to-day responsibilities for organising the work and the progress of their subordinates?

Some have argued that because human resource management is central to the well-being of an organisation and to its ability to perform effectively, the subject has to permeate the responsibilities of every single manager in an organisation. Guest (1987; p.51) argued that: 'If HRM is to be taken seriously, personnel managers must give it away.'

Alternatively, others have claimed that without a knowledgeable, experienced and influential human resources department specialising in the subject, the organisation will never give human resource management the prominence that is needed and will not have the necessary expertise in this crucial area. As a consequence, the organisation will be unable to take the most successful approach to the topic. Does the idea of sharing responsibilities mean that the specialists are in danger of not just giving HRM away, but of 'giving it up' (Blyton and Turnbull, 1992; p.11)?

In historical perspective, it has been argued that, in relation to line management, developments have been almost tidal, ebbing and flowing as the HR specialists move between opposition to the line, through the roles of power-holder, administrative centre, advocate for co-determination and change agent (Scott Myers, 1991). Here we outline the reasons that have been advanced for the growth in line management responsibility and consider some of the problems that it may involve; we examine the evidence for the trends, and particularly explore the differences between countries. Finally, we draw some conclusions about the implications for the HR department and examine some of the dilemmas involved in the management of human resources within the organisation in the future.

We should start with a note on terminology. Although the word 'devolvement' has been used in relation to the allocation of HRM responsibilities to line managers, we have preferred to use the term 'assignment' (Brewster and Larsen, 1992; Brewster et al, 1997). 'Assignment' avoids any assumption of a particular direction of change.

The importance of the line manager in the management of subordinates is often seen as one of the key differentiators between personnel management and human resource management (Freedman, 1991; Legge, 1989; Mackay and Torrington, 1986; Schuler, 1990; Weiss, 1988). Whereas the role of the personnel manager is one of managing and controlling systems, the role of the HRM specialist is one of advising and supporting line managers to achieve their objectives. It is argued that the line manager has to be aware of the synergy between human, financial and physical resources. For line managers, allocating time, money and energy to the management and development of subordinate staff is not only an investment in enhanced effectiveness and future success but a necessary precondition for it. This responsibility cannot be undertaken by the human resource specialist. The HRM function is seen as playing the role of co-ordinator and catalyst for the activities of the line managers – a 'management team player ... working [jointly] with the line manager solving people-related business issues' (Schuler, 1990; p.51).

There are five overlapping reasons why the assignment of HR issues to the line has become such a major feature of human resource management texts in the last few years (Brewster and Larsen, 2000). These are that:

- there has been a trend towards managing organisations through the development of cost-centre- or profit-centre-based approaches

- it is line managers, not the specialist staff in the HR department, who are in frequent, often constant, contact with employees – allocating tasks, enthusing (or upsetting) them, monitoring performance: 'Line management is, and always has been, responsible for the performance of their subordinates' (Lowe, 1992)

- there is a growing influence of the service industries, with their focus on responsiveness to the customer

- staffing decisions are increasingly made in real time, and there has been a widespread movement towards reducing the numbers in 'overhead' departments, such as HRM. In such circumstances the role of line management in HRM can be seen as an alternative to outsourcing the function: the 'internalising' shift (Paauwe, 1995)

- there is plenty of case-study evidence that responsibility for HR is being increasingly allocated to line managers (Gennard and Kelly, 1997; Hutchinson and Brewster, 1995).

International survey evidence (Brewster and Larsen, 1992; Brewster *et al*, 1997; Brewster and Soderstrom, 1994; Holt Larsen and Brewster, 2003) confirms this latter more anecdotal data. The results are unequivocal. They show that, at least in the European sample, organisations have increased line management responsibilities (Mayrhofer and Brewster, 2005). The overall picture is that for each aspect of human resource management and in each country there are always significantly more organisations increasing line management responsibility than decreasing it. The evidence also shows that recruitment and selection, health and safety and the expansion and reduction of the workforce are more likely to have been assigned to the line, while industrial relations and training are more likely to stay with the HR function.

	1991	1992	1995	1999/2000
least devolved	Italy	Rep. of Ireland	Rep. of Ireland	France
	the UK	France	Spain	Italy
	France	the UK	the UK	Rep. of Ireland
	Spain	Spain	France	Spain
	Germany	Germany	Norway	the UK
	the Netherlands	Norway	Germany	Portugal
	Sweden	the Netherlands	Sweden	Germany
	Switzerland	Sweden	the Netherlands	Sweden
	Denmark	Portugal	Italy	Switzerland
		Finland	Switzerland	Norway
		Denmark	Finland	the Netherlands
			Denmark	Denmark
most devolved				Finland

Source: Holt Larsen and Brewster (2003)

Table 14 *A decade of assignment rankings for devolvement in European countries*

There are clear and consistent variations between countries in their overall assignment rankings (see Table 14). Not only are these figures consistent across subject and country, they are also consistent over time. The move toward the devolvement of human resource management responsibilities to line managers may be beyond question, but the countries start from different positions.

Of course, within each country there are considerable variations between organisations. It is important to emphasise that there are elements of choice here. Organisations can exercise their option differently from their neighbours. However, the effect of country differences is clear.

There are six reasons why the assignment of HR responsibilities to the line has not gone further. These are that:

- Line managers are often not enthusiastic about taking on responsibility for HRM for the people in their area.

- Line managers under pressure often give HR responsibilities a low priority – they are often ignorant about legal requirements, trade union agreements or agreed practices.

- There is little evidence that organisations are providing any formal training to help their line managers to handle the human resource management tasks that are being allocated to them.

- They are not particularly interested in HR issues and are unable to keep up to date with the latest HR thinking.

- There will be, however devolved responsibility for HRM in the organisation has become, a need for co-ordination of HRM at some level (Paauwe, 1995).

- Perhaps most significantly, the devolvement of HRM responsibilities to the line will not achieve the objectives hoped for if it is done in a policy vacuum, as it often is, just as a means of cost-cutting.

ACTIVITY

Review

- the reasons for the growth of allocation of HR responsibilities to line managers
- the reasons allocation has expanded no further.

How would you judge the importance of the two sets of explanations?

THE PRESSURE TO OUTSOURCE SOME TRANSACTIONAL ACTIVITIES

The notion of 'outsourcing' certain HRM activities – paying another organisation to carry them out – is part of the new rhetoric of HRM in many countries. We discuss this issue in detail in Chapter 14, but at this juncture it is worth pointing out that this is not new: many management training institutions have existed for well over half a century and would not have been able to do that unless more than 50 years ago organisations had been outsourcing some of their training and development activities. Banks in some counties have long-established and thriving businesses in managing payroll for other organisations. What has happened is that there are now many new providers in the market and they are both creating a demand for outsourcing and trying to talk up the changes that have gone on in order to improve their businesses. Many organisations remain resistant to the notion – and there is a clear country effect such that the 'outsourcers' are finding it very difficult to make any money in certain countries.

THE IMPACT OF SHARED SERVICES

A newer development has been in shared services (Cooke, 2006). Shared services are created when the organisation chooses to concentrate its administrative personnel activities into a centralised 'back office' function. Administrative processing is carried out separately from the main HR group. Although 'shared services' tend to denote centralised provision, a better term to use is 'common provision'. The relevance of this development to international HRM is considerable. Shared service thinking – and the associated technologies used to enhance delivery – represent a force for a fundamental realignment of the HR function. It carries implications for the level of centralisation–decentralisation and devolvement evidenced across countries, regions and corporate headquarters. Moreover, it changes the economics of HR service provision and introduces competing dynamics for not only the standardisation of HR processes but also the potential for mass customisation. Several large organisations have developed shared service models for their HRM. By the beginning of this decade, some multinationals believed that shared services would represent a fundamental change in HRM:

> **'Separation of strategy from service delivery and the creation of shared services is in that league of change with the switch from welfare to personnel in the 1930s and from personnel to human resources in the 1980s.'**
>
> Alf Turner, Director of HR Services, BOC, cited in Reilly (2000; p.2)

The sector that an organisation operates in, however, has a significant impact on the attractiveness of pursuing common technical platforms for the delivery of HR services. For example, in the banking sector the employee cost base is variable across organisations and operations, but would be seen as low in comparison to other sectors – typically from 40% to 60%. Given a lower employee cost base, the pressure to reduce the costs of HR service delivery are not as great as might be seen in other sectors. Yet because the banking business model is itself technology-driven, there is an expectation that HR functions should also be run off common technical platforms.

THE EFFECTS OF ELECTRONIC HRM

In theory, at least, solutions such as outsourcing or developing shared services would be combined with the extension of existing information and communications technology (ICT) systems, and the implementation of new ones, to transform internal operations (CIPD, 2005b; Kettley and Reilly, 2003; Gueutal and Stone, 2005). This process has become known as the e-enablement of HRM (e-HRM), which is qualitatively different from earlier applications of IT to the information function of HR itself (known as HRIS). Meanwhile, e-HR refers to the application of ICT to HRM, in the process changing it from a solely face-to-face relationship to an increasingly virtual one. It is argued that it has the potential to fundamentally transform the nature of the HRM function as e-business has done in sectors such as financial services, retailing and knowledge management. Such transformation is already evident in translating individual e-learning into organisational learning and knowledge management, deep-web mining for talent, interactive self-selection and career management, real-time employee engagement surveys and other forms of interactive communications, creating virtual communities and teams, bringing customers/clients and employees into closer virtual relationships, and e-enabling home-working and other more flexible ways of working (Martin, 2005).

Currently, the application of ICT to HR accounts for a substantial element of total technology-spend in organisations (according to some estimates, perhaps as much as 10% of all ICT investment in British and American organisations). For example, in 2006 SAP claimed that 9,500 companies worldwide use their human capital management (HCM) application, a subset of e-HR, to manage over 54 million employees, while Oracle claimed that 76 of the US top 100 Fortune-500 companies have adopted their software. However, little is known about the long-term cost-effectiveness of generic e-HR systems, whether they promote offshoring and job losses in the UK (or whether this is offset by the creation of high-value jobs), or their overall contribution to organisational productivity and effectiveness. Also, notwithstanding the grandiose claims of their vendors it is not clear how generic systems enable companies to obtain a competitive advantage if they are operating similar business processes to their competitors (Lengnick-Hall and Lengnick-Hall, 2006).

Despite the ubiquity of e-HR systems in large enterprises, at least, their implementation has been fraught with problems, in part because practitioners lack a sound body of theory and evidence on which to proceed (CIPD, 2005b), particularly in the area of innovation, absorptive capacity, technology acceptance and change management. HR specialists cite lack of guidance as one of the most significant problems hindering the adoption of e-HR systems (Martin, 2005). Few studies have systematically explored the nature of e-HR technologies in use, the rationale for their adoption, problems influencing their implementation, technology acceptance and their broader organisational effects. Indeed, the consequences of ICT enablement for HR specialists, line managers and other employees is not well understood, researchers highlighting both significant benefits and problems for these stakeholders (Florkowski and Olivas-Lujan, in press; Lawler and Mohrman, 2003; Shrivastava and Shaw, 2004).

Clearly, the dissemination of e-HR technologies is uneven, reflecting the complex nature of inter- and intra-organisational relationships at regional and sectoral levels and between countries. This process is a relatively under-theorised one, although recent advances in institutional theory have focused on the causes and nature of such diversity in organisational practices, and differing degrees of receptiveness to new technologies (Streeck and Thelen, 2005; Brewster, Wood, Brookes and van Ommeren, 2006).

ACTIVITY

Review

- the growing allocation of HR responsibilities to line managers
- the pressure for outsourcing
- the impact of shared services
- the effects of electronic HRM.

If you can, compare these with the pressures on your own HRM.

What would you expect to be happening to HRM departments in these circumstances? How would you assess the pressure from senior managers to reduce the size of the HRM function?

THE FOCUS ON DOWNSIZING

Some academics (Martin 2005; Snell *et al*, 2001) have proposed that these developments may lead to the 'virtualisation' and/or significant 'leaning' of HR by reducing substantially the numbers of HRM specialists required. However, although it has been argued that e-HR simultaneously improves the quality of the services provided by the HR function by enabling it to play a more strategic role, a counter-argument is that e-enablement of HR leads to routine administrative tasks simply being dumped onto already overloaded managers and employees or else eliminated; it can also have negative consequences on the expectations and benefits of face-to-face relationships between HR staff and employees.

Yet evidence about the size of the HRM department seems to be relatively unequivocal. It varies considerably with the country in which the function is located and with the sector that the organisation is in and the size of the organisation. It is also clear that despite the mooted changes in the nature of the function and the alternative ways in which people management can be carried out, the size of the function has changed very little over the last 15 years (Brewster *et al*, 2006; Mayrhofer and Brewster, 2005). Whether this is because the changes have not been as dramatic as many people have claimed, or because the HR function is finding other roles to perform, is less clear.

SUMMARY

There has been considerable discussion of the implications of these changes for the role of the HR function. How should the human resource specialists relate to the line managers? And what kind of HR department do these implications require?

Using Ulrich's (1997) five roles for the HR department (see above) we can explore some of the implications of the allocation of HR responsibilities to line managers. Sensibly, Ulrich argues that all the roles are still important and will still have to be handled effectively and with credibility. There will, in future, though, be a greater requirement for the function to focus on the latter two roles. These roles have different implications for the relationship with the line manager. Thus, those HR specialists who act as human capital developer or functional expert may be thought of as a valuable source of advice and 'how to get it done' information by the line manager – or may be perceived as the worst kind of bureaucrat, insisting that the systems drive organisational behaviour. Those acting as employee advocate may well find themselves at odds with the line manager, in a kind of 'loyal opposition' role.

Nor are the strategic partner and HR leader roles unequivocal. In theory, HR specialists will have to be closely involved with their line management colleagues if they want to perform that role successfully. As partners, the theory is, they share totally in the creation of policy and also in its implementation. Of course, they expect to, and are expected to, contribute their specific expertise, knowledge and skill to the debate, and to argue their corner on the basis of that expertise. They will not be expected to agree with everything the line manager proposes, or expected to accept something when their professional expertise tells them that it is wrong to do so. To this extent, they will not be such comfortable colleagues as the much-touted 'internal consultants'. There is case study evidence that HR specialists can, indeed, be influential 'strategic change-makers' (Gennard and Kelly, 1997; p.35). On the other hand, it is clear that line managers as such are not a coherent group. Some senior executives may want their HR departments to take a strategic role, but many line managers just want their HR department to deal with the bureaucratic and sometimes difficult issues necessarily involved in managing people. They want a responsive operational partner, not a strategic one. It is a perhaps particular view of partnering that means you ignore what your partner wants to do that you think is necessary …

The less exciting-sounding roles are still required. One implication of the devolvement of personnel work to line managers – the development of smart computer systems and the possibility of outsourcing standard tasks like payroll or training provision – may be that the department's 'administrative expert' work is sharply reduced. The theoretical dividing line that academics draw between policy and practice is not so obvious on the ground. However, there are differences: it is one thing to be charged with placing advertisements or conducting negotiations; quite another to be deciding whether to recruit people for the unit or for long-term careers with the overall organisation, or whether to recognise a union. The fact that this distinction may be less clear on the ground should make us wary of easy assumptions that the way forward would lie in splitting the roles so that specialist HR directors set policy and line managers implement it. In practice, many of these less glamorous tasks still have to be accomplished, and there will in many cases be advantages in having them brought together under one specialist. Alternatively, with the spread of intelligent information and communications systems, much of this work will be available to the line manager without the intervention of an HR specialist.

The structure of the HR department may have to change. One report (Hutchinson and Wood, 1995) argued that increasing devolution would have important implications for HR departments: they would have more status, because those involved would have proved their worth (this, perhaps, requires more research than the first change). The departments would include more generalists able to turn their hand to any aspect of personnel work – and an associated change would see them developing greater skills and competences. Some researchers have found evidence of a move from departments consisting of fragmented specialist functions towards departments where most of the personnel staff undertake integrated generalist roles (Gennard and Kelly, 1997). But Adams (1991) argued the opposite – that there is now a need to be even more of a specialist, and Sisson (1995; p.100) agreed:

> **'Personnel remains a highly fragmented occupational grouping; the image of the personnel manager as the general medical practitioner seems far removed from reality.'**

Hutchinson and Wood (1995) also argued that HR departments would be smaller. This, however, seems not to survive empirical evidence. The ratio of the HR department to the rest of the organisation shows no consistent pattern, at least across Europe, and there are clear differences in those ratios between countries (as there are between sectors and sizes of organisations).

Clearly the interplay between corporate, national and plant-level HR specialists is complex and will vary with context (Farndale and Paauwe, 2005). As Brewster *et al* (2006; p.16) conclude:

> **'The relationship between organisational size, sector, national context, and the size of the HR department within organisations [is] complex. Summarised, the proportion of staff engaged in the HR function will tend to be smaller where the organisation is larger. It will be lower in specific areas of the service sector, retailing and distribution, probably reflecting the predominance of relatively low-value-added HR policies in this area (Wright and Dwyer, 2003); but HR departments are relatively large in the state sector, probably reflecting political pressures against excessive outsourcing. It will be higher in countries in the Large Firms, Anglo-American or Corporatist business systems categories.'**

The relationship between personnel specialists and line managers is complex, ambiguous, dynamic and varied. The nature of the human resource management department has been (Adams, 1991):

> **'a story of ongoing change and adaptation, with organisations unafraid to try out, and often discard, a succession of fairly diverse ways of managing personnel activities.'**

Its responsibilities are continually shifting (Gennard and Kelly, 1997; Torrington, 1989; Tyson, 1995). There is still, within organisations, a requirement for a focus on people management, for skills in people management, for an awareness of new developments and opportunities in this area, and for attention to be paid to the requirements and contribution of the people who make up the organisation. This requirement applies of course to the specialists in the HR department, but it applies equally to line managers. That is the challenge for line managers and personnel specialists alike.

There are significant changes going on in HRM: the strategic involvement of the head of the HR department may be changing; the role of line managers certainly is; the impact of outsourcing, downsizing, shared services and e-HRM are all being felt and even the meaning of the term is being developed day by day. The effects on HRM departments are significant, but there are some notes of caution being raised. However, it is clear that although there may be some general trends and directions, countries start from quite different places and there is little evidence of their converging towards any single model. The influence of country remains strong.

LEARNING QUESTIONS

- In the light of the fact that 'HRM' is understood in some countries to be more 'advanced' than 'personnel management', why might the latter continue to be the preferred terminology in most of Europe?

- Is a high level of assignment of HR responsibilities to line managers a sign of HR influence or of mistrust of HR specialists? How might this vary by country?

- Look at Table 14 (page 87). What are the significant features that link the rankings of different groups of countries?

- What advantages and disadvantages might a line manager see in being asked to adopt greater HR responsibilities?

- Choose three countries for which evidence is presented above. How far does the data presented in this chapter help you to identify the most significant roles in the Ulrich model for each country?

REFERENCES

Adams, K. (1991) 'Externalisation vs specialisation: what is happening to personnel?', *Human Resource Management Journal*, 1 (4): 40–54

Beatty, R. and Schneider, C. (1997) 'New HR roles to impact organisational performance: from partners to players', *Human Resource Management*, 36: 29–37

Bennett, N., Ketchen, D. and Schultz, E. (1998) 'An examination of factors associated with the integration of human resource management and strategic decision-making', *Human Resource Management*, 37: 3–16

Blyton, P. and Turnbull P. (1992) *Reassessing Human Resource Management*. London, Sage

Brewster, C. (2006) 'Comparing HRM across countries', in G. Stahl, and I. Björkman, (eds) *Handbook of Research in International HRM*. London, Edward Elgar

Brewster, C. and Larsen, H. (1992) 'Human resource management in Europe: evidence from ten countries', *International Journal of Human Resource Management*, 3 (3): 409–34

Brewster, C. and Larsen, H. H. (2000) *Human Resource Management in Northern Europe*. Oxford, Blackwell

Brewster, C. and Mayne, L. (1994) *The Changing Relationship between Personnel and the Line: The European dimension*. Report to the Institute of Personnel and Development, Wimbledon

Brewster, C. and Soderstrom, M. (1994) 'Human resources and line management', in C. Brewster and A. Hegewisch (eds) *Policy and Practice in European Human Resource Management*. London, Routledge

Brewster, C., Larsen, H. H. and Mayrhofer, W. (1997) 'Integration and assignment: a paradox in human resource management', *Journal of International Management*, 3 (1): 1–23

Brewster, C., Brookes, M. and Wood, G. (2006) 'Varieties of capitalism and varieties of firm', in G. Wood, and P. James, (eds) *Institutions, Production and Working Life*. Oxford, Oxford University Press

Brewster, C., Wood, G., Brookes, M. and van Ommeren, J. (2006) 'What determines the size of the HR function? A cross-national analysis', *Human Resource Management*, 45 (1): 3–21

Cashman, E. M. and McElroy, J. C. (1991) 'Evaluating the HR function', *HR Magazine*, January: 70–3

CIPD (2005a) *HR Outsourcing: The key decisions*. London, Chartered Institute of Personnel and Development

CIPD (2005b) *People Management and Technology: Progress and potential*. Survey Report. London, Chartered Institute of Personnel and Development

Cooke, F. L. (2006) 'Modelling and HR shared services centre: the experience of an MNC in the United Kingdom', in *Human Resource Management*, Vol 45(2): 211–227

Coulson Thomas, C. (1990) *Professional Development of and for the Board*. London, Institute of Directors

Coulson Thomas, C. and Wakeham, A. (1991) *The Effective Board: Current practice, myths and realities*. London, Institute of Directors

Cunningham, I. and Hyman, J. (1995) 'Transforming the HRM vision into reality', *Employee Relations*, 17 (8): 5–15

Farndale, E. and Brewster, C. (1999) 'Regionalism in human resource management', *Journal of Professional HRM*, 15, April

Farndale, E. and Brewster, C. (2005) 'In search of legitimacy: national professional associations and the professionalism of HR practitioners', *Human Resource Management Journal*, 15 (3): 33–48

Farndale, E. and Paauwe, J. (2005) 'The role of corporate HR functions in MNCs: the interplay between corporate, regional/national and plant level'. Working paper 05–10, Cornell University (http//www.cornell.edu/depts./cahrs/downloads/PDFs/Working Papers/WP05–10.pdf)

Frank, C., Lundmark, A. and Vejbrink, K. (1990) *Personalfunktionen i Statsförvaltningen*. Uppsala, IPF

Freedman, A. (1991) *The Changing Human Resources Function*. New York, The Conference Board

Gennard, J. and Kelly, J. (1997) 'The unimportance of labels: the diffusion of the personnel/HRM function', *Industrial Relations Journal*, 28(1): 27–42

Guest, D. (1987) 'Human resource management and industrial relations', *Journal of Management Studies*, 24 (3): 503–22

Gueutal and D. L. Stone (eds) Gennard, J. and Kelly, J. (1997) 'The unimportance of labels: the diffusion of the personnel/HRM function', *Industrial Relations Journal*, 28 (1): 27–42

Gueutal, H. G. and Stone, D. L (eds) (2005) *The Brave New World of eHR.* San Francisco, Jossey-Bass.

Hedlund, G. (1990) *Personalfragor i Tredje Vägen.* Uppsala, IPF

Hoogendoorn, J. and Brewster, C. (1992) 'Human resource aspects: decentralisation and devolution', *Personnel Review,* 21 (1): 4–11

Holt Larsen, H. and Brewster C. (2003) 'Line management responsibility for HRM: what's happening in Europe?', *Employee Relations,* 25 (3): 228–44

Hutchinson, S. and Brewster, C. (eds) (1995) *Personnel and the Line: Developing the new relationship.* Report to the CIPD, Wimbledon

Hutchinson, S. and Wood S. (1995) 'The UK experience', in S. Hutchinson and C. Brewster (eds) *Personnel and the Line: Developing the new relationship.* Report to the CIPD, Wimbledon

IRS Employment Trends (1991) 'Devolving personnel management at the AA and Prudential Corporation', *IRS Employment Trends,* 479: 4–9

Kettley, P. and Reilly, P. (2003) *An introduction to e-HR.* Report 398. Brighton, Institute of Employment Studies

Lawler, E. and Mohrman, S. (2003) *Creating a Strategic Human Resources Organisation: An Assement of Trends and New Directions.* Palo Alto, Stanford University Press.

Legge, K. (1989) 'Human resource management: a critical analysis', in J. Storey (ed.) *New Perspectives on Human Resource Management.* London, Routledge

Legge, K. (1995) 'HRM: rhetoric, reality and hidden agendas', in J. Storey (ed.) *Human Resource Management: A critical text.* London, Routledge

Lowe, J. (1992) 'Locating the line: the front-line supervisor and human resource management', in P. Blyton and P. Turnbull (eds) *Reassessing Human Resource Management.* London, Sage

Mackay, L. and Torrington, D. (1986) *The Changing Nature of Personnel Management.* London, Institute of Personnel Management

Martin, G. (2005) *Technology and People Management: Transforming the function of HR and the HR function.* London, Chartered Institute of Personnel and Development

Mayrhofer, W. and Brewster, C. (2005) 'European human resource management: researching developments over time', *Management Revue* 16 (1): 36–62

Paauwe, J. (1995) 'Personnel management without personnel managers: varying degrees of outsourcing the personnel function', in P. Flood, M. Gannon and J. Paauwe (eds) *Managing without Traditional Methods.* Wokingham, Addison-Wesley

Pfeffer, J. (1994) *Competitive Advantage Through People.* Cambridge, MA: Harvard University Press

Purcell, J. (1995) 'Corporate strategy and its links to human resource management', in J. Storey (ed.) *Human Resource Management: A critical text.* London, Routledge

Reddington, M., Williamson, M. and Withers, M. (2005) *Transforming HR: Creating value through people.* Oxford, Elsevier: Butterworth-Heinemann

Reilly, P. (2000) *HR Shared Services and the Realignment of HR.* Institute of Employment Studies Report 368. Brighton, IES

Schuler, R. S. (1990) 'Repositioning the human resource function: transformation or demise?', *Academy of Management Executive*, 4 (3): 49–60

Scott Myers, M. (1991) *Every Employee a Manager: More meaningful work through job enrichment*. New York, McGraw-Hill

Shrivastava, S. and Shaw, J. B. (2004) 'Liberating HR through technology', *Human Resource Management*, 42 (3): 201–22

Sisson, K. (1995) 'The personnel function', in J. Storey (ed.) *Human Resource Management: A critical text*. London, Routledge

Sisson, K. (2001) 'Human resource management and the personnel function: a case of partial impact?', in J. Storey (ed.) *Human Resource Management: A critical text*, 2nd edition. London, Thompson Learning

Snell, S. A., Stueber, D. and Lepak, D. P. (2001) 'Virtual HR departments: getting out of the middle', in R. L. Henan and D. B. Greenberger, *Human Resource Management In Virtual Organizations*. Charlotte, NC, Information Age Publishing

Södergren, B. (1992) *Decentralising, Förändring i Företag och Arbetsliv*. Stockholm, Stockholm School of Economics

Stiles, P. (2006) 'The human resource department: roles, coordination and influence', in G. Stahl, and I. Björkman, (eds) *Handbook of Research in International HRM*. London, Edward Elgar

Storey, J. (ed.) (1992) *New Developments in Human Resource Management*. Oxford, Blackwell

Storey, J. (ed.) (1995) *Human Resource Management: A critical text*. London, Routledge

Streeck, W. and Thelen, K. (eds) (2005) *Beyond Continuity: Institutional change in advanced political economies*. Oxford, Oxford University Press

Torrington, D. (1989) 'Human resource management and the personnel function', in J. Storey (ed.) *New Perspectives on Human Resource Management*. London, Routledge

Tregaskis, O., Atterbury, S. and Mahoney, C. (2003) 'International survey methodology: experiences from the Cranet network', in C. Brewster, W. Mayrhofer and M. Morley (eds) *European Human Resource Management: Evidence of convergence?* London, Butterworth-Heinemann

Tyson, S. (1995) *Human Resource Strategy: Towards a general theory of human resource management*. London, Pitman

Ulrich, D. (1997) *Human Resource Champions: The next agenda for adding value to HR practices*. Boston, MA, Harvard Business School Press

Ulrich, D. and Brockbank, W. (2005) 'Role call', *People Management*, 16 June: 24–8

Weiss, D. (1988) *La fonction ressources humaines*. Paris, Éditions d'Organisation

Comparative HRM: recruitment and selection

CHAPTER OBJECTIVES

When they have read this chapter, students will:

- understand the different purposes of recruitment and selection systems
- be able to identify the ways in which recruitment practice can be affected by national legislation
- appreciate some of the most marked differences between countries in recruitment and selection practice
- be able to identify the consequences of the development of global labour markets for recruitment
- understand the different global skills supply strategies available to organisations
- appreciate the role of recruitment as part of an internationalisation strategy

INTRODUCTION: RECRUITMENT

Good recruitment is essential to effective human resource management. The effectiveness of many other human resource activities, such as selection and training, depends largely on the quality of new employees attracted through the recruitment process. Recruitment has to serve several purposes (Sparrow and Hiltrop, 1994):

- to determine present and future staffing needs in conjunction with job analysis and human resource planning
- to increase the pool of applicants at minimum cost
- to increase the success rate of the (subsequent) selection process: fewer will turn out to be over- or under-qualified
- to increase the probability of subsequent retention
- to encourage self-selection by means of a realistic job preview
- to meet responsibilities, and legal and social obligations
- to increase organisational and individual effectiveness
- to evaluate the effectiveness of different labour pools.

As will become evident later in the chapter, such a specification is extremely culturally embedded. Not surprisingly, recruitment practices differ, depending on the type and level of employee required, of course – but they also differ between countries. Governments are involved in the recruitment process, both through the provision of recruitment services and through legislation, mainly concerned with discrimination. In Europe, at least, discrimination against job-seekers for reason of race, gender, age or legal history, or because they belong to disadvantaged groups in society, is seen as undesirable from a moral, legal and, sometimes, organisational point of view. Other countries may be different. India, for example, has laws to privilege its lower castes, and some Arab and Asian states have rules to privilege locals over migrants. In

Europe, though, monitoring staffing practices and outcomes to avoid discrimination is crucial for many HR managers. The breadth of potential legislation that affects recruitment is considerable. HR business partners have to understand the law as it affects:

- the use of employment exchanges and job centres
- outplacement
- temporary work
- fixed-term contracts
- hours of work
- time off work
- termination of employment
- unfair dismissal
- redundancy
- maternity leave
- discrimination and equal opportunities
- health and safety
- recruitment codes of practice
- the use of psychological testing, and
- the disclosure of information.

HR business partners have to understand the nature or source of the law in any particular country, with regard to anything from codified legislation, constitutional rights, national or sectoral collective agreements, to codes of best practice that have set precedents in labour courts. Sparrow (2006) pointed out that the challenges for HR business partners in handling recruitment for an international organisation vary in each country, but a common need is the question of how to ensure rigour and consistency across operations in very different cultures, business markets and labour markets. The whole HR team must devise frameworks that can be applied in the countries in which the organisation already has a presence, but also be aware of the countries into which the organisation *may* enter. In some sectors the business model makes it easier to be forewarned of this. However, the work for an HR business partner is complex as organisations internationalise. Typically, in establishing new country operations the organisation has to:

- set up the legal entities to transfer employees
- decide what is the best mix of local recruitment
- investigate how local job centres should be used and build local networks, and assess what regionalised funding might be available from governments
- understand the implications and ramifications of general employment law
- understand specific legal frameworks (as they apply to issues such as payroll details, salary and reward factors such as contractual benefits or the value of extra work hours, contractual agreement compliance, disciplinary arrangements) both in the country and in relation to the operation of specific sectors in that country.

ACTIVITY

Select a country of your choice and investigate the main elements of employment law in that country in terms of how they affect recruitment.

> *Which aspects of legislation do you find most surprising or might be seen as challenging to your organisation?*

There are three specific areas of country difference that international HR managers must be aware of:

- the type of *labour legislation* – which varies from one country to another in terms of scope, whether it conveys an employer or employee bias, and the recency of codification, and attention therefore to particular areas of deficiency in the behaviour of individuals, organisations and institutions
- the type of *labour market* – which may be internal or external
- the *recruitment sources* usually tapped to attract people.

The scope of labour legislation

The scope of labour legislation and associated collective agreements or custom and practice varies markedly. For example, some constitutions convey rights in relation to appointment. In Norway the Employment Act of 1947 specifies that every citizen has the right to make a living. Article 1 of the Italian Constitution defines the country as a democratic republic based on labour in which the employer is the provider of work and the employee the lender of labour. In France a range of collective agreements at national or industry level shape recruitment practice. For example, in the chemicals sector re-hire arrangements give priority to candidates who were ex-employees in the previous six months. The motive is to stop companies rationalising and then re-hiring to new terms and conditions. In Germany works councils have to agree to the use of personnel questionnaires, can see personal information on all shortlisted candidates and can veto an appointment within one week of offer. The motive is to ensure fairness and an absence of nepotism. In Spain high salary indemnity rates have been associated with a shift by organisations towards temporary employment.

Internal and external labour markets

There are also marked differences across countries in terms of labour markets. Germany, Japan, France and Switzerland are noted for having generally internal labour markets where recruitment tends to be focused on specialised entry points at low levels of the hierarchy, and where promotion is through internal assessment. Internal labour markets are considered to have such benefits as improved morale, commitment and security among employees, more opportunity to assess (and more accurate assessment of) competencies and accrued knowledge, more control over salary levels given lower exposure to market forces, and more specialised HR skills around dedicated entry points (such as graduate recruitment). The downside, however, can be high levels of political behaviour associated with advancement, informal 'glass ceilings' that go unchallenged, complacency, and structural shocks when major market and technological changes force alterations in the whole vocational educational and training system and require a significant overhaul of the entire HR system.

Britain, the USA, Denmark, the Netherlands and Hong Kong tend to be characterised as external labour markets where candidates can move into and out of the hierarchy at any level. How do you get promoted in Britain? You change jobs. The advantages of such labour markets can be the opportunity to bring in new blood as part of culture-change processes, insights into competitor capabilities, and the ability to respond to equal opportunities issues more visibly.

RECRUITMENT METHODS

Data gathered for the Cranet project from 2003 to 2005 (Cranet, 2006) show that it is common around the world for HR and the line to share responsibility for recruitment and selection, but in some countries HR has the assisting role, whereas in others it is the line that assists. For example, the proportion of firms where HR takes the lead is highest in countries such as France (56%), Belgium (50%), Greece (49%), Canada (48%), the UK, Italy and Spain (46%), and the USA and Australia (43%). The line is more likely to take the lead in the partnership in countries such as Sweden (54%), the Czech Republic (52%), the Netherlands (51%), Finland (49%), Germany, Estonia and Tunisia (46%), and New Zealand (41%).

The typical usage of a series of recruitment practices is shown in Table 15. Recruitment occurs through both informal and formal methods. Informal methods rely on the contacts of existing employees or on people just applying. Because it involves the risk of being discriminatory, word-of-mouth recruitment is rarely acceptable in the public sector. In contrast, in the business services sector, word-of-mouth recruitment is common, particularly in those societies rated more collectivist by Hofstede and House *et al* (see Chapter 2). International differences in the use of informal recruitment are substantial but it is widespread throughout the world, especially in poorer countries. Many specialists would defend it. Recruitment of 'family and friends' is very cheap, it aids a sense of community in the workplace, and it provides at least the option of informal control ('If you behave like that, you will embarrass your uncles who got you the job ...').

	Internally	Recruitment agencies/ consultancies	Advertisement	Word of mouth	Vacancy page on company website	Vacancy on commercial job website	Direct from educational institution	Other
United Kingdom	21.2	23.4	49.3	2.1	2.6	0.4	0.4	0.7
France	25.4	10.3	25.4	10.3	6.3	0.8	2.4	19.0
Germany	37.4	1.4	37.4	3.2	8.6	6.1	5.8	0
Sweden	32.8	3.6	36.6	3.8	15.3	4.9	0.8	2.2
Spain	38.4	12.6	13.2	6.0	6.0	11.3	8.6	4.0
Denmark	16.4	7.9	44.7	4.7	11.5	14.0	0.4	0.4
Netherlands	30.1	10.7	39.0	5.1	7.3	2.5	0.3	5.1
Italy	42.2	11.9	13.8	4.6	2.8	2.8	10.1	11.9
Norway	4.5	0	72.3	0.8	11.7	0.8	0	0
Switzerland	17.3	11.8	48.8	6.7	10.2	2.8	0.8	1.6
Turkey	19.4	7.2	20.9	20.1	7.9	15.1	0.7	8.6
Finland	29.4	1.1	50.8	3.8	6.5	3.8	2.7	1.9
Greece	17.2	2.6	50.3	18.5	6.6	1.3	3.3	0
Austria	21.9	4.0	47.8	4.5	8.9	5.3	4.5	3.2
Belgium	20.2	10.4	34.7	2.3	7.5	12.1	5.2	7.5
Australia	21.1	17.8	38.4	4.1	4.1	13.6	0.8	0
New Zealand	18.2	22.1	53.1	1.9	2.3	1.6	0	0.8
United States	16.7	10.4	34.3	10.0	14.3	9.2	1.6	3.6
Canada	43.8	8.4	29.3	2.8	9.2	4.1	0.3	2.3
Slovakia	18.4	7.2	50.0	16.0	0.8	1.6	3.2	2.8

Source: Cranet (2006)

Table 15 *Recruitment practices (by percentage of practices) for clerical positions in selected countries, 2004*

Formal methods are invariably more expensive than informal ones. We make specific mention here of four methods of recruitment that take on more significance for international HR managers:

- headhunting
- cross-national advertising
- Internet recruitment
- international graduate programmes.

Headhunting

The developed countries are also the place where agency recruitment and the use of 'headhunters' for managerial positions are most common. Executive search is defined as the recruitment of senior executives and specialists with an average compensation level of over $100,000. The top 15 global search firms had a net revenue of almost $2 billion in 1997, 19% up on the previous year. Worldwide revenues in the search industry were expected to reach $10 billion by the year 2000 (Garrison-Jenn, 1998). Anecdotal evidence indicates that up to 50% of executive searches are now cross-border. The cross-border capability and geographical spread of individual search firms has therefore become critical (Sparrow, 1999).

Cross-national advertising

Organisations are looking to Europe and beyond to attract professionals to work in the UK, or to work in locations around the globe. If the costs of getting a recruitment campaign wrong are high in the domestic market, then the potential costs of errors in global campaigns are very high. Trends in advertising vary across sectors. There is a shift away from press advertising into creative alternatives, such as targeted outdoor poster sites – airport lounges, airline magazines, and journey-to-work routes. Many recruitment advertising service providers now operate as part of global networks in order to deliver targeted pan-European or global campaigns (Sparrow, 1999). These may be developed and managed from the UK, or developed for local support. Advertising agencies gather a broad spectrum of international intelligence which focuses on the location of the target audience, the kind of market they operate in, sample salaries, recruitment competitors, and whether the job-seeking audience is passive or active. Knowledge about the best recruitment media for target audiences is important. So is awareness of national custom and practice in order to ensure the 'cultural appropriateness' of a campaign. From an advertising perspective, the most important cross-cultural differences concern:

- the role qualities associated with jobs
- the desired company qualities
- softer cultural issues, such as what ideal brochures should look like and the wording of adverts.

National differences in the use of advertising are large. More use is made of newspapers, specialist journals and Internet recruiting in the developed countries; less in the Third World.

Internet recruitment

The Internet offers considerable potential as a source of recruitment for internationally mobile managers, small firms seeking specialist skills, or larger firms wishing to demonstrate their presence. It is proving most useful for international graduate recruitment, attracting MBAs and PhD-level candidates, and for specific roles such as marketing and IT staff. A series of electronic recruiting products and services is re-shaping the job-finding process. E-recruitment (electronic recruitment) has the potential to reduce the barriers to employment on a global scale. Using the Internet allows firms to:

- widen recruitment sourcing at relatively low cost

- attract applicants on a more specialised skills match (by encouraging applicants to use personal search agent facilities)

- target sources of graduates such as MBA career centres

- improve on traditional advertising approaches by targeting particular lifestyle or culture-fit groups (such as expatriates or people who consume services similar to the those provided by the host firm).

Using the Internet for international recruitment has received a mixed reaction but is slowly emerging as a useful tool. Firms have faced a number of problems with web recruitment: many existing service providers do not yet have truly global coverage, and the web is currently not appropriate for all countries. The main impact can be to increase the volume of applicants, and in a time of tight resources within HR this is not always good news.

- Targeting particular populations becomes difficult. For example, in running web pages in Singapore, applications are received from unexpected sources such as Malaysia.

- Generating a larger number of applicants from more diverse social groups may lead to a need for extensive screening activities.

- Company image or brand may not be well known in untried markets.

- Quality becomes more variable and needs managing.

- It can move firms away from relying on targeted universities.

- Equal opportunities issues might exist, in that most applicants still tend to be male and from a small range of countries.

Nonetheless, the Internet has become the primary port of call for a good deal of international talent, and so developing it as a viable recruitment channel is important. It is one of the fastest-growing methods of recruitment – especially for senior professionals, technical specialists and managers. Obviously, its use is restricted to those countries and organisations where the Internet is widely used. Indeed, there are some important differences in privacy attitudes related to the use of the web in recruitment across cultures (Harris, Van Hoye and Lievens, 2003).

International graduate programmes

Another form of international sourcing is the external recruitment of graduates into international roles. Organisations that have initiated international graduate recruitment programmes tend not to replicate the competencies that they use for experienced managers in these programmes. Instead, they have attempted to understand and manage graduates through the process of developing an international management career. A number of significant problems with international graduate programmes must be planned for:

- It only has a slow impact on the level of internationalisation, acting as a slow-burning fuse.

- Retention rates may be low.

- It can be difficult to encourage receiving units to prepare themselves to be able to manage the new international recruits accordingly.

- Visa issues mean that the cadres have to be managed for a significant period of time.

- Many organisations note that graduates (as is also the case for established managers) are becoming more reluctant to move.

- This reluctance to be mobile is also changing attitudes to compensation, forcing organisations to be more responsive to individual circumstances.

SELECTION

Selection involves the identification of the most suitable person from a pool of applicants. The main purposes of selection are (Sparrow and Hiltrop, 1994):

■ to obtain appropriate information about jobs, individuals and organisations in order to enable high-quality decisions

■ to transform information into a prediction on future behaviour

■ to contribute to the bottom line through the most efficient and effective way to produce service/production

■ to ensure cost-benefit for the financial investment made in an employee

■ to evaluate, hire and place job applicants in the best interests of organisation and individual.

Organisations can choose from a wide range of selection methods, including references, interviews and tests. Many organisations use not just one but a combination of selection practices.

If there is one area in HRM where national differences are very apparent, it is in the area of selection (see Table 16). Some selection methods are common in some countries but may not be used at all in others. For instance, graphology – reading character through handwriting – is relatively popular in France and in some parts of Switzerland, but is hardly used at all elsewhere. Such differences reflect different assumptions about the nature of selection. In the UK, for example, an empirical predictive model is the norm. Here the assumption is that selection is about the conversion of good-quality information into accurate, reliable and valid prediction of important outcomes. If a selection method has low validity or reliability, then it is considered inappropriate. In France, by contrast, selection systems work on a principle of clinical assessment. It is considered that accurate prediction of career success and performance at the point of entry is either unnecessary (educational achievement at *grandes écoles* might suffice) or improbable. Rather, selection systems should be designed to take out unnecessary risk. An overall clinical assessment of match is possible, but no finite prediction. Hence although graphology has almost zero predictive validity, it is considered a cheap source of additional information that just might detect extreme risks. Judging selection systems based on the models implicit within one's own system can be misleading.

	Interview panel used for clerical	Psychometric test for clerical	Assessment centre for clerical
United Kingdom	44.1	15.2	6.4
France	5.0	11.4	2.1
Germany	39.2	0.9	5.5
Sweden	30.3	18.0	1.3
Spain	13.3	43.7	4.4
Denmark	69.6	21.3	0.2
Netherlands	54.9	5.5	3.0
Italy	20.5	29.9	12.8
Norway	49.5	6.6	na
Switzerland	22.8	7.7	1.3
Turkey	27.5	14.6	4.7
Finland	35.2	23.5	1.7
Greece	11.1	17.8	11.7

Austria	32.2	7.0	4.8
Belgium	22.6	36.5	7.0
Australia	49.8	12.4	8.5
New Zealand	54.2	15.0	5.9
United States	23.8	6.2	9.2
Canada	48.2	11.2	6.6
Slovakia	33.6	5.0	1.2

Source: Cranet (2006)

Table 16 *Selection practices (by percentage of organisations) for clerical positions in selected countries, 2004*

The most common forms of selection are:

- interviews
- the monitoring and targeting of disadvantaged groups
- assessment centres
- psychological testing.

Interviews

In the USA interviews generally follow a structured format so that each applicant is asked the same questions. Elsewhere this is not the case, even though unstructured interviews have low predictive validity (Cook, 1999). There are also national differences in the number of people involved in the interviews and who they are. Thus, an HR specialist would often be one of the interviewers in northern Europe; less commonly elsewhere. In a simple face-to-face interview, the assessors may be confronted by significant problems (Sparrow, 1999). For example, one US multinational, when recruiting managers in Korea, found that interviewers had to be trained in cross-cultural awareness. It is the cultural norm in Korea, when asked a 'good' question, to keep silent as a sign of respect. The better the question, the longer the period of silence the candidate maintains. In US culture, if you ask a good question and receive silence, you do not attribute the behaviour to respect but to ignorance. Face-to-face interviews can create quite distorted judgements.

The monitoring and targeting of disadvantaged groups

HR policy and practices, including staffing practices, are influenced by national and transnational (eg European Union) employment laws that restrict direct, and sometimes indirect, discrimination based on such factors as gender, race, colour, disability, religion and marital status (Cook, 1999). These laws, and their effects, vary considerably by country, not only in what they outlaw but also in how they interpret discrimination. Thus, for example, evidence of discrimination in the United States includes the proportions of particular groups within the organisation compared with its catchment area. It may be unlawful to employ a white person when the firm has below the appropriate proportion of black employees. In Europe it is unlawful to discriminate in any single case, so that it would be unlawful, for example, to choose between a black and a white person on the grounds of their colour for any single job even when the organisation employs a proportion of black people well below the local average.

Staffing practices are strongly influenced by norms and values that are not covered by the law. For example, most European countries – including the UK – do outlaw discrimination on the grounds of age, but the use of age restrictions varies considerably by country: rare in the UK, common in Germany, for example.

Assessment centres

Because assessment centres are regarded as one of the most robust and valid selection techniques in general, it should be expected that they would be used to assess competence for international managers. This is rarely the case, however. Even where assessment centres are used to select managers in international settings, the key to cross-cultural assessment centres seems to be to design the assessment process so that it is very adaptable to the local environment in which it will be operated (Sparrow, 1999). For example, differences in the HR marketplace often mean that the assumptions made about candidate behaviour in the UK do not translate well abroad. The need for adaptability argues against having overly structured exercises, and most structured tools (such as situational interviews and work simulations) have to be modified. Interviews are easy to adapt, but assessors also have to build as many anchors into the local marketplace as possible in order to give the assessment process meaning. This involves a series of steps, from the simple renaming of case studies and scenarios through to the adoption of local norms for psychometric instruments, and beyond.

Krause and Gebert (2003) have reviewed the international literature on the conception, operation and evaluation of assessment centres, and examined practice in 281 firms from German-speaking countries and compared it to previous work in the USA. Such studies show that the data in Table 16 should be viewed cautiously. Simply showing that, for example, both US and German firms have assessment centres masks some fundamentally different logics. For example, the competencies assessed for job analysis might be identified through the use of interviews with job incumbents in 79% of US organisations but only 39% of German ones; the German firms relied on a much narrower analysis base of interviews with supervisors and job descriptions, compared to job incumbent research and use of critical incidents in US firms. Similarly, in terms of assessment exercises, German firms are much more likely to use interviews, presentations and fact-finding exercises, whereas US firms are more likely to use in-basket exercises, role-playing and skill and ability tests.

Psychological testing

The validity of some psychometric testing methods is also disputed. Psychologists claim that the variability of validity across settings for the same type of job and across different kinds of jobs is small (Schmidt and Hunter, 1998). Nevertheless, some variation is observed, and in particular there are concerns for organisations operating internationally about the cross-cultural transferability of many psychometric tests. Of course, only a small minority of organisations in any country use psychometric testing, and the proportion of organisations that use assessment centres is even smaller. International HR managers are increasingly becoming aware of cross-cultural assessment issues (Van de Vijver, 2002; p.545):

> '**Psychological assessment increasingly involves the application of tests in different cultural contexts, either in a single country (involving migrants) or in different countries ... In the near future the demand for cross-cultural assessment will increase, due to the growing internationalisation of business and the increasing need of migrant groups for culture-informed psychological services.**'

Developing culture-free, culture-fair and more recently culture-reduced instruments has long been a goal for psychologists. Where it is accepted that existing instruments are invalid, unreliable or do not cover the construct they are intended for when used in a different cultural setting, developing culture-specific variations becomes an alternative. This can be costly – so is it necessary and is it cost-effective? Does adaptation add sufficient incremental value to the bad, but common, practice of straightforward applications of existing tests and their norms? The answer to the first part of this question involves more than immediate concerns about fairness and discrimination.

Cross-cultural assessment may be conducted by organisations either within a single country, or as a comparison of characteristics of managers across countries (Van de Vijver and Leung, 1997). The increase in assessment raises important questions (Sparrow, 1999):

- Can organisations use psychological tests fairly in multicultural settings?
- Do the psychometric properties of tests translate to different cultural groups?
- Can 'culture-free', 'culture-fair' or 'culture-reduced' tests be developed?
- Or, if tests do not translate from one culture to another, can new instruments be developed?

The use of psychological tests has become an increasing problem in the international selection field. In the pursuit of the global manager, organisations have to look outside their normal recruitment territory in order to benchmark interview candidates. Because they are aware that interviews or behaviourally based work simulations are subject to culturally different behaviours, from both the candidates and the assessor, international HR managers might be tempted to use more testing. On the surface, psychological tests may be seen as a way of avoiding the subjective bias of other options. Indeed, greater international mobility of candidates has increased the demand for tests to be used on job applicants from a number of different countries, and most test producers now sell their products internationally.

The costs of cultural bias in psychological tests do not lie in reduced performance of the candidates. They lie in the perceived stupidity of the assessment process and the impact on motivation (Sparrow, 1999). There is also the problem of fairness. Candidates whose poor English in the work situation hampers their test performance can find that they do not progress as well through internal selection systems. Such discrimination is inappropriate. Countries also differ greatly in terms of the practices related to user qualification, legal and statutory constraints on test use and the consequences for those tested, and controls exercised over the use of tests.

QUESTIONS

There are no simple answers to the issues posed by the use of testing cross-national samples. International HR managers face several practical dilemmas. How should the following questions be considered in an organisation?

- If a French manager is coming to work in the UK, is it more appropriate to test the manager against the French or against the UK test norm group?
- If you test the manager in the English language, is he or she disadvantaged?
- If international HR managers insist on using standardised tools such as psychological tests, does the degree of confidence in their accuracy have to be tempered?
- Can HR managers make up for this by putting more emphasis on the feedback process?

PUTTING RECRUITMENT AND SELECTION INTO CULTURAL CONTEXT

In the next section we explain the ways in which culture weaves its influence through recruitment and selection practices. We devote considerable attention to culture here, therefore, but point out that these principles can be applied to the other functional areas covered in the book such as reward, training, flexibility, and communication.

A number of studies have looked at international differences in selection practices and the role of national culture in explaining such differences in desirability and usage (Ryan, Wiechmann and Hemingway, 2003). Huo, Huang and Napier (2002) examined data from 13 countries using the Best International Human Resource Management Practices Survey to establish if significant differences existed between nations in terms of commonly used hiring practices. Ryan, McFarland, Baron and Page (1999) surveyed 959 organisations from 20 countries to assess whether differences in staffing practices are due to international differences in some of the factors mentioned above (for example, legislation and labour market factors) or to national cultural values. More than half of the organisations operated in multiple countries. They looked at the extent to which 11 core practices (the number of selection methods used, extent of usage, number of verification methods, extent of verification, number of interviews, number of test types, extent of testing, audit process, use of fixed questions, use of peers as interviewers, and use of peers as decision-makers) were used across the countries and in relation to the cultural values of that country.

Two cultural values – uncertainty avoidance and power distance – could predict some of the practices. Cultures high in uncertainty avoidance used more test types, used them more extensively, conducted more interviews, and audited their processes to a greater extent. For example, 11% of variation in the number of verification methods could be linked to scores on uncertainty avoidance and 5% to scores on power distance. Differences were also found in the use of fixed sets of interview questions or structured interviews, either due to a 'technology lag' whereby information on the effectiveness of certain tools and techniques filters slowly across countries, or more likely due to the fact that certain cultures find that the idea of structured interviews does not sit well with how to conduct interpersonal interactions and the extent to which one should trust the judgement of the interviewer. The study concluded (Ryan, McFarland, Baron and Page, 1999; p.385):

> **'National differences accounted for considerable variance in selection practices. This suggests that those attempting to implement standardised worldwide selection practices may face difficulties beyond the known problems of establishing translation equivalence of test and interview materials ... The identification of staffing practices that "travel well" is needed ... Practices with universal appeal may be easier starting points for those pursuing global selection strategies, but these may not be the "best practices". We need to enhance our understanding of the many practical issues associated with global selection systems.'**

Differences across cultures in terms of factors such as perceptions of fairness (procedural justice) have been linked to the attractiveness or otherwise of specific features of selection systems (Steiner and Gilliland, 2001).

In general, most selection systems give attention to the technical requirements of the job, the person's potential to do a good job and interpersonal qualities. However, the belief that there is a clear link between recruitment practices and organisational effectiveness clearly differs across countries when recruitment cultures are analysed. Sparrow and Hiltrop (1994) pointed out that within Europe, the Anglo-Saxon tradition is based on concepts of predictive validity, underpinned by the belief that variance in employee performance is sufficiently explainable by individual factors (knowledge, skills, abilities and other factors) to enable a cost-benefit and utility analysis of investments in sophisticated HR process on the one hand, and returns through employee performance (on the basis of person-job or person-organisation fit) on the other. For Australian organisations, attention is given to the fit between the person and the organisation's values and ways of doing things. This is an assumption common to most Anglo-Saxon countries, and if assessments of competency are made, it is considered legitimate to ask about a person's values (Patrickson and Sutiyono, 2006). Anglo-Saxon countries – and their MNEs – might consider that an individual's alignment to the organisation's values (rather than his or her qualifications or technical capability) is an important part of the selection mix.

Yet, in contrast, French traditions mean that an examination of an individual's personal values are not considered appropriate to a selection context. You want to know what *my* [private and in personal space] values are? What are my values to do with *you* [my employer to whom I provide labour and appropriate service]? In any event, apart from showing me that if *I* share *your* values it will make life easier for you as my manager, what is your evidence that shared values produce superior performance [considered long-term, across complex changes in business models and environments]? These are difficult questions for an HR business partner to answer or to sell a parent-company's approach to recruitment and selection against! French attitudes towards selection, then, are driven by the view that the prediction of performance is not really sufficiently achievable: other factors intervene over a career and therefore decisions must be influenced by robust processes that enable an assessment of risk rather than processes built on assumptions of predicted outcomes. Hence the tendency towards (Sparrow and Hiltrop, 1994; p.353):

'a more intuitive, interpretative and clinical model [that encourages] wider use of personality questionnaires, multiple one-to-one interviews and graphology. [However,] if the international mobility of managers does increase, then the "cultural fingerprint" of national selection systems will be more widely felt.'

There has been a pan-European trend towards the 'democratisation' of recruitment and selection common to countries such as the UK, the Netherlands, Sweden and Germany, with greater emphasis on the perceptions, attitudes, reactions and rights of the applicant, and common emphasis on the introduction of more interactive procedures, constructive feedback, self-selection and realistic job previews. For example, in the UK, recent legislation on freedom of information means that candidates can apply to see the written notes made by individuals on the interview panel, or the references provided in a promotion process. The attention to due diligence in recruitment processes and shifts in recruitment culture from this are clear to behold. There has also been convergence in social legislation around forms of discrimination and employment rights which has created new influences on the nature of recruitment and selection. Nonetheless, the 'cultural fingerprint' was evident in the direct impact of certain cultural values on the preference for specific tools and techniques. Uncertainty avoidance has been linked to the use of the number of interviews involved in a process.

Values have a deeper relationship than this, though. For example, in Latin America, US principles of recruitment based on objective merit, qualification and equality cannot be applied to the way that employees might evaluate a recruitment and selection process. In countries such as Mexico or Peru, the notion that all men are equal does not hold and reality is not based on perceptions solely of objectivity but also of 'interpersonality', for want of a better word. *Who* the person is is important, and that perception of who he or she is is not just job-related but also reflective of social class and family ties These values influence the way that managers think about justice and the impact they perceive justice has on employee commitment. In the United States, ensuring that fair procedures are in place is essential to gain employee commitment; in Mexico, it is more important to ensure that the treatment of the employee is of a 'high-contact', personalised nature (Gomez and Sanchez, 2005; p.67). Having the right personal connections at the top is an important factor in hiring (Huo *et al*, 2002), but while an MNE's strategic mandate might include objective mechanisms for assessing candidate qualifications:

> 'current employees may, through their relationships, provide a more culturally adept assessment of the true qualifications of an applicant ... US MNCs should consider potential candidates who enjoy "in-group" ties, albeit indirect ones, with current employees. Such ties would help build social capital, but additionally, considering these candidates shows that the MNC looks after the employee's in-group, which hopefully will be expanded to include the organisation in its entirety.'
>
> Gomez and Sanchez (2005); pp.68–9)

In some instances, legal norms prescribe the use of local employees. In Chile, for example, foreign personnel contracts cannot exceed 15% of the total local labour force except for certain specialised technical personnel who cannot be replaced by Chileans.

In an Asia-Pacific context, institutional arrangements reflecting the relationship between the state and organisations becomes more important. For the *chaebol* in South Korea, seen as prestige employers, the culture is one of mass recruitment of graduates. Recruitment takes place biannually, with a preference given to management trainee candidates from the elite universities (Rowley and Bae, 2006). Assessment is thus really made at point of entry into the education system rather than at point of entry into the organisation (which is not unlike the situation in France). However, after the Asian crisis of the late 1990s and the rationalisation and recruitment freezes, slowly there has been a move to more recruitment-on-demand practices and more flexible adjustments to labour demands.

In Japan, too, new graduates have traditionally been hired en masse by large firms in April of each year, usually preceded by substantial written assessments and two to three interviews while at university. Data from the Japan Institute of Labour in Tokyo and Institute for the Study of Labour (IZA) in Bonn show that there has been an increase in the number of individuals seeking positions for themselves via the Internet so that only 5% of firms employing under 100 people now use this system. The collapse of the economic bubble also led to a new social phenomenon known in Japan as 'freeters' – concocted by combining the English word 'free' with the German word *arbeiter* for 'worker' and applied mainly to men and unmarried women aged 15 to 34 working continuously for less than five years on a part-time basis or in side jobs. By 1997 there were 1.51 million such employees, and by 2001, nearly 4 million people were in this category if 'dispatched' (agency employees) were included. The greater availability of non-traditional labour sources has seen an increased tendency for firms to hire workers with experience as needed throughout the year.

In China, deregulation has led to a shift away from the practice of assigning employees to employers, and a greater reliance on the external labour market. Mass rural migration, the downsizing of state-owned enterprises and unemployment have helped fuel negative attitudes to the employment of women, who used to represent 40% of the workforce. New regulations in recruitment are therefore aimed at removing gender discrimination (Cooke, 2001). It is common practice for job adverts to specify gender and to place age limits, making both direct and indirect discrimination likely. In other Asian contexts, such as Malaysia, ethnicity is important, with positive discrimination efforts to create a Malay business class and promote employment of *bumiputras* (ethnic Malays and other native races) in return for the maintenance of a market-based business system favoured by overseas Chinese employers (Mellahi and Wood, 2006). The Islamic work ethic also shapes the sorts of competencies considered important in Malaysia.

In the Middle East, recruitment and hiring practices are also subject to religious and government guidelines. The moral drive in Islam is not to recruit on the basis of favouritism or nepotism (Ali, 1999) but rather on the basis of experience and decency. However, the way in which these latter two qualities may be judged is still, in Western eyes, very socially dependent. In Kuwait, for example, 'Most of the hiring and promotion ... especially in the government sector, is influenced highly by social connectivity, tribal identity, and political and sectarian allegiances ... Social dignitaries, influential individuals and politicians normally interfere in the recruitment, retention and promotion process ... [As] in most societies in the Middle East, it is often difficult to get things done without *wasta* – personal intervention of influential people on behalf of a particular person' (Ali and Al-Kazemi, 2006; pp.89–90). These factors combine to limit the role, function and independence of the HR function. There are social currents arguing for a greater influence of performance and positive participation surrounding recruitment processes (Al-Enzi, 2002). In Algeria, the process of recruitment and selection is a bureaucratic and administrative formality, and friendship and kinship can take precedence over qualifications. The use of *piston* to get jobs (enhanced social prestige and influence resulting from support of administrative personnel recruited from relatives and friends) is still evidenced (Branine, 2006).

Saudi Arabia can be used to exemplify the role of government. There is a minimum legally required flow of desirable Saudi applicants. Problems in attracting sufficient talent has led to the growth of technical and vocational institutions to attract skilled employees, government subsidies for on-the-job training in the initial period of employment, and use of Ministry of Labour facilities and websites to attract candidates (Mellahi, 2006). Recruitment agencies and their identification and screening processes are expensive and used mainly by large firms to attract foreign labour. Selection processes, mainly interviews, are sometimes mentioned in job adverts but little is known about the conduct of such processes.

The role of institutional change is evident in a country like Turkey, where a new labour law introduced in 2003 as part of EU accession arrangements places greater emphasis on the burden of proof for inadequate performance before dismissal, thereby indirectly increasing the likelihood of assessing person-job fit at point of entry (Aycan, 2006) and fuelling the growth of professional training in the area. The competencies that are favoured in recruitment processes – such as taking responsibility, teamwork, conscientiousness, and customer-orientation – would be seen in most European selection systems, but the influence of the collectivistic nature of the culture on recruitment and selection is still seen through suggestions from employees and acquaintances being the most popular recruitment channel, use of social networks which then reinforces a reliance on one-to-one interviews (in 90% of organisations) (Aycan, 2005). As Aycan (2006; p.177) notes:

'The levels of development in the field in Turkey and in industrialised Western countries (mainly US) are very different. For instance, without having an established employee-selection system, HR departments are asked to create an expatriate selection system. Similarly, in some cases where there is no performance-evaluation system, HR departments are asked to implement 360-degree appraisals. Students of HRM use US books and get acquainted with US trends. However, they cannot transfer what they learn in class to real-life situations. Because cross-cultural applicability of North American HRM practices are in question, multinational corporations in Turkey must establish a global-local balance in their HRM practices.'

ACTIVITY

The previous section has noted some of the national practice and current developments in recruitment and hiring. However, does this matter for MNEs operating in those labour markets? Construct two arguments.

- First, list the arguments and suggest the ways in which local labour market practice will influence a local recruitment process conducted by an MNE.

- Second, outline the ways in which an MNE might be able to bypass some of these influences while still seeking local talent.

- Then, imagine you are an in-country HR business partner and write a memo to your HR director explaining your chosen strategy, mixing and matching your reasoning on both sides of the argument if necessary.

GLOBAL PRESSURES ON INTERNATIONAL RECRUITMENT

The recruitment and selection function inside many organisations has experienced particularly rapid global exposure. The need to recruit internationally develops rapidly, but once established, the operations associated with new international recruitment channels can be very volatile and may be scaled down again, re-structured or even disposed of within a fairly short period of time (Sparrow, 2006).

QUESTIONS

In what ways might the following developments change the task faced by an international recruitment function?

- Global business process redesign and the global re-distribution and re-location of work

- The merging of existing operations on a global scale and attempts to develop and harmonise core HR processes within these merged businesses

- The rapid start-up of international operations and the need to manage the development of these operations as they mature through different stages of the business life cycle.

Organisations have to understand the labour markets, local, national or international, within which they recruit. However, despite this, many organisations are caught out and find themselves having to recruit desperately, or to declare redundancies, or find that they have no succession plans when key people leave. Like other aspects of HRM, there is a comparative element here. Planning in tight labour markets, where there may be a shortage of key skills, is a different proposition from planning in markets where appropriately skilled labour is abundant. Shedding staff in countries such as many of those in Europe, where labour laws make that more expensive, is different from reducing numbers in some of the poorer countries of the world or in the United States, where there are few associated costs.

In some cases corporations find that labour costs in one country are significantly higher than those somewhere else, opening up the option of moving their production or, increasingly, their provision of services to the cheaper country. This is what has been called the international division of labour. It is the concept that as companies find labour difficult or expensive to obtain in some of the advanced countries, they move their production or services to other parts of the world where they do not have this problem. This works where the costs of transporting goods back to the markets does not overwhelm the savings made by relocation, or where the service (telephone-answering or information-technology-working, to take common examples) can be provided from anywhere. It remains highly contentious.

For example, there have been long-standing concerns, generally expressed by unions, that a reliance on immigration by UK firms and short-term contracts to fill immediate skills shortages reflects a short-term attitude to skills shortages that provides a disincentive to invest in training for the domestic workforce and indeed for the already-skilled immigrants (Salt and Millar, 2006). The counter-argument from employers, especially global high-technology and service firms, has been that they need to source international skills more flexibly to meet shortages and that by 'injecting' short-term skills into UK operations, they could avoid the jobs in the UK going overseas to offshore centres of excellence. Employers argue that ensuring sufficient skills levels and capability in a domestic market facilitates growth in that market, producing local benefits. This also serves their internal motivations, usually driven by a combination of the need for revenue growth and the need to reduce internal costs. Employers argue that barriers to the movement of expertise must be removed so that they can access and deploy skills more flexibly across internal, but also international, labour markets. They have many strategies at their disposal that can address skills shortages in any one national labour market, including the use of technology to assist remote working, alterations to business process and work standardisation, the development of centres of excellence that can then be used to disseminate organisational learning throughout operations, and offshore outsourcing. There are also institutional pressures supporting flexible skills migration, in particular the General Agreement on Trade in Services Mode 4 which encourages governments to liberalise the supply of services via the temporary movement of people across borders.

GLOBAL SKILLS SUPPLY STRATEGIES

Human resource planning is, then – in theory if not in practice – becoming more important in this area because organisations now have to develop global skills supply strategies. The study of global staffing has traditionally concentrated on the need to resource key positions within multinational enterprises (MNEs) and top management team positions at HQ and subsidiary locations. Harzing (2001; 2004) argues that generally an idiosyncratic mix of strategy is adopted rather than any logical progression of focus that is related to the process of globalisation. Scullion and Collings (2006) point out that the literature therefore gives most attention to:

- the recruitment and selection of expatriates and international managers (see Chapter 12)
- more flexible forms of international business travellers, virtual teams and inpatriates (see Chapter 13), and
- talent management processes at HQ or local level (see Chapter 15).

Our definition of the 'international employee' inside organisations continues to expand (Briscoe and Schuler, 2004; p.223):

> **'The tradition of referring to all international employees as expatriates – or even international assignees – falls short of the need for international HR practitioners to understand the options available ... and fit them to evolving international business strategies.'**

International resourcing activity – and the global skill supply strategies that can be discerned from it – now covers a fragmentary group of individuals. Attention has been given to:

- contract expatriates (Baruch and Altman, 2002)

- assignees on short-term or intermediate-term foreign postings (Morley and Heraty, 2004; Mayrhofer, Hartmann and Herbert, 2004)

- permanent cadres of global managers (Suutari, 2003)

- international commuters (*Economist*, 2006)

- employees utilised on long-term business trips (Mayrhofer, Hartmann, Michelitsch-Riedl and Kollinger, 2004)

- international transferees (moving from one subsidiary to another)(Harvey, Price, Speier and Novicevic, 1999; Salt and Millar, 2006)

- virtual international employees active in cross-border project teams (Janssens and Brett, 2006)

- skilled individuals working in geographically remote centres of excellence serving global operations (Sparrow, 2006)

- self-initiated movers who live in a third country but are willing to work for a multinational (Suutari and Brewster, 2000; Tharenou, 2003)

- immigrants actively and passively attracted to a national labour market (Salt and Millar, 2006), and

- domestically based employees in a service centre but dealing with overseas customers, suppliers and partners on a regular basis.

QUESTION

What factors have led to the increase in demand for these flexible forms of international management?

Not only has international recruitment and resourcing moved away from its traditional focus on managing pools of expatriates, but the changing structure and role of international HR functions also means that these functions and their HR business partners now have to help their organisations manage a very wide range of options associated with global resourcing (Hustad and Munkvold, 2005). This increased demand for new forms of international mobility is due to a number of factors (Salt and Millar, 2006):

- the need for skilled expatriates to help build new international markets (Findlay, Li, Jowett and Skeldon, 2000)

- the growing importance of temporary and short-term access to specialised talent in sending countries to assist the execution of overseas projects (Minbaeva and Michailova, 2004; Hocking, Brown and Harzing, 2004)

- the growing need for highly mobile elites of management to perform boundary-spanning roles to help build social networks and facilitate the exchange of knowledge (Tushman and Scanlan, 2005).

Moreover, the opportunity for broader resourcing strategies has increased markedly in certain labour markets because these labour markets have themselves become globalised (Ward, 2004). For example, considerable attention has been given to the globalisation of health care labour markets (Aiken, Buchan, Sochalski, Nichols and Powell, 2004; Clark, Stewart and Clark, 2006).

Globalisation is also leading to new relationships between a number of corporate functions and the development of many hybrid professionals capable of using the tools and techniques of each function (Sparrow, Brewster and Harris, 2004). A number of tools and techniques strongly influenced by marketing, corporate communications and IT thinking have become part of the mainstream armoury of HR functions when dealing with international recruitment. This convergence of thinking has brought the language of employee value propositions, employer branding, corporate social responsibility, market mapping and recruiting ahead of the curve into the mix of HR activity in this area. The challenge now is to try to manage these approaches on a global scale. An issue for recruitment and selection functions in many organisations is that they have not yet 'internalised' this influence of global markets into their structures and strategies. Many believe that they will increasingly have to do so (Harvey, Novicevic and Speier, 2000; p.382):

> **'What is needed is a global management staffing strategy that enables global consistency among various managerial pools and the foreign subsidiaries.'**

In order to ensure that the correct balance of standardisation versus differentiation is reached, geographical partners have to be treated as equal partners in the ensuing debate. Harvey *et al* (2000) argue that organisations must integrate a transcultural emphasis into their global staffing systems. Often it is the local in-country HR business partner who has to manage these tensions (Sparrow, 2007).

THE ROLE OF RECRUITMENT IN THE INTERNATIONALISATION OF THE ORGANISATION

Organisations can use the development of an increasingly multicultural workforce to the advantage of an internationalisation strategy. However, as the Barclaycard International case study below shows, the sorts of HR issues that have to be managed in relation to recruitment as the internationalisation process proceeds are also quite complex (Sparrow, 2006).

Case study

Barclaycard International: recruitment in the context of an internationalisation strategy

Barclaycard was the UK's first credit card and as one of the largest global credit card businesses now has a rapid growth strategy. Outside the UK, it operates in the United States, Germany, Spain, Greece, Italy, Portugal, Ireland, Sweden, Norway, France, Asia-Pacific and across Africa. A strategy to become as meaningful a contributor to the Group as Barclaycard UK currently is by 2013 has witnessed alliances with Standard Bank of South Africa, acquisition of Juniper Financial Corporation (rebranded as Barclays USA) and a series of in-country launches. It employs 3,000 staff, with 15% based in the UK. To enable expansion, Barclaycard International built a platform of people management processes (processes, structures and frameworks) to bring stability, governance and control. Challenges varied across countries but always included ensuring rigour and consistency across operations in very different cultures, business markets and labour markets.

Primary agenda items for the HR team in 2006 were international resourcing, international mobility, talent acquisition and development of global policies and frameworks. Resourcing, then transferring, capability globally, either within an existing business or during start-up and building of a local business, necessitated a range of preferred recruitment suppliers and the building of networks across them to transfer learning about the management of different types of supplier and agency, assessment of their true global capability, and the availability of skills available in each labour

---

market. Intranets exchanged vacancy information between Hamburg, Zaragoza and Dublin. A new International Resourcing Business Partner role acted as a support mechanism for HR business partners and business leaders to facilitate the acquisition of top talent through negotiation of global preferred supplier arrangements for headhunters and research institutions, the development of an employee value proposition and employment brand across countries, advising on global versus local process, discovering sources of best practice, and ensuring appropriate geographical diversity in the use of international talent.

Barclaycard's call centre in Dublin acted as a central platform and nursery for future international expansion. It grew from 10 to 360 people between 1997 and 2006. Initially intended to support non-UK operations, it grew to serve eight countries including the Republic of Ireland, Italy, Spain, France, Germany, Portugal, Greece, and Botswana. Dublin was chosen because of the nature of the role, the employee base, and the city's labour market. The recruitment population was well-qualified, with intentions to stay in country for around 12 to 18 months. Employees spoke (and were hired for) their mother tongue in the markets they served, requiring principles of cross-cultural management to be applied to a single internal labour market.

The acquisition of Banco Zaragozano enabled a new contact centre in Spain. Thirty-five employees moved from Dublin to Spain to help transfer practices. HR business partners dealt with setting up legal entities to transfer employees, deciding the best mix of local recruitment, using local job centres, assessing funding support, and understanding the implications and ramifications of local employment law and sector agreements. New country operations oversaw other start-up operations (Portugal and Italy were initially resourced under the guidance of the Spanish HR partner). Considerable insight into country capability resided at HR partner level. A 'framework for growth' was established to replicate in-country moves and transfer learning. Many aspects of recruitment and selection could be 'cut and pasted' across operations (procedures, training plans, interview and induction processes, job standards) while others had to be dealt with flexibly (for example, criteria-based interviewing and diversity practices). Dublin acted as a nursery (providing people to facilitate international expansion).

Rapid global expansion required the deployment of skills and experience in a multitude of countries at short notice, not always achievable quickly through local recruitment. A new international mobility framework reduced the cost and complexity of expatriating individuals by securing talented employees on global contracts with a premium for global mobility but only 'light' expatriation benefits. Assignments were designed by HR business partners and international assignments services (IAS) teams located within key global regions. Two initiatives supported a global mindset: awareness-building among the senior leadership community through workshops on the cultures of current and potential labour markets, and cross-cultural training interventions linked to a global induction programme. Talent management tools and techniques supported international resourcing through successive application to top leadership roles, senior cross-Barclays role potential, top 450 leadership potential, and finally a broad business talent population. Succession planning and talent identification processes were integrated with long-term incentives tied to identified capabilities. The top 10% within internal expertise fields were identified on a global basis. Rather than wait until Barclaycard International was in or near market, people were recruited for target markets ('resourcing ahead of the curve') and investments made in forward market mapping (using research agencies and headhunters to map a wider range of geographical labour markets, and researching people working in target roles). Global policies and frameworks operated on an exception basis (even if culturally uncomfortable, explicit guidance and global protocols governed activity unless it was illegal to do so). The aim was to ensure that consistency, rigour, global governance and risk management and control monitoring processes were aligned with institutional requirements such as Sarbanes-Oxley [the US Public Company Accounting Reform and Investor Protection Act, 2002] in areas such as pre-employment screening policy.

ACTIVITY

Recruiting as part of an internationalisation strategy

Read the Barclaycard International case study. Consider the following

- Is there a clear sequence of HR issues that have been managed during the internation-alisation process?

- As an organisation globalises, what decisions have to be made as to which HR processes will be managed at a global level and co-ordinated in-country?

- What is the role of local business partners in relation to recruitment and selection as the activity develops?

The experience of Barclaycard International shows that international resourcing issues cannot be understood without also having to explain developments in the process of creating new in-country operations (Sparrow, 2006), and in particular how this process relates to:

- the varied, dynamic and complex nature of the HR business partner role (see the previous chapter)

- expatriate management (see Chapter 12)

- the challenges of managing more strategic aspects of international resourcing during a period of rapid expansion, such as talent management (see Chapter 15)

- comparative differences in recruitment practice (which have been discussed in this chapter).

Not only has the growth of MNEs meant that they now recruit in many countries, but there has also been a growth in organisations that recruit from abroad for their domestic workforce (Sparrow, 2006). This is particularly the case in the European Union, where work permits and other barriers have been abolished. It applies in such areas as business services and IT, and in the public sector for staff such as nurses. It is more common in the smaller EU countries, and it is dynamic.

SUMMARY

This chapter has shown that although all organisations have to plan, source and select their people, they do not all do these things in the same way. Many of these differences occur within countries; some organisations have more sophisticated systems, some less; some will do it more carefully, some more casually. However, a key to these differences is national cultures and institutions. In broad terms, being in one country means that an organisation is likely to conduct these activities pretty much like other organisations in the same country – and unlike those in other countries. This should not by now be a surprise. When organisations plan their staffing needs, they do so within the context of a particular labour market; they recruit people from the same market and have to do it in ways that fit culturally. What they spend on recruitment and selection is affected by national laws and tax regimes.

However, as organisations internationalise, it is often their recruitment and selection systems that are the first to have to cope with this new context. Moreover, in some sectors, the labour markets themselves are becoming more global, and this is creating both new resourcing strategies and also a need for many domestic organisations to become skilled in overseas recruitment.

A number of lessons can be drawn about international recruitment and selection:

- International HR managers have to consider whether they should internationalise the resourcing systems of the whole organisation.

- International graduate programmes are no 'quick fix' for organisations that need to increase their supply of international recruits.

- In order to be successful, cross-national advertising requires an awareness of the cultural appropriateness of the techniques and media used.

- New recruitment techniques such as Internet recruitment are altering the economics of the international selection process.

- Assessment centres can prove an effective tool for international resourcing, but they require careful modification for an international setting.

- There has been an increase in cross-cultural assessment based on psychological testing.

Organisations employ people within particular cultures and under particular laws and institutional arrangements. This means that organisations have to remain aware of these differences when they determine their HR policies and practices. It also means that notions of good practice in HRM differ from country to country, and this is as true of recruitment and selection as it is of the topic discussed in the next chapter – reward management.

LEARNING QUESTIONS

- What are the main cross-national differences in the nature of recruitment and selection systems?

- How would you characterise the underlying philosophy that British HR professionals have towards selection compared with French HR professionals? Is this evidenced in a different take-up of particular selection tools and techniques?

- What are the main technical challenges faced by firms that wish to internationalise their selection and assessment approaches?

- What are the main issues facing organisations as labour markets become more global?

- What are the different resourcing strategies open to organisations as they operate in these global labour markets?

REFERENCES

Aiken, L. H., Buchan, J., Sochalski, J., Nichols, B. and Powell, M. (2004) 'Trends in international nurse migration', *Health Affairs*, 23 (3): 69–78

Al-Enzi, A. (2002) 'Kuwait's employment policy: its formulation, implications and challenges', *International Journal of Public Administration*, 25 (7): 885–900

Ali, A. (1999) 'The evolution of work ethic and management thought: an Islamic view', in H. Kao, D. Sinha and B. Wilpert (eds) *Management and Cultural Values*. New Delhi, Sage

Ali, A. J. and Al-Kazemi, A. (2006) 'Human resource management in Kuwait', in P. S. Budhwar and K. Mellahi (eds) *Managing Human Resources in the Middle East*. London, Routledge

Aycan, Z. (2005) 'The interface between cultural and institutional/structural contingencies in human resource management', *International Journal of Human Resource Management*, 16 (7): 1083–120

Aycan, Z. (2006) 'Human resource management in Turkey', in P. S. Budhwar and K. Mellahi (eds) *Managing Human Resources in the Middle East*. London, Routledge

Baruch, Y. and Altman, Y. (2002) 'Expatriation and repatriation in MNCs: a taxonomy', *Human Resource Management*, 41 (2): 239–59

Branine, M. (2006) 'Human resource management in Algeria', in P. S. Budhwar and K. Mellahi (eds) *Managing Human Resources in the Middle East*. London: Routledge

Briscoe, D. and Schuler, R. S. (2004) *International Human Resource Management*, 2nd edition. New York, Routledge

Clark, P. F., Stewart, J. B. and Clark, D. A. (2006) 'The globalisation of the labour market for health-care professionals', *International Labour Review*, 145 (1/2): 37–64

Cook, M. (1999) *Personnel Selection: Adding value through people*. Chichester, John Wiley

Cooke, F. L. (2001) 'Equal opportunities? The role of legislation and public policies in women's employment in China', *Journal of Women in Management Review*, 16 (7): 334–48

Cranet (2006) *Cranet survey on Comparative Human Resource Management. International Executive Report 2005*. Cranfield, Bedfordshire, Cranfield University

Economist (2006) 'Travelling more lightly', *The Economist*, 379 (8483): 99–101

Findlay, A. M., Li, F. L. N., Jowett, A. J. and Skeldon, R. (2000) 'Skilled international migration and the global city: a study of expatriates in Hong Kong', *Applied Geography*, 20 (3): 277–304

Garrison-Jenn, N. (1998) *The Global 200 Executive Recruiters*. San Francisco, Jossey-Bass

Gomez, C. and Sanchez, J. I. (2005) 'Managing HR to build social capital in Latin America within MNCs', in M. M. Elvira and A. Davila (eds) *Managing Human Resources in Latin America*. London: Routledge

Harris, M., Van Hoye, G. and Lievens, F. (2003) 'Privacy and attitudes towards internet-based selection systems: a cross-cultural comparison', *International Journal of Selection and Assessment*, 11 (2/3): 230–6

Harvey, M. G., Novicevic, H. M. and Speier, C. (2000) 'An innovative global management staffing system: a competency-based perspective', *Human Resource Management*, 39 (4): 381–94

Harvey, M. G., Price, M. F., Speier, C. and Novicevic, M. M. (1999) 'The role of inpatriates in a globalisation strategy and challenges associated with the inpatriation process', *Human Resource Planning*, 22 (1): 38–60

Harzing, A. W. K. (2001) 'Who is in charge? An empirical study of executive staffing practices in foreign multinationals', *Human Resource Management*, 40: 139–58

Harzing, A. W. K. (2004) 'Composing an international staff', in A. W. K. Harzing and J. van Ruysseveldt (eds) *International Human Resource Management*, 2nd edition. London, Sage

Hocking, J. B., Brown, M. and Harzing, A. W. K. (2004) 'A knowledge transfer perspective of strategic assignment purposes and their path-dependent outcomes', *International Journal of Human Resource Management*, 15 (3): 565–86

Huo, Y. P., Huang, H. J. and Napier, N. K. (2002) 'Divergence or convergence: a cross-national comparison of personnel selection systems', *Human Resource Management*, 41 (1): 31–44

Hustad, E. and Munkvold, B. E. (2005) 'IT-supported competence management: a case study at Ericsson', *Information Systems Management*, 22 (2): 78–88

Janssens, M. and Brett, J. M. (2006) 'Cultural intelligence in global teams: a fusion model of collaboration', *Group and Organization Management*, 31 (1): 124–53

Krause, D. E. and Gebert, D. (2003) 'A comparison of assessment centre practices in organisations in German-speaking regions and the United States', *International Journal of Selection and Assessment*, 11 (4): 297–312

Mayrhofer, H., Hartmann, L. C. and Herbert, A. (2004) 'Career management issues for flexpatriate international staff', *Thunderbird International Business Review*, 46 (6): 647–66

Mayrhofer, H., Hartmann, L. C., Michelitsch-Riedl, G. and Kollinger, I. (2004) 'Flexpatriate assignments: a neglected issue in global staffing', *International Journal of Human Resource Management*, 15 (8): 1371–89

Mellahi, K. (2006) 'Human resource management in Saudi Arabia', in P. S. Budhwar and K. Mellahi (eds) *Managing Human Resources in the Middle East*. London, Routledge

Mellahi, K. and Wood, G. (2006) 'HRM in Malaysia', in P. S. Budhwar (ed.) *Managing Human Resources in Asia-Pacific*. London, Routledge

Minbaeva, D. B. and Michailova, S. (2004) 'Knowledge transfer and expatriation in multinational corporations: the role of disseminative capacity', *Employee Relations*, 26 (6): 663–79

Morley, M. and Heraty, N. (2004) 'International assignments and global careers', *Thunderbird International Business Review*, 46 (6): 633–46

Patrickson, M. and Sutiyono, W. (2006) 'HRM in Australia', in P. S. Budhwar (ed.) *Managing Human Resources in Asia-Pacific*. London: Routledge

Rowley, C. and Bae, J. (2006) 'HRM in South Korea', in P. S. Budhwar (ed.) *Managing Human Resources in Asia-Pacific*. London: Routledge

Ryan, A. M., McFarland, L., Baron, H. and Page, R. (1999) 'An international look at selection practices: nation and culture as explanations for variability in practice', *Personnel Psychology*, 52: 359–91

Ryan, A. M., Wiechmann, D. and Hemingway, M. (2003) 'Designing and implementing global staffing systems: Part II. Best practices', *Human Resource Management*, 42 (1): 85–94

Salt, J. and Millar, J. (2006) 'International migration in interesting times: the case of the UK', *People and Place*, 14 (2): 14–25

Schmidt, F. L and Hunter J. E. (1998) 'The validity and utility of selection methods in personnel psychology: practical and theoretical implications of 85 years of research findings', *Psychological Bulletin*, 124 (2): 262–74

Scullion, H. and Collings, D. G. (eds)(2006) *Global staffing*. Abingdon, Routledge

Scullion, H. and Starkey, K. (2000) 'In search of the changing role of the corporate human resource function in the international firm', *International Journal of Human Resource Management*, 11 (6): 1061–81

Sparrow, P. R. (1999) 'International recruitment, selection and assessment: whose route map will you follow?', in P. Joynt and B. Morton (eds) *The Global HR Manager: Creating the seamless organisation*. London, CIPD

Sparrow, P. R. (2006) *International recruitment, selection and assessment*. London, Chartered Institute of Personnel and Development

Sparrow, P. R. (2007) 'Globalisation of HR at function level: four case studies of the international recruitment, selection and assessment process', *International Journal of HRM*

Sparrow, P. R. and Hiltrop, J. (1994) *European Human Resource Management in Transition*. London, Prentice Hall

Sparrow, P. R., Brewster, C. and Harris, H. (2004) *Globalizing Human Resource Management*. London, Routledge

Spreitzer, G. M., McCall, M. W. and Mahoney, J. D. (1997) 'Early identification of international executive potential', *Journal of Applied Psychology*, 82 (1): 6–29

Steiner, D. D. and Gilliland, S. W. (2001) 'Procedural justice in personnel selection: international and cross-cultural perspectives', *International Journal of Selection and Assessment*, 9 (1/2): 124–37

Suutari, V. (2003) 'Global managers: career orientations, career tracks, life-style implications and career commitment', *Journal of Managerial Psychology*, 18 (3): 185–233

Suutari, V. and Brewster, C. (2000) 'Making their own way: international experience through self-initiated foreign assignments', *Journal of World Business,* 35 (4): 417–36

Tharenou, P. (2003) 'The initial development of receptivity to working abroad: self-initiated international work opportunities in young graduate employees', *Journal of Occupational and Organizational Psychology*, 76: 489–515

Tushman, M. I. and Scanlan, T. J. (2005) 'Boundary-spanning individuals: their role in information transfer and their antecedents', *Academy of Management Journal*, 24 (2): 289–305

Van de Vijver, F. J. R. (2002) 'Cross-cultural assessment: value for money?', *Applied Psychologist: An International Review*, 51 (4): 545–66

Van de Vijver, F. J. R. and Leung, K. (1997) *Methods and Data Collection for Cross-cultural Research*. Newbury Park, CA, Sage

Ward, K. (2004) 'Going global? Internationalisation and diversification in the temporary staffing industry', *Journal of Economic Geography*, 4: 251–73

Comparative HRM: reward

CHAPTER 7

CHAPTER OBJECTIVES

When they have read this chapter, students will:

- be able to describe some of the different ways that organisations approach reward
- be able to quote examples of cross-national variation
- be able to discuss the implications of these differences for the way that reward strategy is to be understood and carried out on an international basis.

INTRODUCTION

Pfeffer (1998) asserts that although people work for money, they also work to find meaning and a sense of identity, and Kohn (1998) goes further, to suggest that extrinsic reward erodes intrinsic interest. Yet a great deal of discussion in the realm of HR now centres on pay, and pay systems almost always feature in broader discussions of the management of high commitment, involvement or performance. It may be a commonplace that employees at all levels typically feel 'underpaid and overworked', but the intensity of their dissatisfaction varies.

The influential expectancy theory suggests that motivation and performance are shaped by the links between effort and reward and by the significance or 'valence' of the reward to the person in question. This underpins Lawler's (1990) notion that 'line of sight' is the crucial issue in the design of reward packages. Accordingly, a good deal of thinking and discussion around reward now centres on motivation and, more specifically, incentivisation. A given in the consideration of senior managers and executives, there is now interest in extending incentivisation via pay beyond these groups, and beyond managerial hierarchies, to the bulk of non-managerial employees, regardless of their prior exposure to such incentives. Discussion of the possibility and potential of various forms of pay for performance or variable pay has become perennial. At the same time, though, with regard to all but the most senior managers of executives, there is an acceptance that the bulk of pay packages must be made up of other elements. Still, in that incentivisation is such a seductive notion, and given the levers held by HR functions in multinationals in this arena, many functions are showing a growing interest in this form of pay in particular.

This chapter briefly surveys the various bases on which pay packages may be constructed. The chapter then turns to outline approaches to understanding cross-national comparative variation in reward practice, focusing on the roles of culture and institutions. It goes on to consider in detail comparative variation in practice, with a focus on the situation regarding the various forms of pay for performance (PfP). The emerging comparative evidence on best practice in reward is then considered. The chapter concludes by considering the 'strategic space' for reward (Vernon, 2005; eg p.217) implied, and thus the international management of reward in MNCs.

REWARD AND BASES OF PAY

Discussions of 'total reward' seek to encompass the entirety of the offer to employees (Antoni *et al*, 2005), relating in many respects to the employers' side of the psychological contract. Notions of total reward thus extend beyond matters of pay, and indeed perquisites (perks) and benefits, to autonomy at work, learning and development opportunities, the quality of working life, and the rather more ephemeral issues of the nature of the company culture (see Armstrong, 2006). For the most part, however, discussion of reward in organisations tends to be more limited, focusing on matters of pay in cash and in kind.

Within this more limited sphere, a good deal of managerial discussion has traditionally focused on perks and benefits, which typically comprise around 20% of the total labour cost. In some respects, though, this agenda seems on the wane. The validity of payment via company cars is increasingly questioned, as environmental issues and indeed concerns over the divisions wrought by such obvious status differentials come to the fore. Despite the erosion of the support and services provided by welfare states in many nations, and the concern of non-managerial employees about their plight in the event of severe sickness and upon retirement in particular, the weight of benefits in managerial discussions has also declined. The strategic use of pay is the new focus for debate. Pay is often seen as a sharper tool for directing and motivating employees than the range of options offered by benefits and perks.

Attachment to benefits?

In China, pay is less important than the range of benefits (housing, food, childcare, etc) typically provided for employees (Verma and Zhiming, 1995). In China, but also Japan and Korea, employees value benefits increases and bonuses above basic pay increases, partly because tax is levied on basic pay. Many benefits are not taxed in the USA either, and in the light of the paucity of national social provision, benefits increases are also popular there. We would expect in countries such as those in the Nordic zone where childcare provision by the state is generous, not to see childcare as a significant part of an employee package. The Nordic countries and France, as examples, prefer to get most of their pay and reward packages in cash and to be free to spend it as they wish. In Europe, benefit provision by employers is less important.

Some elements of pay packages are near ubiquitous, regardless of occupation, industry or country. Almost always, there is a fixed or base element of pay. This base element generally reflects the grade or wider band (or job family) of the job in question, often determined on the basis of some formal job analysis, but also elements of seniority within the organisation or sometimes on sheer age. It may also reflect the qualifications of the employee, even if these exceed the minimum job requirements, or the progression of the employee through some organisation-specific competence ladder. There has been an upsurge of interest in the last decade in increasing the weight of the qualifications or demonstrable competences of employees in determining their base salary. Although qualifications remain the subject of considerable discussion – for example, in considerations of human capital – and competence ladders remain the focus of some attention, the spotlight has fallen increasingly on pay beyond the base. The strategic use of pay has often become synonymous with an emphasis on incentivisation via pay for performance or variable pay.

Traditionally, individual performance has been rewarded by promotion to a new job role or grade. In a sense, one might also suggest that some form of group performance has been implicit in organisation-specific upgradings of pay, but the solidity of the link between organisational performance and reward is rather uncertain. In any event, current discussions of pay for performance centre on reward which is separate from base pay, forming a distinct component of a pay package much more immediately related to the assessed performance of an individual or group. This is very attractive in the context of discussions of reward management linking immediately to the questions 'What do we value?' and 'What do we pay for?'

Agency theory

Compensation for top management has been the subject of considerable discussion since the 1990s, and in relation to it agency theory became an influential perspective from which the issues could be considered (Barema and Gomez-Meija, 1998). The theory posits the existence of a 'principal' who employs an 'agent' to manage on his or her behalf, but accepts that this agent usually has a distinct set of interests, and that information asymmetries imply difficulties for the principal, or owner, in monitoring the agent, or manager, appointed. The problem is then conceived as one of the appropriate framework which can be introduced by the principal to ensure that the agent is working in the principal's best interest. The theory suggests that the principal's two recourses are investment in information-gathering systems which would reveal the manner in which the manager appointed was working, and an incentive system that would motivate the manager to work in the principal's best interest. Agency problems might be thought particularly severe in the context of MNCs, given the extent of information asymmetries, suggesting that the framework might be particularly valuable in this context (Björkman and Furu, 2000). However, the theory implies what is in some respects a rather crude representation of the problem of motivating top managers, or indeed other employees, and of the nature of their response. Ferner and Varul (2000) suggest the relevance of cross-national movements of personnel and international networks as informal means of monitoring and transferring practices across national borders. Moreover, the dangers of incentive systems which reward top managers for favourable movements in share prices have been increasingly obvious since the collapse of Enron and of WorldCom.

Many of the contours of discussions of reward are shared across the nations of the advanced industrialised world and beyond. As we would expect by now, there are some general trends that seem to be spreading across the world, but also some significant differences in the way that each country tends to compensate its workers for the time and commitment that they bring to work. In relation to non-managerial workforces and the external labour pool to which pay policies are applied, the evidence of convergence in rewards behaviour is less marked than in relation to top management or to internationally mobile elites.

Generic processes across cultures

Psychological analysis of rewards behaviour suggests that there is a generic cross-cultural process of pay satisfaction and the subsequent influence that this has on work behaviour. Pay tends to have four meanings. It carries motivational properties. People differ in the extent to which they see pay as a good means of achieving important objectives. Pay signals relative position, both in terms of achievement of tasks or goals, and in relation to performance in comparison with others. Pay carries meaning in relation to the relative level of control an individual has, through the different composition of the pay package and perceived ability to influence others and create autonomy over reward. Finally, pay carries meaning in terms of the utility it creates, the ease or difficulty with which it can be spent. The structure of a pay system (elements of pay, form of payment, and climate factors such as level of secrecy or participation) can determine the meaning that individuals derive from it – and as we have seen, the structure of pay systems varies markedly across societies. So too does the extent to which a pay policy is integrated into the strategic context of the firm, and is tailored to the goals of other HRM policies such as selection, evaluation and management development. Of these four meanings, 'relative position' seems to be the most powerful influence on motivation.

Source: Thierry (1998)

LINKING CULTURE TO EMPLOYEE BEHAVIOURS

In the previous chapter we explained how the conduct of specific practices – we looked at recruitment and selection – can be linked to national culture and institutional factors. This is clearly true too for rewards practices, but there is an important difference. Rewards practices are intended to produce specific outcomes within individuals such as performance, identification with the organisation, commitment to or engagement with a goal. Therefore, the design of any HR practice – and its impact on individual employees living in different countries – has to be informed by a theory or a model of how HR practices produce important performance-related outcomes within the individual (Gelade and Young, 2005). Although, as noted above, the utility of pay and the process of pay satisfaction is similar across cultures, when it comes to engineering complex organisational behaviours, we have to understand the subtle way in way culture impacts on the associated behaviours. Sparrow (2006) argues that HR practitioners need a clearer specification of the generic human functioning and link between the key variables that might be involved, for a number of reasons:

- The assertion that national culture influences work attitudes and behaviours mainly (but indirectly) through organisational practices (Fischer *et al*, 2005; Ostroff and Bowen, 2000) suggests that we need to better understand the processes through which organisational culture and organisational practices mediate national culture effects.

- Bandura's (2002) arguments about the need to incorporate our understanding of cross-culturally generalisable human functions – such as agency theory (see the box above) – suggests that we must develop a more complete functional model that elicits the constructs that are involved in the organisation culture–HR practice–effectiveness chain.

- Erez and Gati's (2004) observations that there are dynamic and two-way (ie top-down and bottom-up) processes involved when studying national culture suggests that this modelling must allow for an understanding of not just how national culture exerts an influence on work attitudes, through its influence on organisational culture and organisational practices (for which we can insert principally human resource management practices), but also of how national culture *as enacted within firms and within individuals also creates a bottom-up influence* on the adoption, customisation and redirection of those practices.

Before we can make sense of the different impacts that national culture has on the various constituent elements – HRM practices, leadership, psychological contract, commitment, and so forth – we must clarify how these elements *generally* relate to and influence each other. It is worth noting that this is not just a problem that applies to international management – it is, for example, also part of the 'black box' problem in the HRM-organisational performance literature.

QUESTIONS

- The pay motivation process has been assumed to be generic across societies, even though the content (ie what motivates people) has long been known to differ across countries. Should we assume that even the pay motivation process is generic?

- National culture should influence many of the causal dynamics between perceived meaning of pay and actual satisfaction. In what ways do you think it does influence rewards behaviour?

Rewards are just one important outcome from an effective employment relationship, but what really has to happen for the desired outcomes to materialise? Sparrow (2006) argues that within any given cultural context (which impacts on all of the variables depicted in Figure 14 at both the organisational and individual level of analysis) – firms that are pursuing globalisation strategies that may be characterised by cross-border alliances (IJVs and mergers and acquisitions), changes to global knowledge management, changing patterns of international employee adjustment and the pursuit of specific organisational competences – there is a specific HRM architecture or set of capabilities. This may be seen in terms of the bundles of HRM practices, the technical effectiveness of these practices within the national context, and the professional HRM capabilities of the HR function. Organisational climates and cultures flow from this set of organisational and HRM practices as reflected by the behaviours that are sanctioned by the system, group perceptions and ways of thinking, culturally embedded leadership styles, and espoused management styles and assumptions.

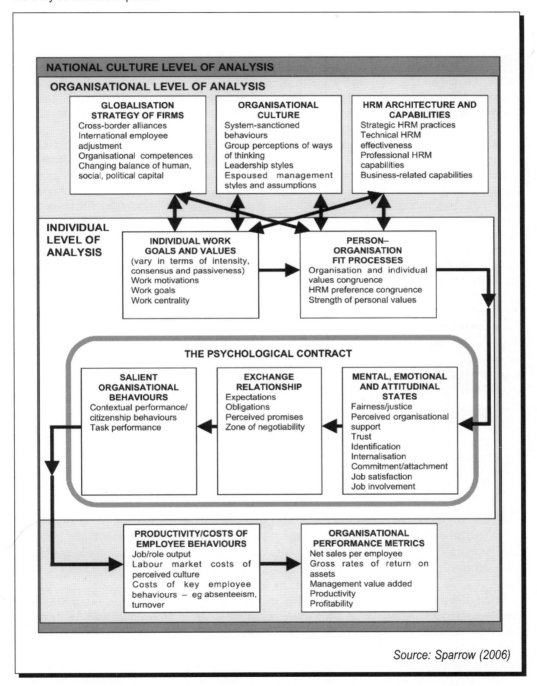

Source: Sparrow (2006)

Figure 14 *Organisational functioning model: cause-effect links within an embedded cultural context*

These organisation-level contexts and the individual work goals and values and consequent fit between the person and the organisation can influence each other either through top-down or bottom-up processes of change in the context of globalisation. In any one cultural context, organisational and individual effectiveness is dependent on there being a fit between the person and the organisation, often seen in terms of there being some congruence in terms of shared values and also shared preferences for the type of HRM. This climate or culture and the fit between the individual and organisation then influences a series of mental (cognitive) and emotional (affective) states, such as levels of trust, perceptions of fairness or organisational support, satisfaction, commitment, motivation and involvement or identification with the organisation.

The broad sequential order of these links, as reflected in the predominantly Western literature, is shown in Figure 14. Via the exchange relationship inherent in the psychological contract (which is culturally embedded and dependent upon the different zones of negotiability associated with different cultures) these states then create a series of employee behaviours that are salient to effectiveness, such as attachment and intention to remain with the organisation, and performance of the task and contextual performance (organisational citizenship behaviour). These behaviours in turn impact on productivity in a number of ways, both indirectly – through problems such as having to cope with the costs of employee disengagement (withdrawal behaviours) and perceived position in the labour market (for example, the employment brand), and directly – through task competence and role capability. These outcome behaviours in turn have a two-way impact, influencing organisational effectiveness but also acting upwards to influence the wider globalisation process via the organisational cultures that they create. With all these in place, organisational productivity can be improved – or, more to the point, any specific rewards practices may have their desired effect – and the employee outcomes that are created can then be directed towards broader aspects of organisational effectiveness.

Employee engagement across cultures

Most survey firms – such as Hay, Gallup and International Survey Research – offer international comparisons of employee engagement. For example, ISR tracked 40 of its global clients from 1999 to 2002, differentiating between three forms of engagement:

- *cognitive* (how employees think about their company) – Is there an intellectual fit between each employee and the organisation? Do employees believe in the organisation's goals and objectives? Do they intellectually support its values?

- *affective* (how employees feel about their company) – Is there an emotional bond between the employees and the organisation? Does this make them proud to be a part of the organisation? Would each employee recommend the organisation as an employer?

- *behavioural* (how employees behave in relation to their company) – This has two dimensions. First, do employees exert maximum effort at their work and do they go the extra mile for the organisation? Second, do they intend to stay with the organisation through its successes and setbacks?

ISR argue that all three elements have to be in place in order for an employee to be engaged. They surveyed 160,000 employees in hundreds of companies across 10 countries, analysing the relationship between growth in net income and employee engagement levels. Organisations with high levels of employee engagement outperformed the industry average over a 12-month period by 6%, whereas those with low levels under-performed by 9%. There were, however, large international differences: 75% of Brazilian and US employees are engaged, compared to 72% in the Netherlands, 70% in Australia and Canada, 67% in Germany, 66% in the UK and Singapore, 65% in Hong

Kong, but only 59% in France. They also found that different factors drove engagement in each of the ten countries surveyed. The type of engagement was also different across countries.

In terms of what people think about their company (cognitive engagement), US employees were most likely to believe in the goals of their company and accept the company's values; the lowest level of engagement was in France. In the UK engagement stems more from a cognitive (intellectual) engagement with the employing company rather than any sense of emotional attachment to its practices and purpose.

In terms of emotional attachment and feelings about the company, this was highest in Brazil but was lowest in Hong Kong.

In terms of how employees actually act (behavioural engagement), employees in France are least likely to put in extra discretionary effort or feel that their company inspires them to give them more, whereas US employees score highly on these questions. Employees in Brazil and the Netherlands are most likely to want to stay with their employer. Singapore, the UK, France and Australia are the countries where employees express the greatest desire to move on.

Source: www.isrsurveys.com

FACTORS THAT CREATE DISTINCTIVE NATIONAL REWARDS SYSTEMS

In sum, it is clear that our current evidence base represents only a limited test of the myriad potential cultural impacts of specific areas of HR practice, but as Figure 14 shows, within individuals there is a very complex set of links that exist between the way that they perceive a specific HR practice and the behaviours and organisational outcomes that might be expected. But how has this issue been thought about when it is applied specifically to rewards practices?

Unravelling the complex set of influences that culture can have on rewards behaviour has become a focus of recent research. Much of the literature on comparative and international HRM stresses the relevance of national cultures to reward, a lot of the discussion building on the work of Hofstede (1980). The suggestion is that typically, in national societies, individuals hold particular attitudes which differentiate them from other national societies. Individuals may not necessarily be conscious of their holding these attitudes and values – indeed, it may be very difficult for them to appreciate their specificity. Although the discussion often proceeds in terms of the attitudes of individuals, there is an implicit understanding in the literature that these attitudes and values are promoted and imbued socially. Bento and Ferreira (1992) distilled earlier work to offer a series of dualities in culture, together taken as a 'cultural lens' through which to view the underlying attitudes or assumptions of workforces regarding reward:

- equality – inequality
- certainty – uncertainty
- controllability – uncontrollability
- individualism – collectivism
- materialist foregrounding – personal foregrounding.

Socially healthy pay versus increasing pay differentials

Some recent discussion has centred on the concept of 'socially healthy pay'. Within societies there are boundaries placed around the range of pay differentials or multiples deemed to be legitimate.

These are generally measured by metrics such as the ratio between the highest- and average-, or the highest- and lowest-paid. In the USA high multiples are both legitimate and expected. In continental Europe much narrower multiples are felt to be appropriate. If differentials move beyond accepted limits, social reaction can be marked. Thus, the influential Swedish confederation of unions, LO, has expressed considerable unease about the recent increase in the gap between the remuneration of workers and that of the most senior managers in organisations, such executives in large private sector Swedish companies now often paid 40 to 50 times as much as front-line employees. Yet in the USA, the multiple is now 400 to 500 – ie the multiple itself is ten times larger, and yet there is little public comment.

The debt to Hofstede (1980) is considerable, although there are differences beyond the terminological. These dimensions and their supposed bearing on reward practices are now outlined in turn.

Equality – inequality

Relating to Hofstede's (1980) notion of power distance, this concerns the national acceptance or toleration of rigid hierarchies featuring levels across which status and reward differ markedly. In the sphere of reward, the key contrast is between a focus on the incentives offered by high pay differentials and a focus on the benefit of of low, 'socially healthy' differentials. It also involves elements of perceived fairness, or justice, within HRM systems.

Distributive justice – shifting perceptions

Studies of distributive justice concern themselves with the rules and standards by which decisions about the allocation of resources (financial or non-financial) are both made and perceived to be fair (Meindl, Cheng and Jun, 1990). Exploring the nature of these decisions and the motives that surround them is perceived as one way in which researchers can gain insight into the social systems that surround rewards behaviour. Allocation problems are resolved by resorting to a series of decision rules that determine the entitlement of recipients. In practice, these rules reflect the familiar, normative rules of a society that concern issues of social and industrial justice. They are also seen to embody decision logics and the value position of individuals and their motives. These logics and value positions are linked to national culture (Meindl, Cheng and Jun, 1990; p.224):

When there is a pot of 'reward' to be shared out, what is the fairest way to do it? Several rule sets have been identified. The two most potent rule sets distinguish between principles of meritocracy and egalitarianism. They are based on principles of:

- 'equity' – whereby entitlements are based on relative contributions, and differential reward is legitimate as long as it is based on an equitable way of differentiating performance. These are felt to be dominant in the USA and related national cultures, such as those of the UK, Australia, and Canada

- 'parity' or 'equality' – in which allocation solutions are insensitive to input differences and call for resources to be distributed equally to all regardless of relative productivity. These are felt to be applicable in collectivist cultures such as those of China and Japan. The decision rule is clearly bounded, in that collectivists make a clear distinction between in-group and out-group members and do not apply equality rules to out-group members. Where teams operate as in-groups, incentives and bonuses should only be given to the group, not to individuals.

There is evidence, however, especially in the special economic zones of China, that a radically altered institutional and social environment can change previously deep-seated psychological determinants of rewards behaviour, such as distributive justice. The 'new glorious rich' in China's free market challenge the underlying value of equality-based rather than equity-based justice.

Morris and Leung (2000) have provided a review of cross-cultural work on various forms of justice and concluded that different forms of justice – particularly, for example, assessments of distributive justice – can be linked to cultural factors, and a number of studies have examined the impact of distributive justice on important performance-related attitudes. Giacobbe-Miller, Miller, Zhang and Victorov (2003) have looked at the adaptation to foreign workplace ideologies of Chinese, Russian and US managers working in joint ventures, and Tata, Fu and Wu (2003) have looked at the link between perceptions of fairness and cultural values of US and Chinese service employees working in foreign-owned enterprises and state-owned enterprises. Murphy-Berman and Berman (2002) examined perceptions of distributive justice amongst managers in Hong Kong and Indonesia, presenting distributive justice dilemmas in the form of vignettes and then attributing justice scores to the actions taken by actors within these scenarios. Although both Indonesia and Hong Kong are collectivist cultures, the value scores differed significantly between the two. Differences in justice assessments were found, and it was argued that culture influenced not only the criteria used to evaluate what was fair but also the degree to which what was seen as fair was additionally judged as good or bad. Lam, Schaubroeck and Aryee (2002) examined the relationship between individual-level measures of individualism and power distance and perceived justice, job satisfaction, perceived competence and absenteeism amongst Hong Kong Chinese and US tellers in a bank. Justice perceptions were related to job satisfaction, performance and absenteeism in both cultures, and the effects were of a stronger magnitude among low power distance individuals. However, once cultural measures were applied at the individual level, country effects disappeared.

Certainty – uncertainty

Related to Hostede's (1980) uncertainty avoidance, this duality generally concerns attitudes to uncertainty or ambiguity in the context or environment of the employment relationship. Where certainty is valued, employees seek rules, standards and clear procedures, are uneasy about the returns from work being subject to risk, most especially where the basis of the variability of reward is not explicitly detailed. Conversely, where uncertainty is tolerated or, indeed, welcomed, employees do not expect that the employment relationship be so structured, and are more open to the possibility that work will deliver uncertain returns, even if the manner in which rewards will ultimately be determined is implicit and ambiguous.

Controllability – uncontrollability

This dimension, not present in Hofstede (1980), concerns the attribution of responsibility for the uncertainty faced by an employee. In high-controllability cultures, the organisation is perceived as having the potential to significantly shape or create the organisational context, and so is seen as largely responsible for the situation faced by employees. Where there is high uncontrollability, the organisational context is regarded as predominantly autonomous, beyond the control of actors at organisational level. In many respects, then, employees see the organisation as unavoidably transmitting unpredictability located beyond organisational borders. Where uncertainty is regarded with unease, high controllability implies that key organisational actors will be held responsible for an undesirable unpredictability of reward. Conversely, where uncertainty is tolerated or welcomed, low controllability may lead employees to assign the credit for a favoured variability in reward to the environment, not to their organisation.

Individualism – collectivism

This duality, present in Hofstede (1980), is of relevance to the motivation of employees, and to their assignment of responsibility for good or bad outcomes to an individual or to a larger grouping. Individualistic cultures favour individuals striking independent poses coming together in loose groupings. With individual approach and action critical, individualistic cultures hold that individuals should be rewarded for their contribution to the success of the wider organisation. Conversely, collectivist cultures favour tightly knit cohesive groups. Rewards are most appropriately shared within the group, and a failure to distribute rewards in this way is disorienting for all and isolating for those seen to be rewarded relatively poorly.

Materialist foregrounding – personal foregrounding

In many respects this facet of attitudes echoes Hofstede's (1980) distinction between masculine and feminine cultures, but with an updating of the terminology. It relates to the relative emphasis placed upon action and achievement as opposed to relationships and empathy. Where the culture is one of materialist foregrounding, symbols of action and success are important, whereas under personal foregrounding, engagement between individuals, nurturing and development are valued in their own right.

National culture and reward practice

Schuler and Rogovsky (1998) present an intriguing quantitative effort to systematically explore the link between national culture and indicators of national prevalence of pay systems across a dozen nations from across and even beyond the advanced industrialised world. They identified many relationships that can be made sense of through the use of the cultural lens.

They found that nations characterised by greater uncertainty avoidance, most commonly the Latin nations, tended to feature pay systems in which seniority and some notion of skill weighed heavily. These nations also featured less focus on individual performance-related pay (PRP). Conversely, nations with lower uncertainty avoidance – Protestant nations, but most of all, Anglo-Saxon nations – tended to feature less focus on seniority or skill, and more on specifically individual PRP.

They also found that nations characterised by greater individualism, most strikingly the Anglo-Saxon nations, tended to feature a greater focus on pay for performance generally, and still more strongly a focus on individual pay for performance. In contrast, nations with less individualism, most prominently Spanish- or Portugese-speaking countries, tended to feature less of such a focus, generally lying at the opposite end of the spectrum. The findings for the focus on share ownership or options are similar.

Nations which rely on a more materialist foregrounding, or greater 'masculinity' in Hofstede's terms, tended to feature more of a focus on individual bonuses. Thus, the Anglo-Saxon area but also Germany and to a remarkable extent Japan generally tended to feature more individual PRP amongst professional and technical staff, amongst clerical staff and amongst manual employees. The contrast here is with the general situation in nations that rely more on personal foregrounding, such as the Scandinavian nations, and indeed the Netherlands, which tended to feature a lesser focus on such payments for these non-managerial employees. Interestingly, there was no significant difference in the focus on individual bonuses for managers specifically between these groups of nations.

There are substantial indications of the usefulness of a consideration of national culture to an understanding of differences in pay practice, but although it has real attractions, and makes good sense intuitively, a focus in discussions of reward on such dimensions of national context also has its disadvantages (Vernon, 2005). Firstly, the evidence that these dimensions are enlightening in capturing and explaining either the basis for the incidence of different approaches to reward in different countries, or the typical reactions of a nation's employees to attempts to apply a single system universally, is still a little patchy. Moreover, in practice, nations display certain tendencies in these respects, but also display a great deal of individual difference in attitudes around the typical. More than this, individuals may display multiple or contradictory identities in these cultural respects, making such dimensions a shaky foundation for thinking about appropriate reward, or even for understanding the current basis of cross-national variability.

A related problem of a focus on national culture in thinking about comparative reward is that it disregards the autonomous influence of social actors and of institutions on pay structures and practices. These may act to shape cultures, cut across a dominant culture, or – perhaps most likely – channel cultural influences in a particular way. An alternative strand of research examines the role of social institutions on pay practices, with particular reference to the role of collective bargaining.

QUESTION

Your organisation has been pursuing a competency-based HR strategy in its UK headquarters and UK operations. It has decided to roll out a competency-based pay approach across its European operations in France, Germany, Sweden and Spain for the top 400 managers. What level of acceptance would you expect for the strategy, and what factors in each country might have to be understood and tackled?

THE ROLE OF UNIONS, EMPLOYERS' ASSOCIATIONS AND COLLECTIVE BARGAINING

Statutory pay minimums have been established in some central and eastern European nations, and are now a common feature of Anglo-Saxon nations, in force in the USA, Canada, New Zealand, and the UK. However, it is in those few nations of continental western Europe featuring such statutory pay minimums that they are set at the highest levels – the minimums in the Netherlands and France the very highest by any criterion (OECD, 1998). Yet even these French and Dutch statutory minimums are set at levels too low to be of direct significance to the pay arrangements of most larger, or multinational, employers (Vernon, 2005). That is to say, the statutory regulation of the level of pay is generally of very limited significance for large companies. Indeed, although there are particular exceptions, the same may be said for other forms of statutory regulation of pay arrangements. Meanwhile, in the sphere of collective bargaining and joint regulation, employers' associations now quite generally favour a derogation of detailed pay arrangements to individual companies (Vernon et al, 2006). It is unions and works councillors who, through collective bargaining and joint regulation, are the crucial social actors in shaping pay arrangements (Vernon et al, 2006).

In a sense, unions simply want pay to be higher. However, although pay is a central area of union consideration, pay is not unions' only priority. Unions do not pursue higher pay blindly. They have typically, to at least some extent, internalised the trade-offs that they face in the conduct of negotiations so that there is widespread acceptance in union circles that pay should not be pursued without regard to the consequences for employment (eg Swenson, 1989). Given a general acknowledgement in union circles of the inadequacy of a crude posturing for more, discussions centre on matters of pay structure and systems. Unions have traditionally tended to favour pay structures in which pay depends predominantly on the job role, qualifications, certificated competences, seniority/age or documented experience. Moreover, they have generally sought to contain pay differentials within their bargaining arena. This still tends to be the case, although unions have not generally buried their heads in the sand in reaction to discussion around PfP.

Instinctively, unions have generally regarded PfP with some suspicion. The concept is quite at odds with the emphasis of unionism on solidarity, and also in tension with the idea that it should be employers that bear risk. Moreover, PfP can seem to threaten the very institutionalisation of the employment relationship. Nonetheless, pressed by employers and indeed by employees, unions which sense some opportunity to shape developments now generally accept the principle of PfP, regarding the devil as in the detail (Vernon *et al*, 2006). Unions are often keen that no groups should be excluded from PfP where it is introduced for some, but simultaneously pursue the containment of any performance-related element of the overall pay package. Typically, unions regard PfP formally comprising 10% of total remuneration as going quite far enough. They are often keen also to compress the variation of such payments in practice, such that the actual spread in the performance-related sums paid out is much more limited. In these respects union concerns with solidarity and the exposure of employees to risk survive.

What, then, of the relationship between collective bargaining and pay arrangements on the ground? The effects of collective bargaining on the pay structure are certainly profound. There is a very strong cross-national and, indeed, historical relationship between union density and the compression of pay differentials of all sorts (Vernon, 2005; Rueda and Pontusson, 2000). Given the status of density as a gauge of the cross-national comparative weight of collective bargaining (Vernon, 2006), the significance of collective bargaining for the pay distribution is clear: more exacting frameworks of collective bargaining compress the pay structure. Thus, for example, the pay distribution in Sweden, with its very significant machinery of joint regulation, is very much more equal than that in the UK or indeed France, which displays high coverage of agreements of very little purchase (Vernon, 2006).

With regard to pay systems, multi-employer agreements at the level of industries, for example, tend not to be directly restrictive of PfP (Vernon *et al*, 2006). Yet their specification of minimum pay rates or increases implies that payment for performance must be made on top of such agreed pay. By implication this allows more room for manoeuvre to larger and more successful companies capable of affording larger pay bills per employee. Beyond the terms of multi-employer agreements, the limited evidence available suggest that local employee representatives rarely refuse it in principle (Vernon *et al*, 2006). However, where there is established local union representation and/or a works council with statutory rights to negotiation or, indeed, co-determination over pay systems, such local employee representatives negotiate over the design and operation of all forms of reward, including PfP. This has no necessary implications for the incidence of PfP, though. To what extent does the comparative pattern of incidence of PfP correspond with what we might expect?

THE INCIDENCE OF PAY FOR PERFORMANCE

As we have seen, organisations may seek to reward performance on a number of bases. Payment may be made on the basis of some assessment of individual performance, of team or group performance, of departmental performance, of the performance of a subsidiary or group. The targets or criteria for reward may take an almost unlimited variety of forms. Sometimes some or all of these bases are used together to create a multifaceted or multi-layered bonus.

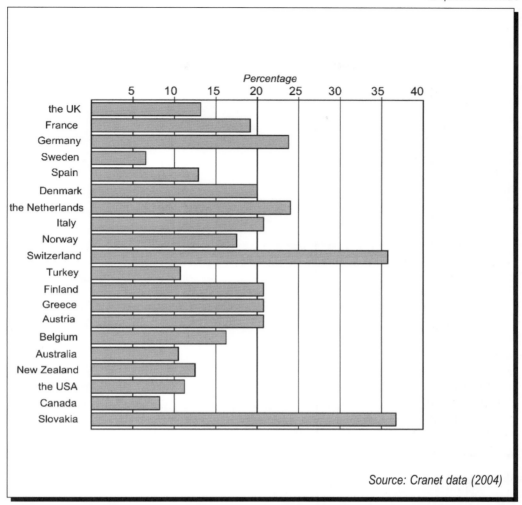

Figure 15 *Use of individualised PfP for manual employees across (selected) countries*

Good comparative data on the usage of different forms of pay for performance is limited, but the large-scale Cranet survey of 2004 afforded particular attention to this form of pay system. Cranet demonstrates the variation in the proportion of organisations in a variety of countries that make use of different forms of PfP for different groups of employees. Cranet provides the best available indication of the extent of organisations' usage of different forms of pay for performance across different groups of the workforce. There are dramatic cross-national comparative differences in the use of PfP.

The situation with regard to organisations' usage of individualised PfP – sometimes termed performance-related pay (PRP) – in the packages of manual employees provides an interesting starting point (see Figure 15). The variation in the use of individualised PfP is intriguing and in many ways surprising. The use of such PRP is much less extensive than might be expected in the USA, often taken to be the leader in such practice. It is continental Europe where organisations make most extensive use of such individualised performance-related pay. The findings for central Europe, represented here by Slovakia, and perhaps even more surprisingly for Switzerland, are notable.

The data for clerical employees (Figure 16) show a similar pattern, although the incidence of PRP varies rather less between the nations for this group. Here it is the Mediterranean nations of Italy and Greece which feature the greatest incidence of individualised PRP.

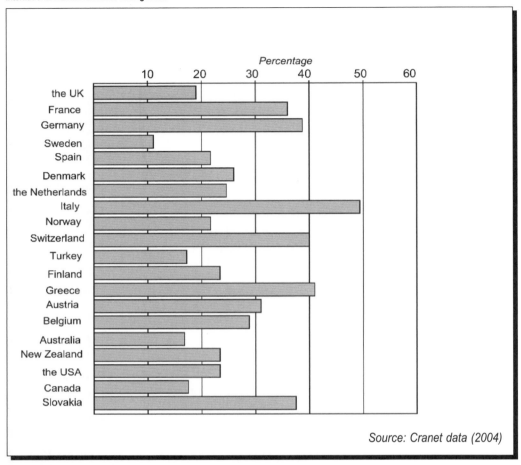

Figure 16 *Use of individualised PfP for clerical employees across (selected) countries*

What, though, of other forms of pay for performance which reward according to the performance not of the individual but of the wider group in which they work? Figure 17 below shows the incidence amongst organisations of the use of team- or department-based pay for manual employees. Italy's position is striking, and is perhaps at least in part influenced by the recent restructuring of collective bargaining, which has encouraged multiple-level bargaining activity, with local bargaining focused on performance-related payments at workgroup or oganisation level. Finland's position shows that powerful unions and significant collective bargaining can co-exist with an extensive use of team- or department-based PfP, even for manual employees. The Slovakian case demonstrates that in central Europe the particularly extensive use of individual PRP can co-exist with an equally extensive use of PfP based on team or department performance.

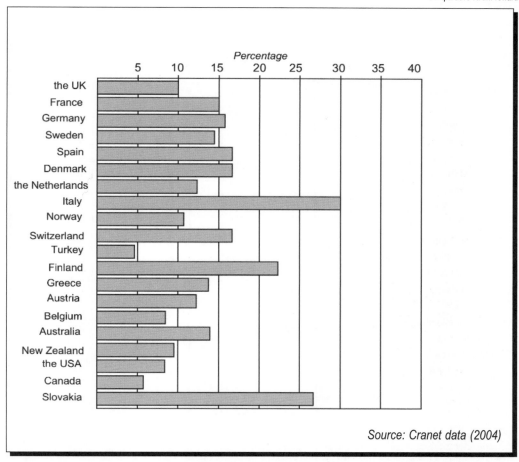

Figure 17 *Use of team- or department-based pay for manual employees across (selected) countries*

The pattern for such payment based on the performance of groups is similar amongst clerical employees, although the much greater use of team- or department-related pay amongst clerical than amongst manual employees in France and in Greece is notable.

Of course, the unit at which performance is assessed may range more broadly, to encompass the organisation as a whole. Employees may be rewarded on the basis of the performance of the entire organisation of which they are a part via share ownership, stock options or profit sharing. Employee share ownership schemes (ESOPs), in particular, were the subject of intense discussion in the UK of the 1980s. Figure 18 below shows the dramatic comparative variation in the extent of the use of such schemes for manual employees. We would expect share schemes to be more widely used in those countries with well-developed stock markets like the USA, the UK, France and the Netherlands. The comparatively high incidence of such schemes in the UK is unsurprising. What might be more surprising is that this level of UK incidence is surpassed in France and Denmark, but surpasses that in the USA by an enormous margin. Clearly, ESOPs should not be seen as a US practice transmitted to Europe via the UK. The pattern of incidence for clerical employees (not shown here) is generally similar, although Norway and Denmark feature much less prominently.

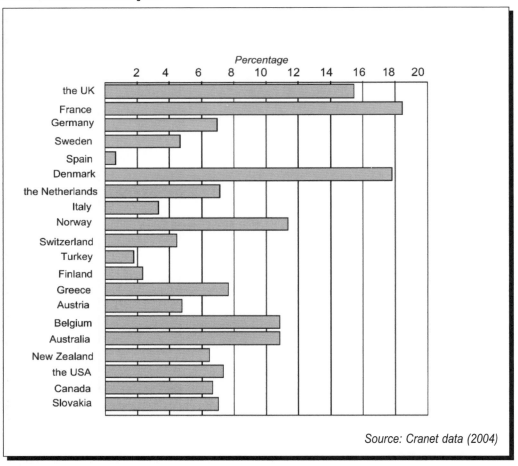

Figure 18 *Use of employee share ownership schemes (ESOPs) for manual employees across (selected) countries*

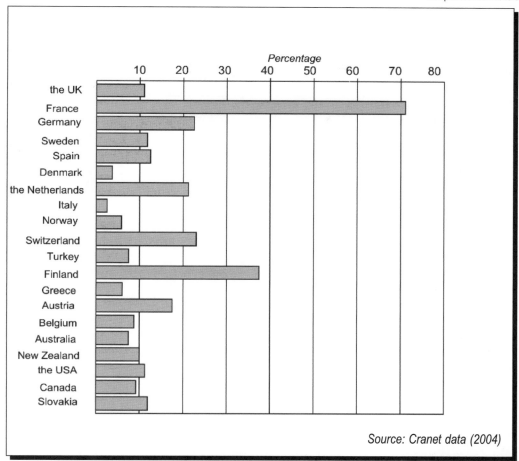

Source: Cranet data (2004)

Figure 19 *Use of profit sharing for manual employees across (selected) countries*

Generally, the extent of the use of profit sharing is quite low. In relation to the situation for manual employees, two exceptions to the general rule are striking (see Figure 19). The situation in France demonstrates the role which law can play in driving a wedge in practice between different nations, even in spheres such as this where there is a cross-border management sympathy towards the broad desirability of a practice. In France profit sharing is now mandatory in private sector organisations with a workforce of over 50 (van het Kaar and Grunell, 2001). The case of Finland shows something quite different – that profit sharing can be quite consistent with powerful unions and significant collective bargaining. The comparative pattern for clerical employees (not shown here) is very similar, although quite generally the use of profit sharing tends to be a little more extensive amongst this group than amongst manual employees.

Surely though there must be some aspect of incentivising reward in which the USA leads the world by incidence across organisations? Cranet suggests that there is – in stock options, at least with regard to the management group (see Figure 20). The use of stock options for management is more extensive in the USA than in any other nation. However, several European nations feature almost as extensive a use, Greece, France and Italy only marginally behind.

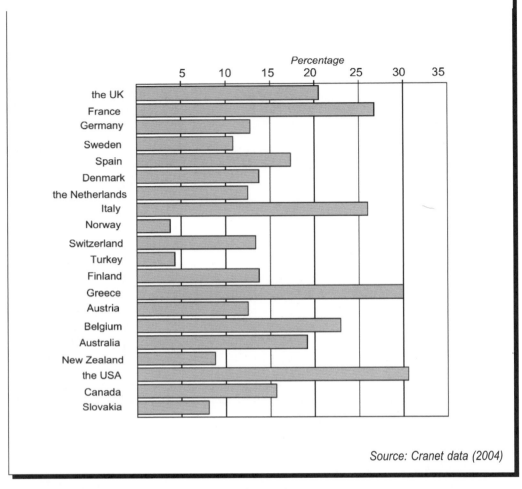

Figure 20 *Use of stock options across (selected) countries*

QUESTIONS

■ What HR rewards practices are indicative of the different pay for performance contexts in the USA, Germany, the Netherlands and Australia?

■ Which PfP practices do you think would be the easiest to converge?

Seductive stock options

Taking lessons from the high-technology start-ups of the US West Coast, larger US corporations began making extensive use of stock options in the 1990s. Stock options afforded those they were offered to the right to buy stock at below-market prices. Stock options were seen as a solution to the principal agent problem introduced by the separation of ownership and control – they could align the interests of managers and shareholders. Moreover, the expense of stock options did not have to be acknowledged until they were exercised. This had huge implications for balance sheets. Perhaps the most striking is the case of Microsoft, at which the cash realisation of stock options would have reduced 2001 profits of $7.3 billion by a third. When they were finally exercised, the extent of the implications for the surplus remaining for shareholders and re-investment was often unclear, particularly in the context of an enduring stock market boom (Stiglitz, 2003).

Very clearly, the incidence of PfP is far from always being what we would expect on the basis of simple cultural characterisations of societies. To the extent that such approaches gave purchase on patterns of organisations' usage of PfP, the relationships appeared by 2004 to be breaking down. Moreover, the findings belie ordinary presumptions about the implications of collective bargaining or joint regulation for pay systems. Whereas it is absolutely clear that more significant collective bargaining compresses overall pay inequality, it has no such clearly demonstrable effect on the intricacies of the pay systems which ultimately deliver this distribution. As the survey findings for Sweden, Finland, Norway and Denmark in particular show, significant collective bargaining is quite compatible with the extensive use of a variety of forms of pay for performance.

Variable pay in German MNCs

Kurdelbusch (2002) explored the emergence of modern forms of variable pay, beyond piecework, in Germany in the 1990s, affording particular attention to the non-managerial employees of large and multinational corporations. There is a very powerful relationship between the extent of internation-alisation of German MNCs, measured by the share of employees employed abroad and in particular by the share of foreign sales in total sales, and the use of incentive-based payment. Interestingly, though, German MNCs did not seem to be adopting practices in their foreign subsidiaries via a process of reverse diffusion. Sheer exposure to an international market appears to encourage the use of variable pay, although it remains unclear whether this is a rational response to a differing competitive context. Independently of the extent of this engagement in international markets, a shareholder value-orientation expressed in the remuneration of top executives, the existence of targets for annual rates of return and the quality of investor relations, also tended to promote variable pay for non-managerial employees.

Performance-related pay in the UK and Finland

Large-scale national surveys of employees in the UK and Finland offer provocative findings (Vernon, 2005). Surveys of the UK show that across the economy as a whole, including the public sector, 25% of employees are subject to individual PRP of one sort or another. In Finland, across the economy as a whole, 23% of manual employees are subject to merit pay specifically. Among lower-level clerical employees the proportion is 40%, and it is still higher among upper clerical employees and managers. Merit pay is the predominant form of individual PRP in Finland, but other forms are present. Conservatively, then, at least a third of Finnish employees are subject to some form of individualised PRP. Clearly, PRP is more common in Finland than in the UK. This strikingly contradicts any notion that individualised PfP occurs where unions and collective bargaining are weaker.

QUESTIONS

- There are extensive discussions in the literature about the influence of national institutions, laws and culture on HRM issues such as rewarding staff. Obviously, there are a range of different practices even within the various national boundaries. Are these boundaries the best level of analysis?

> ■ It has been argued that 'national ... may not be the correct level of analysis' (Bloom and Milkovich, 1999; p.291). What are your views?

THE SIGNIFICANCE TO EMPLOYEES OF PAY FOR PERFORMANCE

As Armstrong (2006; p.35) notes, even when the focus is on the UK, where a great deal of information and data on PfP is available, there is a danger that consideration of it rather neglects the position and views of employees. Information on cross-national comparative variation in reward practice is far from complete, and employees' views of systems particularly lacking. For a few nations, comparative data on pay systems is available from representative surveys of employees, affording an idea of employees' perceptions of the extent to which they are touched by PfP, rather than of managers' views of the usage of PfP in their organisations as does Cranet. This employee-centred data is of particular value because, presumably, employees must be aware of the presence of PfP as a component of their pay package in order for their behaviour to be influenced by it. In a very real sense, it is not managers' views of the usage of PfP but employees' views which are most critical in gauging its meaningful extent.

Antoni et al (2005) summarise data available from the European Survey of Working Conditions of 2000, showing employees' perceptions of the incidence of all forms of PfP. In the UK, 11% of employees reported that they are subject to PfP. This is above the proportion in Belgium, at 9%, but below that in most European nations. The proportion of employees in the Netherlands reporting their exposure to some form of PfP is the same as that in the UK, and short of the proportions of employees in Germany (12%) and Sweden (14%). According to employees, though, the incidence of PfP is by far the greatest in Finland, where 23% are subject to some form. The survey thus confirms the inadequacy of the notion that weightier collective bargaining implies a lower incidence of PfP. Moreover, the proportions are generally rather lower than we would expect given the Cranet results on the use of PfP by organisations, particularly in that Cranet targets larger organisations. To an extent it seems that managers and employees take different views as to whether PfP is in place or not.

There is little data on the proportion of pay packages constituted by PfP, but some data is available for some nations, which is at least indicative. Even in the private sector, despite fairly extensive coverage, PfP of all types accounted for less than 10% of the base pay of Italian employees in 2001. It seems that in Belgium it is of still less importance in terms of the financial reward package as a whole. Perhaps more significantly, evidence from case studies (see Vernon et al, 2006) suggests that in practice there is an extremely tight bunching of the actual payouts from pay for performance. The payouts to individuals from PRP tend to vary little in practice, whereas payouts to teams or departments vary little within a single organisation. In sum, the proportion of income which an employee experiences as at risk under PfP typically tends to be low in principle, and still lower in practice. This may of course mean that some employees formally subject to PfP are not even aware of this component of their pay package.

MANAGING PAY: PROCEDURAL ISSUES

Experience within the UK demonstrates the complexity of the management of PfP in practice. With regard to PRP – an attractive form of PfP to UK managers because it not only signals management's interest in performance (Kessler, 1993) but emphasises the role of the individual and also in principle meets the 'line of sight' criterion – the demands are manifold. Communicating the nature and purpose of initiatives, achieving meaningful objective-setting, eliciting employee acceptance of the legitimacy of the criteria and of the eventual distribution of reward, and avoiding the obscuring of developmental facets of performance management in review meetings have all proved particularly difficult for UK managers (Armstrong, 2006;

pp.276–7). More generally, in organisations that have tried it there is often a view that the proper management of pay for performance is tremendously costly in terms of management training and time (see eg Armstrong, 2006). The limitations of attempts at evaluating PfP schemes also often leave those more intimately involved in managing them unconvinced of their benefits.

As we have already seen, unions across the advanced industrialised world have rather common concerns about PfP. Beyond the containment of the practical effect of PfP on employees' take-home pay already discussed, unions are typically concerned to pursue procedural issues (Vernon *et al*, 2006). They generally regard it as vital that PfP is subject to collective bargaining or joint regulation, usually at multiple bargaining levels, as with other elements of pay. Moreover, they stress transparency in PfP arrangements, pursuing a clear *ex ante* specification of objective criteria for the achievement of specifically identified bonuses. Unions are uneasy not only that a vague promise may not be fulfilled but that there may be victimisation or favouritism by line managers. The rather weaker tendency for unions to favour PfP which is not significantly based on assessments of individual performance but on that of a group, department or firm is a reflection of such fears around individual victimisation, but also expressive of unions' typical belief that individual PRP can be demotivating and undermine crucial team and group co-operation and commitment. The case evidence available suggests that it is in the detailed operation of PfP arrangements, rather than the incidence of the various forms of PfP, that joint regulation has its main effect (Vernon *et al*, 2006). This is of course consistent with the powerful and well-established comparative association between the significance of collective bargaining and the overall pattern of pay inequality which emerges as the implications of pay systems *in toto* are played out.

In many respects, intriguingly, unions' and works councillors' concerns tend to reflect those of employees who have been subject to the reality of PfP. The process of joint regulation in the development and application of PfP may well complicate the enactment of management initiatives in the arena of pay, but may well also contribute to the effective functioning of PfP as it unfolds. Marsden (2004), following his study of performance pay for teachers in the UK, suggests that unions can have just this role.

Competence ladders

An argument that is getting increasingly heard is that what organisations in the modern world need is capability, the resultant flexibility to respond to changing environments, and sufficiently good managements to take advantage of these factors. Hence there has been a growth in the concept of competence-related pay – people are paid for the skills they acquire and what they can do. The organisation then relies on the competence of its managers to ensure that those skills are used in the most effective way. This system aims to reward employees for developing their abilities, not for their current activities.

COMPARATIVE EVIDENCE ON BEST PRACTICE IN REWARD

What of the evidence on the relationship between pay systems and performance? Can we arrive at an evidence-based notion of best practice in the field of PfP?

Systematic examinations of the relationship between pay practices and performance are thin on the ground. This is all the more true in terms of analyses of international coverage. Antoni *et al* (2005) provide a notable exception, with a 10-nation study of the influence of pay systems on the business performance improvements resulting from delegation of tasks to groups of non-managerial employees. The authors focus on what they term 'modern forms of variable pay', comprising reward based on team or department performance, profit sharing schemes and ESOPs (thus excluding not only traditional piece pay but also individual merit pay or performance-related pay). Companies with such modern forms of variable pay report significantly better outcomes from group delegation initiatives in two respects – with regard to reductions in the numbers of managers and increases in output.

The study also explores the moderation of the effect of such modern forms of variable pay – the contingency of their effect – according to its alignment with work organisation. Where intense delegation is combined with modern forms of variable pay there are statistically significant relationships to reductions in management, in costs, and in throughput times. This is not so where there has been relatively little delegation to groups – indeed, there are signs that in such circumstances modern forms of variable pay inhibit performance outcomes to some extent. The alignment of pay systems with the nature of work organisation to give consistent signals to employees emerges clearly as a central issue in the development of pay systems.

Antoni et al's (2005) results suggest a further nuance. Strikingly, although Sweden features by far the most instances of more intense group delegation, national results give no suggestion of a positive impact of modern forms of variable pay on business performance. Indeed, the results for Sweden feature significant indications of a *negative* relationship between modern forms of variable pay and the impact on business performance of direct participation initiatives. Where more intense delegation to groups was combined with modern forms of variable pay in Sweden, companies reported that the delegation initiatives resulted in a *poorer* performance in terms of quality improvement and in terms of the containment of sickness absence. This constitutes suggestive evidence of the contingency of the effects of pay-for-performance on the larger employment relations, and industrial relations, context.

Looking back towards the big picture beyond particular national contexts, what of the matter of the alignment of organisational strategy with the approach to work organisation and to pay? Antoni et al's (2005) findings suggest that the performance-promoting effects of variable pay and of delegation to groups emerge from organisations which do not have a deliberate and systematic product innovation strategy. Where such a product innovation strategy does exist, variable pay and more intense group delegation are not associated with better performance implications of direct participation initiatives in any dimension, alone or in combination. Modern forms of variable pay, in conjunction with intensive delegation to groups, appear a substitute for such a product innovation strategy. This suggests that reward practice may correct for shortcomings in the larger organisational strategy – an intriguing possibility.

SPACE FOR STRATEGY

Although the implications of national culture and systems of joint regulation are not always what we might imagine, it is clear that they have an important effect on pay arrangements.

Case study

Compensation practice in McDonald's across Europe

Perhaps unsurprisingly, McDonald's has sought to export an approach to compensation from their domestic operations across their outlets, regardless of national location. This involves avoidance of and resistance to meaningful collective bargaining over pay, and a focus on containing wage costs. With regard to German operations it is also a matter of an ongoing struggle to prevent the formation at its restaurants of works councils which would have the right to co-determine pay systems (Royle, 2000; 2004). Nonetheless, the real pay levels of McDonald's counter-staff, adjusted for the purchasing power of currencies, shows marked variation within Europe. For example, real pay is typically more than 50% greater in the Nordic countries than in the UK (Royle, 2000). Whatever its corporate stance, McDonald's must both attract staff and offer them a reward package that they consider legitimate, necessitating adjustment not only to legal regulation but to the societal norms and generally prevailing pay practices which legal and bargaining institutions have served to shape.

This is not to say that organisations must simply take up what is existing typical practice with regard to reward. There is variability within nations in the cultures and expectations of employees, as well as in the bargaining institutions with which employers engage. Bloom *et al* (2003) stress the variability *within* nations in the pay practices to which employees are used, a variability present too within particular industries and occupational groups. Managers must of course reflect carefully before positioning their pay practice at the extreme of any existing range of practices, and even greater care is required if this positioning is to be beyond the range of the normal.

However, a recent study (Lowe *et al*, 2002) indicates that the prevalence of a system is no necessary guide to its cultural fit. Examining the attitudes of managers and engineers to pay systems, the research finds that PfP at this level is quite evenly spread across the 10 nations spanned by the study, even across the divide between the established advanced industrialised nations and the newly industrialised countries. Yet employees on the North American continent particularly would like to see more. Moreover, although variable pay tends to be contingent on group performance rather more in Asian nations than in North America, employees across the world are equally keen on such a basis. Perhaps most interestingly, whereas Anglo-Saxon nations displayed less emphasis on long-term performance in their pay systems, employees across the world valued such a long-term emphasis similarly. Clearly, there are culturally permitted alternatives which, for some reason, are not reflected in pay practice.

SUMMARY

Organisations employ people within particular cultures and under particular laws and institutional arrangements. This means that organisations have to remain aware of these differences when they determine their HR policies and practices in reward as in other areas. And it means that notions of good practice in reward still differ from country to country, despite increasing commonalities in the language with which debates are conducted. Importantly, as far as rewards practitioners are concerned, different logics in different nations mean that the 'political' messages that must be communicated in order to 'sell' the convergent policy objective soon become immersed in national culture. A good deal of 'spin-doctoring' becomes necessary in the 'selling strategies' adopted by international HR managers. They have to find 'engagement points' with the national culture on which they can play to make the audience more receptive to the policy objective.

LEARNING QUESTIONS

- What are the main cross-national differences in the nature of pay systems and practices?

- How would you characterise the underlying philosophy that British HR professionals have towards reward, compared with French HR professionals?

- What are the main technical challenges faced by firms that wish to internationalise their reward approaches?

- What are the main ways in which national culture influences rewards behaviour?

REFERENCES

Antoni, C. *et al.* (2005) *Wage and Working Conditions in the European Union – Project No. 0261 Final Report.* European Foundation for the Improvement of Living and Working Conditions

Armstrong, M. (2006). *Employee Reward*, 3rd Edition. London, CIPD

Arrowsmith, J., Marginson, P. and Sisson, K. (2003) 'Externalisation and internalisation in Europe: variation in the role of large companies', *Industrielle Beziehungen*, 10, 3: 363–92

Bandura, A. (2002) 'Social cognitive theory in cultural context', *Applied Psychology: An International Review*, 51 (2): 269–90

Barber, A. E. (1998) *Recruiting Employees*. London, Sage

Bender, K. A. and Elliott, R. F. (2003) *Decentralised Pay Setting. A study of the outcomes of collective bargaining reform in the civil service in Australia, Sweden and the UK*. Aldershot, Ashgate Publishing

Bento, R. and Ferreira, L. (1992) 'Incentive pay and organisational culture', in W. Bruns (ed.) *Performance Measurement, Evaluation, and Incentives*. Boston, MA, Harvard Business School Press

Björkman, I. and Furu, P. (2000) 'Determinants of variable pay for top managers of foreign subsidiaries in Finland'. *International Journal of Human Resource Management*, 11 (4): 698-713

Bloom, M. and Milkovich, G. T. (1999) 'A SHRM perspective on international compensation', in P. M. Wright, L. D. Dyer, J. W. Boudreau and G. T. Milkovich (eds) *Strategic Human Resources Management in the Twenty-First Century*. Stamford, CT, JAI Press

Brown, D. (1999) 'States of pay', *People Management*, 5 (23): 52–5

Cannell, M. and Wood, S. (1992) *Incentive Pay: Impact and evolution*. London, IPM/NEDO

Cook, M. (1999) *Personnel Selection: Adding value through people*. Chichester, John Wiley

Erez, M. and Gati, E. (2004) 'A dynamic, multi-level model of culture: from the micro level of the individual to the macro level of a global culture', *Applied Psychology: An International Review*, 53 (4): 583–98

European Industrial Relations Dictionary. www.eurofound.eu.int/areas/industrialrelations/dictionary/index.htm

Ferner, A. and Varul, M. Z. (2000) 'Internationalisation and the personnel function in German multi-nationals'. *Human Resource Management Journal*, 10 (3): 79–96

Filella, J. and Hegewisch, A. (1994) 'European experiments with pay and benefits policies', in C. Brewster and A. Hegewisch (eds) *Policy and Practice in European Human Resource Management*. London, Routledge

Fischer, R., Ferreira, M. C., Assmar, M. L., Redford, P. and Harb, C. (2005) 'Organisational behaviour across cultures: theoretical and methodological issues for developing multi-level frameworks involving culture', *International Journal of Cross-Cultural Management*, 5 (1): 27–48

Garrison-Jenn, N. (1998) *The Global 200 Executive Recruiters*. San Francisco, Jossey-Bass

Gelade, G. A. and Young, S. (2005) 'Test of a service profit chain model in the retail banking sector', *Journal of Occupational and Organizational Psychology*, 78 (1): 1–22

Giacobbe-Miller, J. K., Miller, D. J., Zhang, W. and Victorov, V. I. (2003) 'Country and organisational-level adaptation to foreign workplace ideologies: a comparative study of distributive justice values in China, Russia and the United States', *Journal of International Business Studies*, 34: 389–406

Goetschy, J. (1998) 'France: the limits of reform', in A. Ferner and R. Hyman (eds) *Changing Industrial Relations in Europe*. Oxford, Basil Blackwell

Gomez-Mejia, I. and Welbourne, T. (1991) 'Compensation strategies in a global context', *Human Resource Planning*, 14 (1): 29–42

Hayden, A. and Edwards, T. (2001) 'The erosion of the country of origin effect: a case study of a Swedish multinational company', *Relations Industrielles*, 56, 1: 116–40

Heery, E. (2000) 'Trade unions and the management of reward', in G. White and J. Druker (eds) *Reward Management. A critical text*. London, Routledge

Hofstede, G. (1980) *Culture's Consequences*. Beverly Hills, CA, Sage

Kohn, A. (1998) 'Challenging behaviourist dogma: myths about money and motivation', *Compensation and Benefits Review*, March-April: 27–33

Kurdelbusch, A. (2002) 'Variable pay in Germany', *European Journal of Industrial Relations*, 8, 3: 325

Lam, S. S. K., Schaubroeck, J. and Aryee, S. (2002) 'Relationship between organisational justice and employee work outcomes: a cross-national study', *Journal of Organizational Behavior*, 23 (1): 1–12

Lawler, E. E. (1990) *Strategic Pay*. San Francisco, Jossey-Bass

Lawrence, P. and Edwards, V. (2000) *Management in Western Europe*. London, Macmillan

Lilja, K. (1998) 'Finland: continuity and modest moves towards company-level corporatism', in A. Ferner and R. Hyman (eds) *Changing Industrial Relations in Europe*. Oxford, Basil Blackwell

Lowe, K., Milliman, J., De Cieri, H. and Dowling, P. (2002) 'International compensation practices: a ten country comparative analysis', *Human Resource Management*, 41: 45–66

Marginson, P., Sisson, K. and Arrowsmith, J. (2003) 'Between decentralisation and Europeanisation: sectoral bargaining in four countries and two sectors', *European Journal of Industrial Relations*, 9 (2): 163–87

Meindl, J. R., Cheng, Y. K. and Jun, L. (1990) 'Distributive justice in the workplace: preliminary data on managerial preferences in the PRC', in *Research in Personnel and Human Resource Management*, Supplement 2. New York, JAI Press

Morishima, M. (1995) 'Strategic diversification of HRM in Japan', in P. M. Wright, L. D. Dyer, J. W. Boudreau and G. T. Milkovich (eds) *Strategic Human Resources Management in the Twenty-First Century*. Stamford, CT, JAI Press

Morris, M. W. and Leung, K. (2000) 'Justice for all? Progress in research on cultural variation in the psychology of distributive and procedural justice', *Applied Psychology: An International Review*, 49 (1): 100–32

Murphy-Berman, V. and Berman, J. J. (2002) 'Cross-cultural differences in perceptions of distributive justice: a comparison of Hong Kong and Indonesia', *Journal of Cross-Cultural Psychology*, 33 (2): 157–70

OECD (1998) 'Making the most of the minimum: statutory minimum wages, employment and poverty', *Employment Outlook*, Paris, OECD

Ostroff, C. and Bowen, D. E. (2000) 'Moving HR to a higher level: HR practices and organisational effectiveness', in J. K. Klein and S. W. J. Kozlowski (eds) *Multilevel Theory, Research and Methods in Organizations: Foundations, extensions and new directions*. San Francisco, Jossey-Bass

Pendleton, A., Poutsma, E., van Ommeren, J. and Brewster, C. (2000) *Financial Participation in Europe: An investigation of profit sharing and employee share ownership*. Report for the European Foundation for the Improvement of Living and Working Conditions, Dublin

Pfeffer, J. (1998) 'Six dangerous myths about pay', *Harvard Business Review*, May-June

Regalia, I. and Regini, M. (1998) 'Italy: the dual character of industrial relations', in A. Ferner and R. Hyman (eds) *Changing Industrial Relations in Europe*. Oxford, Basil Blackwell

Royle, T. (2000). *Working for MacDonalds in Europe. The Unequal Struggle?* London, Routledge

Rueda, D. and Pontusson, J. (2000) 'Wage inequality and varieties of capitalism', *World Politics*, 52, April: 350–83

Schmidt, F. L and Hunter J. E. (1998) 'The validity and utility of selection methods in personnel psychology: practical and theoretical implications of 85 years of research findings', *Psychological Bulletin*, 124 (2): 262–74

Schuler, R. and Rogovsky, N. (1998) 'Understanding compensation practice variations across firms: the impact of national culture', *Journal of International Business Studies*, 29 (1): 159–77

Sparrow, P. R. (1999) 'International recruitment, selection and assessment: whose route map will you follow?', in P. Joynt and B. Morton (eds) *The Global HR Manager: Creating the seamless organisation*. London, CIPD

Sparrow, P. R. (2000) 'International reward management', in G. White and J. Druker (eds) *Reward Management: A critical text*. London, Routledge

Sparrow, P. R. (2006) 'International management: some key challenges for industrial and organisational psychology', in G. P. Hodgkinson and J. K. Ford (eds) *International Review of Industrial and Organizational Psychology*, Volume 21. Chichester, Wiley

Sparrow, P. R. and Hiltrop, J.-M. (1994) *European Human Resource Management in Transition*. Hemel Hempstead, Prentice Hall

Stiglitz, J. (2003) *The Roaring Nineties*. London, Penguin

Swenson, P. (1989) *Fair Shares: Unions, pay and politics in Sweden and Germany*. London, Adamantine

Tang, T. L. P., Tang, D. S. H., Tang, C. S. Y. and Dozier, T. S. (1998) 'CEO pay, pay differentials and pay-performance linkage', *Journal of Compensation and Benefits*, 14 (3): 41–6

Tata, J., Fu, P. P. and Wu, R. (2003) 'An examination of procedural justice principles in China and the US', *Asia-Pacific Journal of Management*, 20 (2): 205–15

Thierry, H. (1998) 'Compensating work', in P. J. D. Drenth, H. Thierry and C. J. de Wolff (eds) *Handbook of Work and Organisational Psychology*. Volume 4: *Organisational Psychology*. Brighton, Psychology Press

Trompenaars, F. (1993) *Riding the Waves of Culture*. London, Economist Books

Van de Vijver, F. J. R. and Leung, K. (1997) *Methods and Data Collection for Cross-cultural Research*. Newbury Park, CA, Sage

van het Kaar, R. and Grunell, M. (2001) 'Variable pay in Europe', *European Industrial Relations Observatory*, April

Verma, A. and Zhiming, Y. (1995) 'The changing face of HRM in China: opportunities, problems, and strategies', in A. Verma, T. Kochan and R. Lansbury (eds) *Employment Relations in the Growing Asian Economies*. London, Routledge

Vernon, G. (2005) 'International pay and reward', in P. Edwards and G. Rees (eds) *International Human Resource Management*. London, FT/Prentice Hall

Vernon, G. (2006) 'Does density matter? The significance of comparative historical variation in unionisation', *European Journal of Industrial Relations*, March

Vernon, G., Andersson, R., Baeten, X. and Neu, E. (2006) 'Unions, employers' associations and the joint regulation of reward in Europe', in C. Antoni, X. Baeten, B. Emans and M. Kira (eds) *Shaping Pay in Europe: A stakeholder approach*. Brussels, Peter Lang (for Uppsala University)

White, G., Luk, V., Druker, J. and Chiu, R. (1996) 'Paying their way: a comparison of managerial reward systems in London and Hong Kong banking industries', *Asia-Pacific Journal of Human Resources*, 36 (1): 54–71

Comparative HRM: training and development

CHAPTER OBJECTIVES

When they have read this chapter, students will:

- understand the range of issues that must be addressed in identifying variations in training and development between nations

- be able to discuss some of the typical variations between T&D in specific states, and the reasons for them

- appreciate the differences between national systems of vocational training and development and their outcomes, organisational training programmes and management development

- understand some of the implications of national variations in T&D for internationally operating organisations.

INTRODUCTION

This chapter outlines cross-national comparative variations in training and development (T&D), and reflects on the implications for the international management of T&D. It begins by describing cross-national variations in systems of initial vocational education and training (VET). It then moves on to consider the role and nature of continuing training. The discussion thereafter broadens to survey the available evidence on job roles, work organisation and job design – issues increasingly central to the employee development agenda. Management development is considered separately, before some conclusions are drawn.

COMPARATIVE TRAINING AND DEVELOPMENT

Discussions of training occurring as an element of broader discussions of HRM have in the last decade given way to discussions employing a host of new concepts and myriad new terminologies. Discussions now proceed around 'learning organisations', 'employee development', 'human resource development' (HRD), 'sustainable development', 'talent management' and, indeed, the nature of learning itself. The terminological shift has seen a broadening of the agenda, which now extends well beyond the conventional territory of training interventions, and its integration with the business plan, to take in many aspects of work and corporate organisation (Reid *et al*, 2004).

To an extent the new development agenda intersects with established discussions around high-performance work systems or high-performance practices for non-managerial employees (eg Appelbaum *et al*, 2004; Ashton and Felstead, 2001). It relates also to a new emphasis on management development, much of which now occurs in the context of organisations which are international and wish to develop an international management cadre (eg Woodall, 2005). Moreover, although the character of national systems of initial VET is often rather neglected in discussions of training and development confined to one nation, no comparative consideration can neglect national systems. A good deal of the discussion on Britain's poor productivity performance has of course been conducted with recourse to unfavourable cross-national comparisons of its system of initial vocational education and training (eg Prais, 1995).

DEBATE

- Who gains from training and development?

- Who is responsible for employees' training and development?

NATIONAL SYSTEMS: INITIAL VET

All advanced industrialised nations provide for a period of compulsory education until young people reach an age of 16 or 17 years. It is the next step – and in particular the forms of initial vocational education and training (VET) – that has been the subject of most attention and debate.

For Hall and Soskice (eg 2001) and other authors seeking to analyse cross-national comparative differences between the forms of capitalism characteristic of the established advanced industrialised world, national systems of VET are critical characteristics of countries' political economic configurations. They draw a contrast between national systems in which extensive provision of VET is coordinated by national governments or other social actors to provide a broad skill base and those in which VET is more limited in its reach, and less coordinated, and there is a greater polarisation in achievement. Broadly, extensive and coordinated provision of VET is characteristic of the nations of at least northern continental Europe whereas VET is more limited and less coordinated in the Anglo-Saxon nations. Although the level of coordination of VET in Japan is questionable, it tends to be grouped together with the continental European nations in such analyses, because it is often suggested that initial training, though grounded within organisations, is particularly sophisticated and broad-based.

Does it matter if VET systems differ in this way? Hall and Soskice (2001) would say that it does. They argue that the extensive and coordinated provision of high-quality VET facilitates certain production and product market strategies, in particular encouraging a focus on continuous improvement and incremental innovation in product strategies and production processes. They contrast this situation with that where VET is limited and weakly coordinated, and where post-compulsory education and training is principally a matter of college and university education resulting in degrees. In these circumstances, evident in the Anglo-Saxon world, Hall and Soskice (2001) argue that radical innovation in products and processes is encouraged. They suggest that this provides a partial explanation for the strength of Anglo-Saxon nations in sectors characterised by rapid change in fundamental technologies, such as IT, and the strength of continental Europe and Japan where gradual innovation within companies themselves is critical, as in mechanical engineering.

Detailed evidence shows that there is rather little difference in the proportions of national populations that have degrees across the countries of the advanced industrialised world. Among the 18 nations analysed by Hall and Soskice (2001, Table 4.3) the proportion of those aged 25–34 who in the late 1990s held a university degree was reckoned by the OECD to be in the range of 10 to 17% for 15 nations. The exceptional nations were Austria and Italy, with outstandingly low proportions, and the USA, with a notably high proportion of 26%. Beyond these exceptional nations, though, there was little difference between the proportion of the cohort who held degrees in continental European nations and in Anglo-Saxon nations.

What, then, of education beyond school that does not result in a degree – the matter of intermediate skills? The form and extent of provision of vocational education and training outside higher education has been the subject of particular attention (eg Crouch *et al*, 1999).

A peculiar benchmark: initial VET in the UK

For much of the twentieth century, VET in the UK revolved around the apprenticeship system, coordinated through employers' associations themselves pressured by the trade unions. It was for most of this period reasonably extensive in terms of the proportion of the workforce it touched, but intensely disputed as craft unions sought to control the numbers of apprentices, and employers sought to break free of craft control.

The apprenticeship system was thus battered by shifts in the balance of power between employers and unions, particularly as unemployment fluctuated, in a way that is not characteristic of other countries. Added to this, committed employers faced problems of other companies' free-riding on their apprenticeship expenditures: labour mobility and poaching of trained apprentices were widespread behaviours. Perhaps relatedly, apprenticeship was subject to further problems of voluntarism in the approach to training – there was considerable informality in terms of the monitoring and enforcement of apprenticeship contracts, an issue in which the British government did not involve itself.

With the great demand for skilled labour in the 1940s and 1950s, apprenticeship surged, and was supported through a subsequent lull by the training levy introduced in 1964. The system came under pressure in the 1970s and collapsed precipitously with the first Thatcher Conservative government of 1979–83. The new approach was one of *laissez-faire* in VET, except with regard to very basic vocational skills – as in the Youth Training Scheme of the 1980s.

In the 1990s, Training and Enterprise Councils (TECs) were established (abolished, 2000) with the intention that they have a key role in the provision of training for the newly introduced National Vocational Qualifications (NVQs) and General NVQs (Crouch et al, 1999). NVQs were designed to demonstrate competence in a particular job, and thus generally taken by those already in work; they do not aim to offer much by way of more general competence. GNVQs then became a basis for a modern apprenticeship, based around competence rather than time served. Support for modern apprenticeships amongst not only unions but employers and their associations has, however, been weak. Limited regulation and monitoring of the consistency of the training remains a problem.

Source: Crouch et al (1999); Thelen (2004)

Form of VET/ Nation	Share of cohort in VET (%)
Dual apprenticeship	
Austria	22
Germany	34
Switzerland	23
Vocational colleges	
Sweden	36
Norway	37
Finland	32

Company-based	
Japan	16*
Italy	35
France	28
Mixed	
Belgium	53
the Netherlands	43
Denmark	31
Variable but weak	
the USA	3
the UK	11
Canada	5
Australia	9
New Zealand	7

Source: Esteves et al (2001)

* Esteves *et al* suggest that this understates the extent of VET, particularly within large firms.

Table 17 *The form and reach of initial VET*

The differences in the reach of initial VET, beyond compulsory education, as shown in Table 17, are enormous. Rubery and Grimshaw (2003; p.124) comment that there is a 'tendency for coverage of training programmes to be higher in consensus-led systems and lower in market-led systems'. Generally, despite the enthusiasm amongst many academics for dual apprenticeships combining workplace and off-the-job learning, it is the mixed regimes, featuring various forms of state and market-led VET, which reach the greatest number of the relevant age cohort. College-based regimes, characteristic of the Nordic countries, with the partial exception of Denmark, are also quite extensive in their reach. Regimes which rely on company training reach proportions of the relevant cohort similar to those that rely on apprenticeships. Finally, VET regimes that are of variable forms and are generally quite weak (perhaps undeserving of the term 'regime' at all) reach a very small proportion of the relevant cohorts.

Of course, education can continue beyond the normal school-leaving age on programmes that are not vocational in strict terms, being more theoretical or academic in emphasis. Post-compulsory education participation rates are everywhere much greater than the participation rates for VET specifically. Yet international comparisons of participation rates show that at age 18, for example, in OECD nations the ranking in overall participation is very similar to that for VET as above. Thus, amongst the nations considered in Table 17 the USA comes bottom in this assessment too, whereas the nations of northern Europe all rank at the top (Ashton and Felstead, 2001; Table 9.1). None of this is, of course, any comment on the quality of these education and training experiences for those who undergo them – this is an issue that is very difficult to assess. Later, though, we will consider the comparative evidence available on workforce attainment.

Current developments in German apprenticeships

Until the mid-1980s trade unions and employers in Germany remained united in their commitment to the country's longstanding system of VET. In part the problems of the so-called dual system of apprenticeship training (workplace plus day-release) have suffered from the unique trauma of German unification since the early 1990s. In an important sense, there are two systems of VET. In the eastern part of Germany the federal government has played a massive role in the transfer of the system from the old West, so that even at the end of the 1990s more than three-quarters of all apprentice places were wholly or partly financed by the government, and indeed 10% of these places were outside of companies, in training centres, etc. This has encouraged some companies in western Germany, with the continuing system of company placements and company investment in training, to question their commitment. The difficulties are not merely those of unification, however.

The acceleration in the pace of technological change, affecting both products and processes, exposes some of the weaknesses of the apprenticeship system, organised as it has been around longstanding occupational categories. The elaborate and carefully certified system of this initial VET in the form of apprenticeships still has much to offer, although Germany's continued strength in this area contrasts strongly with its weakness in continuing vocational education and training [see later]. Moreover, German companies have come under intensified competitive pressure from the 1990s, as other nations – many newly emerging – have become capable of producing high-quality innovative products in engineering and beyond. The traditional niche of German companies has thus been increasingly challenged.

In this new context, German companies have become more cost-conscious, and aware that they may ultimately make redundant those whom they take on as apprentices, bringing an overall reduction in the number of apprenticeships offered. There has also been a reduction in the interest of young people in pursuing apprenticeship. Current erosions in the collective bargaining system, which in the past has resulted in a regulation of the structure of pay that has discouraged the poaching of skilled labour from one company by another, further threaten the commitment of companies to apprenticeships. Moreover, German companies increasingly voice the view that technological change implies a need for education and training which is more general, or more abstractly theoretical, to an extent that the established apprenticeship model of largely workplace-based training is ill-suited. The suggestion is that the government is better placed to provide the training now required, or that individuals should be more prepared to shoulder the burden of training costs, given that the most relevant training does not now result in skills and competences that are so firm-specific.

Indeed, companies are finding the recruitment of graduates with degrees from technical colleges and universities increasingly attractive. It is not surprising that younger people are finding apprenticeships less attractive in this context. Apprenticeship is threatened from all sides, although it should be noted that even as these pressures intensified there was some sign of a stabilisation of numbers from the turn of the millennium. In 2004, however, the then federal government led by Gerhard Schröder was sufficiently concerned to back encouraging companies to take on more apprentices, floating the idea of a training levy, which would mark an enormous departure for the German system. It is too early to say how the new grand coalition led by Angela Merkel will influence the system of VET.

Source: Thelen (2004)

QUESTIONS

- What are the institutional features required to support extensive initial VET?
- Where they are currently in place, are they likely to be sustained in the future?

CONTINUING TRAINING – THE ROLE OF THE EMPLOYER

Technological change and a growing emphasis on life-long learning and, indeed, high-performance work systems have deflected much attention away from the initial provision experienced by individuals before they start work. Increasingly, discussion centres on the continuing training employees experience while employed. Stavrou and Brewster (2005) outline recent international research showing that training provision, particularly in terms of the number of days of training undergone annually by employees, is one of a very few indicators of the stance of HR that is related to organisational performance across the entire array of institutional and cultural contexts.

Training and organisational ambition

To an extent, approaches to training and development express the ambition of organisations. Work in Canada in the late 1990s by Becherman and colleagues identified three approaches to training found in organisations (see Ashton and Felstead, 2001). Under the first, on-the-job learning is less of a focus than incidental, informal, learning, with formal training limited to that required by statute, or confined to a very small proportion of the workforce who need to be able to operate some specific equipment. This tended to be associated with a rather conservative organisational approach overall, and operating in traditional or well-established markets. Under the second approach, training is a response to specific events such a general upgrading of equipment, or perhaps some critical incident recognised as actually or potentially severely damaging to the organisation. Training is then formal and delivered systematically, but is quite narrowly focused. Under the third approach, training is directed at supporting the development of a learning organisation. Arrangements are bureaucratised via training budgets, formal assessment of training needs and also an evaluation of the outcomes of training interventions. Organisations adopting this approach saw training as an essential element of organisational success, supporting and complementing employee commitment, motivation and autonomy. They tended to be organisations seeking product and process innovation, and operating in high-value-added markets.

DEBATE

- Can an organisation seek to be innovative without extensive training provision?

- Can an international organisation use other processes to overcome the weaknesses that might be inherent in the VET systems of some of the countries in which it operates?

Despite the wider horizons presented by the new discussions of employee development and HRD, such continuing training remains an important element of the package that employers can offer. International evidence shows that in the vast bulk of organisations, in almost every nation covered, there is a written policy for training and development – indeed Cranet data shows that generally speaking written policies on T&D are more common than written policies on any other aspect of HRM excepting pay and benefits. Moreover, T&D is an area in which HR departments retain an important responsibility, and the vast majority of organisations are internationally involved in the formation of training and development policies just as in the early 1990s (Holden and Livian, 1993; Table 6.11). It remains the case that, as Crouch et al (1999) observed, continuing training tends typically to be concentrated on those relatively highly educated and trained already.

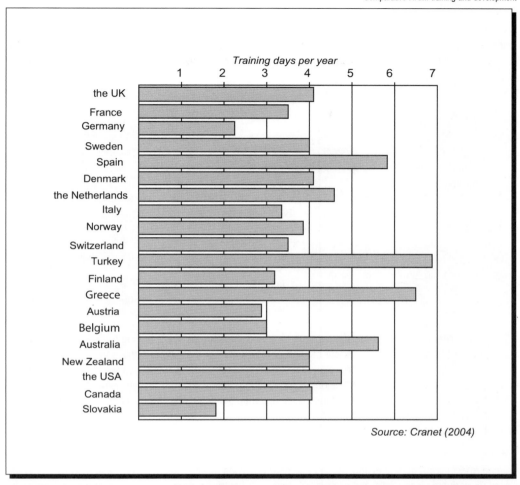

Figure 21 *Average number of days of training per year for manual employees across (selected) countries*

Despite these general truths and cross-national similarities, cross-national comparative training provision varies dramatically, as is clear in the data on the distribution of average training days for manual employees (see Figure 21). In the UK very few organisations report that their manual employees, on average, experience no days of training whatever each year. Just over 40% of organisations report that manual employees experience on average 1–2 days of training annually. Just over 20% report that the average is 3–4 days, and just over 30% report 5–10 days. The pattern is near identical in Canada and similar in the USA and other Anglo-Saxon countries, with the exception of Australia. Australian provision, like that in Sweden, Denmark, the Netherlands, and, according to the limited data available, in Bulgaria, tends to be more generous. In contrast, the pattern of provision in Belgium, Austria and most strikingly, Germany, shows that continuing training for manual employees in these nations is much more limited than in the UK. It is extremely limited in Slovenia, where over 70% of organisations report that training is limited to at best 1–2 days annually.

Comparison of current Cranet data on training days with that for the early 1990s (Holden and Livian, 1993; Table 6.5) reveals marked differences in national trends over the last decade or so. Provision for manual employees in Germany is very little changed, whereas that in France appears to have fallen off a little. In contrast, there has been a very marked expansion in training provision in the cases of Sweden, Denmark and also the UK. Other countries have typically seen a more limited growth. There is thus little sign of convergence across national borders in training provision, despite the typical tendency for companies to set aside more days for the training of employees. It should also be noted that there has been little change in the uncertainty in many organisations about the extent of training provision. In 2004, more than a third of organisations responding to the Cranet survey could not offer an answer to questions about training days, much as in the early 1990s.

Training in Sweden

By the 1990s Sweden had extensive provision for competence development post-full-time education. Although comparative evidence on such job-related training beyond that of Cranet is fragmentary, it confirms the suggestion that by the mid-1990s there were, relatively, very many more training episodes in Sweden than for example in France, Germany, Italy or the USA (Crouch *et al*, 1999; Table 3.5). Much of this was centred around the active labour market policy, even after its partial privatisation, although there has been an effort to adapt provision to the increasing importance of internal labour markets. Yet evidence for the 1990s has suggested that the extent of continuing training at work varied enormously between employees, particularly by gender, by certificated education and by the size of the employing organisation, being greatest for highly qualified men in large organisations.

Source: Kjellberg (1998)

What of the extent of companies' commitment of financial resources to continuing training? Organisations are often rather uncertain of the extent of their commitment, as they were in the early 1990s. Generally, whereas in most cases they feel able to state a spending range, organisations typically spend less than 2% of their total pay bill on training provision, a situation little changed from the early 1990s (Cranet, 2004; Holden and Livian, 1993; Table 6.3). France is exceptional, spending considerably above these levels, such that the bulk of companies spend more than 2% of their payroll on training. Sweden ranks second in terms of such financial commitments to continuing training.

Strikingly, however, it is not only that expenditure on training in France is comparatively great. In France the training effort is particularly evenly spread across employees of all grades (Cranet, 2004). Uniquely in the advanced industrialised world, the number of days of training experienced by non-managerial employees in France is almost as great as that experienced by managerial employees. This egalitarianism in training provision contrasts even with the situation in Sweden and the other Nordic countries.

Much, but not all, of this French exceptionality is explained by law. French statute compels French employers of more than 10 employees to devote 1.5% of their pay bill to continuing training. A substantial proportion of this total must be assigned specifically to the training of young employees, who tend to be on lower grades (IDS, 1993). However, it seems clear that training provision by French employers typically exceeds this statutory requirement. Some part of expenditures beyond the statutory minimum may be nurtured by the procedural requirements applying to those organisations subject to the terms of a collective agreement; the vast bulk in the French case (see Chapter 10). Such organisations must formally consider training requirements several times each year, in conjunction with works councils where appropriate, and establish an annual training plan. Statute and multi-employer agreements provide what amounts to a conceptual framework for the consideration of training needs (IDS, 1993). This both heightens awareness of training issues and eases their consideration.

Joint regulation of continuing training: the case of Germany

Trade union involvement has long been central to the famous dual system of apprenticeship training in Germany, and industry agreements make certified skills central in the grading of employees. Moreover, statute requires the involvement of works councillors in the organisation of training provision at workplace level (IDS, 1993). Employers must consult works councils on the nature of training provision. Works councils ultimately have co-determination rights with regard to training provision, implying the power of veto. In effect, particularly in comparison to other countries, it seems as though works councils in Germany practically co-determine appointments of managers charged with shaping training arrangements.

Germany features continuing training which is largely ad hoc and, where certificated, this certification is of uncertain meaning (Thelen, 2004). In the last decade or so, German unions have shown great interest in the further development of continuing training, and in skill-based pay structures which take account not only of apprenticeship but of such continuous development (see eg IDS, 1993). This is despite their inevitable reservations about the dangers of a less clear-cut skill hierarchy. However, although the deficit in continuing training may become an increasing problem as technological change continues at a rapid pace, for employers have shown little enthusiasm for the development of continuing training for non-managerial employees, and in particular the least skilled (see eg IDS, 1993).

The strictness of existing industry agreements severely limits the extent to which employees may be upgraded on the basis of continuing training and development rather than apprenticeship (Marsden, 1999). The reorganisation of notions of skill and reward for skill is problematic for both sides, and would require effort and compromise on both sides.

ACTIVITY

Skills and international productivity

The briefing

You are an International HR manager looking at your organisation's possible investment in UK operations. You have been sent the following worrying analysis by HQ about the level of skills and productivity in the country.

'In conducting due diligence before making further investment decisions, we see that an analysis by Her Majesty's Treasury (2002) shows that gross domestic product per worker [a general measure of the efficiency of national economies] in the UK is 38% lower than in the USA, 15% worse than in France and 9% less than in Germany. The UK still falls below both the EU and the OECD averages. This gap exists across most sectors of the economy, and is not just a manufacturing issue but also applies to the service sector. GDP per hour is probably a better measure of productivity than GDP per worker [because there are international differences in things like double job-holding, hours worked, and holidays] but this shows that the situation is even worse. In manufacturing, output per hour is 55% higher in the USA than in the UK, 32% higher in France, 29% higher in Germany. The figures in the service sector are 32% higher in the USA, 25% higher in France and 25% higher in Germany. In relation to France and Germany the recent higher growth of the UK economy is a result simply of longer working hours in the UK and a larger percentage of the population (ie women returners) at work.

When the National Institute for Economic and Social Research reported to the Department of Trade and Industry on the factors that explained relative productivity performance (O'Mahoney and De Boer, 2002), they found that the four biggest productivity drivers were: exposure to foreign trade, skills, investment in physical capital, and innovation and technological progress.

However, apart from trade exposure (the biggest drive for productivity improvement), it was the difference between countries in terms of their stock of human capital that was the single most important reason for growth differentials in the OECD. Nearly 20% of the productivity gap between Germany and the UK can be explained by the skills gap. Similarly, 10% of the gap with France, and nearly one-fifth of productivity differences between companies can be explained by differences in HR practices. Bloom *et al* (2004) put the skills and productivity issues down to higher education and company levels of investment in training. Despite a large increase in the number of people getting managerial qualifications in the UK, it still lags behind – 49% of UK managers have now got degrees, compared with 61% in France, 72% in Germany, 74% in the USA and 78% in Japan.

The number of days off per year spent in training is 8 on average for the UK, compared to 12 days in the rest of Europe and Japan, and 15 days in the USA. The UK invests about 0.6% of GDP in training and education, France 0.9%, Germany 1% and the Republic of Ireland 1.4%. (The USA invests only 0.3% – but, of course, of a very much larger GDP.) We are aware of there being concern in that country about the level of skills development in the economy and that the UK continues to lag behind many European competitors as well as the USA in terms of productivity. Why should we continue to invest in these local operations?'

The task

Your task is to persuade people in your company that you understand the need to do something about this (or to allay any concerns and explain why it is not an issue). Devise a presentation that:

- identifies the key issues that HQ is likely to be worried about

- puts forward a local in-country strategy to handle these issues and deals with any institutional weaknesses.

FROM TRAINING TO DEVELOPMENT

Increasingly, discussion of training corresponds to an element of a broader discussion about high-performance work systems or working practices. An institutionalised commitment to training often occurs as an element of a wider approach to HRM that involves the structuring of work, appraisal, reward and promotion possibilities. Now, the differentiation between organisations in their approach to the development of non-managerial employees extends beyond their approach to training.

	Management assessed by appraisal (%)
the UK	88.9
Sweden	87.4
Germany	81.5
Greece	88.0
Slovakia	65.4

Source: Cranet (2004)

Table 18 *Comparative use of appraisal: the proportion of management assessed via a formal appraisal system*

Increasingly, discussions of employee development take in the context of job roles, the organisation of work and job design. Employee involvement or employee participation is generally a central reference in these discussions, and attention is paid most particularly to the extent and intensity of team- and group-working, problem-solving activity and the scope of employee autonomy. At minimum, implicitly, there is growing recognition that where extensive responsibility resides with teams or groups of employees, such that they take on many of the traditional functions of management, accelerated development is likely. Of course, such delegation presupposes appropriate training, and also the agreement to stretching but realistic targets.

	Not at all	To a small extent	To a large extent	Totally
the United Kingdom	19.5	62.1	18.4	0
France	22.8	53.7	22.1	1.5
Germany	15.8	56.1	27.5	0.6
Sweden	12.9	58.0	29.1	0
Spain	31.3	56.3	11.8	0.7
Denmark	14.3	52.8	32.5	0.4
the Netherlands	14.8	61.3	22.6	1.3
Italy	14.3	42.9	42.9	0
Norway	26.7	56.7	15.5	1.1
Switzerland	15.0	53.1	29.3	2.7
Turkey	28.6	51.0	16.3	4.1
Finland	24.1	53.2	22.7	0
Greece	23.4	35.1	39.6	1.9
Austria	19.2	53.5	25.0	2.3
Belgium	27.6	45.2	22.6	4.5
Australia	17.0	60.5	22.5	0
New Zealand	9.8	61.8	27.6	0.7
the United States	11.0	54.9	33.7	0.4
Canada	18.6	57.6	22.5	1.2
Slovakia	48.4	33.2	17.6	0.8

Source: Cranet (2004)

Table 19 *Comparative use of special tasks or projects for non-managerial employment*

QUESTIONS

- What are the opportunities and problems posed by delegating tasks traditionally seen as those of management to non-managerial employees?

- Might these opportunities and problems be more or less keen in different national contexts of employment?

A large-scale survey of work organisation in 10 nations conducted through the European Foundation's Employee Direct Participation in Organisational Change programme (EPOC, 1997) together with the European Survey of Working Conditions of 2000 (see eg Antoni *et al*, 2005) demonstrate the diversity of experience even within Europe. Despite the currency of the rhetoric of employee involvement, management delegation in the UK is comparatively limited. Sweden stands out, in terms of the incidence and typical scope of delegation to working groups as well as in the extent of employee representatives' involvement in the introduction and joint regulation of such group work. It is also noteworthy that Swedish management accords particular significance to such (semi-autonomous) work organisation. In many respects, particularly in terms of direct participation of employees as opposed to the representative participation of employee representatives, the Netherlands ranks second to Sweden among the countries considered. Surprisingly, in the light of some commentaries (eg Streeck, 1992; Marsden, 1999), in these large-scale surveys Germany appears if anything to feature less delegation than the UK, contrasting strikingly with Sweden in particular in terms of the incidence of employee autonomy and team- or group-working of substance.

What of the situation beyond Europe? In the USA, despite celebration of the effectiveness of such management delegation to groups, the limited diffusion of such initiatives is widely acknowledged even by enthusiasts for high-performance work systems (eg Appelbaum et al, 2000). Moreover, although in many respects the agenda in this area has been influenced by interpretations of the Japanese experience, Vernon (2006) shows that the nature of delegation and teamwork in Japan is more circumscribed than is often suggested. In the newly industrialised and developing world, the limited evidence available suggests that employee involvement and participation is typically still less advanced (eg Zhang et al, 2005).

QUESTION

- Why might a shift in work organisation towards more team- and group-working be expected in the newly industrialising and developing countries?

Research on the cross-national comparative differences in the manner in which the various facets of training and development are bundled to produce coherent but contrasting bundles is at an early stage. It would seem plausible, however, that in countries where most employees undergo thorough initial training at the beginning of their working lives, particularly if it combines substantial theoretical and practical components, there might be less need for a focus on continuing training. Such thoroughgoing initial training might also make autonomous working groups more likely to succeed, might make more fragmented forms of work organisation less appropriate, and might have implications for the identity of employees, and thus for the means by which they might meaningfully be appraised.

QUESTIONS

- What implications might the difference in initial training provision between the USA and Germany have for the organisation of work and the character of relationships between managers and non-managerial employees?
- How might performance management differ in Sweden from that in Japan?

SYSTEMS OF EMPLOYEE DEVELOPMENT

Marsden's (1999) examination of the relationships between different facets of the employment relationship suggests a powerful nexus between job roles and work organisation, training arrangements and forms of appraisal and performance management. He argues that in Germany, but also still the UK, job design prioritises employees' skills, such that there is considerable potential mobility of employees across organisations. In contrast, in France, the USA and Japan, job design is structured principally by the production technology, and rewards for seniority and internal labour markets are more heavily featured. He distinguishes also between the character of employees' accountability in these countries, arguing that in France, the USA, but also the UK (despite the role of skill in job design), the assignment of work and the responsibility of employees tends to centre on specific tasks. In contrast, in Germany, and also Japan, assignment and accountability are organised around employees' functions, with less segmentation of work roles, including that between hierarchical levels of the organisation. Marsden's account of the basis of these comparative differences stresses the differing character and extensiveness of initial VET but also of collective bargaining.

WORKFORCE ACHIEVEMENT: LITERACY AND NUMERACY

So much for initiatives and systems of training and development at national and organisational level. What of the typical achievement of the citizens and workforces? Until the late 1990s indications of the comparative capabilities of countries in this regard were weak and fragmented. The International Adult Literacy Survey (IALS) of the late 1990s offered a systematic assessment of literacy, broadly conceived, across 20 OECD nations (Crouch *et al*, 1999). The survey showed that the people of Sweden were the most literate and numerate. Sweden had the highest average scores on all three scales employed, ranking first on each of prose, document and quantitative literacy. The UK ranked 13th, 16th and 17th respectively on these scales, although better than the Republic of Ireland. The USA and other Anglo-Saxon nations did a little better than the UK and the Irish Republic, but there was a clear gulf between the better-performing countries of continental Europe and those of the Anglo-Saxon world.

There was also a marked contrast in the extent of variation in achievement amongst the citizens of the different nations surveyed. Each of the Anglo-Saxon nations displayed very much greater variation in the literacy of its citizens than did the nations of continental Europe. Chile and Poland footed the rankings in terms of overall average and also showed the greatest variation in their citizens' achievements. The IALS suggests very strongly that whatever its basis in cross-national comparative variation in education and training provision and development opportunities, there is great difference in the structure of achievement of the populations of the various countries of the established advanced industrialised world. We would expect that this difference between countries would be even greater if newly emerging nations were considered.

The OECD (2001) also set up its Programme for International Student Assessment (known as PISA). This study was designed to monitor educational outcomes against internationally agreed frameworks. Rather than simply accept various government statistics, the OECD independently supervised tests of 250,000 15-year-old students (out of a total population of 17 million) in 32 countries. The tests scored the attainments of people at school-leaving age in three basic areas that employers find important: knowledge in reading, knowledge in mathematics, and scientific literacy.

Countries such as Finland, New Zealand, Korea and Japan scored consistently well across areas. The UK and the Republic of Ireland were in the top 10 (out of 32). France was poor in two areas but came into the top 10 for maths. The USA scored only at average levels in all areas. Surprisingly, post-unification Germany scored between 20th and 22nd. Mexico and Brazil were in the two bottom places. The study was repeated in 2003. The results show that basic skills acquired immediately post-school can be a good indicator of the subsequent load that is placed on VET systems.

MANAGEMENT DEVELOPMENT

In line with the received wisdom in many countries – most significantly, of course, the USA – that it is senior managers who are critical to organisational performance, considerable attention now focuses on the development of managers.

The significance of informal learning in conjunction with formal training for managers has long been recognised. Increasingly, however, there is recognition of the reality of individuals' differing learning styles. Moreover, learning is increasingly seen as embedded and promoted in particular contexts, and as occurring in teams rather than in individuals. Interactive learning techniques and action learning projects are increasingly deployed in management development initiatives. Yet consideration of the manner in which effective learning may vary in texture across national boundaries is only now emerging in many organisations.

Discussion now centres on the identification and operationalisation of international leadership competencies. A significant literature has codified such supposedly generic competencies, stressing the significance and potential of individuals who are, for example, action-oriented, risk-taking, analytical, and in touch with the needs of themselves and others. Yet the evidence for the universal importance and transferable relevance of such characteristics or behaviours is somewhat lacking (eg Woodall, 2005).

There is a particular focus on the development of high-flyers or hi-pos (high-potential managers) in the USA and across much of Europe. Notions of the generalist manager in the USA have resulted in specialist training in business schools, whereas rotation through different functions is more common in Japan and France. Woodall (2005) considers an attempt to forge an integrated organisation via management development following a hostile takeover of a French by a UK company. The experience shows that different conceptions of the appropriate nature of such development activities still prevail. The elite cadres emerging from the *Grandes Écoles* to populate the higher reaches of management are rather wary of typical Anglo-Saxon attempts to identify high-potential individuals within an already demonstrably elite group. Moreover, French participants in executive education programmes seek more abstract discussion, broad principles and critical contemplation of complex situations. They are rather impatient with the pragmatic orientation and prescriptive direction that the British favour in their dash for practical application (Woodall, 2005).

Since the early 1980s, China's economy has grown at an average annual rate of around 10% per annum, making it one of the most exciting markets for the products of companies of the established advanced industrialised world. The accumulated stock of FDI by foreign MNCs in China has grown more than 500-fold since 1980. Despite the continued relevance of the *guanxi* tradition of reciprocal relationships, and a continuing tendency that lines of authority be strong and clear, MNCs operating in China have found that there is substantial room for manoeuvre (Zhang *et al*, 2005). Thus Gamble (2003) showed that a British retailer established relatively flat hierarchies in its Chinese operations, despite the departure that this represented from common local practice. Where China is chosen as a low-cost location for manufacturing, a sophisticated approach to (non-managerial) employee development is often not a priority (Zhang *et al*, 2005). Generally, however, foreign MNCs have devoted considerable attention to management development (see box).

Management development for localisation in China

European multinationals operating in China have shown an increasing interest in localising their Chinese operations – passing more and more responsibility for their running to Chinese-born managers. Meanwhile, Chinese employees have shown great interest in achieving management status in such foreign enterprises. European MNCs have generally regarded localisation in China as requiring a significant investment in promising individuals, yet still have on occasion underestimated the extent of the investment needed.

ABB achieved a substantial presence in China with a relatively few expatriate managers. Its formal planning of the localisation process was viewed as critical to the success of the company in China, in the light not only of their language skills but of their sensitivity to the cultural and political context, and to the conventions of business in China. Localisation was regarded as a business goal to stand alongside profit and market share. In recognition of the importance of the goal – and of the dangers posed by expatriates' being asked to work to render themselves superfluous – expatriates were offered substantial bonuses tied to targets emerging from the localisation plan. This also helped to mitigate the danger that line managers would regard the immediate bottom line as the key objective. Interestingly, expatriate assignments were normally expected to be for two to three years, ABB stressing to assignees the significance of such international experience for them, and the importance for ABB of imparting ABB experience to the Chinese. They discouraged expatriates' attempts to learn Chinese, since they were only to be there for a short while. ABB moved from the identification of high-potential Chinese candidates for management through to their socialisation, making use also of local business schools.

Qualifications are important in China. Chinese managers often give preference to those with degrees, and also often expect to have their development certificated. The action-learning-based programmes offered by the Siemens Management Institute to employees of Siemens and others suit Chinese managers well. Focused on the actual problems they face in their roles, and involving extensive group work, this sort of programme avoids the theoretical study that Chinese managers often find demotivating. From the organisation's point of view, the projects emerging result in initiatives with measurable economic impact.

As in other forms of management development, on-the-job training is critical. Indeed, given that authority structures tend to be centralised in China, it has a particular relevance because the absence of managers undergoing off-the-job training can have a severe impact on progress in their team. Sometimes, however, MNCs seeking localisation in China have deployed job rotation insufficiently, despite the willingness of local managers to be rotated. Job rotation can not only aid management development, but can form one element of a career and development path which encourages Chinese-born managers to remain with the organisation that has invested in their initial development. These development opportunities, alongside a good relationship with those to whom they report, are more important to the retention of the local managers than relative salaries (Worm, 2001).

SUMMARY

Considerable interest centres on the development of international management elites, and there are many indications of the establishment of international notions of best practice in the nurturing of development amongst such groups. However, examination of prevailing practice in training and development beyond such elites reveals stark and continuing differences across national borders. There seems some coherence in the character of these national systems, practices fitting together according to different logics of development. It may be that development initiatives aimed at international management cadres would benefit from greater sensitivity to cross-cultural variation in management identity and learning styles.

Innovation in training and development is of course possible in all national settings. To some extent, cross-national variation in practice seems buttressed by national management approaches to the framing of reflection on employment and work which have their own life, rather than emerging from a rational consideration of what is possible or effective in a particular institutional or cultural context. This implies opportunities for MNCs to innovate successfully. However, adherence to typical local practice offers benefits in terms of the comprehensibility and legitimacy of arrangements in the eyes of employees. Forms of job design, or of performance management, accepted as natural in one country may be perplexing to employees, and thus be disruptive, in another. As in other spheres, in that of training and development the task for international organisations is to meld innovation with a sensitivity to key dimensions of the national settings in which they operate.

LEARNING QUESTIONS

- What are the implications for international HR departments of the range of levels of literacy and numeracy that they will encounter in different countries?

- Describe the likely effects of the different concepts of management in, say, the USA and Sweden on management development programmes.

- What would be the implications for a training manager of moving from performing that role in western Europe to performing that role in China?

- For an internationally operating organisation, what aspects of training and development policies are best retained centrally and what are best handled locally? Why?

REFERENCES

Antoni, C. *et al.* (2005) *Wage and Working Conditions in the European Union – Project No. 0261 Final Report*. European Foundation for the Improvement of Living and Working Conditions

Appelbaum, E., Bailey, T., Berg, P. and Kalleberg, A. L. (2000) *Manufacturing Advantage: Why high-performance work systems pay off*. Ithaca, Cornell University Press

Ashton, D. and Felstead, D. (2001) 'From training to lifelong learning: the birth of the knowledge society?' in J. Storey (ed.) *HRM: A citical text*. London, Thomson Learning

Bloom, N., Conway, N., Mole, K., Neely, A. and Frost, C. (2004) *Solving the Skills Gap*. London, Advanced Institute of Management Research/Council for Industry and Higher Education

Crouch, C., Finegold, D. and Sako, M. (1999) *Are Skills the Answer? The political economy of skill creation in advanced industrial countries*. Oxford, Oxford University Press.

EPOC (1997) *New Forms of Work Organisation: Can Europe realise its innovative potential? Results of a survey of direct employee participation in Europe*. Dublin, European Foundation for the Improvement of Living and Working Conditions

Esteves-Abe, M., Iversen, T. and Soskice, D. (2001) 'Social protection and the formation of skills: a reinterpretation of the welfare state', in P. A. Hall and D. Soskice (eds) *Varieties of Capitalism: The institutional foundations of comparative advantage*. Oxford, Oxford University Press

Gamble, J. (2003) 'Transferring HR practices from the UK to China: the limits and potential for convergence', *International Journal of HRM*, 14 (3): 369–87

Hall, P. A. and Soskice, D. (2001) 'An introduction to varieties of capitalism', in P. A. Hall and D. Soskice (eds) *Varieties of Capitalism: The institutional foundations of comparative advantage*. Oxford, Oxford University Press

Her Majesty's Treasury (2002) *Pre-Budget Report 2002*. London, HM Treasury

Holden, L. and Livian, Y. (1993) 'Does strategic training policy exist? Some evidence from ten European countries', in A. Hegewisch and C. Brewster (eds) *European Developments in HRM*. London, Kogan Page.

IDS (Income Date Services), (1993), *Training and Development*. London, IPD

Kjellberg, A. (1998) 'Sweden: restoring the model?', in A. Ferner and R. Hyman (eds) *Changing Industrial Relations in Europe*. Oxford, Blackwell

Marsden, D. (1999) *A Theory of Employment Systems: Micro-foundations of societal diversity*. Oxford, Oxford University Press

O'Mahoney, M. and de Boer, W. (2002) *Britain's Relative Productivity Performance: Updates to 1999*. National Institute for Economic and Social Research, Final Report to DTI

OECD (2001) *Knowledge and Skills for Life: First results from PISA 2000*. Paris, OECD

Prais, S. J. (1995) *Productivity, Education and Training: An international perspective*. Cambridge, Cambridge University Press

Reid, M. A., Barrington, H. and Brown, M. (2004) *HRD: Beyond training interventions*. London, Chartered Institute of Personal Development

Rubery, J. and Grimshaw, D. (2003) *The Organisation of Employment: An international perspective*. Basingstoke, Palgrave-Macmillan

Stavrou, E. T. and Brewster, C. (2005) 'The configurational approach to linking strategic human resource management bundles with business performance: myth or reality?', *Management Revue*, 16 (2): 186–201

Streeck, W. (1992) *Social Institutions and Economic Performance*. Sage, London

Thelen, K. (2004) *How Institutions Evolve: The political economy of skills in Germany, Britain, the United States and Japan*. Cambridge, Cambridge University Press

Vernon, G. (2006) 'The potential of management-dominated work reorganization: the critical case of Japan', *Economic and Industrial Democracy*, 27, 3 (August): 399–424

Woodall, J. (2005) 'International management development', in T. Edwards and C. Rees (eds) *International Human Resource Management: Globalization, National Systems and Multinational Companies*. Harlow: FT/Prentice Hall. London, Prentice Hall

Worm, V. (2001) 'HRD for localisation: European MNCs in China', in J. B. Kidd and F.-J. Richter (eds) *Advances in HRM in Asia*. Basingstoke, Palgrave

Zhang, M., Edwards, T. and Edwards, C. (2005) 'Internationalisation and developing countries: the case of China', in T. Edwards and C. Rees (eds) *International Human Resource Management: Globalization, National Systems and Multinational Companies*. Harlow: FT/Prentice Hall. London, Prentice Hall

Comparative HRM: flexibility and work–life balance

CHAPTER OBJECTIVES

When they have read this chapter, students will:

- be familiar with concepts of flexible working practices and work–life balance and the relationship between them

- be aware of developments in working-time flexibility, non-permanent forms of employment and work–life balance

- identify similarities and differences at country level, in relation to flexibility and work–life balance

- understand the principal factors associated with country- and institution-level differences

- be able to draw conclusions about managing flexible working and work–life balance across country borders.

INTRODUCTION: THE CONCEPT OF FLEXIBILITY

In many respects, flexibility and work–life balance are flip sides of the same coin. Discussions of flexibility begin with the employer or manager and his/her notion of what is required for effective operations to meet fluctuations in throughput or demand, and sometimes to take advantage of the structure of taxation on employment and employers' social insurance contributions. Necessarily, managers must take account of the possibilities that the labour market presents of pursuing a certain policy, with a focus on effective resource planning to meet operational need. Discussions of work–life balance begin with the employee, as employers and managers seek to interpret and accommodate employees' needs and situations. Necessarily, of course, there must be reference to organisational objectives, but a focus on work–life balance implies a rather softer approach to HRM, beginning with a more holistic view of the employee. Despite the differing starting points and emphases, there is of course a relationship between the agendas of flexibility and work–life balance.

Flexible working is an area bedevilled with terminological problems. 'Flexibility', which is the term used here, is the common term in Europe, even though it has certain linguistic connotations that may be inaccurate. Even in Europe some commentators prefer the phrase the 'peripheral workforce' (Atkinson, 1984) or the (equally inaccurate) term 'atypical working'. Others have referred to the 'just-in-time workforce' (Plews, 1988). Some trade unionists talk about 'vulnerable work'.

A broad definition of 'atypical' employment is that adopted by Delsen (1991; p.123), who describes it as deviating 'from full-time open-ended work employment: part-time work, … seasonal work …'. In the United States the most common term that largely overlaps what is referred to in Europe as flexible working patterns is 'contingent work' (Freedman, 1986), although some consultants have tried to foster the term 'complementary working'. Polivk and Nardone (1989; p.10) define contingent employment as 'any arrangement that differs from full-time, permanent, wage and salary employment'. Morishima and Feuille (2000) note that contingent employment can include a wide variety of workers. They conclude that:

> 'The common themes that unite the individuals in these diverse catego-
> ries are that they receive few or no fringe benefits, they have little or no
> expectation of long-term employment with the firm on whose premises
> they work at any given time, and they occupy a secondary position to
> the regular, full-time (or core) employees in the firm's status hierarchy.'

Although an accurate account of the situation for most flexible workers in the USA and Japan, within the European context such distinctions do not hold true. Apart from the fact that in many European countries local employment protection helps guard against discrimination, the EU has passed legislation guarantee-ing the rights of part-time and temporary workers, which apply across the EU. Furthermore, there will be a minority, but an important minority, of highly in-demand and successful people on flexible work contracts to whom none of these factors apply.

QUESTION

■   What implications might be inherent in these different terminologies?

The concept of 'labour flexibility' remains, both in theoretical and practical terms, highly problematic. In the literature, the term 'flexibility' is applied to a series of quite distinct (if related) theories and practices. The concept that some kinds of work are peripheral or atypical carry with them the idea that they are in some way less significant or worthy than other, more standard, kinds of work. Thinking about this kind of work as 'contingent', 'just in time' or 'disposable' is clearly looking at such work from an employer's perspective, focusing on the positive side from that position, so that the individuals concerned are almost defined out of existence as real people. By contrast, 'vulnerable' work implies thinking from the employees' point of view – and moreover, from that viewpoint, is focused on the downside.

The labour that an organisation employs is, in nearly all cases, the most expensive item of its operating costs. There is increasing pressure on operating costs. In the private sector, competition – particularly internationally – is getting tougher. In the public sector, ever-tightening public-sector financial constraints mean that organisations here too are having to use their most expensive resource in ever more cost-effective ways. Standard employment has built-in inefficiencies unless work comes in exactly the standard employment patterns. That is rarely the case now, and many organisations are attempting to match their employment patterns more closely to the work (Brewster and Holt Larsen, 2000).

These changes and the development of a more flexible labour market have been controversial. There are those who see the development of the flexible workforce as a long-overdue move away from rigid forms of employment towards forms that can be more responsive to the needs of employees, or can be 'family-friendly'. There are many who would argue that part-time, shift- or home-working allows them to spend more time with their children or elderly or disabled family members (Bevan, 1996). However, the growth in flexibility at the end of the last century and the beginning of this one has been driven by employer demands. In a comparative study of German, French and UK industries, Lane (1989) found that each country responded differently to the same economic pressures for flexibility. She argued that whereas German industry embraced flexible specialisation, British industry tended to adopt a combination of Fordist and contractual flexibility principles of management.

INSTITUTIONAL DIFFERENCES

Brewster and Tregaskis's (2003) analysis showed that the country of operation has the largest effect on levels of uptake of flexibility, accounting for 25% of the variance. The sector of operation accounts for another 17% of variance. Multinational corporate status in contrast accounts for very little variance – a mere 1%. Dickmann (1999) stresses the significance of corporate finance and governance for the extent of the commitment that employers make to employees, but also the relevance of labour law, collective bargaining and systems of vocational education and training for the deployment of flexibility.

There are still significant differences in labour relationships and institutions between countries (see Chapter 10). In Germany, for instance, the co-determination regulations promote greater employee influence in employment relations than in many other countries, enhancing the use of contracts that are more favourable to employees in terms of job security and skill acquisition opportunities. The influence of trade unions and collective bargaining arrangements has played a significant role in the restriction of weekend working in Germany. Unions are significantly less powerful in the UK (Lane, 1992) and weaker and more adversarial in Spain (Miguelez and Prieto, 1991; Filella and Soler, 1992). The well-known German 'duales' vocational education and training systems, combined with the longer-term German investment perspective, encourages strong internal labour markets (Muller, 1997; and see Chapter 8). In contrast, the low value placed on educational qualifications in the UK context, in combination with the lower level of vocational training, encourages poaching and reliance on external labour markets. This places more of a premium on contractual flexibility.

Overall, there are clear benefits for employers in deploying these various contingent practices, even when they do not pay lower wages. Employers, that is, pay just for the hours that are productive, have limited commitment and enjoy increased flexibility. In some cases, moreover, these contingent employment practices are also advantageous for employees. For example, part-time employment can allow those with other responsibilities (young children, elderly relatives, etc) to be away from work when they need to be. Across Europe, EU surveys show that most people on part-time employment tend to prefer those kinds of contracts. They tend to be less common in the southern European countries where pay levels are lower (part-time work = part-time pay: and if the pay is low anyway, that may not be attractive) and where family support for working mothers is higher. By contrast, the evidence is that most employees with a temporary or fixed-term contract would prefer a permanent one. In general it is the poorer countries that have the highest levels of employees on such contracts. Nevertheless, we should also note that fixed-term contracts in occupations that are in high demand and in low supply – such as software designers – can prove quite advantageous for individuals in terms of reward packages and opportunities for skill enhancement.

De Grip et al (1997) found that the prevalence of part-time and temporary employment varies across countries, showing distinctive patterns. Tregaskis et al (1998) and Brewster and Tregaskis (2001) reported similar findings, and Tregaskis and Brewster (2006) found that these differences are not diminishing.

CONTRACTUAL FLEXIBILITY: 'NON-PERMANENT' EMPLOYMENT

Many of the developments in flexibility relate to contractual flexibility. There is a range of methods by which organisations can get work done. In some cases these involve contracts of employment which are quite distinct from 'typical' contracts in more significant ways than just a change to the time at which the employee works – they may involve short-term or even casual employment, for example. Or they may involve getting the work done through a non-employment option. Brewster (2000) has provided the following analysis:

Short-term employment

This is a phrase used to cover any form of employment other than permanent open-ended contracts. To some extent 'temporary', 'fixed-term' and 'casual' contracts are substitutes, and which is used most heavily in a country depends largely on legal and quasi-legal regulations and national expectations. Temporary contracts are those that can be terminated with just the appropriate notice and are recognised by both parties as not intending to lead to permanent employment commitments. They can range from a few weeks' work (for example, on building sites) to as many as three years', although typically they are at the lower end of such a distribution. Fixed-term contracts, in contrast, are those which the parties agree will end on a certain date, often after 12 or 24 months. By law, the terminations of these contracts are not treated as terminations of employment *per se* since the contracts have simply been completed, not broken. Temporary and fixed-term contracts tend to overlap, but often appear to substitute for each other depending on local legislation. Temporary contracts tend to be set with lower-skilled workers, whereas fixed-term contracts tend to be set with higher-skilled employees. Employers avoid expectations that either type of contract will lead to permanent employment and, consequently, avoid some of the legal obligations, as well as trade union reactions, that the termination of employment might otherwise prompt. Casual contracts occur when both employer and employee accept that the employment will be on an 'as necessary' basis. Thus, students working in certain occupations over the Christmas and New Year sales period or catering staff called in to a restaurant just to cover children's parties, would be examples of casual work. Similar examples can be found in many industries.

QUESTION

- When and why might an employer prefer to offer a short-term contract rather than a permanent one?

In general, it seems that employers are likely to offer short-term contracts in three broad sets of circumstances: when, for one reason or another they are not sure whether or how long a job will last (for example, in the construction industry or when government funding for a charity project might be of limited duration); when they seek to avoid the commitments to employees that come with permanent work (employment rights, pensions, etc); and when they are uncertain that they have chosen the right person. In practice, the first reason has always existed and probably has not changed much and the capacity to avoid obligations has been much reduced in places such as the countries of the European Union by legislation. The third reason seems to be growing. Many employees are now appointed on short-term contracts while the employer checks whether they will be good employees (see Chapter 6).

Detailed evidence from Cranet 2004 shows that the use of fixed-term contracts remains limited, generally, but there is considerable variability across countries. Despite their reputations as nations displaying great flexibility in the character of their employment relationships, the Anglo-Saxon nations cluster towards the bottom end in terms of organisational use. Nor does the Slovakian experience suggest that central/eastern European organisations are extreme in their use of fixed-term contracts. It is in the western part of continental Europe that use is more common. Regarding the proportion of organisations featuring more than 5% of employees on fixed-term contracts (see Figure 22), Finland stands out, more than half of all organisations in that country reporting such use. With the interesting exception of Denmark, where labour markets are tight, the other Nordic countries are not so very far behind. Organisations in southern Europe also feature prominently, while still remaining within the confines of the general tendency for the use of fixed-term contracts to remain quite limited. The Netherlands is the exception to this general tendency in a striking sense. Although being placed second to Finland in the figure here, many more Dutch organisations report very heavy use of fixed-term contracts. One third (33.6%) of Dutch organisations report that more than half of their employees are on fixed-term contracts, compared to 14.6% in Turkey and the 1 to 5% characteristic of other nations.

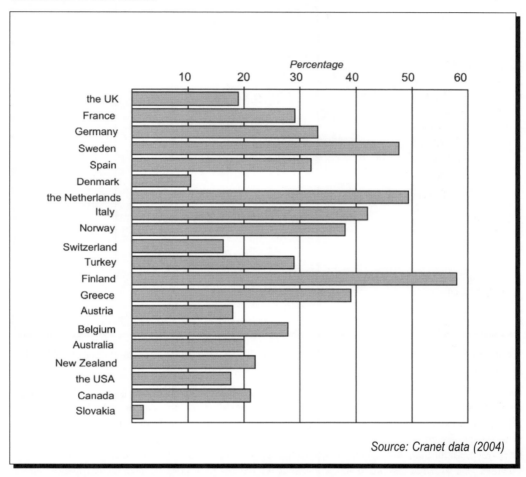

Source: Cranet data (2004)

Figure 22 *Proportion of organisations with more than 5% of employees on fixed-term contracts, across (selected) countries*

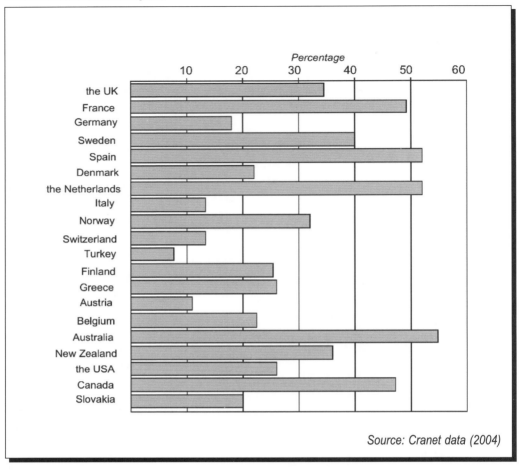

Figure 23 *Proportion of organisations with more than 5% of employees as temporary or casual, across (selected) countries*

Generally, the extent of organisations' usage of temporary and casual employees also remains limited, but as with their use of fixed-term contracts, there are some marked variations across countries (see Figure 23). To some extent, temporary work and fixed-term work seem to substitute for each other. Organisations in the Anglo-Saxon nations tend to secure numerical flexibility via the use of temporary and casual employees, rather than through fixed-term contracts. The UK, the US and New Zealand, but most of all Australia and Canada feature quite prominently in Figure 23. Some continental European nations, specifically France, Spain and the Netherlands, figure more prominently, whereas most of continental Europe features more limited use. Considered alongside the findings for the use of fixed-term contracts above, the precariousness of the situation of many Dutch employees is striking. To an extent this is expressive of the efforts made by the Dutch government to reduce unemployment in the 1990s (Visser and Hemerijck, 1997).

Subcontracting

Subcontracting is 'the displacement of an employment contract by a commercial one as a means of getting a job done' (Atkinson and Meager, 1986). For some employees this will make little difference in terms of flexibility: they might well be permanent full-time employees in the contractor firm. In many other cases, however, this system – which has always been common in industries like construction, and in countries in Asia and Africa – means the displacement of more traditional contracts of employment with individuals by contracts for services with other organisations. The employment relationship will have been superseded by a commercial relationship. The organisation that is giving out the contract will have no further concern with employment issues – these will have been passed on to the contractor. This is a common system in many of the poorer countries around the world, but is beginning to spread again among the richer countries due to cost concerns and a move towards outsourcing.

WORKING TIME FLEXIBILITY

Part-time work

The degree of flexibility in part-time work has been debated. The argument is that if someone is doing regular part-time work and has other commitments which cannot be moved, he or she is not individually very flexible. However, from the viewpoint of management, part-time employment – which in some cases can in practice be readily reduced, extended or moved to a different place in the day – is more flexible than standard full-time work.

> ### QUESTION
>
> ■ What advantages might accrue to employers and to employees from employing people on a part-time basis?

Part-time work helps managers to match the labour available to peaks and troughs in demand during the working day and week. Recruiting a few part-time workers to cover particularly busy periods, for example, can mean that other employees can work more standardised hours and the total full-time equivalent headcount can be kept down. It is also argued that judicious use of part-time employment allows employers to pay only for the most productive hours of an employee's time (the longer one works the less productive per hour one becomes). On the other hand, such arrangements can be beneficial for those with, for example, family care responsibilities who find that longer working hours exclude them from participating in the labour market. Approximately 85% of part-time workers in Europe, it can be noted, are female.

Part-time employment varies around the world. Since a substantial majority of part-time workers are female, it is no surprise to find that there is also a correlation with female participation in the labour force (Rubery and Fagin, 1993; Rubery *et al*, 1996) and indeed with childcare arrangements (Rees and Brewster, 1995). It is much used in northern Europe (over one third of the workforce in the Netherlands, a quarter of all employment in the UK and Sweden) and common in northern America, but much less common in other parts of the world.

Part-time work is an example of flexible working that provides something for the employee, involving lower pay for fewer hours, but allowing the employee time outside work for caring for children, relatives and friends, charitable work or self-actualising or emancipatory activities of his or her choosing. Most employees with part-time contracts express satisfaction with working less than full-time, given their other commitments, responsibilities and interests.

Definitions across national boundaries can be complex. Part-time work, for example, will apply to any work hours short of the normal working week for each country, which vary across the globe. Thus, in France and Belgium, part-time work is defined as four-fifths or less of the collectively agreed working time; in the Netherlands and the USA as less than 35 hours per week; in the UK as less than 30 hours, with lower thresholds in relation to social security contributions. Elsewhere, the norm is concentrated around 25–30 hours per week (see Bolle, 1997, or Brewster *et al*, 1996, for more complete listings).

Nonetheless, the detailed evidence offered by Cranet 2004 (see Figure 24) shows marked comparative variation in the use of what employers themselves regard as part-time employees. The Anglo-Saxon nations are quite heavy users comparatively speaking. However, the heaviest users are amongst the smaller nations of continental Europe, although this is not to say that all small continental European nations feature heavy use – witness Finland. The position of the Netherlands is again striking, over three-quarters of organisations reporting that more than 10% of their employees are part-time. To a degree this can be considered expressive of the notion of part-time in the Netherlands – those working less than 35 hours. But this definition of part-time is the same as that held in the USA, and rather similar to that held in the UK (less than 30 hours).

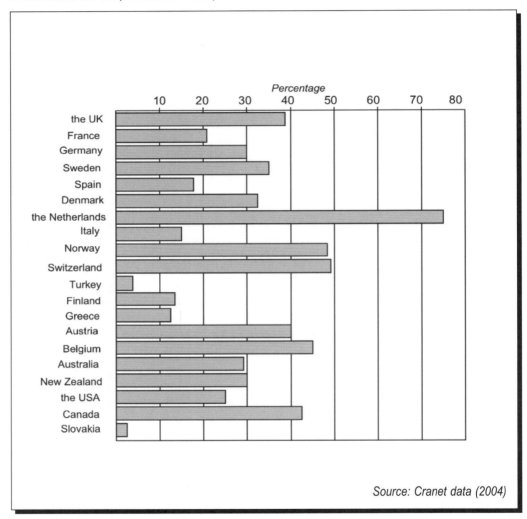

Source: Cranet data (2004)

Figure 24 *Proportion of organisations with more than 10% of employees as part-time, across (selected) countries*

In some respects, job-sharing represents a development of the established idea of part-time work. It remains rather uncommon, Cranet 2004 showing only 5–10% of organisations in the vast bulk of nations reporting that more than 5% of their employees job-share. However, as usual there are some exceptions to the general tendency. Over two-fifths (42.4%) of Slovakian organisations report that more than 5% of their employees job-share. In Turkey, the proportion is more than a quarter (27.6%). These comparatively very high incidences are perhaps the flip side of the very limited use of part-time employment in these two countries.

Other forms of working time flexibility

Annual hours contracts typically offer full-time employment without necessarily offering consistency in hours week-to-week. From the employers' point of view, they offer a means of adapting to variations in the amount of work to be done. From the employees' point of view, though, they can be very disruptive. Although annualised hours contracts have been becoming increasingly common (see Figure 25), their incidence across nations varies markedly. It is in France that they figure most prominently, around half of organisations there reporting that more than 50% of their employees are on annual hours contracts. This is in large part a response to the French working hours legislation, which reduced the length of the working week. Employers and employees often came to the view that the mutually beneficial way of handling this working time reduction was that employees would work more variable hours across the weeks of the year. In principle, annualised hours offer the possibility that parents might be able to work heavier weeks in school terms in order to be able to take the entirety of school vacations with their children, although it is not clear that this is common in practice. This is an indication of a more general principle – that annualised hours tend to imply flexibility from the point of view of the employer.

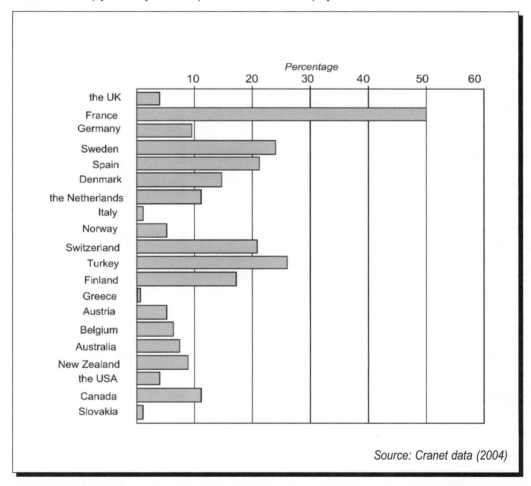

Source: Cranet data (2004)

Figure 25 *Proportion of organisations with more than half of employees on annual hours contracts, across (selected) countries*

There is a great variety of other flexible working time patterns available – some of them very new – but in general they are less widespread. They include such approaches as shift-working, weekend-working and term-time working, networking, working as consultants or government-sponsored trainees, and tele-working. All are much smaller in extent – but all are growing.

The rationales for flexibility

Working patterns and contracts are established according to a complex set of factors – employers' needs, competition, the sales market, the availability of particular skills, the bargaining power of trade unions, managerial understanding, tradition, and employment legislation. The use of these various practices varies considerably by country. And so do the implications. Being on a short-term contract in a country with generous social security provision has a completely different connotation from being on such a contract in a country where such provision is very limited.

In some versions of HRM, particularly those that deal with the soft, friendly face of HRM, concentrating on 'high commitment', 'high performance', 'competence' and 'human resource development', the evidence in this chapter is particularly challenging. How are organisations to develop highly committed, energised and enthusiastic contributors to managerial objectives when the organisations' commitment to the employees is severely limited? Why should organisations train and develop people when the costs of doing so are the same as the costs for the long-term full-time employees, but the payoff is obviously limited to the proportion of time the employee is at work or the length of his or her association with that organisation? It is no surprise to find that, in practice, employers provide much less training or development for atypical workers (Brewster *et al*, 1996).

THE IMPLICATIONS OF FLEXIBILITY

ACTIVITY

- Describe some of the implications of the development of flexible working patterns and work–life balance policies for employers, for individuals, and for the state.

For employers, flexibility offers significant advantages. They are able to develop ways of employing people, or even getting the work done without employing people, that more closely match the need for the work. Organisations need flexibility, and in particular time and contractual flexibility, in order to ensure the most economic use of labour. But increased flexibility is not without its problems for organisations. Less training of flexible workers means lower skill levels in a society. Other problems centre on the difficulty of establishing policies, administering the system, communication and commitment. There are obviously benefits for employers in matching better the work they pay for and the work they get done. Arguably, however, the major benefit of the use of flexibility for organisations lies in the transfer of cost and risk from the organisation to individuals and to the state, or to society as a whole (Brewster, 1998; Sparrow and Cooper, 2003).

For individuals, flexible working patterns can provide additional opportunities to work, can enable family incomes to be supplemented, and can allow work to be fitted in with family responsibilities. However, the transfer of the costs means that flexible work is often low-paid. It is the individual and the family who bear the cost of not working standard hours and contractual arrangements. In addition, workers may well be expected to arrange for and to pay for their own training and skill updating. The transfer of risks means that many individuals and the families that they support cannot be sure of employment much beyond the immediate future. This becomes more than just an immediate financial problem for the families involved; it has a major effect on the rest of their lives, because so much of our society is built on the assumption that most people have standard employment. Thus the ability to purchase goods on credit, to have bank loans, to arrange housing and to provide pension arrangements are still sensitive to some degree in every European country on individuals' having a full-time, long-term job.

Governments also have to address these changes in labour markets more directly. One important implication concerns the effect on government finances. Even if it reduces unemployment, flexible working tends to increase the number of those in employment who, because they do not work enough hours a week, or enough weeks in the year, end up paying no taxes.

For society in general the costs have been transferred directly, because the state supplements low earnings and provides support for the unemployed. The costs have also been transferred indirectly in that the requirements for training, for health and safety and for the provision of other relevant benefits have to be borne by the state. The transfer of risk means that during periods of unemployment – between short-term contracts, for example – the state is again expected to provide support. And there are arguably many indirect aspects of this transfer in terms of the effects of insecurity and stress on health levels, in terms of pension arrangements and in terms of housing support.

It appears, for instance, that part-time jobs are likely to be replacing full-time jobs on a one-for-one basis, rather than that full-time jobs are being replaced by two part-time jobs to cover the same number of hours. Even if two people were getting work rather than one, though, the overall benefit might be extremely limited if one or both remain on income support, do not pay tax (or even in many cases National Insurance) and have little extra money to spend in the economy. The increased flexibility in Europe means that risks and costs have been transferred from employers to individuals and to the state. This may make the employing organisations more efficient, but not necessarily make the country more competitive.

WORK–LIFE BALANCE

Debate around work–life balance occurs in the context of the changing future of work, flexible working patterns, a feminisation of the labour force in many countries, and, increasingly and perhaps belatedly, a reassessment by many employees of the priorities in their lives. Organisational initiatives may range from symbolic devices to counteract poor publicity, through efforts to deal with an immediate problem of recruitment or retention, to efforts to foster a new atmosphere and perhaps greater personal integrity and a more sincere workplace. Currently, rhetoric about a new balancing often exceeds the reality in many workplaces.

There is currently little cross-national comparative research on work–life balance. Wood's (1999) research on the UK suggested that the work–life balance agenda may be more prominent in the public sector (due to political accountability), in larger private sector companies (due to visibility but also due to the greater influence of unions), in organisations taking a broader performance-informed approach to HRM, and in organisations with a higher percentage of women employees. This rather understates the importance of the labour market to the differential development of work–life balance policies for different grades or job families. Often, attention is focused on a particular segment of the workforce regarded as particularly valuable or likely to leave, so that the scope of discussion of work–life balance is heavily conditioned by the labour market situation and its perceived implications for organisational performance.

To some extent the language of 'work–life balance', like the language of flexbility, is problematic. In practice, life and work overlap and interact, work giving substantial meaning to peoples' lives:

> '**In the experience of most people no clear-cut distinction can be established between the world of work and the world of family, friends and social networks and community. In practice, over the length of our lives it is impossible to establish neatly-constructed demarcation lines. Moreover, the word – balance – implies the existence of a settled**

> **equilibrium that can be achievable between paid employment and a life outside the job. This is highly questionable.'**
>
> *Taylor (2002)*

In this context, terms such as 'reconciliation' or 'synergy' may be more appropriate to the discussion, crystallising better the issues at stake (Taylor, 2002). The terms 'work–family conflict' and 'family–work conflict' capture the agenda in a more striking way. Whatever the terminology, the work–life balance agenda implies a questioning of the effectiveness of the rigidity of many of the established dimensions of paid work, around the regularity of hours, work location, and indeed the effectiveness of long hours where employees feel torn, resentful or experience self-loathing as a result of their time-commitment to work. Initiatives in work–life balance offer employees more autonomy in seeking to reconcile their differing roles, allowing them to re-order the boundaries between work and non-work.

Very often, discussion of work–life balance revolves around a need for 'family-friendly' policies, in recognition of the very severe difficulties which work can pose for family roles, and of the significance of those roles to so many employees, most obviously in terms of parenting but also in terms of caring for older relatives or friends. Of course, the work–life balance agenda can also encompass consideration of the implications of employees' commitments to voluntary work, or any activity that in some respects competes for attention with paid work roles.

The 'encompassing' service-intensive welfare states of the Nordic countries feature more or less universal childcare provision, the bulk of which is orchestrated by national or regional government (Esping-Andersen, 1999). Though less comprehensive, France has extensive provision by the state, particularly for children aged three and over. To a significant extent, the work–life balance agenda in the Nordic countries in particular has, through childcare initiatives and other support for parents, been taken out of the hands of employers. The quality of working life agenda pursued systematically by the Nordic trade unions has also sought to reduce working time and to allow employees more easily to balance home and work responsibilities. Employers have often responded creatively to the pressure applied by unions in negotiations at multiple levels, bringing, as we have seen, more flexible working in the Nordic nations, and productivity and competitiveness has been combined to a remarkable extent with improvements in the quality of working life (see Gallie, 2003).

Chandola *et al*'s (2006) comparison of the UK with Japan and Finland shows that it is in the latter that employees have the best mental health, and in which work–family and family–work conflicts have the least severe impacts on mental health. This is particularly the case for those employees who are single parents. Japanese employees experience the poorest mental health, their work–family and family–work conflicts showing the most severe impact. Where employers act with less institutional encouragement and support for the work–life balance agenda than experienced in Finland, or the Nordic countries more generally, the development of an informed and sophisticated approach is more problematic in important respects. Increasingly, however, organisation- or workplace-level initiatives can draw on wider debate and experience.

QUESTION

- What advantages might accrue to an organisation from the introduction of 'family-friendly' policies?

Employers rarely introduce policies that make for a better work/non-work balance because they feel altruistic. Those in the private sector need to make money and those in the public sector need to provide cost-effective services. But there are arguments that employers can gain considerable benefits from such policies: more motivated and committed staff, less absenteeism, less labour turnover, etc (see box below for an example from BT).

Family-friendly policies in the UK

Bond *et al* (2002) found that in the UK organisations adopting family-friendly policies did so to retain staff. They also found, though, that arrangements were often not formalised and considerable discretion was left to line managers. Moreover, their work suggested that where unions were present, family-friendly provision was more widespread. The latest Workplace Employment Relations Survey of the UK showed that family-friendly practices are spreading rapidly, but by 2004 most managers still felt that it is employees', not employers', responsibility to balance life and work. This view is on the decline, however, perhaps in response to a series of public policy initiatives aimed at improving the position of working parents.

Case study

Work–life balance at BT

British Telecom's Work–Life Balance project evolved over two decades of continual development and experimentation, and is remarkable in the UK context. In 1998 the results of a staff survey revealed that 62% of its managers felt that their lives were too skewed towards work and 33% said they were not prepared to accept promotion or greater responsibilities because of the effect on their domestic life. In response, BT committed to substantial investment in pursuing a flexible employment strategy. The HR team piloted a Freedom to Work programme, offering staff the chance of arranging their own work hours and patterns, subject to the achievement of business objectives, although usually these hours are organised around a total 41-hour working week. BT extended the initiative to 8,000 employees. The key reference is the psychological contract between employer and employee, and the need for people to feel that they are valued. There is evidence of an improvement in productivity within teams, a reduction in absenteeism, and, most strikingly, a continued improvement in the return rate after maternity leave, which now stands at 96%. A number of key roles support the development and extension of such policies – the Director of Employment Policy, the Social Policy Finance Manager and the Manager of Employment Philosophy – and a senior executive forum also helps to develop the strategy. The BT intranet is used to promote and enable the Work–Life Balance programme.

Source: Higginbottom (2001)

Flexi-time

In some respects flexi-time offers something similar to annual hours contracts, although it tends to be led by the employee rather than the employer. The comparative variation in incidence is enormous. Flexi-time is very common in the Nordic nations, approximately 35% of all organisations across the four mainland countries reporting its use for more than half of their employees. Among these nations, usage in Sweden is the heaviest, and we might reckon its incidence to be expressive of the extent of the feminisation of the labour force, particularly as this extends to full-time work, given the high figures for female participation in the Nordic countries. However, incidence even in Sweden is not as great as in Germany, which stands out in Figure 26. High incidence also in Austria, Switzerland and Belgium suggests that flexi-time is more common where collective bargaining is weightier and industrial relations more heavily subject to legislation. In these circumstances it seems that employees often expect, and employers often grant, the flexibility which flexi-time gives.

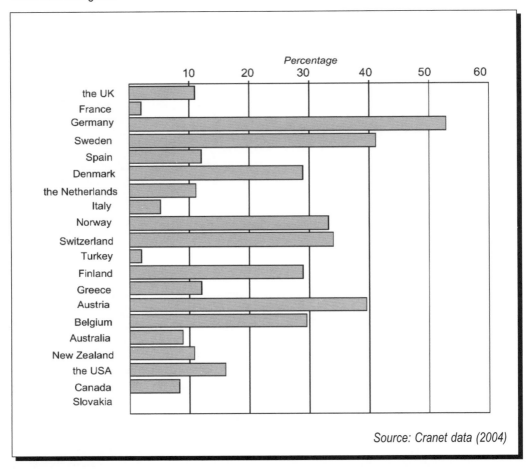

Source: Cranet data (2004)

Figure 26 *Proportion of organisations with more than half of employees on flexi-time, across (selected) countries*

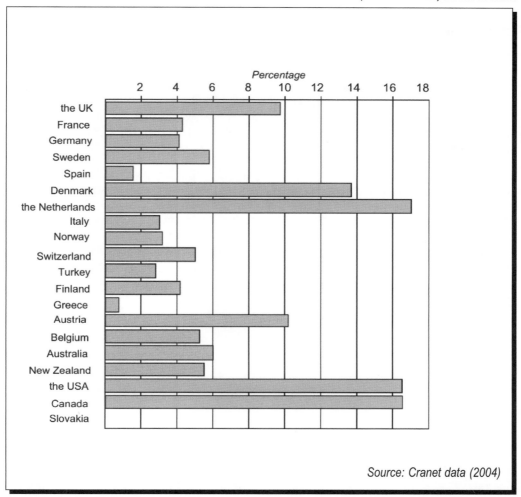

Figure 27 *Proportion of organisations in which more than 5% of employees are on a compressed working week, across (selected) countries*

Compressed working weeks

Compressed working weeks offer an alternative means of balancing commitments to and outside work, and are often used by parents of pre-school children. Cross-national comparative variation in organisational use is marked. North America and the UK feature comparatively extensive use of this relatively new practice, around 10 to 20% of organisations having 5% or more employees on compressed working weeks (see Figure 27). In continental Europe, Dutch and Austrian organisations are comparatively commonly making some use of compressed working weeks, as are Danish organisations, although interestingly the practice is not particularly common in the remainder of the Nordic countries. Mediterranean countries feature very little use of compressed working weeks, whereas the practice is completely unknown in Slovakia. Clearly, there is not only much comparative variation in the extent of use of compressed working weeks, but in the intensity of the concentration of this use within nations. To a degree, the remarkable cross-national comparative variation probably expresses the use of other practices with similar implications. It is notable, for example, that the Anglo-Saxon nations feature relatively limited use of flexi-time. In addition, of course, there are real differences in the extent to which the organisations of different nations have begun to operationalise forms of working which accommodate work–life conflicts more readily.

Total working hours

Much of the debate around work–life balance centres on the manner in which working time is structured, in particular with regard to the rigidity of the commitment which employees must make. Yet total working time is of obvious relevance to work–life balance. The comparative differences are immense. Within the EU, the number of public holidays per year ranges from 8 to 14, with the UK at the bottom and Portugal at the top. This is just the beginning of differences even in holidays, however. The average number of vacation days (including public holidays) taken by employees around the world varies enormously, from 13 days in the USA, to 28 days in the UK and 42 days in Italy (ONS, 1999).

Weekly working hours in the UK are famously long compared to other European countries, such that the EU's Employment in Europe survey reported that almost half of the 7 million male workers working over 48 hours a week in the EU were employed in Britain. Much of this overtime is not specifically rewarded. The 1999 Social Trends survey reported that 42% of UK employees said that they always or often left work in a state of exhaustion. The Working Time Regulations have had little effect on reducing these extreme working weeks (CIPD, 2001). Working hours seem to be longer in the USA and very long indeed in Japan; the accompanying problems manifest in those countries too.

Country	Average annual hours, manufacturing
the USA	1,980
Japan	1,978
Canada	1,902
the UK	1,839
Italy	1,741
Austria	1,668
Norway	1,659
Sweden	1,646
Finland	1,633
France	1,610
Germany	1,521

Table 20 *Average annual working time in manufacturing, Vernon, 2000*

Unsurprisingly in this context, 'working sick' is a common experience for British employees, and appears shared with employees in the USA and Japan. Indeed, increasingly in the UK, as in Japan, a small but growing minority of employees are expected to take days off as part of their holiday entitlement rather than to take them as 'off sick' not only when their children are sick but when they themselves are so sick that they cannot work. This sort of situation is much rarer in the bulk of the advanced industrialised world.

Differences in vacation time, in the normal working week, in overtime, and in sickness absence, but also in study leave, result in striking differences in average annual hours actually worked across countries. There has been little comparative change in this regard since the mid-1990s, for which Vernon (2000; Table 20) provides comparative data centring on from the manufacturing sector. The very long hours worked in the UK are exceeded by those in the USA, Canada and Japan. Hours in emerging and developing nations are, as far as we can tell, generally much longer than the longest reported here for the established advanced industrialised world. Vernon (2000) shows that within the advanced industrialised world annual hours are strongly related to the significance of collective bargaining – this would of course also account for the very long hours of work in emerging countries, where collective bargaining is generally weak.

It is clear that there are associations between total working hours and health. Sparks *et al* (1997) established correlations between work hours and poorer physiological health, gauged by indicators including headaches, work accidents, coronary heart disease and general health symptoms. Long hours also showed a stronger correlation with psychological health, gauged by (for example) irritability/tension, problems with relationships, lack of concentration, tiredness, role strain, anxiety, frustration, insomnia, depression, and general mental stress.

SUMMARY

This chapter has examined the concept of flexibility and work–life balance. We saw how the established systems and procedures are changing so that the nature of work becomes more varied, more difficult to manage and, potentially, more cost-effective for employers and, increasingly, more appropriate for employees. There are some general trends in flexibility which seem to be happening in many countries: there is a widespread move to increase the extent of flexibility within the workforce. We also noted, however, that different countries are doing very different things in each of these areas, with sustained idiosyncrasies. The nature, extent and implication of flexible working and work–life balance initiatives vary markedly between countries. Companies are constrained or influenced at a national level by culture, financial and corporate governance arrangements, legislation, training provision and multi-employer agreements. At the organisational level, companies are constrained by trade union involvement and consultative arrangements. In the light of the differences in the institutional, regulatory and cultural arrangements we might expect these different patterns of contingent employment use to continue.

LEARNING QUESTIONS

- Do the differences in flexible and work–life balance practices discussed in this chapter constitute a barrier to multinational corporations' transferring personnel policies and practices across borders?

- Why do countries respond differently in terms of flexibility and work–life balance to what seem similar economic pressures?

- What country factors does an HR manager need insight into in order to understand the flexibility and work–life balance trade-offs that are preferred in any particular country?

Given the imperatives of modern capitalism, should we expect convergence across countries, or at least convergence across the national operations of multinational corporations?

REFERENCES

Aparicio-Valverde, M. and Soler, C. (1996) 'Flexibility in Spain', in *E Working Time and Contract Flexibility.* Report prepared for the European Commission, Directorate-General V. Centre for European HRM, Cranfield University

Arthur, L. (2002) 'Work–life balance: towards an agenda for policy learning between Britain and Germany'. Survey report. Anglo-German Foundation for the Study of Industrial Society

Atkinson, J. (1984) 'Manpower strategies for flexible organisations', *Personnel Management*, 16 (8): 32–5

Atkinson, J. and Meager, N. (1986) 'Is flexibility just a flash in the pan?', *Personnel Management*, 18 (9): 26–9

Bevan, S. (1996) *Who cares? Business benefits of carer-friendly employment policies*. Brighton, Institute for Employment Studies

Bielenski, H., Alaluf, M., Atkinson, J., Bellini, R., Castillo, J. J., Donati, P., Graverson, G., Huygen, F. and Wickham, J. (1992) *New Forms of Work and Activity: A survey of experiences at establishment level in eight European countries*. European Foundation for the Improvement of Working and Living Conditions, Working Papers, Dublin

Blyton, P. (1992) 'Flexible times? Recent developments in temporal flexibility', *Industrial Relations Journal*, 23 (1): 26–36

Bolle, P. (1997) 'Part-time work: solution or trap?', *International Labour Review*, 136 (4): 1–18

Bond, S., Hyman, J., Summers, J. and Wise, S. (2002) *Family-friendly working: putting policy into practice*. York, Joseph Rowntree Foundation

Brady, D. (2002) 'Rethinking the rat-race', *Business Week*, 26 August: 142–3

Brewster, C. (1998) 'Flexible working in Europe: extent, growth and challenge for HRM', in P. Sparrow and M. Marchington (eds) *HRM: The new agenda*. London, Pitman

Brewster, C. and Holt Larsen, H. (2000) 'Flexibility in HRM', in C. Brewster and H. Holt Larsen (eds) *Human Resource Management in Northern Europe*. Oxford, Blackwell

Brewster, C. and Tregaskis, O. (2001) 'Adaptive, reactive and inclusive organisational approaches to workforce flexibility in Europe', *Comportamento Organizacional e Gestão*, 7 (2): 209–32

Brewster, C. and Tregaskis, O. (2002) 'Convergence or divergence of contingent employment practices? Evidence of the role of MNCs in Europe', in W. Cooke (ed.) *Multinational Companies and Transnational Workplace Issues*. New York, Greenwood

Brewster, C., Tregaskis, O., Hegewisch, A. and Mayne, L. (1996) 'Comparative research in human resource management: a review and an example', *International Journal of Human Resource Management*, 7 (3): 585–604

Brewster, C., Mayne, L., Tregaskis, O., Parsons, D., Atterbury, S., Hegewisch, A., Soler, C., Aparicio-Valverde, M., Picq, T., Weber, T., Kabst, R., Waglund, M. and Lindstrom, K. (1996) *Working Time and Contract Flexibility*. Report prepared for the European Commission, Directorate-General V. Centre for European HRM, Cranfield University

Buckley, P. and Muccielli, J. (1997) *Multinational Firms and International Relocation*. Cheltenham, Edward Elgar

Chandola, T., Martikainen, P., Bartley, M., Lahelma, E., Marmot, M., Sekine, M., Nasermoaddeli, A. and Kagamimori, S. (2006) 'Does conflict between home and work explain the effect of multiple roles on mental health? A comparative study of Finland, Japan and the UK', *International Journal of Epidemiology*, London, University College

Chartered Institute of Personnel and Development (2001) *Working Time Regulations: Have They Made A Difference?* London, Chartered Institute of Personnel and Development

Covaleski, M. A. and Dirsmith, M. W. (1988) 'An institutional perspective on the rise, social transformation, and fall of a university budget category', *Administrative Science Quarterly*, 33: 562–87

De Grip, A., Hoevenberg, J. and Willems, E. (1997) 'Atypical employment in the European Union', *International Labor Review*, 136 (1): 49–72

Delsen, L. (1991) 'Atypical employment relations and government policy in Europe', *Labor*, 5 (3): 123–49

Dickmann, M. (1999) *'Balancing Global, Parent and Local Influences: International human resource management of German multinational companies'*. PhD thesis, University of London, March

Due, J., Madsen, J. S. and Jensen, C. S. (1991) 'The Social Dimension: convergence or diversification of IR in the Single European Market?', *Industrial Relations Journal*, 22 (2): 85–102

Economist (1999) 'A survey of Germany: the Berlin Republic', *Economist,* 350, 8105: 10

EIU (1994) *Country Report: Spain*. London, Economic Intelligence Unit

Esping-Andersen, G. (1999) *Social Foundations of Post-Industrial Economies*. Oxford, Oxford University Press

Filella, J. and Soler, C. (1992) 'Spain', in C. Brewster, A. Hegewisch, L. Holden and T. Lockhart (eds) *The European Human Resource Management Guide*. London, Academic Press

Freedman, A. (1986) 'Jobs: insecurity at all levels', *Across the Board*, 23 (1): 4–5

Gallie, D. (2003) 'The quality of working life: is Scandinavia different?', *European Sociological Review*, 19 (1): 61–79

Goodhart, D. (1994) *The Reshaping of the German Social Market*. London, Institute of Public Policy Research

Higginbottom, K. (2001) 'Flexible working policy rings in rewards for BT', *People Management*, 27 September: 11

Hyman, R. and Ferner, A. (eds) (1994) *New Frontiers in European Industrial Relations*. Oxford, Blackwell

Lane, C. (1989) *Management and Labour in Europe*. Aldershot, Edward Elgar

Lane, C. (1992) 'European business systems: Britain and Germany compared', in R. Whitley (ed.) *European Business Systems*. London, Sage

Miguelez, F. and Prieto, C. (1991) *Las Relaciones Laborales en España* (Industrial Relations in Spain). Madrid, Siglo Veintiuno

Morishima, M. and Feuille, P. (2000) 'Effects of the use of contingent workers on regular status workers: a Japan US comparison'. Paper presented at the IIRA conference, Tokyo, Japan

Morley, M., Brewster, C., Gunnigle, P. and Mayrhofer, W. (2000) 'Evaluating change in European industrial relations: research evidence on trends at organisational level', in C. Brewster, W. Mayrhofer and M. Morley (eds) *New Challenges for European Human Resource Management*. Basingstoke, Macmillan

Muller, M. (1997) 'Institutional resilience in a changing world economy? The case of the German banking and chemical industries', *British Journal of Industrial Relations*, 35 (4): 609–26

O'Brien, L. (2001) 'Unions seek big break in bank holiday drive', *People Management*, 13 September: 12

Office for National Statistics (1999) *Social Trends*. London, Office for National Statistics

Plews, T. J. (1988) 'Labour force data in the next century', *Monthly Labour Review*, 113 (4): 3–8

Polivk, A. E. and Nardone, T. (1989) 'The definition of contingent work', *Monthly Labour Review*, 112, 9–16

Rees, B. and Brewster, C. J. (1995) 'Supporting equality: patriarchy at work in Europe', *Personnel Review*, 24 (1): 19–40

Rubery, J. and Fagin, C. (1993) 'Occupational segregation of women and men in the European Community', *Social Europe* 3

Rubery, J., Fagin, C., Almond, P. and Parker, J. (1996) *Trends and prospects for women's employment in the 1990s*. Report for DGV of European Commission, UMIST, Manchester

Seneviratna, C. and Turton, S. (2001) 'Dependents' day', *People Management*, 7 (24): 38–40

Sparks, K., Cooper, C. L., Fried, Y. and Shirom, A. (1997) 'The effects of hours of work on health: a meta-analytic review', *Journal of Occupational and Organizational Psychology*, 70: 391–408

Sparrow, P. R. and Cooper, C. L. (2003) *The Employment Relationship: Challenges facing HR*. London, Butterworth-Heinemann

Taylor, R. (2002) *The Future of Work–Life Balance*. Swindon, Economic and Social Research Council

Tregaskis, O. and Brewster, C. (2006) 'Converging or diverging? A comparative analysis of trends in contingent employment practice in Europe over a decade', *Journal of International Business Studies*, 37 (1)

Tüsselmann, H.-J. (1999) 'Standort Deutschland: German Direct Foreign Investment – exodus of German industry and export of jobs', *Journal of World Business*, 33 (3): 295–313

Vernon, G. (2000) 'Work Humanization: comparative historical developments in the manufacturing sectors of advanced capitalist societies, 1960–1995'. Unpublished PhD thesis, University of Warwick, June

Visser, J. and Hernerijck A. (1997) *A Dutch Miracle*. Amsterdam: Amsterdam University Press

Wood, S. (1999) 'Family-friendly management: testing the various perspectives', *National Institute for Economic Research*, 168, April 2/99: 99–116

Comparative HRM: employee relations and communications

CHAPTER OBJECTIVES

When they have read this chapter, students will:

- understand the range of approaches to communication and consultation between managers and subordinates in Europe and around the world, especially the link between collective and individual communications

- understand the role of national cultures and institutions in influencing those communications

- be aware of the differences in the meaning and role of trade union membership in different countries, and how that relates to communication.

INTRODUCTION: COMMUNICATIONS WITHIN ORGANISATIONS

Effective communication is at the heart of effective human resource management (Buckley *et al*, 1997). It is argued that it can:

- foster greater commitment (Dutton *et al*, 1994; Kane, 1996; Lippit, 1997)

- increase job satisfaction (Miles *et al*, 1996)

- act as a conduit for the promotion and development of collaboration between organisational stakeholders (Folger and Poole, 1984; Monge and Eisenberg, 1987; Bolton and Dewatripont, 1994; Mintzberg *et al*, 1996)

- facilitate the diffusion of teamwork (Mulder, 1960; Barnes and Todd, 1977; Daft and Macintosh, 1981; Lawson and Bourner, 1997; Pettit, 1997)

- improve internal control and facilitate strategy development (Baird *et al*, 1983; Fiol, 1995; Smyth, 1995; Steinberg, 1998).

The importance of communications in organisations is not confined to HRM. For management as well as organisational theorists, communication is a key element and theoretical construct, respectively, for describing and explaining organisational phenomena (see Blake and Mouton, 1976; Mosco, 1996). In his classic study, Mintzberg (1975) demonstrated that communication in its various forms is one of the key tasks of the managerial role. From a different point of view, Weick states that 'interpersonal communication is the essence of organisation because it creates structures that effect what else gets said and done by whom' (Weick, 1989; p.97). Phillips and Brown (1993), in their analysis of communication in and around organisations, suggest that it lies at the intersection of culture and power and represents a process in which actors present particular understandings of the world in the hope of creating and/or sustaining preferred patterns of social relations.

The importance of communication

In the modern organisation, the importance of effective communication is emphasised by:

- the increasing recognition that it is only through exploiting employees' ideas and talents that organisations will be able to compete and survive

- the need to convince employees that working for the organisation is something that they should be committed to and to which they should devote their ideas, their energy and their creativity

- the increased emphasis on knowledge management as a factor of competitive advantage (see Chapter 15).

It has been argued that employees are the most important stakeholders in an organisation (Garavan *et al*, 1995) and, hence, employee communication and consultation are often seen as central tenets of HRM (Buckley *et al*, 1997).

In Europe, at least, there is now clear evidence that organisations are going beyond trite statements about their employees being their major asset, to developing and increasing the amount of communication and consultation in which they involve those employees (Mayrhofer *et al*, 2000; Sisson, 1997). The European Commission's Works Councils Directive, which requires the establishment of employee works councils in organisations initially with 100 or more employees, has brought the debate on communication and consultation into even sharper focus.

However, as Morley, Mayrhofer and Brewster (2000) point out, this is a difficult area for organisations, and the literature abounds with reports of obfuscation in corporate communications (Filipczak, 1995), information distortion (Gill, 1996; Janis, 1982; Larson and King, 1996), miscommunication and problematic talk (Coupland *et al*, 1991). Calls have been made for the development of a more systematic framework for the conceptualisation, development and implementation of communication and consultation in organisations (IPC, 1987; Campbell, 1995).

Our focus in this chapter is specifically on communication within organisations – and particularly communication between managerial and non-managerial employees. We are concerned with the full range of hierarchical communications, including communications through representative structures and trade unions.

QUESTION

- Why do communication and consultation seem to be moving from the representative to the individual forms?

Types of communication

A useful distinction has been made between two types of consultation and communication, variously called 'collective', 'indirect' or 'representative' to represent one type, and 'individual' or 'direct' for the other (Gold and Hall, 1990). Within each form, the influence of employees on decision-making within the organisation may be greater or less. A useful categorisation of subjects for communication has been made (Knudsen, 1995) which divides managerial decisions into strategic, tactical, operational, and welfare. In general, the representative form has tended to address the wider strategic and tactical issues (such as investments, mergers, labour issues and pay systems), whereas the direct forms have tended to concentrate on operational workplace and working practice issues.

There are two kinds of reasons it might be argued that communication is becoming more individualised. First, because of the dominance of the US literature in our understanding of HRM and the use there of non-union companies as exemplars of good practice, there has been a tendency to associate the concept of HRM with the individualisation of communication. In addition, there is perceived to be a move away from, or even antagonism towards, the concept of industrial relations (IR), which is seen as typified by communication and consultation that is collective, particularly that which is trade-union-based (see, for example, Salaman, 1991; Bacon and Storey, 1993; Blyton and Turnbull, 1993). Many of these authors have argued that communication in modern forms of HRM will necessarily be anti-union. The focus of writings on HRM in the United States of America has been on communication with the individual.

This unitarist approach has created a picture of simple common interest between managers and the managed, an interest supposedly centred solely on the organisation's success in the marketplace (Blyton and Turnbull, 1993; Storey and Sisson, 1993). Such a development might be intended to replace or in some way subvert the practice, traditional in Europe, of involvement through trade union channels. For example, it has been argued that because of the inherent conflict of interests in the employment relationship and the indeterminate nature of labour effort, management will constantly seek to exert control over the labour process. This is aimed at serving the interests of the firm's owners. The introduction of some consultation mechanisms is designed principally to integrate employees into the organisation, but is also designed to ensure that there is no challenge to the basic authority structure of the enterprise (Marchington et al, 1992; Blyton and Turnbull, 1993).

Second, from a practical point of view, the shift of emphasis from representative to individual forms of communication may lie in the changing nature of work itself (see Chapter 9 on flexibility). Where organisations previously tended to be highly structured with clearly identifiable categories of professional and vocational groups, they are now more heterogeneous, complex and network-based. Diversity in education, experience, ethnic background, gender and/or age makes it in itself more difficult to establish or maintain a representative communication system. People may be in the organisation at different times, or may not come to any physical site, or may have a variety of different contractual relationships with the organisation. Getting people together to arrange representative consultation becomes difficult. And ensuring that the individuals chosen for that role are a fair representation of heterogeneous groups of fellow-workers becomes extremely complicated. Direct communication is more appropriate.

In all organisations there is anyway a requirement for direct communication between managers and their subordinates in order to get the work done. As organisations become increasingly knowledge-intensive (Winch and Schneider, 1993), and indeed knowledge-dependent (Conner and Prahalad, 1996; Doz et al, 2001; Grant, 1996; Mowery et al, 1996; Tallman and Fladmoe-Linquist, 1994), so it becomes ever clearer that the crucial knowledge in the organisation rests not with the senior management but with those who make up the organisation and contribute to its work. A key management task becomes understanding the people within the organisation, appreciating their talents and abilities, and being able to motivate and commit them to the organisation so that it can draw on this reservoir of skills and understanding in the most effective way.

At the same time, communication is a mechanism for the managers in the organisation to handle some of the difficulties involved in the processes of work. Managers have to develop performance requirements that are clearly recognised, set disciplinary standards that are understood and adhered to, and encourage grievances to be surfaced and dealt with. In each case, communication is vital. The question is not whether there is direct as well as indirect communication: the question concerns the balance between the two and the trends.

We examine, firstly, the representative approach, focusing on trade unions, industrial relations and various forms of 'works council' arrangements. Then we explore the growth in the various different forms of direct communication and consultation.

ACTIVITY

In your organisation – or one that you know of – what forms of up and down communication are used? Write down as many as you can.

TRADE UNION CHANNELS

The definition, meaning and reliability of union membership figures vary across countries. However, it is quite clear that in general the European countries, particularly the northern European countries, are more heavily unionised than most other areas of the world. Trade union membership in North America is much lower, and in Asia it varies considerably (Kim, 2006). Much more importantly, perhaps, the meaning of trade unionism varies considerably too. In some of the Nordic countries, for example, almost everyone at work is a trade union member and the unions see their task as looking after the interests of their members by ensuring that their employers are successful and the members have good social arrangements for when they are not employed. In other countries – in Africa, for example – only the employed elite tend to be union members and they see their task either as sustaining their position or as political (see Wood and Brewster, 2007). In some countries unions are organised by the government; in others by political parties. In some countries unions split along 'confessional' lines (linked to different religions); in others by politics, by profession or skill, by position in the hierarchy, or by employment status.

Membership

Trade union membership and influence varies considerably by country (see Table 21). Sweden has union membership of 85% of the working population, and the other Nordic countries also have union density figures of over two-thirds. Some countries have no union members at all – and there are all variations in between. The union movement lost members over the last decade and in some respects the union movement is struggling to come to terms with the modern economy. The decline of the traditional areas of union strength in primary industries and giant manufacturing plants, the unions' failure to deal effectively with internationalisation and with the developments in flexible working (Croucher and Brewster, 1998), and government and employer strategies have all led to reductions in union membership and influence. In the hostile environment of recent years, unions have suffered at least some membership loss and some level of loss of influence even in the northern European countries (Morley, Mayrhofer and Brewster, 2000). Although membership is declining slowly, there is a remarkable level of stability. Even in the UK, where there was a sustained governmental attack throughout the 1980s and much of the 1990s on the unions, trade union membership levels amongst organisations with over 200 employees remained remarkably stable (Morley et al, 1996) and have declined only very steadily since. As was noted in Chapter 4, most European countries are more heavily unionised in terms of union membership than the USA.

Country	Trade union coverage (%)	Collective bargaining coverage (%)
Austria	37	95+
Belgium	56	90+
Germany	25	68
Denmark	74	80+
Spain	15	80+
France	10	90+
the UK	31	30+
the Netherlands	23	80+
Portugal	24	70+
Sweden	79	90+
Finland	76	90+

Australia	25	80+
Japan	22	15+
the USA	13	14

Source: OECD Employment Outlook (2004); Rigby, Smith and Brewster (2004)

Table 21 *Trade union density and collective bargaining coverage, across selected countries, 2000*

Recognition

A more important issue is that of trade union recognition – whether the employer deals with a trade union in a collective bargaining relationship which sets terms and conditions for all or most of the employees (Morley *et al*, 2000). Numbers are important, but not all-important (Ferner and Hyman, 1992). The number of employees who are union members in a workplace is of less relevance than whether the employer deals with a trade union in a collective bargaining relationship that sets terms and conditions for all or most of the employees. In many European countries trade union recognition for collective bargaining is required by law. Some states, such as Germany, France and the Benelux countries, have legislation requiring employers over a certain size to recognise unions for consultative purposes. Thus, although union membership varies, bargaining coverage is high in all the countries of northern Europe: 90–95% in Denmark, Sweden, Finland and Germany, over 80% in the Netherlands, around three-quarters of the working population in Norway, and half in the UK (OECD, 1996). As Table 21 shows, in many European countries, but not generally elsewhere in the world, collective agreements that are reached through negotiations with trade unions are spread, by law in most cases, to other employees, ensuring a much wider coverage of collective bargaining than trade union membership figures alone would suggest.

The last quarter of the twentieth century saw major challenges to the established institutions of industrial relations (Hyman, 1994). The social and economic environment became increasingly hostile to unionism and to many traditional union practices and policies (Blanchflower and Freeman, 1992) and many of the gains made by the labour movement were reversed (Baglioni, 1990). The potentially convergence-encouraging processes of the European Union have, for the most part, produced little apart from working parties (Baldry, 1994).

In other parts of the world acceptance of the unions may be greatly contested, and many union members have no employer recognition of their union, so that bargaining coverage may well be far less than the coverage of the unions. For example, in Australia the decline of unions (especially in manufacturing) has meant that employers are gaining more power over the conditions of employment. Australian workplace agreements (AWAs) now cover 3,000 organisations but only a small proportion of employees (De Cieri and Kramar, 2003). In non-unionised workplaces, effective consultations about AWAs has created positive outcomes, and in line with findings from the USA and the UK, 60% of employers believed their introduction had enhanced management–employee relations by assisting in change and productivity arrangements (Patrickson and Sutiyono, 2006).

QUESTIONS

■ What are the benefits for an organisation of recognising a trade union?

■ How might this differ across countries?

Influence

The breadth of trade union membership and recognition is a critical indication of the nature of the employment relationship in European countries, but it gives no more than an indication of union influence.

Assessing trade union influence is an altogether more complex task. Unlike membership or recognition, influence is largely perceptual. (If two parties believe one is influential, then that one will be influential, regardless of how an objective observer of the 'power balance' might assess the position.) Inevitably, perceptions of union influence vary widely.

The effective influence of unions varies considerably, but is almost impossible to measure comparatively. Do the unions in South Africa, closely linked to the ANC government, exert a lot of power? Or are they limited as their key leaders join government and they feel that opposing government policy is disloyal? Research has shown that there is a higher differential between union and non-union wages in the United States (Blanchflower and Freeman, 1992), but this is probably a reflection of the weakness of the unions there since – unlike the unions in most European countries, for example – they are unable to ensure widespread coverage of the deals they make.

WORKS COUNCILS/CONSULTATION

Formal trade union recognition and influence may or may not be linked to employee involvement. In Europe it is – and employee consultation is legally required (see Brunstein, 1995; Hees, 1995; Wachter and Stangelhofer, 1995). Generally in Europe there is a close relationship between the presence of trade unions and other representational bodies (Brewster *et al*, 2007); in the USA and other countries employee consultation may be seen as an alternative to unionisation.

Employers have to deal with workplace (and often wider) works councils wherever the employees request it in, for example, the Netherlands, France and Germany. These works councils have differing degrees of power, but in this example, employee representatives can resort to the courts to prevent, or to delay, managerial decisions in such areas as recruitment, termination, or changing working practices.

Furthermore, many of the largest companies in Europe are now covered by the same European legislation – the European Works Councils Directive. There is, within the Directive, scope for differing arrangements, but again it can be seen as, and was designed to be, another pressure towards increasing communication and consultation.

Beyond the workplace, legislation in countries such as the Netherlands and Germany requires organisations to have two-tier management boards, employees having the right to be represented on the more senior supervisory board. Employee representation can, depending on country, size and sector, comprise up to 50% of the board. These arrangements give considerable (legally backed) power to the employee representatives and tend to supplement rather than supplant the union position. In relatively highly unionised countries it is unsurprising that many of the representatives of the workforce are, in practice, trade union officials. In most countries, the majority of them are union representatives. The major exception to this legally backed establishment of consultation is clearly the UK, but the European Union Directive currently requires the introduction of national works councils even here.

Sisson (2006) points out that historically the issue of international employee representation has been the concern of trade unions and organisations such as the International Labour Organisation and United Nations, but not of MNEs. However, globalisation – and within this, moves towards more regionalisation – has led to senior managers of MNEs giving more attention to the matter. There are around 47 MNEs in which there are worldwide groupings of union and works council representatives that meet regularly: 12 of these are US-owned, 7 Japanese, 6 French, 4 German, 3 Swedish and 3 UK-owned. The metalworking sector has by far the largest contingent, followed by transport, utilities, telecommunications and food sectors. By 2003 639 MNEs had established European Works Councils, thought to be about about a third of those MNEs eligible.

DIFFERENCES IN COLLECTIVE COMMUNICATION

Communication through representative bodies continues to be a growth area in most European countries (Mayrhofer *et al*, 2000). The evidence shows that more organisations have increased their use of representative bodies than have decreased them over the previous three years, except in Norway, where the latter is much above the former. Of course the most common pattern for most organisations is 'no change'. A similar pattern can be found in upward communication, although here France, Finland and Sweden, as well as the UK, report slightly more organisations decreasing their use of representative upward channels of communication.

Apart from the Republic of Ireland and the UK, in every country in northern Europe three-quarters or more of its organisations with more than 200 employees have a joint consultative or works committee. Nine out of every ten of these have existed for more than three years. In all countries, the most common response to a question about changes in the use of such committees is that there has been no change in the last three years. Where there has been a change, the number of organisations increasing their use of consultative bodies for communicating major issues to employees outweighs the number reducing their use in every country except the UK. On average, 23% of all organisations across Europe are increasing their use of representative channels of communication and only 8% are decreasing their use.

Country	Increased	Same	Decreased	Not used
the UK	25.3	42.0	4.6	28.1
France	15.3	75.9	5.1	3.6
Germany	17.1	67.9	6.5	8.5
Sweden	22.6	63.3	7.3	6.7
Spain	28.8	56.9	2.6	11.8
Denmark	37.0	46.3	4.2	12.5
the Netherlands	35.0	49.9	6.9	8.2
Italy	24.3	57.0	9.3	9.3
Norway	5.4	32.3	58.6	3.8
Switzerland	17.8	34.9	3.6	43.6
Turkey	11.9	41.5	5.1	41.5
Finland	34.7	57.3	5.2	2.8
Greece	10.6	47.5	2.1	39.7
Austria	19.4	66.0	7.8	6.7
Belgium	18.8	54.6	8.3	18.3
Australia	9.4	37.7	9.4	43.5
New Zealand	14.4	46.4	3.2	36.0
the USA	11.4	30.6	2.3	55.7
Canada	20.2	47.8	3.9	28.2
Slovakia	15.7	42.7	2.0	39.6

Source: Cranet data (2004)

Table 22 *Change in communication through representative staff bodies over the previous three years, by percentage of organisations*

INDIVIDUAL COMMUNICATION

Given the popular notions spread in the scientific and practitioner-oriented literature, individualised communication should be an important element of organisational practices. Indeed, the evidence is very clear on that point: communication to individuals is extensive – and is increasing.

We analyse developments in first downward and then upward direct communication, and we thereafter outline lateral communication.

Downward communication

Downward communication is the flow of information from management to the employees. With regard to the information channel used, the use of direct ways of communications has increased. Across Europe, direct verbal communication is increasing in up to 63% of organisations (the maximum figure, found in both Sweden and the UK), with a European average of 53%. Only 2% of organisations across Europe are using less direct verbal communication. A similar picture arises from the evidence on direct written communication to employees. Of course, with computerisation, human resources information systems and mail-merge techniques it becomes much easier for managers to write 'individually' to all staff involved in a particular change – and the opportunity is being taken. Between 30% (Norway) and 64% (the Netherlands), with a European average of 50%, of organisations have increased their use of direct written communication; 37% of organisations have increased their use of electronic communication with employees, and 47% have increased their use of team briefings. In all these cases, almost no organisations have decreased their use of communication mechanisms.

Regular meetings of the workforce are another way in which management is able to talk directly with all employees. Again, and following a by now expected pattern, increases in the use of such mechanisms outweigh the decreases by a considerable margin in nearly all European countries.

The writers on HRM who are advising employers that individual communication with their employees is vital to the future success of the organisation can take comfort from these figures. Of course, when the question is asked of senior personnel practitioners (as it was in this survey) it is possible that they are exaggerating the extent of the improvement in communication: there may be an element of wishful thinking here. However, the figures are so large and so consistent that it seems likely that they reflect some kind of reality. We are encouraged in this view by the fact that in other respects the same data does indicate that respondents are likely to report that their organisations are not following the received wisdom. Furthermore, these figures reflect similar findings in the European Foundation's EPOC survey (Sisson, 1997). It would seem that organisations are indeed communicating more with their employees.

With regard to what is communicated through these channels, this varies from case to case. Two areas of central interest for management and employees are information on:

- organisational strategy
- organisational finances.

In Europe, at least nine out of every ten organisations formally brief their managers about the organisation's strategy and financial results. However, there is a marked 'slope' in the provision of information below the managerial level. The further down the organisation one goes, the less likely employees are to be given this information. Information on strategy is provided for manual workers by 12% of organisations in Germany and 57% in Finland. Other countries in Europe have figures between these two, half having less than a quarter of organisations that inform manual workers about strategy. These are not high figures, even allowing for an expected differential between the information that would be given to managers and manual workers. Organisations become increasingly dependent on employees' knowing the corporate strategy, understanding how their own performance contributes to the implementation of the strategy, wanting to contribute in this way and being able to communicate this strategy to co-workers and external parties (customers, suppliers, public agencies, etc). The more the organisation is providing services, know-how or other types of immaterial 'products', the more an understanding of – and acceptance of – the overall corporate strategy is a prerequisite for competent performance. This is not the case to the same extent when the job involves the manipulation of physical production processes.

A similar reasoning applies to the communication of financial information about the organisation, although here the slope indicating the difference in providing information for different groups of employees is not so steep. The financial performance of the organisation is made known to employees to a greater extent than is the case in the area of strategy. In nearly two-thirds of the countries, 50% or more of the organisations also brief manual workers, the least informed group within the organisation, about financial performance. Figures 28 to 30 show the briefing patterns for various employee groups in three European countries in the area of strategy and financial performance. What is noticeable is that the slope of information reduces from management to manual worker grades, and that the slope varies in each country – so that manual workers in Sweden are considerably more likely to get such information and manual workers in Germany much less.

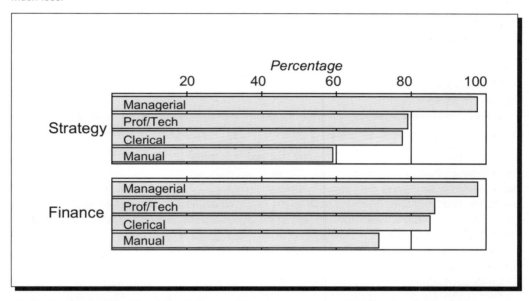

Figure 28 *Strategic and financial briefing of different groups of employees – Sweden*

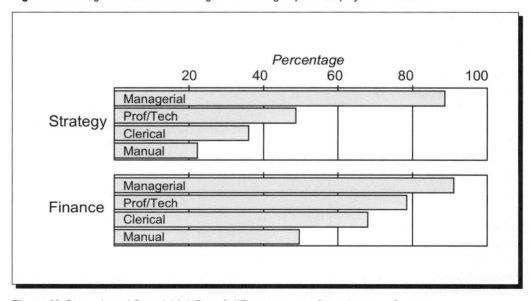

Figure 29 *Strategic and financial briefing of different groups of employees – Germany*

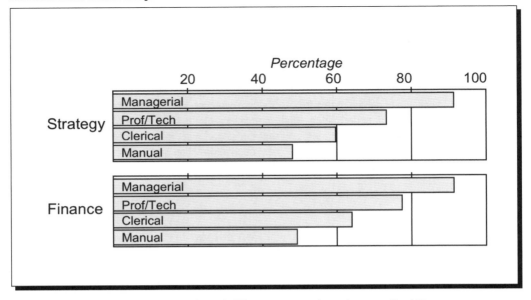

Figure 30 *Strategic and financial briefing of different groups of employees – the UK*

Northern European countries generally present their non-managerial employees with more data on these matters than countries elsewhere in Europe (Morley *et al*, 2000). In many Pacific countries information on these issues is generally only given to senior managers (Zanko, 2002). It seems that there is a widespread assumption that those lower down the organisation simply do not need to know what the organisation is trying to do, or the value or constraints imposed on the organisation by the extent to which it is succeeding in reaching those objectives.

Upward communication

Upward communication is the other key issue in terms of management/non-management communication – the feeding of information, concerns or ideas from the employees to the management. Again, we can differentiate between various communication channels especially relevant for the question of individualist- or collectivist-oriented communication.

Communication to the employee's immediate superior is, perhaps inevitably, the most important form of direct upward communication. However, we can also include here direct access to senior management, quality circles and suggestion schemes as ways in which some organisations have tried to provide channels to encourage employees to make their individual grievances known or to draw on the innovative and entrepreneurial skills of their workforce.

Both communication up to the immediate superior and direct communication with senior management has increased. In the case of communication to the immediate superior, the figures vary from 18 to 44% of the organisations, depending on the European country involved. In the case of direct communication between employees and senior management, the figures range from 12 to 39%. However, the increase in the use of quality circles tends to be less, and the net increases in the use of suggestion schemes is marginal.

Lateral communication

In recent years, considerable attention has been devoted by companies and researchers to the notions of knowledge management and knowledge flows within employing organisations. It has, indeed, been argued (Kostova and Roth, 2003; Nahapiet and Ghoshal, 1998; Tsai and Ghoshal, 1998) that this may be the factor that distinguishes the successful from the unsuccessful organisation. A company's strategic advantage is usually found in its specific knowledge (Penrose 1959; Caves 1982), and this specific knowledge (eg advanced technological expertise or specific marketing knowledge) can only be acquired within the company. It is obviously in the organisation's interests that this knowledge is shared as widely as possible. This is not as easy as it sounds. In many countries knowledge is perceived as power and individuals are reluctant to give it away. The kind of knowledge that can be shared through computerised systems tends to be the explicit knowledge that can be readily captured through such systems – and that is often much less potent than the tacit knowledge that people hold in their heads – sometimes without realising that they do. Thus, knowing how to deal with key clients in different countries may be something that an individual has only developed through extensive experience ... and it is not always straightforward to pass what has become an intuitive skill on to others.

QUESTION

- What might create difficulties in the transfer of information and knowledge between individuals within an organisation?

Among the factors that might create 'stickiness' in the passing of information are lack of understanding, or even antipathy, between different functions within the organisation; a feeling that information is power, so that those with it want to hang on to it; strong notions of hierarchy; a desire not to pass on anything that is not polished and complete; and personal predilections to share. It should be obvious by now that many of these are influenced by the culture of the country in which the individuals operate – high power distance and strong uncertainty avoidance may make knowledge-sharing less likely.

Given the differences we have identified in communication practices between countries, it is no surprise to find that cross-national communication is particularly problematic. The cultural dimensions examined in Chapters 2 and 3 have an impact here. Clearly, where, for example, hierarchies are seen as very important (power distance is high), the flow of information between different levels of the hierarchy may be more difficult – and probably so too will be the flow of information between departments. The assumption will be that this should be passed up the management chain until more senior figures can relate to each other: passing information to another department rather than to the boss may not be seen as appropriate.

The consensus now seems to be (Foss and Pedersen, 2002; Riusala and Smale, 2007; Szulanski, 1996; Zander and Kogut, 1995) that there are various factors that make knowledge 'sticky' – it does not move around organisations, and especially across national boundaries, easily. Establishing systems that allow the information to be transferred more readily becomes a key task – often one of the reasons for using expatriates. For example, in an analysis of knowledge management and expatriation within professional legal service firms (Beaverstock, 2004) it was shown that expatriation was not homogeneous for every region of the world. In some areas, expatriation followed a one-way knowledge diffusion from headquarters. In these cases, expatriates represented the traditional managerial role. In contrast, expatriates from HQs in other regions worked with locally qualified employees and expatriates of other nationalities in an environment where these different groups of people joined partnerships and led teams. The type of learning and its impact on careers is probably quite different in these two cases.

Increasingly, researchers believe that although information can be made to move more easily around organisations, knowledge cannot be captured. Systems that attempt to do that are doomed to failure – what can be done is to develop systems that enable people to meet, exchange and share information, because that way knowledge can be deployed by the individuals who are the ones who need it.

SUMMARY

Three basic themes seem to develop through our analysis of organisational communication:

- There is a new balance between individualised and collective communication.

- Although industrial relations have a stable place in European organisations, they are under threat in many other countries.
- There is a need for a modified concept of HRM.

First, although the evidence in northern Europe in particular is that both individual and representational communication are growing, it would seem that elsewhere collective communication is ceding ground to direct individual communication. The considerable moves that have been made by many employers in Europe to expand the degree of information given to the workforce, irrespective of legal requirements, is clear. This reflects a central theme of standard concepts of HRM – the requirement to involve the workforce and to generate significant workforce commitment. In Europe, however, this provision of information to and from the workforce includes communication through the formalised employee representation or trade union channels as well as the more frequently discussed individual communication.

The second, and a closely related, theme is that although trade unionism remains widespread and important among larger employers and the public sector in particular in Europe, indicating a significant degree of continuity, there have been substantial reductions in union membership even here. The figures do not reveal whether these organisations have reduced the range of issues that they bargain over, or have withdrawn recognition for some groups of staff.

Third, a theme which develops the practical implications of the first two is that, well into the new millennium, organisations in Europe will still be working with trade unions even as individual communication grows. Many of these organisations will have clearly strategic, well-thought-through and successful approaches to the management of their human resources and their relationships with the trade unions and other representative bodies within the organisation. As we argued in Chapter 4, the universalist conceptions of HRM are unable to encompass that. In practice – and we need to ensure that in our theory, as well – important and successful organisations in Europe and elsewhere will be working with their trade unions and their individual workers to ensure maximum communication up and down the organisation.

QUESTIONS

Review the national differences identified in this and the previous two chapters.

- On the basis of that evidence, what are your views about the divergence and convergence of HRM practices around the globe?

(*Try to be clear in your own mind about what is known, what exactly is diverging or converging, and what is unknown or speculation.*)

- On balance, why do you prefer one argument to the other?

LEARNING QUESTIONS

- How important, would you argue, is up and down communication within an organisation to the organisation's achieving its objectives?

- Which are the best methods to facilitate communication to and from senior managers? Are they likely to vary with different cultures?

- What might explain the fact that trade union membership is higher in some countries than in others?

- Are trade unions a positive or negative in organisational communications? Is the answer dependent upon or independent of country? Give reasons for your answers.

- Consultation with representative bodies is now required for all organisations over a certain size by the European Union. What reasoning might have led the EU to take such a step?

- In what ways might formal consultation arrangements weaken a trade union? And in what ways strengthen it? Is this dependent on country?

- What steps could be taken to facilitate communication across the national boundaries within an organisation?

REFERENCES

Bacon, N. and Storey, J. (1993) 'Individualisation of the employment relationship and the implications for trade unions', *Employee Relations*, 15 (1): 5–17

Baglioni, G. (1990) 'Industrial relations in Europe in the 1980s', in G. Baglioni and C. Crouch (eds) *European Industrial Relations: The challenge of flexibility*. Newbury Park, CA, Sage

Baird, L., Meshoulam, I. and DeGive, G. (1983) 'Meshing human resources planning with strategic business planning: a model approach', *Personnel*, 60 (5): 14–25

Baldry, C. (1994) 'Convergence in Europe: a matter of perspective', *Industrial Relations Journal*, 25 (2)

Barnes, D. and Todd, F. (1977) *Communication and Learning in Small Groups*. London, Routledge & Kegan Paul

Beaverstock, J. (2004) 'Managing across borders: knowledge management and expatriation in professional service legal firms', *Journal of Economic Geography*, 4 (2): 157–79

Blake, R. and Mouton, J. (1976) *Consultation*. Reading, MA, Addison-Wesley

Blanchflower, D. and Freeman, R. (1990) *Going Different Ways: Unionism in the US and other advanced OECD countries*. Centre for Economic Performance Discussion Paper 5, LSE, London

Blanchflower, D. and Freeman, R. (1992) 'Unionism in the United States and other advanced OECD countries', *Industrial Relations*, 31 (1): 56–80

Blyton, P. and Turnbull, P. (1993) *Dynamics of Employee Relations*. London, Macmillan

Bolton, P. and Dewatripont, M. (1994) 'The firm as a communication network', *Quarterly Journal of Economics*, 109 (4): 809–40

Brewster, C., Wood, G., Croucher, C. and Brookes, M., (2007) 'Are works councils and joint consultative committees a threat to trade unions? A comparative analysis', *Economic and Industrial Democracy*, 28 (1): 53–81

Brunstein, I. (1995) *Human Resource Management in Western Europe*. Berlin, Walter de Gruyter

Buckley, F., Monks, K. and Sinnott, A. (1997) *Communication Enhancement: A process dividend for the organisation and the HRM department?* Dublin, Dublin City University Business School

Campbell, D. (1995) *Learning Consultation: A systematic framework*. London, Karnac Books

Caves, E. (1982) *Multinational Enterprise and Economic Analysis*. Cambridge, Cambridge University Press

Conner, K. and Prahalad C. K. (1996) 'A resource-based theory of the firm: knowledge versus opportunism', *Organization Science*, 7 (5): 477–501

Coupland, N., Giles, H. and Wienmann, J. (1991) *Miscommunication and Problematic Talk*. Newbury Park, CA, Sage

Croucher, R. and Brewster, C. (1998) 'Flexible working practices and the trade unions', *Employee Relations*, 20 (5): 443–52

Daft, R. and Macintosh, N. (1981) 'A tentative exploration into the amount and equivocality of information processing in organisational work units', *Administrative Science Quarterly*, 26 (2): 207–24

De Cieri, H. and Kramar, R. (2003) *Human Resource Management in Australia: Strategy, people, performance*. Sydney, McGraw-Hill

Doz, Y., Santos, J. and Williamson, P. (2001) *From Global to Metanational: How companies win in the knowledge economy*. Boston, MA, Harvard Business School

Dutton, J., Dukerich, J. and Harquail, C. (1994) 'Organisational images and membership commitment', *Administrative Science Quarterly*, 39 (2): 239–63

EIRO (2002) *Industrial Relations in the EU Member States and Candidate Countries*. Foundation for the Improvement of Living and Working Conditions, Dublin

Ferner, A. and Hyman, R. (1992) *Industrial Relations in the New Europe*. Oxford, Blackwell

Filipczak, B. (1995) 'Obfuscation resounding: corporate communication in America', *Training*, 32 (7): 29–37

Fiol, C. (1995) 'Corporate communications: comparing executives' private and public statements', *Academy of Management Journal*, 38 (2): 522–37

Folger, J. and Poole, M. (1984) *Working Through Conflict: A communication perspective*. Glenview, IL, Scott, Foresman

Foss, N. and T. Pedersen (2002) 'Transferring knowledge in MNCs: the role of sources of subsidiary knowledge and organisational context', *Journal of International Management*, 8: 1–19

Garavan, T., Costine, P., Heraty, N. and Morley, M. (1995) 'Human resource management: a stakeholder perspective', *Journal of European Industrial Training*, 19 (10): 1–45

Gill, J. (1996) 'Communication: is it really that simple? An analysis of a communication exercise in a case study situation', *Personnel Review*, 25 (5): 23–37

Gold, M. and Hall, M. (1990) *Legal Regulation and the Practice of Employee Participation in the European Community*. European Foundation for the Improvement of Living and Working Conditions, Paper EF/WP/90/40/EN, Dublin

Grant, R. M. (1996) 'Prospering in dynamically-competitive environments: organisational capability as knowledge integration', *Organization Science*, 7 (4): 375–87

Hees, M. (1995) 'Belgium', in Brunstein, I. (ed.) *Human Resource Management in Western Europe*. Berlin, Walter de Gruyter

Hyman, R. (1994) 'Industrial relations in Western Europe: an era of ambiguity?', *Industrial Relations*, 33 (1): 1–24

IPC (1987) *Joint Consultation in Practice: A study of procedures and actions*. Dublin, Irish Productivity Centre

Janis, I. (1982) *Groupthink: Psychological studies in policy decisions and fiascos*. Boston, MA, Houghton Mifflin

Kane, P. (1996) 'Two-way communication fosters greater commitment', *HR Magazine*, 41 (10): 50–4

Kim, D.-O. (2006) 'Industrial relations in Asia: old regimes and new orders', in M. Morley, P. Gunnigle, and D. Collings (eds) *Global Industrial Relations*. Abingdon, Routledge

Knudsen, H. (1995) *Employee Participation in Europe*. London, Sage

Kostova, T. and Roth, K. (2003) 'Social capital in multinational corporations and micro-macro model of its formation', *Academy of Management Journal*, 45: 215–33

Larson, E. and King, J. (1996) 'The systematic distortion of information: an ongoing challenge to management', *Organizational Dynamics*, 24 (3): 49–63

Lawson, J. and Bourner, T. (1997) 'Developing communication within new workgroups', *Journal of Applied Management Studies*, 6 (2): 149–68

Lippit, M. (1997) 'Say what you mean; mean what you say', *Journal of Business Strategy*, 18 (4): 17–21

Marchington, M., Goodman, J., Wilkinson, A. and Ackers, P. (1992) *New Developments in Employee Involvement*. Research Series, No 2. Sheffield, Employment Department

Mayrhofer, W., Brewster, C., Morley, M. and Gunnigle, P. (2000) 'Communication, consultation and the HRM debate', in C. Brewster, W. Mayrhofer and M. Morley (eds) *New Challenges for European Human Resource Management*. Basingstoke, Macmillan

Miles, E., Patrick, S. and King, W. (1996) 'Job level as a systematic variable in predicting the relationship between supervisory communication and job satisfaction', *Journal of Occupational and Organizational Psychology*, 69 (3): 277–93

Mintzberg, H. (1975) 'The manager's job: folklore and fact', *Harvard Business Review*, July–Aug: 49–61

Mintzberg, H., Jorgensen, J., Dougherty, D. and Westley, F. (1996) 'Some surprising things about collaboration: knowing how people connect makes it work better', *Organizational Dynamics*, 25 (1): 60–72

Monge, P. and Eisenberg, E. (1987) 'Emergent communication networks', in F. Jablin, L. Putnam, K. Roberts and L. Porter (eds) *Handbook of Organizational Communication: An interdisciplinary perspective*. Newbury Park, CA, Sage

Morley, M., Mayrhofer, W. and Brewster, C. (2000) 'Communications in Northern Europe', in C. Brewster and H. Holt Larsen (eds) *Human Resource Management in Northern Europe*. Oxford, Blackwell

Morley, M., Brewster, C., Gunnigle, P. and Mayrhofer, W. (1996) 'Evaluating change in European industrial relations: research evidence on trends at organisational level', *International Journal of Human Resource Management*, 7 (3): 640–56

Mosco, V. (1996) *The Political Economy of Communication: Rethinking and renewal*. Thousand Oaks, CA, Sage

Mowery, D. C., Oxley, J. E. and Silverman, B. S. (1996) 'Strategic alliances and interfirm knowledge transfer', *Strategic Management Journal*, 17: 77–99

Mulder, M. (1960) 'Communication structure, decision structure and group performance', *Sociometry*, 23 (1): 1–14

Nahapiet, J. and Ghoshal, S. (1998) 'Social capital, intellectual capital and the organisational advantage', *Academy of Management Review*, 23: 242–66

Patrickson, M. and Sutiyono, W. (2006) 'HRM in Australia', in P. S. Budhwar (ed.) *Managing Human Resources in Asia-Pacific*. London, Routledge

Penrose, E. T. (1959) *The Theory of Growth of the Firm*. London, Basil Blackwell

Pettit, J. (1997) 'Team communication: it's in the cards', *Training and Development*, 51 (1): 12–16

Phillips, N. and Brown, J. (1993) 'Analysing communication in and around organisations: a critical hermeneutic approach', *Academy of Management Journal*, 36 (6): 1547–77

Riusala, K. and Smale, A. (2007) 'Predicting stickiness factors in the international transfer of knowledge through expatriates', *International Studies in Management and Organization*, Fall, 37 (3)

Salaman, G. (ed.) (1991) *Human Resource Management Strategies*. Milton Keynes, Open University

Sisson, K. (1997) *New Forms of Work Organisation: Can Europe realise its potential? Results of a survey of direct employee participation in Europe*. European Foundation for the Improvement of Living and Working Conditions, Dublin

Sisson, K. (2006) 'International employee representation – a case of industrial relations systems following the market?', in T. Edwards and C. Rees (eds) *International Human Resource Management: Globalization, national systems and multinational companies*. Harlow, Prentice Hall

Smyth, J. (1995) 'Harvesting the office grapevine: internal communication', *People Management*, 1 (18): 24–8

Steinberg, R. (1998) 'No, it couldn't happen here', *Management Review*, 87 (8): 68–73

Storey, J. and Sisson, K. (1993) *Managing Human Resources and Industrial Relations*. Buckingham, Open University Press

Szulanski, G. (1996) 'Exploring internal stickiness: impediments to the transfer of best practice within the firm', *Strategic Management Journal*, 17: 27–43

Tallman, S. and Fladmoe-Lindquist, K. (1994) 'A Resource-based Model of the Multinational Firm'. Paper presented at the Strategic Management Society Conference, Paris, France

Tsai, W. and Ghoshal, S. (1998) 'Social capital and value creation: the role of intrafirm networks', *Academy of Management Journal*, 41: 464–76

Wachter, H. and Stangelhofer, K. (1995) 'Germany', in I. Brunstein (ed.) *Human Resource Management in Western Europe*. Berlin, Walter de Gruyter

Weick, K. E. (1989) 'Theorising about organisational communication', in F. Jablin, L. Putnam and K. Roberts (eds) *Handbook of Organisational Communication. An interdisciplinary perspective*. Newbury Park, CA, Sage

Winch, G. and Schneider, E. (1993) 'Managing the knowledge-based organisation: the case of architectural practice', *Journal of Management Studies*, 30(6): 923–37

Wood, G. T. and Brewster, C. (eds) (2007) *Industrial Relations in Africa*. Basingstoke, Palgrave

Zander, U. and Kogut, B. (1995) 'Knowledge and the speed of the transfer and imitation of organisational capabilities: an empirical test', *Organizational Science*, 6 (1): 76–92

Zanko, M. (ed.) (2002) *The Handbook of HRM Policies and Practices in Asia-Pacific Economies*. Cheltenham, Edward Elgar

International HRM

International HRM: theory and practice

CHAPTER OBJECTIVES

When they have read this chapter, students will:

- be able to link the choice of strategic international HRM approach with international business strategy approaches
- be able to identify the strengths and weaknesses of alternative theoretical perspectives on strategic international HRM
- be able to describe the components of international HRM.

INTRODUCTION

International HRM (IHRM) examines the way in which international organisations manage their human resources in the different national contexts in which they operate. Usually, these are private sector international organisations, generally referred to in the literatutre as either multinational corporations (MNCs) or multinational enterprises (MNEs). We have already seen the extent and complexity of environmental factors such as different institutional, legal, and cultural circumstances. These affect what is allowed and not allowed in the different nations and regions of the world, but more significantly also create differences in what is seen to make for cost-effective management practices. Organisations working across national boundaries, therefore, have to agree HR policies and practices which maintain some coherence while still being sensitive to critical aspects of difference.

Traditionally much of our understanding of IHRM has been based on the study of multinationals, although this provides us with quite limited insight into the challenges that have to be managed (Sparrow and Brewster, 2006). Multinationals are presented as being economically dominant – the world's 1,000 largest companies produce 80% of the world's industrial output. Around 60% of international trade involves transactions between two related parts of multinationals. This means that the physical location of economic value creation is now difficult to ascertain:

> **'Multinational companies may increasingly operate as seamless global organisations, with teams of workers based all over the world, passing projects backwards and forwards via the Internet or the companies' private in-house intranets. This will make it more difficult for the tax authorities to demand that economic activity and value creation be attributed to a particular physical location.'**
>
> *Economist (2000; p.9)*

Global trend

Analyses by the United Nations Conference on Trade and Development show a clear trend towards increasing globalisation (as measured by the average of the ratios of foreign to total assets, sales and employment) driven primarily by an expansion of foreign direct investment (FDI) and an enlargement of international production in the world economy. 63,000 transnational corporations' trade patterns account for about two-thirds of all world trade. Indeed, the top 100 of these corporations (just 0.2% of the total number of such corporations) account for 14% of worldwide sales, 12% of assets and 13% of employment (UNCTAD, 2004).

There is clearly a trend towards globalisation and as a process it is exerting an effect inside organisations. The topic of international HRM (IHRM), or more appropriately, strategic international HRM (SIHRM), has become a separate, and crucial, field of study in its own right.

This chapter provides the theoretical underpinning of this section of the book. We explore IHRM in the following way:

- First, we explore a number of different lenses (life cycle and organisational design models) through which we can examine the subject of IHRM.

- Then we consider the key issue of differentiation *v* integration.

- Next we examine contingency approaches to strategic international HRM.

- We explore five theoretical models that can be applied to the subject.

- And we present a model of 'global HRM'.

However, before looking in detail at SIHRM theory and practice, three criticisms of the existing literature should be noted and borne in mind throughout this chapter:

1   *An over-statement of current levels of globalisation within multinationals* – In reality, stateless organisations operating independently of national borders under global rules of economic competition are few and far between (Ferner and Quintanilla, 1998; Edwards, Almond, Clark, Colling and Ferner, 2005). Multinationals continue to have assets, sales, ownership of workforces and control concentrated in home countries or regions (see the discussion of institutional theory towards the end of this chapter).

2   *The need for a broader geographical base to our understanding about IHRM* – Until recently, most of the writing in this area has reflected a predominantly US focus. There are now ever greater numbers of countries with substantial international organisations, and ever more internationally operating organisations that are *not* based in the USA. There are in practice US-global firms, European-global firms, Japanese-global firms, and others, each operating in distinctive national business systems with their own patterns of corporate governance and human resource management (Sparrow, Brewster and Harris, 2004). The strategies that they pursue towards globalisation of human resource management, and the associated shifts in centralisation and decentralisation, are therefore bounded by this inheritance. Strategic decision-making inside organisations has elements that are driven simultaneously by global, regional and national logics and these logics may not always be mutually supportive.

3   *The need to study a wider and more diverse set of organisations, beyond just multinationals* – Strategic IHRM theory has tended to overlook important areas of internationalisation. Parker (1998) noted that a true understanding of global operation must also incorporate the learning from international family business units, overseas networks of entrepreneurs, and even illegal

gangs, all of which have learned how to operate more globally. Inter-governmental international organisations, such as the United Nations, the European Union and the regional banks, and internationally operating non-governmental organisations (NGOs), such as charities and churches, employ increasing numbers of people around the world (Brewster and Lee, 2006).

ACTIVITY

Taking a global perspective

In some parts of the world, such as the Middle East (Budhwar and Mellahi, 2006), the Asia-Pacific region (Budhwar, 2004) and China (Cooke, 2005), the influence of locally based multinational enterprises (MNEs) is becoming more important. The economic and industrial development of Africa has created a harsh set of global realities that both domestic and foreign firms now have to understand (Kamoche, Debrah, Horwitz and Nkombo Muuka, 2004). Exploring IHRM issues in the Latin American context has been relatively unexplored until recently (Elvira and Davila, 2005), and even in North America there are a series of new challenges that relate to the study of IHRM (Werner, 2007). The continued expansion of the EU also adds a different flavour to the concept of internationalisation in Europe. One of the key missions of the EU – the dismantling of the barriers to the international movement of goods, labour and capital within Europe – has led to a substantial increase in cross-border trade in a region that was already well down that road. It is, therefore, unsurprising to note the extensive growth in the amount of research into IHRM now being conducted in Europe (Larsen and Mayrhofer, 2006; Brewster, Sparrow and Dickmann, 2007).

What do you think might be the unique influences on IHRM in each of the following geographies, and why are they important?

- western Europe
- transitional economies in eastern Europe
- North America
- Latin America
- Africa
- Asia-Pacific
- the Middle East.

Case study

Global consensus and regional differences on top HR issues

A survey of over 200 organisations in over 35 countries by the World Federation of Personnel Management Associations (2005) found that there was a global consensus around a range of issues and evidence of some clear regional variations. The top three global challenges were: change management (48%), leadership development (38%) and the measurement of HR effectiveness (27%). In addition to the above common challenges, in Africa 31% of organisations cite health and welfare benefit costs and learning and development as key issues. In Asia-Pacific and North America 32% and 34% respectively cite succession planning as a challenge. In Europe the additional concern for 34% of organisations is staffing, recruitment and availability of local labour. In South America 38% cite compensation.

Different levels of analysis can be used to explore the consequences of globalisation.

KEY FRAMEWORK

Different levels of globalisation

Sparrow and Brewster (2006) note that the main models and frameworks that have been used in the field concentrate on four different levels of analysis, each of which can present a different picture of the true extent of globalisation and the HRM issues that consequently have to be managed:

The globalisation of industries

Global industries are ones in which a firm's competitive position in any particular country is dependent upon competition that might exist in other countries (Makhija, Kim, Williamson, 1997). The level of international trade, intensity of international competition, worldwide product standardisation and presence of international competitors in all key international markets are all high and firms can only achieve efficiencies through global scale, local responsiveness and worldwide learning.

The relative levels of internationalisation of the firm

Estimating the degree of internationalisation of the firm is still an arbitrary process and both the choice of constructs to evidence it and the actual measures used are contentious (Sullivan, 1994). The most popular single measures used are things like foreign subsidiaries' sales as a percentage of total sales, export sales as a percentage of total sales, foreign assets as a percentage of total assets as an estimate of the material international character of an organisation, the number of foreign subsidiaries (to distinguish the degree of foreign investment), tallying of the cumulative duration of top managers' international assignments, or the dispersion of subsidiaries across cultural groupings and zones in the world.

The progressive building of international capabilities within firms

The concept of organisational capability focuses on the ability of a firm's internal processes, systems and management practices to meet customer needs and to direct both the skills and efforts of employees towards achieving the goals of the organisation. This level of analysis emphasises the way in which firms manage the resources that enable them to develop core competences and distinctive capabilities. International expansion is only possible when firms can transfer their distinctive knowledge-assets abroad into new international markets (Caves, 1996). Organisation structures have to respond to a series of strains faced by the process of globalisation (eg growth, increased geographical spread, and the need for improved control and co-ordination across business units) and organisations have to build capability in each stage sequentially in order to maintain integrated standards for some business lines but remain locally responsive in others (Hamel and Prahalad, 1985; Yip, 1992; Ashkenas, Ulrich, Jick and Kerr, 1995).

Functional realignment within globalising organisations

At this level of analysis it is argued that globalisation within organisations is driven by what happens within business functions as they seek to co-ordinate (develop links between geographically dispersed units of a function) and control (regulate functional activities to align them with the expectations set in targets) their activities across borders (Kim, Park and Prescott, 2003).

As the framework shows, we need to understand how organisations enhance the ability of specific functions to perform globally.

DEBATE

Malbright (1995; p.119) argues that true 'Globalisation occurs at the level of the function, rather than the firm.' Is this right? Using the Key Framework above, what evidence would satisfy you that an organisation was becoming truly global?

LIFE CYCLE MODELS

Theoretical frameworks in SIHRM have been – and still are – influenced by three developments that emerged in broad historical sequence (Sparrow and Braun, 2006):

- early attention to life cycle models based on the concept of 'fit' between HRM and the progressive stages of HQ management attitude to international operations, product life cycles, or organisational life cycles

- subsequent development of ideas about organisational design and the process through which strategy and structure can be matched, or ideal MNEs created

- development of integrative 'contingency' frameworks premised on the need to both integrate and differentiate HRM policies.

At first, attention was given to a series of 'life cycle models'. These models reflected the need for strategic fit between HRM policies and practices and the international evolution of the firm. One of the earliest set of studies to leave a strong mark on future SIHRM frameworks was put forward by Perlmutter (1969) and Heenan and Perlmutter (1979). Staffing decisions within MNEs were seen as a consequence of attitudes of the management at headquarters. The authors identified four main approaches to describe how MNEs deal with the staffing and management of their subsidiaries.

KEY FRAMEWORK

Attitudes to internationalisation

- In *the ethnocentric approach*, few foreign subsidiaries have any autonomy; strategic decisions are made at headquarters. Key positions at the domestic and foreign operations are held by headquarters' management personnel. In other words, subsidiaries are managed by expatriates from the parent country (PCNs).

- In *the polycentric approach*, the MNE treats each subsidiary as a distinct national entity with some decision-making autonomy. Subsidiaries are usually managed by local (host-country) nationals (HCNs) who are seldom promoted to positions at headquarters. Likewise, PCNs are rarely transferred to foreign subsidiary operations.

- *The regiocentric approach* reflects the geographic strategy and structure of the multinational. Personnel may move outside their countries but generally only within a particular geographic region (eg Europe or Asia-Pacific). Regional managers may not be promoted to headquarters positions but enjoy a degree of regional autonomy in decision-making.

- In *the geocentric approach*, the MNE takes a worldwide stance in respect of its operations, recognising that each part makes a unique contribution with its overall competence. It is accompanied by a worldwide integrated business, and nationality is ignored in favour of ability.

> PCNs, HCNs and third-country nationals (TCNs) can be found in key positions anywhere, including those at the senior management level at headquarters and on the board of directors.

Adler and Ghadar (1990), early writers in this field, suggested that organisations inevitably develop through certain stages and have to follow very different IHRM policies and practices according to the relevant stage of international corporate evolution – stages they identify as:

- domestic
- international
- multinational
- global.

Proponents of life cycle models argue that there is a link between the variation in an MNE's HRM policies and practices and either their product life cycle or the organisation's life cycle. Consequently, in all these models, human resource flexibility becomes central to effective internationalisation, and is dependent upon the capacity of HRM to facilitate the ability of the organisation to adapt to changing demands from within the MNE or from its context both effectively and in a timely manner.

These models are perhaps less useful in today's world, where many organisations are international from start-up and do not appear to progress in measured steps through all stages of internationalisation. Although these models are not without their critics (see, for example, Mayrhofer and Brewster, 1996, who argue that the vast majority of firms are ethnocentric), these classifications provide indicators for defining the predominant approach to IHRM within an international organisation.

QUESTIONS

Think about the main features of your current organisation – or one you have read about – in terms of its international HR policies and practices.

- Which orientation do they most closely resemble?
- Is this the same with key features of your organisation's international business strategy?
- Does the reality match where the organisation would like to be in theory?

DEBATE

Must organisations work through each phase in a linear sequence to build organisational capability, or can new organisational forms short-circuit the process? Does the assumption of linear and broadly sequential phases of organisational development fit the modern business environment? Can we accelerate the pace at which organisations progress through the constituent phases? Or is it foolhardy to assume that you can 'jump' a stage of development? Will there be key capabilities that an organisation will not have learned?

ORGANISATIONAL DESIGN MODELS
International organisational structures

Another development was the advent of organisation design models. The challenge of considering *how* an MNC can best implement international policies and practices was taken up by giving attention to organisation design and the match between strategy and structure.

Information processing theory

Many of the assumptions about organisation design in MNEs are driven by information processing theory. This makes a basic assumption that organisations are open social systems exposed to both external and internal sources of uncertainty (defined as the difference between information possessed and information required to complete a task). They need to develop information-processing mechanisms capable of dealing with this uncertainty (Tushman and Nadler, 1978; Egelhoff, 1991). Information processing in organisations includes the gathering of data, the processing and transformation of data into information, and the communication and storage of information in the organisation. Effective organisations create a 'fit' between their information-processing capacities and the information-processing requirements determined by such factors as their strategy, task characteristics, inter-unit interdependence and their organisational environment. MNEs are large and complex and have very high information-processing requirements because:

- a transnational strategy requires a reciprocal interdependence between affiliates and headquarters

- their focus on flexible, people-based co-ordination and control mechanisms requires high levels of informed action.

MNEs frequently reach the limits of their information-processing capacity and the competing demands of globalisation and localisation influence the choice of structure and management control processes within international organisations. A number of typologies of organisational forms have been developed. In general, these typologies denoting a move away from hierarchical structures toward network or heterarchical structures.

KEY FRAMEWORK

Different international forms

Hierarchy approaches

Under this form, control rests at the MNE's headquarters, with strong reporting and control systems for subsidiaries. Senior management is composed of parent-country nationals (PCNs). Birkinshaw and Morrison (1995) synthesise earlier work on hierarchical MNE structures to arrive at three basic assumptions underlying these configurations:

- Co-ordination costs are economised by grouping tasks according to the geographic or product markets on which they are focused.

- Critical resources (including management expertise) are held at the centre to ensure the most efficient use of scarce resources.

- The development of an appropriate system to monitor and control divisional managers ensures that the likelihood of opportunistic behaviour on their part is minimised.

Polycentric approaches

Organisations adopting this type of structure reflect less parent control and much greater autonomy of subsidiaries. The term 'multinational' is used by Bartlett and Ghoshal (1986) to define this type of organisation in that it operates in multiple geographic contexts, and functions may be duplicated internationally.

Network/heterarchy approaches

In this type of organisation the driving force is to capitalise on the advantages of global spread by having multiple centres. Subsidiary managers are responsible for their own strategy and the corporate-wide strategy. Co-ordination is needed across multiple dimensions (eg functions, products, and geography). Each subsidiary is aware of the role of the others; no subsidiary sees itself in isolation from the rest of the global organisation (Hedlund, 1986). This type of organisation has been called a transnational by Bartlett and Ghoshal (1987). Transnational organisations aim to develop a truly global culture and mindset amongst their employees.

QUESTIONS

Consider the Key Frameworks presented so far.

■ How might you combine the different forms of international operation and the different attitudes to globalisation?

■ How might the different levels of globalisation impact on an organisation's forms and attitudes?

DIFFERENTIATION AND INTEGRATION

A unifying theme throughout all SIHRM studies is the tension between differentiation and integration – sometimes referred to as the 'global v local' dilemma – as a defining characteristic of the international perspective on HRM (Ghoshal, 1987; Galbraith, 1987; Punnett and Ricks, 1992; Schuler *et al*, 1993; Evans *et al*, 2002).

QUESTIONS

Think about the answers to the following questions – questions that all international organisations face.

■ What freedom does an international organisation have in regard to imposing its own approaches to HRM on its operations throughout the world?

■ How can an international organisation, aware of the need to be sympathetic to local cultures, still ensure that it gains optimum value from its internationalism?

■ What is the relationship between the strength of organisational culture and national cultures?

Evans *et al* (2002) see this tension as a critical component of duality theory. Proponents of this perspective argue that opposites and contradictions are not 'either-or' choices but 'both-and' dualities that must be reconciled. Fit or contingency theories are seen as too static for the fast-moving modern age and do not provide an adequate conceptual basis for understanding organisational dynamics. Explaining the nature of the *local responsiveness/global integration duality*, these authors (Evans *et al*, 2002; p.83) write:

'All firms maintain corporate integration through rules, central procedures and planning, and hierarchy. But as the needs for integration grow, more rules, more control and more bosses at the centre simply

will not work, but instead will only kill local entrepreneurship and drive away good people. So these classic tools need to be complemented with more informal mechanisms for coordination: lateral relationships, best practice transfer, project management, leadership development, shared frameworks, and the socialisation of recruits into shared values. These tools of "glue technology", as we call them, are to a large degree the application of human resource management.'

A key determinant of an organisation's eventual positioning on the integration–differentiation continuum is the nature of the international business strategic approach adopted.

QUESTIONS

Ask yourself:

- What range of options is open to international organisations carrying out operations across national boundaries?
- How might each of the 'tools of "glue technology"' described by Evans *et al* (2002) affect the strategic positioning of the IHRM function?

The ways in which MNEs organise their operations globally has been the subject of extensive research by international management scholars (leading names include Prahalad and Doz, 1987; Bartlett and Ghoshal, 1989; Porter, 1990). Recurrent themes in the literature are the link between the strategy–structure configuration in MNEs and the competing demands for global integration and co-ordination versus local responsiveness. Where global integration and co-ordination are important, subsidiaries must be globally integrated with other parts of the organisation and/or strategically co-ordinated by the parent. In contrast, where local responsiveness is important, subsidiaries should have far greater autonomy and there is less need for integration.

Factors that influence the need for integration in global business strategy include:

- operational integration
- strategic co-ordination
- multinational customers.

Operational integration

This might be the case in technology-intensive businesses such as chemicals and pharmaceuticals where a small number of manufacturing sites can serve wide geographical markets. Equally, universal products or markets, such as in the case of consumer electronics, lead to high demands for integration.

Strategic co-ordination

Organisations can select specific areas where there is a need for centralised management of resources in line with strategy. For instance, significant resources such as research and development may be co-ordinated in terms of strategic direction, pricing and technology transfer, while other functions such as sales are not.

Multinational customers

Global competition places greater demands on the co-ordination of resources, equipment, finance and people. For example, it is important to co-ordinate pricing, service and product support worldwide, because a multinational customer can compare prices in different regions.

Factors that influence the need for differentiation in global business strategy include:

- market demands
- legislative demands
- political demands.

Market demands

Local responsiveness is more common where local competitors define the market competition. This is equally true where products have to be customised to local taste or regulations, such as in the case of processed foods or fashion.

Legislative demands

Local legislation may prevent full standardisation of services across the globe, leading to a requirement for more tailored approaches.

Political demands

Barriers to entry in some markets may require an organisation to set up a more autonomous subsidiary primarily staffed by host-country nationals (HCNs).

ACTIVITY

You are the HR manager of a UK-based small to medium-sized enterprise about to expand into several European countries. Based on your reading of the earlier chapters and this one so far,

prepare a brief report for the board outlining:

- the key HR issues you will face with internationalisation
- an initial project plan for the internationalisation activity.

STRATEGIC INTERNATIONAL HRM: CONTINGENCY APPROACHES

A full understanding of strategic IHRM in MNEs requires an integration of multiple disciplinary bases and theoretical perspectives (Sundaram and Black, 1992). Taylor *et al* (1996; p.960) provide a definition of strategic IHRM derived from the strategic HRM literature:

> **'Strategic Human Resource Management (SHRM) ... is used to explicitly link HRM with the strategic management processes of the organisation and to emphasise co-ordination or congruence among the various human resource management practices. Thus, SIHRM (strategic international HRM) is used explicitly to link IHRM with the strategy of the MNC.'**

Schuler *et al* (1993) offer an integrative framework for the study and understanding of strategic IHRM which incorporates features unique to the international context (Figure 31). They define strategic IHRM as (Schuler *et al*, 1993; p.720):

> **'human resource management issues, functions and policies and practices that result from the strategic activities of multinational enterprises and that impact on the international concerns and goals of those enterprises.'**

The breadth of issues is illustrated by their framework, which links strategic IHRM orientations and activities to the strategic components of the inter-unit linkages and internal operations of the MNEs. These authors again argue that the key determinant of effectiveness for MNEs is the extent to which their various operating units across the world are to be differentiated and at the same time integrated, controlled and co-ordinated. Evidence of different solutions adopted by MNEs to the tension between differentiation and integration are seen to result from the influence of a wide variety of external and internal factors.

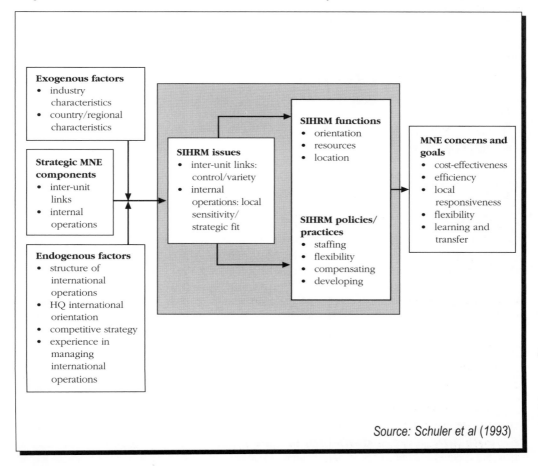

Source: Schuler et al (1993)

Figure 31 *The Schuler framework*

External factors include:

- industry characteristics, such as type of business and technology available
- the nature of competitors
- the extent of change
- country/regional characteristics (political, economic and socio-cultural conditions and legal requirements).

Internal factors include:

- the structure of international operations
- the international orientation of the organisation's headquarters
- the competitive strategy
- the MNE's experience in managing international operations.

So how does theory help international managers to make sense of these complex considerations? A recent overview of theoretical and empirical developments in the study of SHRM in MNEs identified five theoretical perspectives (Sparrow and Braun, 2006):

- resource dependency theory
- the resource-based view (RBV) of the firm
- the knowledge-based view of the firm, and organisational learning theory
- relational and social capital theory
- institutional theory.

Resource dependency theory

The resource dependency perspective focuses predominantly on power relationships and resource exchanges between an organisation and its constituencies (Pfeffer and Salancik, 1978). In this respect, organisational decision-making is not seen as an outcome of strategic choice. Rather, the theory assumes that all organisations depend on a flow of valuable resources (eg money, technology, management expertise) into the organisation in order to continue functioning. An MNC affiliate may have more or less dependence and power, as these resources are controlled by various actors, internal to the MNC (eg parent company or regional operations) or external to it (eg the stock market or government institutions). The higher the scarcity of the valued resource, the more the power of the entity that controls that resource increases. An example might be the lack of suitably qualified people in a certain country of operation, thus necessitating the costly transfer of personnel from other countries in the organisation's set-up. Equally, work permit restrictions in many countries limit the extent to which labour is completely mobile. If external parties control vital resources, an organisation is vulnerable and will strive to acquire control in order to minimise its dependence (De Cieri and Dowling, 1999). The resource dependency perspective highlights the important influence of external environmental conditions on the ability of an organisation to maximise the effectiveness of its human resources. It is one of the key building-blocks of the SIHRM frameworks discussed earlier (see Schuler *et al*, 1993; Taylor *et al*, 1996). It has been used to explain the findings of a number of studies that have looked at MNE HR practices and HR practices in joint ventures (Rosenzweig and Nohria, 1994; Hannon *et al*, 1995; Lu and Björkman, 1997).

The resource-based view of the firm

The resource-based view (RBV) of the firm has become, perhaps, the most common theoretical perspective (Wright, Dunford and Snell, 2001; Morris, Snell and Wright, 2005). This perspective sees the firm as a unique bundle of tangible and intangible resources (Wernerfelt, 1984). It stresses the inherent 'immobility' of valuable factors of production and the time and cost required to accumulate those resources. Firms accumulate different physical and intangible assets. It is only possible for others to imitate these assets if they have gone through the same process of investments and learning. This historical evolution of a firm constrains its strategic choice.

KEY FRAMEWORK

Qualities needed for a resource to provide competitive advantage

Barney (1991) and Peteraf (1993) argue that in order for firm resources to hold the potential of sustained competitive advantage they must be:

- valuable – ie the resource exploits opportunities and/or neutralises threats in a firm's environment

- rare among a firm's current and potential competitors

- imperfectly imitable – ie other firms do not possess the same resources and cannot obtain them easily

- non-substitutable with strategically equivalent resources.

The resource-based view of the firm presents the clearest argument as to *why* firms must transfer capabilities globally. MNEs operate in multiple environments and so possess variations in both their people (reflecting the skill-sets created by national business systems) and in their practices (which reflect local requirements, laws, and cultures). SIHRM practices allow a firm to capitalise on its superior skills and exploit the cultural synergies of a diverse workforce (Morris, Snell and Wright, 2005). Strategists argue that in a competitive marketplace the act of integrating disparate sources of knowledge *within the organisation*, utilising 'organisational capabilities' worldwide, becomes a source of advantage (Ghoshal, 1987; Grant, 1996; Nohria and Ghoshal, 1997). In the HR field the term 'organisational capability' was coined by Ulrich (1987). As a concept it combines ideas from the fields of management of change, organisational design and leadership. It concerns the ability of a firm's internal processes, systems and management practices to meet customer needs and to direct both the skills and efforts of employees towards achieving the goals of the organisation and is therefore about competing 'from the inside out'.

The resource-based view of the firm has been questioned recently. Although it relates to the importance of learning and knowledge transfer, it has tended to emphasise the role of the corporate centre in MNEs, which is generally assumed to be one of shaping the strategic direction of the organisation and designing the strategic change programmes pursued in the subsidiaries. Knowledge-transfer processes inside MNEs are central to the global transfer of capabilities (Foss and Pedersen, 2004; Morris, Snell and Wright, 2005). Recently, more attention has been given to the mechanisms that explain why *mutual* transfer of capability (to and from the corporate HQ and subsidiaries) is beneficial to the organisation, and how it actually happens.

QUESTIONS

- What does the pursuit of 'organisational capability' mean for the design of IHRM functions and for the role of HR business partners?

- Why might the organisational capabilities associated with strategic goals such as 'meeting customer needs' be constituted in the same way in different international operations of the firm?

- How would you use the resource-based view of the firm to explain how the following mechanisms can develop the business and technological skills needed to ensure the mutual transfer of capabilities?

    - international diversification into multiple markets

    - collaborating with organisations that have mutually complementary competences (for example, through joint ventures)

    - emphasising strategic leadership roles for national subsidiaries

    - gaining access to foreign-based clusters of excellence

    - building internal centres of excellence based on global best practice.

Although resources *can* provide a global advantage to the MNE as a whole, this is only if the knowledge, skills, and capabilities can be leveraged appropriately. We must draw upon organisation learning perspectives to understand how this can be done.

The knowledge-based view of the firm, and organisational learning theory

Given the increasing focus of attention that is given to knowledge transfer, knowledge-based views of the firm and theories of organisational learning have come to influence the field of SIHRM. We return to these issues in Chapter 16, but at this stage outline some of the relevant theory. The knowledge-based view focuses explicitly on the role of tacit knowledge as a resource.

There are two different aspects that dominate this area and can be used to explain the strategies taken by organisations (Tallman and Fladmoe-Lindquist, 2002):

- *Capability-recognising* – This strategy or perspective notes that although MNEs possess unique knowledge-based resources, these are typically treated as being home-country-based or belonging to central corporate functions and top teams. These capabilities are only disseminated to international operations on a 'need-to-know' basis.

- *Capability-driven* – This perspective (also called the dynamic capability perspective in the strategy literature) is more proactive. It is concerned with a wider process of how firms build, protect and exploit mutual capabilities between, for example, corporate HQ and subsidiaries. In terms of international management, the world is not just a source of new markets but also an important source for new knowledge.

DEBATE

In the light of the two aspects of the knowledge-based view of the firm, capability-recognising and capability-driven:

- What are the HRM implications for an organisation that pursues a capability-driven strategy rather than a capability-recognising strategy?

- How feasible is it for organisations to put this into practice?

- Will it matter to them if they cannot deliver this strategy? Why, or why not?

The organisational learning literature has had a major influence on the SIHRM frameworks discussed earlier in the chapter. These frameworks stress the effect that time and experience has on organisational learning. The capability-driven perspective has begun to dominate theory and research. It takes a very clear stance with regard to the question 'Should firms transfer HR systems?' It argues that by deploying these resources and progressively integrating them into their most-value-adding activities, organisations can build a series of important capabilities such as industry-specific skills, networks and relationships, and appropriate organisational knowledge and structures.

An important capability that must be developed has been called 'absorptive capacity' (Cohen and Levinthal, 1990) or 'knowledge transfer capacity' (Martin and Salomon, 2003). Prior related knowledge gives organisations the ability to recognise the value of new information, assimilate it, and then apply it to new ends. Organisations learn by 'encoding' inferences from history into their structures, designs, rules and procedures. These routines also serve to help individuals learn, because they socialise employees into desired ways of behaving, educate them about the business environment they face and ensure that practices imitate the assumed best ways of coping with this world. Knowledge transfer – and the integration of this knowledge into the routines of the organisation – is however only facilitated when the respective parties have the absorptive capacity or prior experience that is necessary to understand the new ideas (Szulanski, 1996; Tsai, 2002). Groups with large amounts of international experience, for example, are more likely to be able to integrate knowledge from other parts of the organisation than those that do not have such experience.

Globalisation is forcing organisations to improve their capability to transfer knowledge. If an organisation learns to do this well, it can develop a superior 'knowledge transfer capacity'. This means that the organisation has to develop two mutually reinforcing capabilities (Martin and Salomon, 2003):

- the ability of the organisation (or business unit) to articulate the uses of its own knowledge, assess the needs and capabilities of the main recipients for that knowledge, and then transmit knowledge so it can be used in another location ('source transfer capacity')

- the ability of the transferee to assimilate and retain information from a willing source – ie evaluate external knowledge, take in all its detail, and modify or create organisational procedures to accommodate the new knowledge ('recipient transfer capacity').

QUESTIONS

Can organisations enhance their 'absorptive capacity'?

- If so, what managerial actions are the most important?

- What sort of organisational culture becomes important?

- What sorts of abilities and motivations do employees need?

- What does this mean for the design of IHRM policies and practices?

There have been some recent attempts to specify the contribution that HRM makes to global knowledge management processes. The topic is considered in more detail in Chapter 16.

Relational and social capital theory

The organisational learning theories discussed here have provided us with a much clearer focus on *how* organisations must navigate their way through the internationalisation process. This focus on the need to better understand the 'how' has also been improved by work on relational and social capital theory.

'The process of globalisation is ... not only reorganising power at world level but also at national and subnational levels. As domestic firms move part of their production to other countries, technology, knowledge and capital become more important.'

Buckley and Ghauri (2004; p.83)

ACTIVITY

Think about the impact that e-commerce and more flexible networks of organisations have had on the way international business is conducted. How has it created new complexities in the relationships between organisations or new opportunities in how they deal with each other?

One response to globalisation has been the development of complex cross-business networks. These networks might be built around groups of independent firms, or neighbouring firms within a regional industrial cluster or district that share a common need (Rugman *et al*, 1995). A number of changes inside organisations – such as more transparent internal transfer pricing arrangements or service-level agreements – have brought internal prices more in line with external prices. This has sometimes allowed divisional managers to bypass what are considered to be weak or incompetent sections of their own organisation and develop supply or production arrangements that service all members of these broader cross-business networks. The literature on inter-organisational trust has considerable relevance to the study of global organisations. It gives attention to the role of what is termed 'relational capital' (Chen, Chen and Ku, 2004).

So why is relational capital important, and how does it help organisations build competitive advantage?

Relational capital is primarily concerned with business networks and the inter-firm relationships that exist within these networks. It concerns the sets of interdependent business relationships upon which repeated business transactions are based. This includes things like goodwill and trust that exists between a firm and its customers, suppliers, partners, government agencies, research institutions and so forth. Competitive advantage is assumed to result from this form of capital primarily for four reasons:

- Knowledge-sharing across these relational networks reduces the cost of transactions between network members, and thereby facilitates value creation and innovation.

- Organisations can access and deploy their existing capabilities within this network in ways that help them seek new markets, resources, efficiencies and assets.

- The social networks inherent in the relationships affect the rate of creation of new inter-firm links, and this improves the organisation's ability to align its structure and design with its global strategy.

- The ability of partners to absorb and learn from each other at more equal rates is facilitated, thereby extending the life cycle of arrangements such as joint ventures.

However, despite the growth of such cross-business networks, often made easier also by technology, face-to-face contacts with foreign partners are still crucial in cultivating trust, providing access to the flow of information within the network, and providing the opportunity for international managers to create new relationships. Many of these relationships can be captured in what is called an individual or group's 'social capital'. This is defined as:

> **'the sum of the resources, actual or virtual, that accrue to an individual or group by virtue of possessing a durable network of more or less institutionalised relationships of mutual acceptance or recognition.'**
>
> *Bourdieu and Wacquant (1992; p.119)*

It can be something that an international manager builds up after years of working as an expatriate or consultant, or it might be something that an important unit within the organisation develops because of the resources that it controls and influences. In the international context, it has been defined as 'the intangible resource of structural connections, interpersonal interactions, and cognitive understanding that enables a firm to (a) capitalise on diversity and (b) reconcile differences' (Lengnick-Hall and Lengnick-Hall, 2005; p.477).

Possessing the right relationships makes possible the achievement of certain ends that would not be attainable otherwise. The management of social capital has become viewed as a critical business competence. Whereas human capital theory assumes that people, groups or organisations do better (ie receive higher returns for their efforts) because of their personal traits and characteristics, social capital theory assumes that they do better because they are better 'connected' (Sparrow and Braun, 2006). This 'connection' might be realised in the form of trust, obligation or dependency. A certain network structure, or having a job or role that is located in a powerful place amongst this set of exchange relationships, may become an asset in its own right. The management literature has long pointed to the role of international managers and expatriates as 'information brokers' or 'transferrers of knowledge' (Bonache and Brewster, 2001). This is discussed in the next chapter.

QUESTIONS

- In what ways, and through which structures, does greater social capital make international managers more effective?

- Is social capital separate from human capital, or are there particular skills and competencies that help an international manager build social capital?

- What other attributes must be combined with social capital in order to lead to the creation of a global mindset? (What, for example, is the role of cultural intelligence, discussed in Chapter 3?)

- What is the role of HR processes in building, protecting and utilising social capital?

KEY FRAMEWORK

Structural holes and social capital

International managers and expatriates often possess a lot of influence because their position in the organisation gives them 'brokerage' opportunities, in relation to their participation in, and control of, information diffusion across international operations. Central to this process of information diffusion is the concept of 'structural holes' (holes in the social structure within a network). The 'hole' might not reflect a total unawareness of the other parties, but it certainly reflects a lack of attention given to them (Burt, 2000). Structural holes are often implicit in the boundaries that exist between cohorts of employees, teams, divisions and subsidiaries, and between firms. Individuals, units or organisations that have relationships that 'span' these holes or implicit boundaries can create a competitive advantage for themselves, depending on the nature of their 'brokerage'. Holes act as buffers, people on each side of the hole circulating in different flows of information. They therefore offer an opportunity to broker the flow of information between people and to control the projects that bring people together from opposite sides of the hole. Knowing the holes that exist inside the organisation and one's ability to broker across these boundaries can be of benefit both to an individual's career, or more altruistically to the process of internationalisation.

Would it help to know what relationships and social capital a candidate for an important international role has? Would these relationships be more or less important than his or her international skills?

Across which holes inside your organisation would it be useful to force employees to work in order to foster their international mindset?

Institutional theory

The final theoretical perspective we discuss here is institutional theory. Much of this discussion relates to the material in Chapter 4 on comparative HRM, indicating how the fields of international HRM and comparative HRM have begun to combine. International organisations are under pressure to work through partnerships, and to localise much of their management. Consequently, they have to understand how HRM operates in different national contexts.

Institutional theory focuses on the 'taken-for-granted' character of social institutions such as religion, work, family, politics (Berger and Luckman, 1967) and explains how these realities are created and then institutionalised. In the management sphere, structures, for example, are not determined by an organisation's work activities, and the demands made by competition and the needs for efficiency as much as we might believe (DiMaggio and Powell, 1983). Rather, they arise as a reflection of rules that become rationalised in the search for legitimacy and recognition. From the perspective of institutional theory, organisational decision-making is not an outcome just of strategic choice, but also of powerful social forces within and outside organisations. External 'institutional agencies' can create a drive for similarity in unrelated forms (called 'isomorphic processes') within any particular organisational field (which is defined as an aggregate set of organisations that constitute a recognised area of institutional life). There are three isomorphic pulls (DiMaggio and Powell, 1983):

- coercive – eg pulls resulting from pressures of external institutions such as the state, the legal environment, the cultural expectations of societies
- mimetic – eg where organisations model themselves on other organisations in their field as a standard response to uncertainty (triggered, for example, through attempts at benchmarking, global performance metrics, employee transfers or through agencies such as consultancies)
- normative – eg pulls that result from the professionalisation of functions and individuals, such as through educational institutions or through practice dissemination by professional networks.

Institutional theory also focuses on the role of agencies from *within* an organisation:

'The beliefs, norms, rules, and understandings are not just "out there" but additionally "in here".'

Scott (1983; p.16)

Institutional pressures from multiple stakeholders may be powerful influences on HR strategy. The environment is considered to 'enter' the organisation through processes of 'imposition', 'acquisition', 'authorisation'. There is also a series of 'pulls' exerted by the internal agents from within an organisation (Scott, 1987; Westney, 1993). These include:

- 'inducement' of organisational structure (eg where an organisation that lacks power to impose patterns on other organisations instead offers inducements such as funding or certification)

- 'incorporation' (eg where organisations come to replicate salient aspects of differentiation that can be found in their environment within their own structures)

- 'bypassing' (eg where shared values are so institutionalised they can substitute for any formal structure)

- 'imprinting' (eg where an organisational form retains some of the patterns that were institutionalised at the time its industry was founded).

Most use of institutional theory has examined sectoral or occupational variations, but the theory has left a strong mark on conceptual work in the area of SIHRM (Amable, 2003; Hall and Soskice, 2001; Westney, 1993; Whitley, 1999) and increasingly on the empirical work where institutional theory has been used to:

- examine the HRM practices found in foreign-owned subsidiaries of multinationals in terms of the degree of global 'integration' or 'standardisation' versus local 'responsiveness' or 'local adaptation' (Rosenzweig and Nohria, 1994; Björkman and Lu, 2001; Rosenzweig, 2005)

- attempt to identify how differently foreign MNCs manage their people compared with indigenous MNCs (Ferner and Quintanilla, 1998; Wood *et al*, 2006)

- compare HRM practices across countries (Brewster *et al*, 2006; Gooderham, Nordhaug and Ringdal, 1999; Tregaskis and Brewster, 2006).

Rosenzweig and Nohria (1994), using institutional theory, argued that, of all functions, HRM tends to most closely adhere to local practices, in that they are often mandated by local regulation and shaped by strong local conventions. Within HRM they see the order in which six key practices most closely resemble local practices as: time off, benefits, gender composition, training, executive bonus and participation. Where there are well-defined local norms for the HRM practices, and they affect the employees of the affiliate organisation, practices are likely to conform to practices of local competitors.

QUESTION

Think of three or four other HR practices.

In what order would they fit onto this list, in terms of their likely alignment with local practices?

Given this, MNEs from different countries still differ systematically in their overseas operations (Björkman, 2005). The current consensus is that organisations are not as global or international as is often assumed. A country-of-origin effect is still clearly evident. US MNEs, for example, tend to be more centralised and formalised than others in their management of HRM issues, ranging from pay systems through to collective bargaining and union recognition. They tend to innovate more and import leading-edge practices from other nation states. Japanese MNEs, on the other hand, have been at the forefront of work organisation innovations through lean production, but expect their subsidiaries abroad to fit in with this approach. Even though standard worldwide policies and formal systems are not as apparent as in US MNEs, there is stronger centralised direction and ethnocentric attitudes. In short:

> 'MNCs, far from being stateless organisations operating independent of national borders in some purified realm of global economic competition, continue to have their assets, sales, work-force ownership and control highly concentrated in the country where their corporate headquarters are located.'

> *Ferner and Quintanilla (1998; p.710)*

ACTIVITY

Consider the recent analysis of the 500 largest MNEs. Rugman and Verbeke (2004) found that 84% had an average of just over 80% of their sales concentrated in one of the three regional trade blocks (EU, Asia or North America). Only 11 of the 500 MNEs could be deemed to have truly penetrated markets across the globe. Few firms are considered to have developed an effective capability to locate, source and manage human resources anywhere in the world.

- Given the discussion of the various theories throughout this chapter, what organisational attributes does the development of the capability to locate, source and manage human resources throughout the world really entail?

From the perspective of institutional theory, three factors are identified as being important in determining the extent to which an organisation adopts standard practices worldwide or adapts them to suit local conditions:

- the degree to which an affiliate is embedded in the local environment – through its method of founding and its age, as well as its size, its dependence on local inputs and the degree of influence exerted on it from local institutions
- the strength of flow of resources such as capital, information and people between the parent and the affiliate – the stronger and more important the flow, the more there is a need for global co-ordination
- the characteristics of the parent – for example, the degree of uncertainty avoidance (see Chapter 2) of the home country will affect the freedom of subsidiaries. Equally, if the culture of the home country is perceived to be very different from the culture of the subsidiary country, more cultural control will tend to be exercised by headquarters (ie an ethnocentric approach) in order to achieve internal consistency.

QUESTION

Each of these theoretical perspectives has value, but assume for a moment that you were asked to choose between them.

What order would you put them into, based on their value in explaining SIHRM?

Ferner, Quintanilla and Sánchez-Runde (2006) have analysed recent developments in the national-institutional approach. They note that the tendency to concentrate on the conditions and interlocking mechanisms that maintain integrity within institutional arrangements overstates the level of stability within MNEs and the host and subsidiary country national business systems. Citing the work of Streeck and Thelen (2005), they note that MNCs are 'rule makers as well as rule takers' (p.2) and institutions usually leave space that can be contested and influenced. Institutional influences surrounding MNEs go through periodic phases of re-adjustment but also continually evolve. The national-institutional approach must therefore be integrated with phenomena seen at others levels of analysis, one of which concerns the micro-organisational level of the MNE itself and, indeed, we would argue, at the level of functions (such as HR) within the organisation.

A MODEL OF GLOBAL HR

Brewster, Sparrow and Harris (2005) build on the results of the original CIPD-funded research programme into the impact of globalisation on the role of the HR professional to argue that the field of SIHRM is changing significantly and rapidly, and that there is a need for better understanding of these developments. The study used questionnaires and a longitudinal case study design, involving organisations from both the private and public sector with a broad sectoral range of sizes and contexts.

The authors note that extant models of the SIHRM process tend to be static and do not include many key drivers and enablers. They identify five distinct, but linked, organisational drivers of international HRM:

- efficiency orientation

- global service provision

- information exchange

- core business processes

- localisation of decision-making.

These factors (which are addressed in Chapter 14) are creating a new set of pressures on HRM specialists. Three distinct, but linked, enablers of high-performance international HRM are being developed by multinational enterprises:

- HR affordability – the need to deliver global business strategies in the most cost-efficient manner possible. Both people and activities are now examined to identify their added value, and organisations are devoting considerable attention to ensuring that people are operating where they can be most cost-effective and that central overheads are as low as possible

- central HR philosophy – the need to ensure a common philosophy and coherent practice across disparate countries and workforces

- e-enabled HR knowledge transfer – the use of networks and technology to assist organisational learning. In relation to this factor, Sparrow (2006) has outlined five main forms of global knowledge management, or integration mechanisms that are currently dominating the actions of organisations: organisational designs and the use of centres of excellence; managing systems and technology-driven approaches to global knowledge management systems; capitalising on expatriate advice networks; co-ordinating international management teams; and developing communities of practice (COPs) or global expertise networks.

These enabling competencies are in turn are delivered through a series of important HR processes, which are addressed at various points in the subsequent chapters:

- global leadership through international assignments (Chapter 12)
- managing an international workforce (Chapter 13)
- talent management (Chapter 15)
- employer branding (Chapter 15)
- evaluation of HR contribution.

This research illustrates the need for global HR functions to be able to position themselves in a range of ways in order to deliver the enablers and processes that lead to organisational capability (see Figure 32).

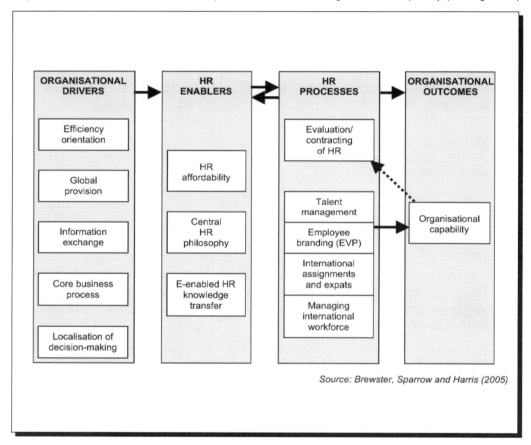

Source: Brewster, Sparrow and Harris (2005)

Figure 32 *Processes involved in globalising HRM*

SUMMARY

This discussion of strategic IHRM demonstrates the complexity of HR decisions in the international sphere and the broad scope of its remit – going far beyond the issue of expatriation to an overall concern for managing people effectively on a global scale. In adopting a strategic IHRM perspective, HR practitioners in international organisations would be engaging in every aspect of international business strategy and adopting HR policies and practices aimed at the most effective use of the human resource in the firm.

LEARNING QUESTIONS

- Which of the theoretical approaches to SIHRM are the most useful in explaining your organisation's current IHRM policies and practices?

- To what extent can there be such a thing as 'best practice' in IHRM?

- Describe the key features of a typical HR approach under each of Heenan and Perlmutter's orientations to internationalisation.

- Plot your current organisational approach to HRM on the model of processes associated with globalising HRM.

REFERENCES

Adler, N. and Ghadar, F. (1990) 'International strategy from the perspective of people and culture: the North American context', in A. Rugman (ed.) *Research in Global Strategic Management*, Vol.1. Greenwood, CT, JAI Press

Amable, B. (2003) *The Diversity of Modern Capitalism*. Oxford, Oxford University Press

Ashkenas, R., Ulrich, D., Jick, T. and Kerr, S. (1995) *The Boundaryless Organization*. San Francisco, Jossey-Bass

Barney, J. B. (1991) 'Firm resources and sustained competitive advantage', *Journal of Management*, 17: 99–120

Bartlett, C. A. and Ghoshal, S. (1986) 'Tap your subsidiaries for global reach', *Harvard Business Review*, 4 (6): 87–94

Bartlett, C. A. and Ghoshal, S. (1987) 'Managing across borders: new strategic requirements', *Sloan Management Review*, 28, Summer: 7–17

Bartlett, C. A. and Ghoshal, S. (1989) *Managing across Borders. The Transnational Solution*. Boston, MA, Harvard Business School Press

Berger, P. L. and Luckman, T. (1967) *The Social Construction of Reality*. Garden City, NY, Doubleday

Birkinshaw, J. M. and Morrison, A. J. (1995) 'Configurations of strategy and structure in subsidiaries of multinational corporations', *Journal of International Business Studies*, 4: 729–53

Björkman, I. (2005) 'International human resource management research and institutional theory', in G. Stahl and I. Björkman (eds) *Handbook of Research in International HRM*. London, Edward Elgar

Björkman, I. and Lu, Y. (2001) 'Institutionalisation and bargaining power explanations of HRM practices in international joint ventures – the case of Chinese–Western joint ventures', *Organization Studies*, 22 (3): 491–512

Bonache, J. and Brewster, C. (2001) 'Knowledge transfer and the management of expatriation', *Thunderbird International Business Review*, 43 (1): 145–68

Bourdieu, P. and Wacquant, L. J. D. (1992) *An Invitation to Reflexive Sociology*. Chicago, University of Chicago Press

Brewster, C. and Lee, S. (2006) 'HRM in not-for-profit international organisations: different, but also alike', in H. H. Larsen and W. Mayrhofer (eds) *European Human Resource Management*. London, Routledge

Brewster, C., Sparrow, P. R. and Dickmann, M. (eds) (2007) *International Human Resource Management: Contemporary issues in Europe*. London, Routledge

Brewster, C., Sparrow, P. and Harris, H. (2005) 'Towards a new model of globalising HRM', *International Journal of Human Resource Management*, 16 (6): 953–74

Brewster, C., Wood, G., Brookes, M. and van Ommeren, J. (2006) 'What determines the size of the HR function? A cross-national analysis', *Human Resource Management*, 45 (1): 3–21

Buckley, P. J. and Ghauri, P. N. (2004) 'Globalisation, economic geography and the strategy of multinational enterprises', *Journal of International Business Studies*, 35 (2): 81–98

Budhwar, P. S. (ed.) (2004) *Managing Human Resources in Asia-Pacific*. London, Routledge

Budhwar, P. S. and Mellahi, K. (eds) (2006) *Managing Human Resources in the Middle-East*. London, Routledge

Burt, R. S. (2000) 'The network structure of social capital', in B. M. Staw and R. I. Sutton (eds) *Research in Organizational Behavior: An annual series of analytical essays and critical reviews*. Volume 22. New York, JAI Press

Caves, R. E. (1996) *Multinational Enterprise and Economic Analysis*. Cambridge, Cambridge University Press

Chen, T.-J., Chen, H. and Ku, Y.-H. (2004) 'Foreign direct investment and local linkages', *Journal of International Business Studies*, 35 (4): 320–33

Cohen, W. M. and Levinthal, D. A. (1990) 'Absorptive capacity: a new perspective on learning and innovations', *Administrative Science Quarterly*, 35: 128–52

Cooke, F. L. (2005) *HRM, Work and Employment in China*. London, Routledge

Coviello, N. E. and Munro, H. J. (1997) 'Network relationships and the internationalisation process of small software firms', *International Business Review*, 6 (2): 1–26

De Cieri, H. and Dowling, P. (1999) 'Strategic human resource management in multinational enterprises', *Research in Personnel and Human Resources Management*, Supplement 4: 305–27

DiMaggio, P. J. and Powell, W. W. (1983) 'The iron cage revisited: institutional isomorphism and collective rationality in organisational fields', *American Sociological Review*, 48: 147–60

Economist (2000) Special Report: A survey of globalisation and tax, *The Economist*, 354, (8155), 29 January: 1–18

Edwards, A., Almond, P., Clark, I., Colling, T. and Ferner, A. (2005) 'Reverse diffusion in US multinationals: barriers from the American business system', *Journal of Management Studies*, 42 (6): 1261–86

Egelhoff, W. G. (1991) 'Information-processing theory and the multinational enterprise', *Journal of International Business Studies*, 22 (3): 341–69

Elvira, M. M. and Davila, A. (2005) *Managing Human Resources in Latin America*. London, Routledge

Evans, P., Pucik, V. and Barsoux, J.-L. (2002) *The Global Challenge: Frameworks for international human resource management*. Boston, MA, McGraw-Hill Irwin

Ferner, A. and Quintanilla, J. (1998) 'Multinational, national business systems and HRM: the enduring influence of national identity or a process of "Anglo Saxonisation"?', *International Journal of Human Resource Management*, 9 (4): 710–31

Ferner, A., Quintanilla, J. and Sánchez-Runde, C. (2006) 'Introduction: multinationals and the multilevel politics of cross-national diffusion', in A. Ferner, J. Quintanilla and C. Sánchez-Runde (eds) *Multinationals, Institutions and the Construction of Transnational Practices*. Basingstoke, Palgrave Macmillan

Foss, N. J. and Pedersen, T. (2004) 'Organising knowledge processes in the multinational corporation: an introduction', *Journal of International Business Studies*, 35 (5): 340–9

Galbraith, J. R. (1987) 'Organisation design', in J. Lorsch (ed.) *Handbook of Organization Behavior*. Englewood Cliffs, NJ, Prentice Hall

Ghoshal, S. (1987) 'Global strategy: an organising framework', *Strategic Management Journal*, 8: 425–40

Gooderham, P. N., Nordhaug, O., and Ringdal, K. (1999) 'Institutional and rational determinants of organisational practices: human resource management in European firms', *Administrative Science Quarterly*, 44: 507–31

Grant, R. M. (1996) 'Toward a knowledge-based theory of the firm', *Strategic Management Journal*, 17 (S2): 109–22

Hall, P. and Soskice, D. (eds) (2001) *Varieties of Capitalism: The institutional foundations of competitive advantage*. Oxford, Oxford University Press

Hamel, G. and Prahalad, C. K. (1985) 'Do you really have a global strategy?', *Harvard Business Review*, July/August: 139–48

Hannon, J. M., Huang, I.-C. and Jaw, B.-S. (1995) 'International human resource strategy and its determinants: the case of subsidiaries in Taiwan', *Journal of International Business Studies*, 26: 531–54

Hedlund, G. (1986) 'The hypermodern MNC – a heterarchy?', *Human Resource Management*, 25 (1): 9–35

Heenan, D. A. and Perlmutter, H. V. (1979) *Multinational Organizational Development: A social architectural approach*. Reading, MA, Addison-Wesley

Jackson, S. E., Hitt, M. A. and DeNisi, A. S. (2003) 'Managing human resources for knowledge-based competition: new research directions', in S. E. Jackson, M. A. Hitt and A. S. DeNisi (eds) *Managing Knowledge for Sustained Competitive Advantage: Designing strategies for effective human resource management*. San Francisco, Jossey-Bass

Kamoche, K., Debrah, Y., Horwitz, F. and Nkombo Muuka, G. (2004) *Managing Human Resources in Africa*. London, Routledge

Karagozoglu, N. and Lindell, M. (1998) 'Internationalisation of small and medium-sized technology-based firms: an exploratory study', *Journal of Small Business Management*, 36 (1): 44–59

Kim, K., Park, J-H. and Prescott, J. E. (2003) 'The global integration of business functions: a study of multinational businesses in integrated global industries', *Journal of International Business Studies*, 34: 327–44

Larsen, H. and Mayrhofer, W. (2006) *Managing Human Resources in Europe*. London, Routledge

Lengnick-Hall, M. L. and Lengnick-Hall, C. (2005) 'International human resource management research and social network/social capital theory', in G. Stahl and I. Björkman (eds) *Handbook of Research in International HRM*. London, Edward Elgar

Lu, Y. and Björkman, I. (1997) 'HRM practices in China-Western joint ventures: MNC standardisation versus localisation', *International Journal of Human Resource Management*, 8: 614–27

Makhija, M. V., Kim, K. and Williamson, S. D. (1997) 'Measuring globalisation of industries using a national industry approach: empirical evidence across five countries and over time', *Journal of International Business Studies*, 28 (4): 679–710

Malbright, T. (1995) 'Globalization of an ethnographic firm', *Strategic Management Journal*, 16: 119–41

Martin, X. and Salomon, R. (2003) 'Knowledge transfer capacity and its implications for the theory of the multinational corporation', *Journal of International Business Studies*, 34: 356–73

Matlay, H. (1997) 'The paradox of training in the small business sector of the British economy', *Journal of Vocational Education and Training*, 49 (4): 573–89

Mayrhofer, W. and Brewster, C. (1996) 'In praise of ethnocentricity: expatriate policies in European multinationals', *International Executive*, 38 (6): 749–78

Minbaeva, D., Pedersen, T., Björkman, I., Fey, C. F. and Park, H. J. (2003) 'MNC knowledge transfer, subsidiary absorptive capacity, and HRM', *Journal of International Business Studies*, 34: 586–99

Morris, S. S., Snell, S. A. and Wright, P. M. (2005) 'A resource-based view of international human resources: towards a framework of integrative and creative capabilities', in G. Stahl and I. Björkman (eds) *Handbook of Research in International HRM*. London, Edward Elgar

Nohria, N. and Ghoshal, S. (1997) *The Differentiated Network: Organizing multinational corporations for value creation*. San Francisco, Jossey-Bass

Parker, B. (1998) *Globalization and Business Practice: Managing across boundaries*. London, Sage

Perlmutter H. V. (1969) 'The tortuous evolution of the multinational corporation', *Columbia Journal of World Business*, 1: 9–18

Peteraf, M. A. (1993) 'The cornerstones of competitive advantage: a resource-based view', *Strategic Management Journal*, 14 (3): 179–91

Pfeffer, J. and Salancik, G. (1978) *The External Control of Organizations: A Resource Dependence Perspective*. New York: Harper & Row

Porter, M. E. (1990) *The Competitive Advantage of Nations*. London, Macmillan

Powell, W. and DiMaggio, P. (1991) *The New Institutionalism in Organizational Analysis*. Chicago, University of Chicago Press

Prahalad, C. K. and Doz, Y. (1987) *The Multinational Mission: Balancing local demands and global vision*. New York, Free Press

Punnett, B. J. and Ricks, D. A. (1992) *International Business*. Boston, MA, PWS-Kent

Reed, M. (1996) 'Organisational theorising: a historically contested terrain', in S. R. Clegg, C. Hardy and W. R. Nord (eds) *Handbook of Organization Studies*. London, Sage

Rosenzweig, P. M. (2005) 'The dual logics behind international human resource management: pressures for global integration and local responsiveness', in G. Stahl and I. Björkman (eds) *Handbook of Research in International HRM*. Cheltenham, Edward Elgar

Rosenzweig, P. and Nohria, N. (1994) 'Influences of human resource management practices in multinational firms', *Journal of International Business Studies*, 20 (2): 229–52

Rugman, A. and Verbeke, A. (2004) 'A perspective on regional and global strategies of multinational enterprises', *Journal of International Business Studies*, 35: 3–18

Rugman, A. M., D'Cruz, J. R. and Verbeke, A. (1995) 'Internationalisation and de-internationalisation: will business networks replace multinationals?', in G. Boyd (ed.) *Competitive and Co-operative Macromanagement*. Aldershot, Edward Elgar

Schuler, R. and Jackson, P. (1987) 'Linking competitive strategy and human resource management practices', *Academy of Management Executive*, 3 (1): 207–19

Schuler, R. S., Dowling, P. J. and De Cieri, H. (1993) 'An integrative framework of strategic international human resource management', *Journal of Management*, 19 (2): 419–59

Scott, W. R. (1983) 'Health care organizations in the 1980s: the convergence of public and professional control systems', in J. W. Meyer and W. R. Scott (eds) *Organizational Environments: Ritual and Rationality*. Beverly Hills, CA, Sage

Scott, W. R. (1987) 'The adolescence of institutional theory', *Administrative Science Quarterly*, 32: 493–511

Sparrow, P. R. (2006) 'Knowledge management in global organisations', in G. Stahl and I. Björkman (eds) *Handbook of Research in International HRM*. London, Edward Elgar

Sparrow, P. R. and Braun, W. (2006) 'HR strategy theory in international context', in R. S. Schuler and S. E. Jackson (eds) *Strategic Human Resource Management*. London, Blackwell

Sparrow, P. R. and Brewster, C. (2006) 'Globalising HRM: the growing revolution in managing employees internationally', in C. L. Cooper and R. Burke (eds) *The Human Resources Revolution: Research and practice*. London, Elsevier

Sparrow, P. R., Brewster, C. and Harris, H. (2004) *Globalizing HR*. London, Routledge

Streeck, W. and Thelen, K. (2005) (eds) *Beyond Continuity: Institutional change in advanced political economies*. Oxford, Oxford University Press

Sundaram, A. K. and Black, J. S. (1992) 'The environment and internal organisation of multinational enterprises', *Academy of Management Review*, 17: 729–57

Szulanski, G. (1996) 'Exploring internal stickiness: impediments to the transfer of best practice within the firm', *Strategic Management Journal*, 17: 27–44

Tallman, S. and Fladmoe-Lindquist, K. (2002) 'Internationalisation, globalisation and capability-based strategy', *California Management Review*, 45 (1): 116–35

Taylor, S., Beechler, S. and Napier, N. (1996) 'Towards an integrative model of strategic international human resource management', *Academy of Management Review*, 21 (4): 959–65

Tregaskis, O. and Brewster, C. (2006) 'Converging or diverging? A comparative analysis of trends in contingent employment practice in Europe over a decade', *Journal of International Business Studies*, 37 (1)

Tsai, W. (2000) 'Social capital, strategic relatedness and the formation of intra-organisational linkages', *Strategic Management Journal*, 21: 925–39

Tushman, M. L. and Nadler, D. A. (1978) 'Information processing as an integrating concept in organisational design', *Academy of Management Review*, 3: 613–24

Ulrich, D. (1987) 'Organisational capability as competitive advantage: human resource professionals as strategic partners', *Human Resource Planning*, 10: 169–84

Ulrich, D. and Lake, D. (1990) *Organization Capability: Competing from the inside out*. New York, Wiley

UNCTAD (2004) 'World Investment Report 2004: the shift towards services', Research note. *Transnational Corporations*, 13 (3): 87–124

Werner, S. (2007) *Managing Human Resources in North America*. London, Routledge

Wernerfelt, B. (1984) 'A resource-based view of the firm', *Strategic Management Journal*, 5 (2): 171–80

Westney, D. E. (1993) 'Institutional theory and the multinational corporation', in S. Ghoshal and D. E. Westney (eds) *Organization Theory and the Multinational Corporation*. New York, St Martin's Press

Whitley, R. (1999) *Divergent Capitalisms: The social structuring and change of business systems*. Oxford, Oxford University Press

Wood, G., Brookes, C. and Brewster, C. (2006) 'Varieties of capitalism and varieties of firm', in P. James and G. Wood (eds) *Institutions and Working Life*. Oxford, Oxford University Press

World Federation of Personnel Management Associations (2005) *Survey of Global HR Challenges: Yesterday, today and tomorrow*. New York, PriceWaterhouseCoopers

Wright, P. M. and McMahan, G. C. (1992) 'Theoretical perspectives for strategic human resource management', *Journal of Management*, 18 (2): 295–320

Wright, P. M., Dunford, B. B. and Snell, S. A. (2001) 'Human resources and the resource-based view of the firm', *Journal of Management*, 27: 701–21

Yip, G. S. (1992) *Total Global Strategy*. Englewood Cliffs, NJ, Prentice Hall

Managing international working

CHAPTER 12

CHAPTER

CHAPTER OBJECTIVES

When they have read this chapter, students will:

■ understand how international assignments link to an organisation's international strategy

■ be able to evaluate trends in the nature of expatriation

■ be familiar with the critical components of the expatriate management cycle

■ be able to critique theory versus practice in international manager selection

■ recognise antecedents to adjustment in international assignments

■ be able to design appropriate pre-departure preparation programmes for expatriates

■ know how to compare ways of measuring the performance of expatriates

■ be able to describe best practice in relation to repatriation.

INTRODUCTION: LINKING INTERNATIONAL ASSIGNMENTS WITH ORGANISATIONAL STRATEGY

A critical component of IHR strategy is the management of internationally mobile staff. Traditionally, international organisations have deployed groups of managers and experts to disseminate corporate strategy and culture to local units and to transfer competence across borders. In addition, high-potential managers from headquarters have been sent abroad as a developmental method prior to progression to senior management. Changes at both organisational and individual level are causing a fundamental rethink of international staffing policies. This chapter explores how international mobility fits within an organisation's overall strategic IHRM approach. It also examines critical components in the effective management of international assignees.

Aligning international assignments with organisational strategy can be thought of in relation to the dominant orientation of the international organisation. The generic patterns of expatriation associated with the four main modes of international orientation (ethnocentric, polycentric, regiocentric and geocentric) were outlined in a Key framework in Chapter 11.

A perceived link could be seen between adopting a primarily geocentric orientation and planning for international assignments as part of global HR planning. This trend towards a more global approach to international staffing represents a major move away from the traditional mode of international assignments, particularly the ethnocentric approach. Mayrhofer and Brewster (1996), however, counsel against a wholehearted rejection of an ethnocentric approach to international staffing, pointing out the numerous advantages, as well as the disadvantages, of such an approach (see Table 23). They point out that most MNEs are still fundamentally ethnocentric.

Advantages	Drawbacks
■ efficient coordination ■ effective communication ■ direct control of foreign operations ■ diffusing central values, norms and beliefs throughout the organisation ■ broadening the view of expatriates and chance of growth for expatriates ■ rapid substitution of expatriates possible ■ no need for a well-developed international internal labour market ■ appropriate for entry into international business	■ adaptation of expatriates uncertain ■ selection procedures prone to errors ■ high costs ■ complicated personnel planning procedures ■ private life of expatriates severely affected ■ difficulties in mentoring during stay abroad ■ reduced career opportunities for locals ■ potential failure rate likely to be higher ■ government restrictions

Source: Mayrhofer and Brewster (1996)

Table 23 *The advantages and drawbacks of ethnocentric staffing*

Case study

HSBC: the international manager programme

HSBC is a major financial services organisation that employs 284,000 employees worldwide and operates in over 80 countries. The bank has colonial roots and was originally based in Hong Kong. It was managed by 'international officers' who were largely British expatriates. In the early 1990s, Midland Bank was acquired. Major acquisitions in North America have also made HSBC the largest foreign bank in Canada and the USA. The corporate centre is now in the UK. The bank's vigorous advertising campaign features the need to be sensitive to local culture and customs in order to succeed in business, proclaiming it to be 'the world's local bank'.

The expanding geographical reach of HSBC and its growth through acquisitions increased the need for international deployment of people. It has operated a traditional elite expatriate model, virtually all senior managers being drawn from a tight-knit cadre of international managers (IMs) who were perceived as 'the DNA of the organisation' (*Economist*, 2006; p.99). This currently outweighs the decreasing need for expatriates in some of HSBC's earlier markets, where more highly skilled local people are now available.

HSBC has retained a specific group of 'international managers'. IMs are globally mobile, generalist commercial bankers who provide a pool of resources, often at short notice, to meet the Group's needs. They are exposed to a wide range of commercial banking business areas across a range of geographical, operational, functional and cultural barriers. HSBC recruits and plans for IMs to stay with the Group in the long term. Individuals are recruited direct into the International Manager Programme either from higher education or internally. The career deal for IMs is clear. They can be sent anywhere and at short notice, and so give high commitment to the organisation. In return, the individual has a good employment package, a wide range of challenging jobs and good career prospects leading to general management positions. Realistic job preview is an important feature of the recruitment process. Attention is drawn to the potential downsides, such as not being able to choose where you work; having to be prepared to spend an entire career outside your native country; being trained as a generalist and not a specialist; having to work and live amongst a range of cultures, customs, nationalities and languages; having an ever-changing circle of friends; and living in a world where partners and children must accept an IM lifestyle. Once the initial development programme has been completed after five years, the managers are deployed on new postings every two to three years on a rolling basis. Each move is planned to provide a steep learning curve. By their early forties successful managers become country managers or the chief executive of an operation. Development is measured against core skills throughout the process through a systematic Executive Performance Development Programme.

The scheme, which peaked with around 800 expatriates, has now been scaled back to 380 employees who come from 33 countries. But although the IM programme has been downsized, there has been a large expansion in other types of foreign posting. In addition, there are 1,600 people working as secondees, contract executives and short-term assignees (mainly technical staff). Each group has its own compensation and benefits package.

QUESTIONS

Ask yourself:

- In what circumstances might ethnocentric staffing be valuable, and why?
- And when should it be avoided?

ASSIGNMENT PLANNING

Discussions of overall orientation to internationalisation and its impact on staffing practices provide the context for the more detailed formulation of strategic operational goals and their link to international assignments.

Bonache and Fernandez (1999) used the resource-based view of the firm (Chapter 11) to address the question 'What relationship exists between the MNE's international strategy and the expatriate selection policy?' According to this view, competitive advantage can occur only in situations of heterogeneity (resources are unevenly distributed and deployed across firms) and immobility (they cannot be transferred easily from one firm to another). A sustainable competitive advantage is achieved when firms implement a value-creating strategy that is grounded in resources that are valuable, rare, imperfectly imitable and non-substitutable. In an international context, resources that provide the company with a competitive advantage in the firm's home country are also useful in other countries.

Depending on the extent to which subsidiaries develop these dimensions of internationalisation, Bonache and Fernandez classified them in four categories:

- implementor
- autonomous unit
- learning unit
- globally integrated unit.

In line with the resource-based view of the firm, it is the transfer of intangible resources – in particular, knowledge – which is most important to the firm both in value and as a basis for competitive advantage.

Implementor subsidiaries apply the resources developed in the headquarters or other units of the organisation to a specific geographic area. Skills knowledge transfer is expected to be a critical reason for using expatriation here due to the high need for tacit knowledge transfer.

Autonomous units are much less dependent on the human and organisational resources existing in the rest of the company's international network. They therefore will have little use for expatriates for knowledge transfer and coordination, and would tend to use local country nationals in key positions.

Learning units acquire and develop new resources that may later be exported to other parts of the organisation. The dominant pattern of international transfer will therefore be one of managers from these units to another country.

Finally, *globally integrated units* develop new expertise but also use the resources generated in other subsidiaries or in the headquarters. Expatriates are used for knowledge transfer, but also for coordination.

Research reveals an extensive list of possible strategic targets for international assignments (see checklist box below).

Strategic targets addressed by an international assignment

- to improve business performance
- to foster the parent corporate culture in the subsidiary, or share the cultural view
- to break down barriers between the parent company and subsidiaries
- to solve technical problems
- to develop top talent and future leaders of the company
- to open new international markets
- to handle politically sensitive business
- to control business improvement initiatives
- to improve the trust/commitment of the subsidiary
- to reduce risks
- to train host-national employees in order to improve individual skills
- to improve team skills
- to implement knowledge practices – eg development, sharing, codification, combination, transfer and mapping of the organisation's knowledge
- to develop, share, and transfer best practices
- to improve business relationships
- to develop networking processes at intra- and inter-organisational level
- to develop an international leadership
- to control financial results.

At this level management has to answer a fundamental question: why do we need to send people on an international assignment to perform the strategic goals? Since expatriates are very expensive, an organisation has to clarify why it is sending them on an assignment. For an organisation they represent a high-cost investment. This cost should be justified against a set of payoff benefits (see Chapter 13).

The situation with regard to the use of expatriates as both a vanguard for international recruitment and as a form of 'corporate glue' has been changing quite rapidly in recent years. Rising costs and staff expectations and greater risks associated with certain locations mean that each assignment is increasingly viewed on the basis of a cost-benefit analysis. Many organisations are in the process of reconsidering the role of their internationally mobile employees (Sparrow, 2006).

Today's context for global mobility

The latest GMAC (2005) survey suggests the following situation with regard to global mobility:

- Around 40% of organisations deploy 50 or fewer expatriates, 9% from 51 to 100 expatriates, 13% up to 1,000, and 13% claim to have over 1,000 expatriates.

- 23% of expatriates now are women (up from 10% in 1994) and 54% are aged between 20 and 39 (compared to 41% in 1994).

- Family concerns and spouse career issues continue to dominate reasons for failure to accept an assignment and also assignment failure.

- Only around 12% of employees in the surveyed organisations were considered to have international experience.

- In 1997 81% of organisations expected an increase in their expatriate population, but the early 2000s also saw a period of cost-cutting (currently this may be easing a little). In 2001 only 23% of organisations expected growth in the size of their expatriate workforce, but by 2005 this had recovered to 47%.

- Formal cross-cultural training is made available to 20% of employees.

- 70% of organisations require a clear statement of objectives, 52% some kind of cost-benefit analysis, but only 37% compare estimated costs with actual costs, and 14% measure the return on investment.

Assignment failure is still reported as the most frequent problem in destinations such as China, Japan, the USA, the UK, Saudi Arabia and Iraq. Causes of assignment failure in order of importance are spouse/partner dissatisfaction, other family concerns, inability to adapt, job not meeting expectations, poor job performance, poor candidate selection, quality of life, dissatisfaction with remuneration, and security and safety issues. Expatriate attrition rates are at least double those of other employees, 21% of expatriates leaving the organisation during the assignment, 23% leaving within one year of return, and 20% leaving between the second and third year.

There have thus been major changes recently in terms of the profiles of individuals undertaking international assignments and their expectations. The traditional expatriate profile is changing. We are moving away from the traditional career-expatriate model, usually filled by white, middle-class male employees from headquarters. Key features of the modern expatriate population include:

- There are more people from outside the headquarters country – 'third-country nationals' (not from the home or the host country) and inpatriates (ie people brought into headquarters) – as part of a more geocentric staffing policy.

- There are more women: overall, there still remains only a small proportion of female expatriates – although the numbers vary with country (Bonache et al, 2007), estimates range between 2% and 15% (Adler, 1986; Scullion, 1994; Harris, 1995; Caligiuri and Tung, 1998) – but the number of women expatriates is increasing. Women, however, continue to face numerous barriers to participation (see Chapter 13).

- The number of 'dual-career couples' has increased significantly. For them, an international assignment presents a series of challenges (Caligiuri and Tung, 1998; Harvey, 1995, 1996, 1997, 1998; Punnett *et al*, 1992; Reynolds and Bennett, 1991). Fewer partners, male or female, are prepared to accept a 'trailing' role – not working, but being expected to act as support to their MNE-employed partner, and even to act as (typically) 'hostess' for corporate functions. Partners now more frequently have their own career, and expect to work in the new country (see Chapter 13).

- The expatriate population is now better educated than it used to be. Increasing demands for expatriates to deliver value during assignments, linked to the use of expatriate assignments for developmental purposes for high-potentials, have resulted in an expatriate population made up substantially of well-educated individuals, with degrees or MBAs.

- Changes have occurred in employee expectations that international assignments will lead to career progression, in line with changes in the psychological contract. Research suggests that managers increasingly view an international assignment as enhancing their careers (Tung, 1998). Emerging notions of 'internal' or 'boundary-less' careers (Arthur and Rousseau, 1996) suggest that managers value an international assignment for the opportunity it brings for skill acquisition, personal development and career enhancement, even though it may not help them advance within their company. Many expatriates now find their own way to another country rather than being sent by their organisation (Inkson *et al*, 1997; Inkson and Myers 2003; Suutari and Brewster, 2003; Banai and Harry, 2004). This trend has major implications for organisational policy and practice in terms of repatriation and career management.

- The increasing development of new communications technology – and new transport options – means that many, though not all, of the advantages of using expatriates can be achieved by other means: short-term assignments and frequent flying (Welch 2006) and virtual teamworking (Zimmerman and Sparrow, 2007).

The different ways in which expatriates are used

An analysis of company practice with regard to the role of expatriates to assist international strategy signposts five different types of organisation (Baruch and Altman, 2002):

Global

The archetypal role in large global multinationals with established reputations for expatriate management. Comprehensive sets of procedures are put in place, centres of excellence set up to manage knowledge of best practice. Expatriation is expected by employees to form the basis of a professional and managerial career inside the organisation. Being an expatriate is seen as a necessary part of the career path to senior roles in the organisation. Recruitment and selection systems concentrate on the internal labour market (see the Hong Kong and Shanghai Bank [HSBC] case study earlier in this chapter).

Emissary

Organisations have established overseas markets and a long-term view as to their positioning in these markets. However, resourcing systems are still firmly rooted in the domestic home culture. Expatriates may be excused from international assignments, but when assigned their role is to represent the power and ideology of the headquarters and export its systems. Assignments act as a mission away from the corporate centre. Comprehensive back-up is provided to compensate for the burden of an overseas post. The key challenge is to maintain the motivation of expatriates.

Peripheral

Characteristic of companies operating in geographies where expatriation is still a sought-after option and a reward in its own right. The globalisation process has resulted in new international expansion opportunities and limited growth opportunities in the home market means that overseas assignments are seen as a perk, facilitating the temporary migration of candidates to overseas posts. The domestic workforce might itself be sourced from several countries and multi-ethnic and so there are ample employees willing to now be dispersed throughout the world.

Professional

A preference to use external people and buy in expertise and knowledge, in effect outsourcing the expatriation process. The goal is to concentrate on the home country strengths and keep people within specified geographical borders. Skills are bought in from the external labour market at the periphery of the organisation. Expatriates are hired to act as 'foreign legion troopers' and have careers that span expatriate assignments in several companies. Recruitment and selection is focused around work history and previous assignments rather than personal skills and attributes. There is a cost-driven and transactional psychological contract. Critical issues concern loyalty and commitment of the foreign legion.

Expedient

An emergent approach for organisations newly internationalising and developing policies and procedures. Ad hoc and pragmatic choices are made across the other policies.

Morley and Heraty (2004, p.634) point out that 'there is an emerging recognition that international assignees may impact the bottom-line performance of multinational enterprises, and thus, as Dowling and Welch (2004) observe, finding and nurturing the human resources required to implement an international strategy is of critical importance'.

HOW SHOULD WE THINK ABOUT THE RECRUITMENT OF INTERNATIONAL EMPLOYEES?

In this section we consider general debates about the issue of recruiting employees specifically for international work. How best should we think about the recruitment of people into international roles inside organisations?

QUESTIONS

In reading the following sections, bear the questions below in mind, with a view to answering them in due course.

- Can the competencies that become important for international management be developed?

- Are some competencies so complex, rare on the ground or time-consuming to build that the real issue is to select and motivate a small elite of managers?

- Can we identify a clear hierarchy of international management skills, from the most basic to higher levels of performance and sophistication, or must we be left with endless lists of desirable characteristics with assumed relevance?

- Do internal resourcing systems realistically make such graded and calibrated decisions about managers?

> ■ Are line managers just happy to find candidates who are half-competent, but are willing and mobile?

The consensus view from HR practitoners for some time now has been that it is possible (if not actually realistic to try and put into practice) to specify a set of competencies for the international manager, and that they can be used to assist the selection of some people in some jobs. However, there are very different views about the practicality of using them to select international managers – and there is certainly considerable debate about the feasibility of developing the full spectrum of international management competencies in a sufficiently large pool of employees.

The first point of contention concerns the overall resourcing philosophy that should be adopted. The second point of contention – reflecting much of the discussion in Chapter 6 about the fragmentation of resourcing options – concerns the sorts of international managers from whom evidence of success (and therefore potential recruitment criteria) might be gathered. Should we look at expatriates, frequent commuters, international team members, immigrants, and so forth, under this umbrella?

In relation to the first debate, Sparrow (1999) reported two competing resourcing philosophies:

■ the traditional psychometric approach, whereby role analyses and corporate competency systems recognise the importance of competencies associated with international management and these are then used to predict individual capability for assignment

■ a clinical risk assessment approach which investigates the individual psychological transitions and adaptations that international managers have to undergo, but recognising that there is no choice but for that person to undertake the assignment, directs attention to the design of the assignment around the manager in order to minimise risks to the organisation.

The first traditional 'psychometric' approach argues that there is an identifiable set of competencies that are associated with success and that these can be used to predict effective performers in international roles (see Chapter 11 for a review of this work). Few professionals doubt that selecting someone for an international assignment draws attention to quite stringent criteria and that there is a tension between the skills and competencies that organisations think they should be looking at when they recruit, and the skills that are actually needed to make a success of working abroad. It is also accepted that factors that become essential when operating internationally (such as openness to experience, tolerance of ambiguity, introversion, the ability to generate and inspire trust in others, and proactive information-seeking) can be understated in domestic selection systems and therefore have to be given some attention when internationalising the organisation.

A second philosophy, described as a 'clinical risk assessment approach', finds favour amongst HR professionals who argue that there are limits to the use of personal competencies as a selection criterion for international employees. The reasons for failure of international management assignments often go beyond problems of the managers' cultural adaptability, maturity and stability. Adaptability of the partner, dual career difficulties, national attitudes to mobility, and pay arrangements clearly all play a role in the success of the assignment. The supporting structures that surround the international manager (in terms of localisation policies, management structures, reporting relationships, accountabilities and responsibilities, and the technical difficulty of assignment) all play a part in determining the success of the international manager. The need for greater cost control over international managers, and the growth of joint ventures and strategic alliances all serve to reduce the position power of international managers and often means that there is limited supply of willing employees. This limits the selection context. In relation to this clinical risk approach, with its criticism of the competency approach to international selection, Scullion and Collings (2006) argue that companies need better systems to be able to work with the more limited range and quality of candidates that they in practice must work with. They cite NCR as an example of an organisation that pursues the strategy of designing the assignment to match the skills of the manager, rather than the other way round. An earlier study of 30 leading UK multinationals showed that skills databases and tracking systems were increasingly important in tracking talent across the organisation (Scullion and Starkey, 2000). Qualitative data on 'soft' resourcing issues were collected for populations such as the top 150 to 400 in the organisation on issues such as willingness to move to particular countries and dual career status. Using talent management systems, rather than focusing solely on recruitment and selection of specific competencies, can be a more practical solution. We return to the topic of talent management in Chapter 15.

The second point of contention concerns the sorts of international managers who should be studied if we are to elicit potential recruitment criteria for successful international managers. Those concerned with the early identification of international management potential often argue that many of the lessons learned about the recruitment of expatriates can be generalised to people working in other international contexts. The majority of expatriate skills are learned through experience – they learn how to manage across cultures in most instances without training or education in cross-cultural skills. So too must international managers who, although not having to become totally immersed in a new culture because they are expatriates, still encounter individuals of different cultures through overseas trips to customers or suppliers, short visits to international operations, or work in international management teams. Increasingly, these managers too can no longer work in the comfort of their home culture (Spreitzer, McCall and Mahoney, 1997).

Taking a strategic view of managing international staffing does not end at the planning stage. Effective management of international mobility entails the need to take a holistic approach to all aspects of the assignment process. The 'global assignment cycle' (see Figure 33) identifies the key components of this approach.

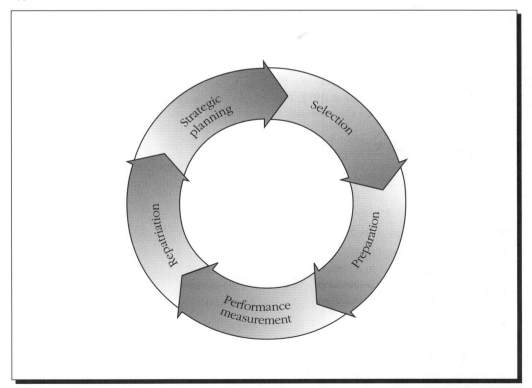

Figure 33 *The global assignment cycle*

MANAGING THE GLOBAL ASSIGNMENT CYCLE: SELECTION

The complexities of managing this cycle have been the focus of sustained academic research over many years. Despite this focus, key challenges still remain under each of the cycle components.

Selection for international assignments

The cycle starts with identifying the right person for the post. For the organisation, we are generally discussing selection rather than recruitment, because in most cases the candidates are already employed by the organisation (although note that Suutari and Brewster, 2003, found a substantial proportion of people working outside their own country had made their own way there). These appointments normally fall into the category of transfers or promotions and are often linked with prior identification of potential (particularly in the case of developmental assignments). Research into selection criteria for international assignments shows a split between theory and practice. The literature on the criteria used for expatriate manager selection also has a tendency towards prescription and a heavy North American bias.

Selection criteria: the theory

We discussed in Chapter 6 some of the assumptions and competing perspectives about the desirability of selecting people against individual characteristics for successful international working. In the context of selecting expatriates, sometimes theoretical lists of competencies for international managers can look amusing. One book on cross-cultural management (Harris and Moran, 1996) cites 68 dimensions of competency, of which 21 are perceived to be 'most desirable'. Staff with these competencies should probably be chief executive officer rather than expatriates! Others (eg Phillips, 1992) suggest that there is not much difference between the competencies required for an international manager and those required for a domestic manager. Most studies dealing with the skills needed for expatriates have focused on lists of criteria, competencies and personal characteristics that should be assessed. Studies have also analysed the reasons for assignment failure and recommended the HR practices that can help organisations select, develop and retain competent expatriate managers. Yamazaki and Kayes (2004) reviewed the expatriate literature and analysis of the skills necessary for cross-cultural learning and identified 73 skills that clustered into 10 high-level competencies! In terms of characteristics to be considered, an amalgam of recent studies (see Aycan, 1997; Pucik, 1998; Yamazaki and Kayes, 2004; and Stroh, Black, Mendenhall and Gregersen, 2005) reveals the characteristics listed in the box below.

> *Characteristics of the successful expatriate manager*
>
> *Professional and technical competence and experience on the job*
>
> - experience in the company
> - technical knowledge of the business
> - previous overseas experience
> - managerial talent
> - overall experience and education
>
> *Relational ability 1: personality traits and relational abilities*
>
> - communicative ability and interpersonal skills
> - maturity and emotional stability
> - tolerance for ambiguity in personal relations, unfamiliar situations/new experiences

- behavioural and attitudinal flexibility: willingness to acquire new patterns
- respect for culture of host country
- adaptability and flexibility in new environment

Relational ability 2: perceptual dimensions and life strategies

- information-seeking skills: listening and observation
- modelling capacities: ability to draw upon observational learning to acquire knowledge, attitudes, values, emotional proclivities and competences
- non-judgemental frameworks
- non-evaluative in interpreting the behaviour of host-country nationals

Self-maintenance factors

- ability to substitute traditional reinforcements with other activities
- stress reduction techniques
- self-maintenance, confidence in own ability to perform specific behaviours (self-efficacy)

Leadership and motivational factors

- relationship development and personal influence skills
- willingness to communicate
- action and initiative skills
- belief in the mission
- interest in overseas experience
- congruence with career path

Cultural awareness

- cultural robustness: understanding of the differences between countries
- host-country language skills and translation of concepts, ideas and thoughts in verbal form
- understanding non-verbal communication

Family situation

- stability of family situation
- spouse and family's adaptability and supportiveness

There have, then, been many attempts to distil the key criteria from the more extensive lists. However, it may be the case that expatriates from some countries are more successful than others (Waxin and Brewster, 2005), either because of their cultural similarity with the host country (Gong, 2003) or because some cultures (for example, those with a higher tolerance of uncertainty (see Chapters 2 and 3), make better expatriates. A key observation from this literature is the emphasis on interpersonal and cross-cultural skills as determinants of success for international assignments. The stress on 'soft' skills reflects a more general departure from reliance on traditional 'hard' skills for successful management. A major drawback of lists, however, is that few are drawn from empirical data and the tendency is for such lists to end up describing a superman (or less frequently, a superwoman).

Mendenhall, Kühlman, Stahl and Osland (2002) argued that if we are to move beyond our currently limited views of the skills needed by people operating in this environment, then we need more research that employs longitudinal designs and that also includes the host-country perspective on the determinants, processes and outcomes of international adjustment. From a theoretical perspective our models of international management skills can be classified as being driven by four sets of assumptions about learning, stress-coping, development and personality.

Assumptions about the skills need by international managers

Learning models

These assume that the adjustments that international employees have to make (and therefore the skills and competencies that they need) are related to learning new skills and techniques of adaptation; the impact of the 'other' culture can be seen as a change in behavioural reinforcement contingencies. The major task facing expatriates is to adjust their social skills so that they can learn the salient characteristics of the new environment in terms of new roles, rules and norms of social interaction. Cross-cultural training is generally designed on the principle that the rules and values of a new culture have to be learned (and a repertoire of cognitive and behavioural schema and responses developed) before adjustment can take place.

Stress-coping models

These assume that feelings of anxiety, confusion and disruption associated with culture shock are akin to individual stress reactions under conditions of uncertainty, information overload and loss of control. The adjustment reaction is characterised by a variety of symptoms of psychological distress associated with any critical life event. Moreover, role theory argues that competing assignment demands make role conflicts unavoidable and it is this that impacts effectiveness. Stress management (coping strategies), rather than stress avoidance, is necessary in order for expatriates to engage in necessary engagement behaviours. International employees have to draw from a wide range of such strategies to manage problems, although there may not be congruence between what is necessary to manage stress and what is required for effective management of the assignment.

Developmental models

These assume that there are a series of phases of adjustment that an international employee has to go through (for example, contact, disintegration, reintegration, autonomy and independence) that reflect progressive stages of cultural awareness. Individuals undertake adaptive activities only when environmental challenges threaten their internal equilibrium. Processes of periodic (rather than linear) disintegration, regrouping/regeneration, then higher maturation (progressive inter-cultural sensitivity often also associated with global leadership competence) are an inevitable consequence of exposure to other cultures. In a rare qualitative study of returned expatriate stories, researchers adapted the metaphor of heroic adventures to note the importance of personal transformations that accompany adjustment processes.

Personality-based models

These assume that such development can in part be predicted by a set of generalisable attitudes and traits, such as adaptation, cross-cultural and partnership skills or personality variables that are associated with model cross-cultural collaborators. The importance of these prerequisites depends on the nature of the position and task variables, organisation characteristics and host country. Empirical support is, however, still weak, and again there may be contradictions between what is required for interaction adjustment and work adjustment. Moreover, as found in a study of German international employees assigned to work in Japan and the USA, each country presented different problems and conflicts to the employees and therefore required differential personality-related coping strategies.

A recent study has collated evidence across 66 studies that examined the role of 50 determinants and consequences of adjustment in 8,474 expatriates. The study looked at the trajectory of adjustment over time and how this affected any adjustment. The results showed the centrality, criticality and complexity of adjustment and strongly supported the impact that it has on job satisfaction, withdrawal cognitions and performance (Bhaskar-Shrinivas, Harrison, Shaffer and Luk, 2005). Language skills helped international managers engage in rewarding interpersonal exchanges but had no impact on work adjustment. Previous experience of international assignments had a minimal impact on subsequent adjustment. Two individual factors were important in predicting adjustment: the ability to be a self-starter and relational skills, the latter exceeding other predictors by 30% in terms of explaining variance in adjustment. Finally, non-work factors such as culture novelty and spouse adjustment were extremely potent predictors of successful overseas adjustment.

Selection criteria: the practice

Certainly, global leaders must possess some very specific skills and competencies simply because the roles that they perform are complex:

'[global leaders] have to possess a complex amalgamation of technical, functional, cultural, social and political competencies to navigate successfully the intricacies of changing cross-border responsibilities.'

Harvey and Novecevic (2004; p.1173)

However, Harvey and Novicevic (2004) also point out that there are many sorts of capital that people need in international roles, and recruitment can only help manage some of them:

■ social capital (which leads to trust)

■ political capital (which leads to legitimacy)

■ human capital (which leads to competencies), and

■ cultural capital (which leads to social inclusion and acceptance).

Although many recruitment and selection systems focus on human capital (the skills and competencies needed for the job), external context factors have much to do with the building of an international manager's social and political capital. A recent study of managers working in international teams, and the skills that were needed for the team to mutually adjust, showed that an expatriate's adjustment within a team is not influenced solely by his or her own competencies. Instead, the power balance between team members is likely to have a major influence on the course of adjustment (Zimmermann and Sparrow, 2007). Depending on the distribution of the nationality of headquarters, leadership, and the customer interface, the international manager will have more or less power to demand changes from the other side, and instead may have to achieve his or her aims through teaching and control.

Given the emphasis on interpersonal skills in management theory, it is somewhat surprising to find that the research into current practices of MNEs consistently identifies the continuation of more traditional criteria for selection of expatriates.

There are two main findings from the empirical research into selection practices among MNEs. The first is that expatriates are primarily selected on the basis of their technical competence (see, for example, Tung, 1981, 1982; Zeira and Banai, 1984,1985; Harris, 1999). The second finding is that there is an underlying assumption of the universal nature of managerial skills, as first identified by Baker and Ivancevich (1971).

QUESTION

Before you read on, think for a moment.

■ What might explain the gap between the advice of those who have studied the subject and the practices of companies?

Companies' perceptions of international selection as a high-risk operation lead to a tendency to place emphasis in recruitment on technical and managerial qualifications, to ensure that the job can be done competently (Miller, 1972; Antal and Izraeli, 1993). Put another way, an expatriate who is not at least competent in the job he or she is performing is really going to struggle to bring any other competencies into play.

Another factor may be the selection process. Research into expatriate selection practice (see Mendenhall and Oddou, 1985; Dowling *et al*, 1994) highlights the predominance of informal selection processes – what Harris and Brewster (1999) called the 'coffee machine system' – which leads to selection from a small pool known to senior managers, to potentially discriminatory outcomes and to some serious failures. Lack of attention to developing formal expatriate selection systems can be extremely costly to an organisation. Many leading-edge organisations, however, have been employing more sophisticated procedures, which may include psychometric assessments of competencies and other approaches to suitability assessment.

One such approach is outlined by Sparrow (1999). This consists of a cultural adaptability assessment developed by Kaisen Consulting. The assessment is focused on helping employees understand the personal qualities required to work overseas and the implications of an international assignment for themselves and their families. It also draws attention to the mechanisms that can assist them in coping with their new environment. The approach concentrates on identifying the psychological adaptations that have to take place on an international assignment. One potential drawback with such an approach is the reluctance on the part of an employee to be completely honest about family problems when the assignment is seen to be critical to progression. The discussion in Chapter 11 about political and social capital also has relevance to this kind of 'risk assessment' approach to international resourcing.

ASSIGNMENT IMPLEMENTATION

Selecting the right person is only the first stage of managing the assignment. The rest of the global assignment cycle also has to be managed effectively. Expatriate failure in the usually defined sense, the premature return home of an expatriate manager (Tung, 1981), is rare. Some US literature has claimed very high failure rates, and it does seem that expatriate failure may be a less significant issue for European MNEs (Brewster, 1991; Scullion, 1994; Suutari and Brewster, 1998; PriceWaterhouseCoopers, 2000). Harzing (1995) showed that the myth of high expatriate failure rates seems to have been created by poor research. However, the cases that occur are invariably traumatic for the individual and the organisation. And perhaps more serious are the many more numerous cases of poor performance. Preventing or minimising these will involve the HRM specialists in work on:

- preparation
- adjustment
- rewards
- performance measurement, and, finally,
- repatriation.

Preparation

One of the key ways in which organisations can support individuals undertaking international assignments is through the provision of pre-departure preparation, which can include training and other forms such as briefings, visits and shadowing. Expatriates are very positive about the value of training programmes (Brewster and Pickard, 1994; Harris and Brewster, 1999a; Waxin and Panaccio, 2005). However, the latest GMAC (2005) survey found that formal cross-cultural training was mandatory in only 20% of organisations – the lowest percentage in the survey's history – even though 73% rated it as having great or high value.

Cross-cultural training has long been advocated as a means of facilitating effective interactions (Brislin, 1986). Tung's (1981) framework for selecting cross-cultural training methods has two main dimensions: degree of interaction required in the host culture, and the similarity between the expatriate's home culture and the host culture. Mendenhall and Oddou (1985) developed this framework to include the degree of integration and level of rigour required, and translated this into the needed duration of time for each type of training programme. This framework consisted of three levels: information-giving approaches (eg factual briefing and awareness training), affective approaches (eg culture assimilator training, critical incidents and role-plays) and immersion approaches (eg assessment centres, field experience and simulations).

Mendenhall himself (Mendenhall *et al*, 1995), however, points out that this model does not specify how the level of rigour is determined and refers only to cross-cultural training. A framework developed by Black and Mendenhall (1989) based on social learning theory suggested a decision-tree model which logically links and integrates the variables of culture novelty, required degree of interaction with host nationals, job novelty and training rigour (see Figure 34).

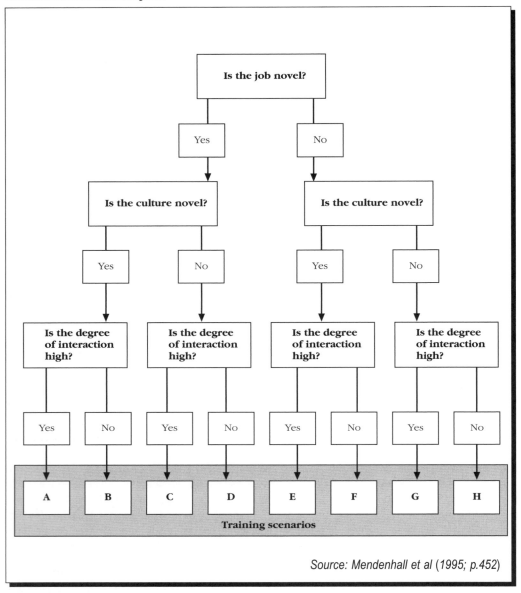

Figure 34 *Decision-tree for selecting appropriate training methods*

QUESTION

Think about your own organisation – or about one that you know.

■ What forms of pre-departure training does it offer?

After reviewing existing approaches to pre-departure preparation, Harris and Brewster (1999a) argued that organisations should take a more holistic approach to pre-departure preparation for expatriates. The authors suggested an integrative framework that takes into account job variables at the home- and host-country level, including the nature of the international operation, size of home-country organisation, host-country location, objective of assignment, nature of job and level of organisational support, together with individual variables in terms of the expatriate profile and partner considerations (see Figure 35). These antecedents are considered alongside an assessment of the individual's existing level of competency before deciding on an appropriate preparation scenario.

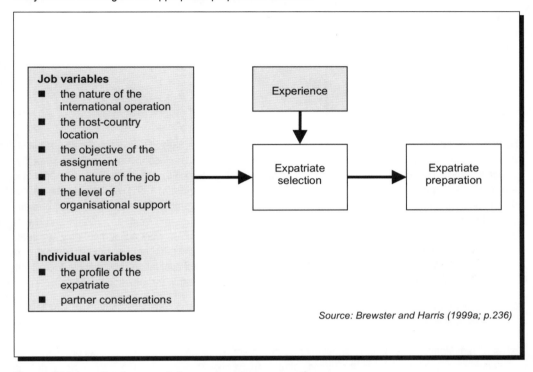

Figure 35 *Integrative framework for pre-departure preparation*

Adjustment

A key issue concerns the ability of the expatriates – and their families – to adjust to their new environment. McCaughey and Bruning (2005) review evidence on expatriate satisfaction and a range of important outcomes such as assignment completion. They look at how three sorts of support strategies impact on satisfaction (and adjustment): pre-assignment support strategies (such as career planning and development, training in deficits in knowledge, skills and abilities, partner/family involvement); assignment support strategies (such as using mentors and partner employment counselling); and repatriation support strategies (utilisation of knowledge, skills and abilities learned on assignment).

The prevalent model describes linear causal relationships between antecedents and three narrowly conceived and one-dimensional adjustment outcomes: interaction adjustment, general adjustment, and work adjustment. These categories are an artificial construct from the adjustment measure used (Black and Stephens, 1989) and are not comprehensive or, more critically, analytical or discrete. Further, the model excludes feedback loops to account for the real-life dynamics of expatriate adjustment. It thus does not reflect the complexities of expatriate adjustment (Haslberger, 2005). Finally, the model addresses adjustment only on one level – that of the individual expatriate. Recent research indicates that about three-quarters of expatriates are accompanied by at least one family member (Dickmann, Doherty and Brewster, 2007).

The dimensions of adjustment include cognitions and emotions (Searle and Ward, 1990; Ward *et al*, 1998; Ward and Kennedy, 1999) as well as behaviours, as distinct outcome components (Kim, 1988). Note, too, that adjustment may not be entirely one-way – one of the roles of expatriates is often to introduce new practices into the subsidiary organisation: local employees will have to adjust, to some extent, to the ways of the expatriate and perhaps to the new practices he or she is bringing in (Brewster, 1993, 1995).

Adjustment in each of these three domains is determined by a variety of factors. These fall into four main groups:

- factors to do with the individual
- non-work factors
- organisational factors
- job factors.

The *individual factors* include self-efficacy, relational and perception skills, flexibility, a desire to adjust, tolerance of ambiguity, leadership qualities, interpersonal skills and self-confidence, cultural empathy, emotional stability (Hiltrop and Janssens, 1990; Coyle, 1992; Collins, 1995), language ability and previous international experience (Black and Stephens, 1989; Black and Gregersen, 1991). A study examined the link between expatriate personality, the sorts of social ties that the expatriate developed (number, breadth and depth), and different types of adjustment (Johnson, Kristof-Brown, van Vianen, de Pater and Klein, 2003). Depth and breadth of relationships with other expatriates predicted work adjustment only, whereas social ties with host nationals predicted all forms of adjustment, and the number of social ties formed was not predicted by extraversion, but rather by what was called core self-evaluation (how people feel about themselves, measured through self-esteem, self-efficacy, locus of control and emotional stability).

Non-work factors include some of these, but particularly important is the family situation. Cross-over effects exist between expatriate and spouse (eg Takeuchi *et al*, 2005). An inability of the spouse and children to adapt to the cultural environment is a common source of difficulty (Moore and Punnett, 1994; Collins, 1995; Jones, 1997). If a spouse or family member is undergoing severe culture shock or experiencing difficulty in making the cross-cultural adjustment, the morale and performance of the expatriate may be affected adversely (Torbiörn, 1997). Children may also be very resistant to moving due to the educational and social disruption it may cause. The older the children, and the more there are of them, the greater the likelihood of adjustment problems (Church, 1982). A positive family situation is likely to enhance the expatriate's cross-cultural adjustment and increase the chances of a successful assignment (Punnett and Ricks, 1992; Collins, 1995). The degree of cultural difference between the home and host country can have a significant influence on ability to adapt. If the host-country culture is very different from the home culture, the expatriate may have to develop a complete set of new behaviours in order to 'make sense' of this new macro-environment and to be able to work successfully in the culture.

The expatriate may find it difficult to perceive and learn these behaviours, thus increasing the period of time required for expatriate acculturation. Glanz (2003) has examined how sense-making – the use of rational thought to re-analyse and bring order to confusion and surprise – can be engendered through the use of narratives about the expatriate experience. This perspective shows that expatriate experience is not simply an incremental development towards adjustment but involves periods in which previous learning becomes overturned and revelations occur at an accelerated pace.

Organisational factors were classified by Black *et al* (1991) as organisation culture novelty, social support and logistical help. If the international job is high in organisational culture novelty, the expatriate will have a difficult time adjusting to the work situation and will in turn have a more difficult time adjusting to the culture in general. This is made easier in an organisational culture that encourages social support from co-workers and where superiors provide new expatriates with clear information about what is and is not acceptable work behaviour. Social support has an important impact on the expatriate's ability to adapt to the new environment (Coyle, 1992; Brewster and Scullion, 1997). If the firm offers support for the expatriate and family in the form of housing, payment of school tuition, practical information about shopping, etc, the expatriate will feel part of a larger social group. Logistical support such as information on housing, education and travel should help to reduce this uncertainty, so facilitating adjustment. Mendenhall *et al* (1995), however, warn that too many 'buffers' may reduce the learning that the expatriate gets from the experience.

Job factors which affect adjustment include role novelty, role clarity, role discretion, role conflict and role overload. Role novelty is the degree of difference between the expatriate's previous position and his or her new one (Morley *et al*, 1997). Role clarity is the extent to which expatriates know what duties they are expected to perform in the overseas assignment. If the role is ambiguous, the expatriate may find it difficult to choose the necessary behaviours, which may cause him or her to feel ineffective and frustrated (Black, 1988). Role discretion reflects the expatriate's authority to determine the parameters of the new position. Greater role discretion will enable the expatriate to use past actions that proved effective in a previous role. This should make adjustment easier because it reduces uncertainty and increases the expatriate's confidence in his or her ability to perform in the new environment. Role conflict and overload may negatively affect the adjustment of the expatriate. This is likely to vary with the expatriate's home culture: some will prefer fewer restrictions on the way they perform their role, some will prefer greater clarity.

Hechanova *et al* (2003) applied meta-analytical methods to research into expatriate adjustment. Based on 42 empirical studies covering 5,210 expatriates, the most important and consistent predictive relationships were identified. These are shown in Figure 36.

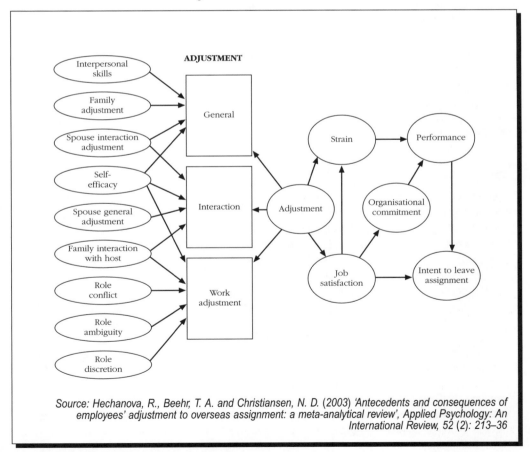

Source: Hechanova, R., Beehr, T. A. and Christiansen, N. D. (2003) 'Antecedents and consequences of employees' adjustment to overseas assignment: a meta-analytical review', Applied Psychology: An International Review, 52 (2): 213–36

Figure 36 *A model of expatriate outcomes*

A recent study of managers working in international teams, and of the skills that were needed for the team to mutually adjust, showed that an expatriate's adjustment within a team is not influenced solely by his or her own competencies (Zimmermann and Sparrow, 2007). Instead, the power balance between team members is likely to have a major influence on the course of adjustment. Depending on the distribution of the nationality of headquarters, leadership, and the customer interface, the expatriate will have more or less power to demand changes from the other side, and to achieve them through teaching and control.

QUESTION

Take any one of the adjustment factors shown in Figure 36 and ask yourself:

- What might the individual – and what might his or her employer – do to make it less of a problem?

The reward package

Managing compensation and benefits for international assignments has traditionally been one of the core functions of the IHR manager (Bonache, 2006; Suutari and Tornikoski, 2001). The high costs of assignments mean that considerable attention is focused on developing more cost-effective systems that will still provide an incentive to move. Key determinants of the type of system to be employed include (Evans *et al*, 2002; p.131):

- cost-efficiency – making sure that the plan delivers the intended benefits in the most cost-effective manner (including tax consequences)

- equity issues – making sure that the plan is equitable irrespective of the assignment location or nationality of the expatriate

- system maintenance – making sure that the plan is relatively transparent and easy to administer.

Developments in international reward and recognition

There is increasing focus on how expatriates perform and add value across global networks inside the organisation. The study by Perkins (2006; p.26) found that rewards strategists at Boots, BT, Cable and Wireless, CadburySchweppes, Citigroup, Diageo and Shell are reappraising the basis on which expatriation has to be managed, 'integrating organisational networks around common governance principles'. This brings tensions into the relationships between expatriates and local employees, and renewed attention to reward comparability factors. Package design is moving towards generically designed frameworks that can be flexed to ensure a fair reflection of the mobility pressures. Organisations are exerting more control over the reward–effort bargain by standardising aspects of their rewards systems. Motivating talented employees to undertake assignments in an environment of regionalised political tensions continues to require idiosyncratic reward solutions, but there are moves to eliminate personal deals, increase transparency and knowledge about the assignment, and encourage ownership amongst local line managers. A philosophy of 'value creation' is being exported across operations (a 'one organisation, one global reward system' strategy), reducing the difference between rewards systems designed purely for expatriates and those that are designed to manage an (internationally mobile) set of talented managers. There is a process of directional convergence, not final convergence, in rewards policies. 62% of rewards specialists claimed that rewards systems were still adapted to local context, but 78% would prefer a globally integrated approach and 84% wanted to integrate the rewards approach with global strategy. Multinationals are combining tools and techniques across the whole HR process and applying them to all populations of internationally mobile managers. Unilever combined the talent management, organisational effectiveness, learning and reward functions in order to help its international managers better understand how they add value. The balance between what the business wants and what is fair to employees is increasingly reflecting the underlying reason for mobility and estimate of business value, which varies according to factors such as skills shortages, project logics, employee-initiated or career development motivations.

Table 24 provides a summary of the current approaches to expatriate compensation systems.

Compensation system	For whom most appropriate	Advantages	Disadvantages
Negotiation	Special situations Organisation with few expatriates	Conceptually simple	Breaks down with increasing number of expatriates
Localisation	Permanent transfers and long-term assignments Entry-level expatriates	Simple to administer Equity with local nationals	Expatriates usually come from economic conditions different from those experienced by local nationals
Headquarters-based balance-sheet	Many nationalities of expatriates working together	No nationality discrimination Simple administration	High compensation costs Difficult to repatriate TCNs
Home-country-based balance-sheet	Several nationalities of expatriates on out-and-back-home assignments	Low compensation costs Simple to repatriate TCNs	Discrimination by nationality Highly complex administration Lack of conceptual purity
Lump-sum approaches	Consistently short assignments (less than three years), followed by repatriation	Resembles domestic compensation practices Does not intrude on expatriate finances	Exchange rate variation makes this unworkable except for short assignments
International pay structures	Senior executives of all nationalities	Tax- and cost-effective Expatriates and local nationals may be on the same compensation plan	Inhibits mobility for lower levels of expatriates Lack of consistency among locations
Cafeteria approaches	Senior executives	Tax- and cost-effective	To be effective, options needed for each country Difficult to use with lower levels of expatriates
Regional plans	Large numbers of expatriates mobile within region(s)	Less costly than global uniformity Can be tailored to regional requirements	Multiple plans to administer Discrimination between regionalists and globalists

Multiple programmes	Many expatriates on different types of assignments	Can tailor compensation programmes to different types of expatriates Possible lower compensation costs	Difficulty of establishing and maintaining categories Discrimination by category Highly complex administration

Source: Evans et al (2002; p.132)

Table 24 *A summary of expatriate compensation systems*

One of the most popular methods is the 'balance-sheet' approach. This is designed to maintain standards of living for expatriates irrespective of their assignment location. Under this approach, expatriates are kept on the home pay system, while allowances and differentials are used to maintain home equity for items such as goods and services, housing and income tax. The idea is that the expatriate should neither gain nor lose, thus encouraging mobility. The system is administratively simple.

QUESTION

- What are the potential disadvantages of the balance-sheet approach for a) the individual, and b) the organisation?

Alternatives to the balance-sheet approach include a 'global' compensation structure in which national origin or home has no impact. This type of scheme is more often applied to senior executives who are regarded as truly global employees. However, such systems are fraught with standard-of-living issues, not to mention complexities of tax and pension planning.

Expatriate compensation is becoming more problematic as the profile of the typical expatriate becomes more diverse. Packages based on the traditional white male with a trailing spouse and children may be completely inappropriate for a woman from the Indian subcontinent who leaves her children at home. In addition, the role of the compensation package as a key motivator for international mobility may well differ, depending on the life-stage and/or career intentions of the assignee. The trend towards rationalisation of expatriate compensation and benefits packages, linked with increasing numbers of dual-career couples, makes the decision whether to accept an international assignment or not a much more complex one.

A developing trend in Europe is for companies to treat the whole of the EU and its related partners in EFTA as one country: no work permits are required, there is a right to residence in every country, medical help is available everywhere, etc. Moving people within the EU means providing the same sort of support that a transfer within one country would attract, but no 'expatriate' allowances.

Performance measurement

Given that expatriates are among the most expensive people an organisation employs, it is surprising how little is known about the assessment of their performance and contribution. Of course it involves a complex range of issues, and research to date suggests that rigorous performance appraisal systems for expatriates are far from universal (Brewster, 1991; Schuler *et al*, 1991; Fenwick *et al*, 1999). The assessment of expatriate performance requires an understanding of the variables that influence an expatriate's success or failure in a foreign assignment.

An objective appraisal of expatriate performance is likely to be highly complex. This is because the general difficulties of performance measurement are compounded in the case of expatriates by HQ's lack of knowledge of the local situation.

The already problematic relationship is further complicated by the necessity of reconciling the tension between the need for universal appraisal standards with specific objectives in local units. It is also important to recognise that more time may be needed to achieve results in markets which enjoy little supporting infrastructure from the parent company (Schuler *et al*, 1991).

QUESTION

- What techniques might an organisation use to assess the performance of an expatriate?

Multinational companies are aware that there are no easy answers here and tend to use a variety of methods. Thus they may combine formal performance appraisal with visits from HQ; visits back to HQ; an assessment of results in the area under the expatriate's command; reports; emails – in short, anything that will help them make a judgement. Formal appraisal systems for expatriates may either be local (with the value of cultural sensitivity and local knowledge, but with little comparability between results from different parts of the world) or be worldwide, with the opposite advantages and disadvantages.

Repatriation

The final element in the global assignment cycle is the repatriation phase. The relationship between the foreign assignment and the future human resource needs of the organisation has become more important, with an increasing focus on the need to develop international/global mindsets (Harvey *et al*, 1999; Osland *et al*, 2006) and the role of expatriates as mechanisms of knowledge transfer (Bonache and Brewster, 2001). In this respect, evidence of major problems with repatriation for multinational companies is worrying. Surveys suggest that 10 to 25% of expatriates leave their company within twelve months of repatriation (Black, 1992; Black and Gregersen, 1999; Solomon, 1995), a figure notably higher than for equivalent non-expatriates (Black and Gregersen, 1991), and that between a quarter and a third of repatriates leave their firms within two years of returning (Suutari and Brewster, 2000). Since nearly half the companies did not keep records of the career outcomes of repatriates, the true figure is likely to be higher. In a sample of Finnish expatriates, even among those who stayed with the same employer, well over half had seriously considered leaving (Suutari and Brewster, 2003). About one-third of the repatriate group studied by Suutari and Brewster (2003) had changed their employer. From those, one-third had done so while they were still abroad. The timing indicates that they had changed employer earlier than the average repatriation job negotiations started.

The problem has been emphasised in recent years, particularly in Europe, because the expansion of foreign operations has taken place coincident with a rationalisation of HQ operations. In the leaner HQ operations of today's world there are few spaces for expatriates to 'fill in' while the organisation seeks for a more permanent position for them. A majority of organisations nowadays do not provide post-assignment guarantees ((GMAC GRS/Windham International, 2000; ORC, 2000). From the repatriate perspective, other problems associated with re-integrating into the home country are loss of status, loss of autonomy, loss of career direction, and a feeling that international experience is undervalued by the company (Johnston, 1991). Alongside these there may also be a loss of income and life-style, and family readjustment problems.

A critical issue in repatriation is the management of expectations (Pickard, 1999: Stroh *et al*, 1998; Welch, 1998). Work-related expectations of repatriates can include job position after repatriation, standard of living, improved longer-term career prospects, opportunities to utilise skills acquired while abroad, and support and interest from supervisors and colleagues in the home country. There are few empirical studies concerning the expectations of repatriates. The ones that have been reported note generally high expectations. Most expatriates expect the return to enhance their career prospects and their return to be exciting and/or challenging (Suutari and Brewster, 2003). Often it is not.

For most expatriates, the experience is hugely positive and of great value in their careers. Frequently, however, such value is obtained for a company other than the one that paid for the international experience. This is a substantial loss for the company, made worse by the fact that these individuals rarely change their careers radically: they are more likely to go and work for competitors than move into an entirely different industry.

Together, these findings suggest that organisations should devote more attention to their handling of repatriation, and that it should be part of the overall planning of the international assignment. Examples of best practice in this area include:

- pre-departure career discussions

- a named contact person at the home-country organisation

- a mentor at the host location

- re-entry counselling

- family repatriation programmes

- employee debriefings

- succession planning.

In any international company, effective handling of all stages of an international assignment is critical to ensuring the full utilisation and development of human resources. Mishandling of returning expatriates means that a good deal of critical knowledge is lost to the organisation.

SUMMARY

This chapter has examined the literature on one aspect of international working – the management of expatriates. It has noted that the international aspect adds many difficulties in addition to those involved in managing staff in one country, and that those difficulties occur at each point of what we have called the 'global assignment cycle'. This is likely to be an ever-growing part of the work of HR departments. Given that expatriates are almost invariably amongst the most expensive people for companies to employ, and that they are usually in important positions, the necessity of taking a strategic view of the use and management of expatriates becomes obvious.

The next chapter explores this issue further, and also examines the issues related to other kinds of international working.

LEARNING QUESTIONS

- Expatriation is an expensive process: what are the reasons that cause companies to continue to use it?

- Given the ease with which we can communicate internationally through electronic means, and the increasing ease of air transport, is it likely that there will be fewer expatriates in the future? Give reasons for your answer.

- Compare the advantages for companies and individuals of using permanent, career expatriates who go from country to country as opposed to single-assignment expatriates.

- What would be the best and most cost-effective form of pre-departure training and development for an expatriate?

■ Why should a company be worried about expatriates leaving it at the end of an assignment? What should it do to minimise the possibility?

REFERENCES

Adler, N. J. (1986) *International Dimensions of Organizational Behavior*. Boston, MA, PWS-Kent

Antal, A. and Izraeli, D. (1993) 'Women managers from a global perspective: women managers in their international homelands and as expatriates', in E. Fagenson (ed.) *Women in Management: Trends, issues and challenges in management diversity, Women and Work*, Vol. 4. Newbury Park, CA, Sage

Arthur, W. and Rousseau, D. M. (1996) *Boundaryless Careers*. Oxford, Blackwell

Aycan, Z. (1997) 'Expatriate adjustment as a multifaceted phenomenon: individual and organisational-level predictors', *International Journal of Human Resource Management*, 8 (4): 434–56

Baker, J. and Ivancevich, J. (1971) 'The assignment of American executives abroad: systematic, haphazard or chaotic?', *California Management Review*, 13 (3): 39–44

Banai, M. and Harry, H. (2004) 'Boundaryless global careers', *International Studies of Management and Organization*, 34 (3): 96–120

Baruch, Y. and Altman, Y. (2002) 'Expatriation and repatriation in MNCs: a taxonomy', *Human Resource Management*, 41 (2): 239–59

Bhaskar-Shrinivas, P., Harrison, D. A., Shaffer, M. A. and Luk, D. M. (2005) 'Input-based and time-based models of international adjustment: meta-analytic evidence and theoretical extensions', *Academy of Management Journal*, 48 (2): 257–81

Black, J. S. (1988) 'Work role transitions: a study of American expatriate managers in Japan', *Journal of International Business Studies*, 30 (2): 119–34

Black J. S. (1992) 'Coming home: the relationship of expatriate expectations with repatriation adjustment and work performance', *Human Relations*, 45 (2): 177–92

Black, J. S. and Gregersen, H. B. (1991) 'Antecedents to cross-cultural adjustment for expatriates in Pacific Rim assignments', *Human Relations*, 44: 497–515

Black, J. S. and Mendenhall, M. (1989) 'A practical but theory-based framework for selecting cross-cultural training methods', *Human Resource Management*, 28: 511–39

Black, J. S. and Stephens, G. K. (1989) 'The influence of the spouse on American expatriate adjustment in overseas assignments', *Journal of Management*, 15: 529–44

Black, J. S., Mendenhall, M. and Oddou, G. (1991) 'Toward a comprehensive model of international adjustment: an integration of multiple theoretical perspectives', *Academy of Management Review*, 16: 291–317

Bonache, J. (2006) 'The compensation of expatriates: a review and a future research agenda', in G. Stahl and I. Björkman (eds) *Handbook of Research in International Human Resource Management*. Cheltenham, Edward Elgar

Bonache, J. and Brewster, C. (2001) 'Expatriation: a developing research agenda', *Thunderbird International Business Review*, 43 (1): 3–20

Bonache, J. and Fernandez, Z. (1999) 'Multinational companies: a resource-based approach', in C. Brewster and H. Harris (eds) *International Human Resource Management: Contemporary issues in Europe*. London, Routledge

Bonache, J., Brewster, C. and Suutari, V. (2007) 'International mobility and careers: editorial', special edition *International Studies in Management and Organization*

Brewster, C. (1991) *The Management of Expatriates*. London, Kogan Page

Brewster, C. and Pickard, J. (1994) 'Evaluating expatriate training', *International Studies of Management and Organisation*, 24 (3): 18–35

Brewster, C. and Scullion, H. (1997) 'Expatriate HRM: an agenda and a review', *Human Resource Management Journal*, 7 (3): 32–41

Brislin, R. W. (1986) 'The working and translation of research instruments', in W. J. Lonner and J. W. Berry (eds) *Field Methods in Cross-Cultural Research*. Beverly Hills, CA, Sage

Caligiuri, P. M. and Tung, R. L. (1998) 'Are masculine cultures female-friendly? Male and female expatriates' success in countries differing in work value orientations'. Paper presented at the International Congress of the International Association for Cross-Cultural Psychology: The Silver Jubilee Congress, Bellingham, WA

Caligiuri, P., Hyland, M., Joshi, A. and Bross, A. (1998) 'A theoretical framework for examining the relationship between family adjustment and expatriate adjustment to working in the host country', *Journal of Applied Psychology*, 83 (4): 598–614

Cendant International Assignment Services (1999) *Policies and Practices Survey 1999*. London, Cendant International Assignment Services

Church, A. (1982) 'Sojourner adjustment', *Psychological Bulletin*, 91 (3): 540–72

Collins, S. (1995) *Expatriation: A moving experience*. Dublin, Michael Smurfitt Graduate School of Business

Coyle, W. (1992) *International Relocation*. Oxford, Butterworth-Heinemann

Dickmann, M., Doherty, N. and Brewster, C. (2007) 'Why do they go? Individual and corporate perspectives on the factors influencing the decision to accept an international assignment', *International Journal of Human Resource Management*

Dowling, P. J. and Welch, D. (2004) *International Human Resource Management: Managing people in a multinational context*, 4th edition. London, Thomson Learning

Dowling, P. J., Schuler, R. S. and Welch, D. (1994) *International Dimensions of Human Resource Management*, 2nd edition. Belmont, CA, Wadsworth

Economist (2006) 'Travelling more lightly', *The Economist*, 379 (8483): 99–101

Evans, P., Pucik, V. and Barsoux, J.-L. (2002) *The Global Challenge*. Boston, MA, McGraw-Hill Irwin

Fenwick, M. S., De Cieri, H. and Welch, D. E. (1999) 'Cultural and bureaucratic control in MNEs: the role of expatriate performance management', *Management International Review*, 39 (3): 107–24

Glanz, L. (2003) 'Expatriate stories: a vehicle of professional development abroad?', *Journal of Managerial Psychology*, 18 (3): 259–74

GMAC Global Relocation Services (2005) *Global Relocation Trends 2005, Survey Report*. Woodridge, IL, GMAC

Gong, Y. (2003) 'Subsidiary staffing in multinational enterprises: agency, resources and performance', *Academy of Management Journal*, 46: 728–39

Harris, H. (1995) 'Women's role in international management', in A. W. K. Harzing and J. van Ruysseveldt (eds) *International Human Resource Management*. London, Sage

Harris, H. (1999) 'Women in international management: why are they not selected?', in C. Brewster and H. Harris (eds) *International HRM: Contemporary issues in Europe*. London, Routledge

Harris, H. and Brewster, C. (1999a) 'The coffee-machine system: how international selection really works', *International Journal of Human Resource Management*, 10 (2): 488–500

Harris, H. and Brewster, C. (1999b) 'A framework for pre-departure preparation', in C. Brewster and H. Harris (eds) *International HRM: Contemporary issues in Europe*. London, Routledge

Harris, P. R. and Moran, R. T. (1996) *Managing Cultural Differences*, 2nd edition. Houston, TX, Gulf

Harvey, M. (1995) 'The impact of dual-career families on international relocations', *Human Resources Management Review*, 5 (3): 223–44

Harvey, M. (1996) 'Addressing the dual-career expatriation dilemma in international relocation', *Human Resource Planning*, 19 (4): 91–109

Harvey, M. (1997) 'Dual-career expatriates: expectations, adjustment and satisfaction with international relocation', *Journal of International Business Studies*, 28 (3): 627–57

Harvey, M. (1998) 'Dual-career couples during international relocation: the trailing spouse', *International Journal of Human Resource Management*, 9 (2): 309–22

Harvey, M. and Novicevic, M. M. (2004) 'The development of political skill and political capital by global leaders through global assignments', *International Journal of Human Resource Management*, 15 (7): 1173–88

Harvey, M. Speier, C. and Novicevic, M. M. (1999) 'The role of inpatriation in global staffing', *International Journal of Human Resource Management*, 10 (3): 457–75

Harzing, A. W. K. (1995) 'The persistent myth of high expatriate failure rates', *International Journal of Human Resource Management*, 6 (2): 457–75

Haslberger, A. (2005) 'The complexities of expatriate adaptation', *Human Resource Management Review*, 15: 160–80

Hiltrop, J.-M. and Janssens, M. (1990) 'Expatriation: challenges and recommendations', *European Management Journal*, March: 19–27

Inkson, K. and Myers, B. (2003) 'The big O.E.: international travel and career development', *Career Development International*, 8 (4): 170–81

Inkson, K., Arthur, M. B., Pringle, J. and Barry, S. (1997) 'Expatriate assignment versus overseas experience: contrasting models of international human resource development', *Journal of World Business*, 32 (4): 351–68

Johnson, E. C., Kristof-Brown, A. L., van Vianen, A. E. M., de Pater, L. E. and Klein, M. R. (2003) 'Expatriate social ties: personality antecedents and consequences for adjustment', *International Journal of Selection and Assessment*, 11 (4): 277–88

Johnston, J. (1991) 'An empirical study of repatriation of managers in UK multinationals', *Human Resource Management Journal*, 1 (4): 102–8

Jones, B. (1997) 'Getting ahead in Switzerland', *Management Review*, 86 (6): 58–61

Kim, Y. Y. (1988) *Communication and Cross-Cultural Adaptation*. Clevedon, UK/Philadelphia, PA, Multilingual Matters

Mayrhofer, W. and Brewster, C. (1996) 'In praise of ethnocentricity: expatriate policies in European multinationals', *International Executive*, 38 (6): 749–78

McCaughey, D. and Bruning, N. S. (2005) 'Enhancing opportunities for expatriate job satisfaction: HR strategies for foreign assignment success', *Human Resource Planning*, 28 (4): 21–9

Mendenhall, M. and Oddou, G. (1985) 'The dimensions of expatriate acculturation: a review', *Academy of Management Review*, 10: 39–47

Mendenhall, M. and Oddou, G. (1986) 'Acculturation profiles of expatriate managers: implications for cross-cultural training programs', *Columbia Journal of World Business*, Winter: 73–9

Mendenhall, M. E., Kühlmann, T. M. and Stahl, G. D. (eds) (2001) *Developing Global Business Leaders*. Westport, CT, Quorum

Mendenhall, M., Punnett, B. J. and Ricks, D. (1995) *Global Management*. Cambridge, MA, Blackwell

Mendenhall, M. E., Kühlman, T. M., Stahl, G. and Osland, J. S. (2002) 'Employee development and expatriate assignents', in M. J. Gannon and K. L. Newman (eds) *Handbook of Cross-Cultural Management*. London, Blackwell

Miller, E. (1972) 'The selection decision for an international assignment: a study of the decision-makers' behaviour', *Journal of International Business Studies*, 3: 49–65

Moore, S. and Punnett, J. (1994) 'Expatriates and their spouses: a pilot study in the Limerick region and directions for future research', *Irish Business and Administration Research*, 15: 178–84

Morley, M. and Heraty, N. (2004) 'International assignments and global careers', *Thunderbird International Business Review*, 46 (6): 633–46

Morley, M., Burke, C. and Finn, G. (1997) 'The Irish in Moscow: a question of adjustment', *Human Resource Management Journal*, 7 (3): 53–67

Organization Resources Counselors (ORC) (1998) *North American Survey of International Assignment Policies and Practices*. New York, ORC

Organization Resources Counselors (ORC) (2000) *Worldwide Survey of International Assignment Policies and Practices*. London and New York, ORC

Osland, J., Bird, A., Mendenhall, M. E. and Osland, A. (2006) 'Developing global leadership and global mindsets: a review', in G. Stahl and I. Björkman (eds) *Handbook of Research in International Human Resource Management*. Cheltenham, Edward Elgar

Perkins, S. (2006) *International Reward and Recognition*. London, Chartered Institute of Personnel and Development

Phillips, N. (1992) 'Cross-cultural training', *Journal of European Industrial Training*, 17 (2): 3–11

Pickard, J. (1999) 'Successful repatriation: organisational and individual perspectives'. PhD Thesis. Cranfield, Cranfield University

PriceWaterhouseCoopers (2000) *International Assignments: European policy and practice 1999/2000*. London, PWC

Pucik, V. (1998) 'Selecting and developing the global versus the expatriate manager: a review of the state of the art', *Human Resource Planning*, 21 (4): 40–54

Punnett, B. J. and Ricks, D. A. (1992) *International Business*. Boston, MA, PWS-Kent

Punnett, B. J., Crocker, O. and Stevens, M. A. (1992) 'The challenge for women expatriates and spouses: some empirical evidence', *International Journal of Human Resource Management*, 3 (3): 585–92

Reynolds, C. and Bennett, R. (1991) 'The career couple challenge', *Personnel Journal*, March: 46–9

Schiuma, G., Harris, H. and Bourne, M. (2002) *Assessing the Value of International Assignments*. Centre for Business Performance/Centre for Research into the Management of Expatriation, Cranfield School of Management

Schuler, R. S., Fulkerson, J. R. and Dowling, P. J. (1991) 'Strategic performance measurement and management in multinational corporations', *Human Resource Management*, 30: 365–92

Scullion, H. (1994) 'Creating international managers: recruitment and development issues', in P. Kirkbride (ed.) *Human Resource Management in Europe*. London, Routledge

Scullion, H. and Colings, D. (2006) *Global Staffing* London, Routledge

Scullion, H. and Starkey, K. (2000) 'In Search of the changing role of the corporate human resource function in international firms', *International Journal of Human Resource Management* 11(6): 106–81

Searle, W. and Ward, C. (1990) 'The prediction of psychological and sociocultural adjustment during cross-cultural transitions', *International Journal of Intercultural Relations*, 14: 449–64

Solomon, C. M. (1995) 'Repatriation, up, down or out?', *Personnel Journal*, 74 (1): 28–35

Sparrow, P. R. (1999) 'International recruitment, selection and assessment: whose route map will you follow?', in P. Joynt and B. Morton (eds) *The Global HR Manager: Creating the seamless organisation*. London, IPD

Sparrow, P. R. (2006) *International Recruitment, Selection and Assessment*. London, Chartered Institute of Personnel and Development

Spreitzer, G. M., McCall, M. W. and Mahoney, J. D. (1997) 'Early identification of international executive potential', *Journal of Applied Psychology*, 82(1): 6–29

Stroh, L. K. and Caligiuri, P. M. (1998) 'Increasing global competitiveness through effective people management', *Journal of World Business*, 33 (1): 1–16

Stroh, L. K., Black, J. S., Mendenhall, M. E. and Gregersen, H. B. (2005) *International Assignments: An integration of strategy, research and practice*. London, Lawrence Erlbaum

Stroh, L. K., Gregerson, H. B. and Black, J. S. (1998) 'Closing the gap: expectations versus reality among expatriates', *Journal of World Business*, 33 (2): 111–24

Suutari, V. and Brewster, C. (1998) 'The adaptation of expatriates in Europe: evidence from Finnish companies', *Personnel Review*, 27 (2): 89–103

Suutari, V. and Brewster, C. (2000) 'Making their own way: international experience through self-initiated foreign assignments', *Journal of World Business*, 35 (4): 417–36

Suutari, V. and Brewster, C. (2003) 'Repatriation: empirical evidence from a longitudinal study of careers and expectations among Finnish expatriates', *International Journal of Human Resource Management*: 14 (7): 1132–51

Suutari, V. and Tornikoski, C. (2001) 'The challenge of expatriate compensation: the source of satisfaction and dissatisfaction among expatriates', *International Journal of Human Resource Management*, 12 (3): 1–16

Takeuchi, R., Tesluk, P. E., Yun, S. and Lepak, D. P. (2005) 'An integrative view of international experience', *Academy of Management Journal*, 48: 85–100

Torbiörn, I. (1997) 'Staffing for international operations', *Human Resource Management Journal*, 7 (3): 42–53

Tung, R. (1981) 'Selection and training of personnel for overseas assignments', *Columbia Journal of World Business*, 16 (1): 68–78

Tung, R. (1982) 'Selection and training procedures of US, European and Japanese multinationals', *California Management Review*, 25 (1): 57–71

Tung, R. L. (1998) 'American expatriates abroad: from neophytes to cosmopolitans', *Journal of World Business*, 33(2): 125–144

Ward, C. and Kennedy, A. (1999) 'The measurement of sociocultural adaptation', *International Journal of Intercultural Relations*, 23: 659–77

Ward, C., Okura, Y., Kennedy, A. and Kojima, T. (1998) 'The U-curve on trial: a longitudinal study of psychological and sociocultural adjustment during cross-cultural transition', *International Journal of Intercultural Relations*, 11(22): 277–91

Waxin, M. F. and Panaccio, A. J. (2005) 'Cross-cultural training to facilitate expatriate adjustment: it works!', *Personnel Review*, 34 (1): 51–67

Waxin, M. F. and Brewster, C. (2005) 'Expatriates' time to profiency: antecedents and country of origin effects'. Paper for the 8th Conference on International Human Resources Management, Making a Difference in a World of Differences, Cairns, Australia

Welch, D. (1998) 'The Pyschological contract and expatriation: a disturbing issue for HRM?' Paper presented at 6th Conference on International Human Resource Management, University of Paderborn.

Welch, D. and Worm, V. (2006) 'International business travellers: a challenge for IHRM', in G. Stahl and I. Björkman (eds) *Handbook of Research in International Human Resource Management*. Cheltenham, Edward Elgar

Yamazaki, Y. and Kayes, C. (2004) 'An experiential approach to cross-cultural learning: a review and integration of competencies for successful expatriate adaptation', *Academy of Management Learning and Education*, 5 (4): 362–79

Zeira, Y. and Banai, M. (1984) 'Selection of expatriate managers in MNEs: the lost environment point of view', *International Studies of Management and Organisation*, 15 (1): 33–51

Zeira, Y. and Banai, M. (1985) 'Present and desired methods of selecting expatriate managers for international assignments', *Personnel Review*, 13 (3): 29–35

Zimmermann, A. and Sparrow, P. (2007) 'Mutual adjustment processes in international teams: lessons for the study of expatriation', *International Studies in Management and Organisation*, 37(3), Fall

Managing diversity in international working

CHAPTER OBJECTIVES

When they have read this chapter, students will:

■ be able to evaluate the strengths and weaknesses of various forms of diversity initiatives in international organisations

■ be able to recommend ways of increasing the number of women in international management

■ be familiar with the various theoretical perspectives relating to work–life balance and international working

■ be able to assess the pros and cons of using various forms of international working

■ know how to measure the value of international assignments.

INTRODUCTION

In order to become truly global in orientation, organisations must ensure that they maximise their human resources wherever they are located. As we have seen in the preceding chapters, achieving this entails a clear understanding of a wide range of factors, particularly cultural differences, which might impact on the development of a truly diverse workforce and management cadre. In Chapter 6 we explained how the population of international employees inside organisations has become very fragmented. Diversity management has therefore become a key feature of human resource policies for both domestic and internationally based organisations over the last decade.

Diversity management refers to initiatives that capitalise on the diversity in a firm's workforce (including such characteristics as race, ethnicity, national origin, gender, age and disability) as a 'strategic approach to business that contributes to organisational goals such as profits and productivity'.

In this chapter we examine first the nature of diversity programmes within international organisations. We then focus on fostering diversity within the international assignee population, because this is perceived to be a critical step in progression to senior management positions. We examine research into the role of women in international management, drawing conclusions for broader diversity initiatives, and investigate the implications of dual-career and work–life balance considerations on the nature of international working. Finally we consider the issues concerned in measuring the value of international assignments in order for more objective planning decisions to be taken.

DIVERSITY MANAGEMENT PROGRAMMES

Despite a prevalence of diversity programmes in the USA, and anti-discrimination programmes in the European Union, it is unclear how much this type of approach has been taken up in organisations in other parts of the world. For example, in the late 1990s the International Labour Organisation attempted to survey workplace anti-discrimination diversity training programmes in 14 industrial nations. The survey was only completed in three nations – the United States, Great Britain and the Netherlands – principally because of an inability in the other nations to identify samples of workplaces where such training existed.

Common features of US diversity management approaches include:

- a broad definition of diversity, often known as 'universal inclusion' – This is a broader definition than employment discrimination legal compliance and can encompass any personal characteristics that affect employees' workplace treatment or productivity

- a 'business case' motivation for diversity initiatives – Typical objectives include: being an employer of choice, attracting and retaining talent, developing high-potential employees, increasing productivity, and keeping up with competitors

- administrative structures for diversity, which may include: a small, *specialist consulting group* at headquarters, either reporting directly to a senior executive or located in the firm's human resources department; *diversity councils* at corporate and local levels; and *affinity groups* (eg women or ethnic minority networks) to link and represent employees who are members of specific demographic groups. Short training programmes are a key feature of the diversity approach

- integration of the organisation's diversity initiatives into organisational change programmes.

DIVERSITY MANAGEMENT IN INTERNATIONAL ORGANISATIONS

For those organisations committed to diversity management operating in international contexts, a key debate is the extent to which their diversity programmes should be standardised across subsidiaries. In principle, the organisational structure of a multinational enterprise's diversity management activities should support the one the firm has adopted for its overall activities. This would assume that an organisation adopting an ethnocentric or geocentric approach would have more or less standardised programmes across the world. However, this area is particularly influenced by local institutions and culture, which may render company-wide programmes inappropriate. Many organisations therefore allow a considerable degree of autonomy to their subsidiaries in developing their own diversity programmes, often providing expert assistance from headquarters if needed.

Case study

Internationalising diversity management in a US-based telecom company

Telco (not the company's real name) adopts a 'multilocal' approach in all aspects of internationalisation. Internationalising diversity is therefore driven from the bottom rather than the top. Each international facility is responsible for developing, designing, implementing and funding its own diversity management work. The role of the corporate headquarters is an advisory one, communicating the corporate-wide diversity message and responding to requests for assistance.

The experience of Telco in running a multi-domestic diversity approach has highlighted both the strengths and weaknesses of such a system. Making local staff responsible for shaping diversity activities was perceived as having the following positive benefits:

- harnessing the energy of managers who feel personally involved in the outcomes
- unleashing considerable creativity and commitment
- resulting in activities well targeted toward issues of local relevance.

On the negative side, localised efforts were perceived as problematic due to:

- lack of time to invest in diversity initiatives on an ongoing basis

---

- lack of training and expertise in diversity management on the part of local managers, which led to 'reinventing the wheel' on occasions.

Initiatives were limited to training interventions due to managers' lack of resources and authority to explore system-wide diversity problems embedded in HR systems.

QUESTION

- What steps would you take to implement a global diversity strategy, taking into account the issues raised in the Telco case study above?

WOMEN IN INTERNATIONAL MANAGEMENT

The development of a global mindset – the goal of many transnational organisations – can only be achieved through exposure to diversity. It is hardly likely that a homogeneous group of managers will develop a global mindset unless the composition of the group is changed to reflect the diversity within the organisation and potentially within its client base. A key indicator of a transnational organisation is a diverse population amongst board members. However, despite making up almost half the workforce in many industrialised countries, the number of women at board level is minimal. In the UK, for instance, women comprise only 2% of executive directors and 10% of non-executive directors.

Many aspiring global organisations strive to develop a broad international cadre of managers amongst their most promising junior and middle-management-level employees who are intended to feed into the most senior positions in the company. International management assignments constitute a vital component of the development of a geocentric mindset amongst this body of managers. Adler and Bartholomew (1992; p.18) stress the importance of international assignments to developing a 'global firm':

'Foreign assignments become a core component of the organisational and career development process. "Transpatriates" from all parts of the world are sent to all other parts of the world to develop their worldwide perspective and cross-cultural skills ... Foreign assignments are used ... to enhance individual and organisational learning in all parts of the system.'

Despite this increase in demand for international assignees, the numbers of women in such positions is increasing only slowly. Research in the USA and the UK puts the percentage of women on international management assignments as between 2 and 15% (Adler, 1984a; Brewster, 1991; Florkowski and Fogel, 1995; Harris, 1999; ORC, 1998; Reynolds and Bennett, 1991; Tung, 1997). It is probably higher in multinationals from the Nordic countries (Suutari and Brewster, 2002). There is evidence that this situation might slowly be improving. For example, the latest GMAC survey (GMAC, 2005) suggests that with regard to global mobility 23% of expatriates are now women (up from 10% in 1994). Nonetheless, given that women now constitute almost 50% of the UK workforce and form approximately 26% of junior and middle management positions (Labour Force Survey, 1995), assumptions that diversity is being acknowledged and incorporated in the development of a geocentric mindset must be questioned.

The rising but still low incidence of women on international management assignments is puzzling when one looks at research into the criteria for effective international managers. Here, as noted in Chapter 12, the emphasis is on interpersonal, intuitive and co-operative styles of management as the key skills for working internationally. These same skills have been argued to be typical of a 'female' style of management (Fondas, 1997; Marshall, 1984; Rosener, 1990; Sharma, 1990; Vinnicombe, 1987). Why, therefore, do organisations continue to under-use such a valuable source of diversity and a potentially powerful aid towards developing a truly global mindset?

Reasons why women are not sent

One of the earliest and most influential bodies of work on women in international management was that of Adler (1984a, 1984b, 1984c, 1986, 1987). Working with a predominantly North American sample, she undertook a series of studies to investigate both the participation rates of women in international management and the reasons for the low rates revealed. In particular, she tested the veracity of three 'beliefs' which had emerged from the academic literature and from managers themselves in attempting to explain the scarcity of females on international assignments. These beliefs or 'myths' were:

- Women do not want to be international managers.

- Foreigners' prejudice against women renders them ineffective, even when they are interested in international assignments and are actually sent.

- Companies refuse to send women abroad.

Adler addressed the first myth in research (Adler, 1984b) amongst graduating MBA students in Canada, the United States and Europe. Her findings showed that new women graduates expressed as much interest in international careers as their male colleagues. Women, however, saw organisational barriers facing females as greater potential constraints to achieving this goal than did the male sample. A later study by Lowe et al (1999) amongst graduate and undergraduate business students in the United States reported that gender was a significant predictor when specific referent countries were identified. Differences in cultural distance and human development explained substantial variance among males and females in their willingness to accept international assignments. Political risk was not deemed to be a significant factor

The second myth was also shown to be questionable by research carried out by Adler in 1987 among North American female expatriates in Asia: 92% of this sample reported their assignment as being successful, backed up by supporting organisational evidence. Adler concluded that this finding revealed that the female expatriates were seen as foreigners who happened to be women and were not therefore subject to the same cultural constraints as local women (Adler, 1993; Jelinek and Adler, 1988; Westwood and Leung, 1994). Caligiuri and Cascio (1998) attribute such a phenomenon to the cognitive process of stereotyping subtypes (Brewer et al, 1981; Kunda and Thagard, 1996). They argue that according to this theory, Asian host nationals in Adler's study would have a sub-stereotype of 'Western working women' and a very different sub-stereotype for 'Asian working women'. Reactions to the two groups might well therefore be very different.

The third myth – organisational reluctance to send women overseas – turned out, however, to be true. In a survey of international personnel managers from 60 Canadian and US corporations, Adler (1984c) found that the major perceived barriers to women moving into international management assignments were foreigners' prejudice (72.7%) and dual-career marriages (69.1%). In addition, more than half of the managers saw their own company's reluctance to select women as a major barrier. This reluctance was attributed to:

- traditional male chauvinism

- recognition of the higher risk involved in sending an unproven quantity
- lack of suitably qualified or experienced women.

The role of organisational processes

Organisational processes form part of Caligiuri and Cascio's (1998) four-factor model for predicting the success of female global assignees. The four antecedents in the model are:

- personality traits
- organisational support
- family support
- host nationals' attitudes towards female expatriates.

Organisational support is defined in the model in terms of cross-cultural and gender-specific training for women on assignments, and projecting female expatriate managers as being most suitable and highly qualified for the job to local nationals. The model does not, however, include the role of organisational selection systems for international assignments as a critical variable in organisational support.

Harris (1999) examined the impact of organisational selection systems for international assignments on the participation rates of women. She drew on the wider research into discrimination in selection to assess the extent to which differing types of selection system would influence ideas about 'fit'. From a sociological perspective, selection is seen as a *social* process, to be used by those in power within the organisation as a means of determining the continuing form of the organisation by recruiting and promoting only those individuals who most closely conform to organisational norms. Individuals would therefore be judged more on the basis of their acceptability than their suitability (Jewson and Mason, 1986).

Social psychological studies explore the role of individual values in perpetuating discrimination in selection through the use of schema and stereotyping (see, for example, Futoran and Wyer, 1986; Heilman 1983). Such studies suggest that individual selectors will develop schema of 'ideal job-holders' and use them as a yardstick against which all prospective candidates are measured during the process of selection. In groups where there is a dominance of one gender, job-holder schema are likely to be gender-typed. In addition, the less distinct the information concerning the vacancy and/or the candidate, the more likely selectors are to use schemata and stereotypes.

Harris's research with UK-based MNEs revealed the existence of four typologies of selection systems for international manager positions. These were constituted in two dimensions. The first related to the extent to which organisations operated open or closed selection systems for international management assignments. An 'open' system is one in which all vacancies are advertised and anyone with appropriate qualifications and experience may apply and candidates are interviewed with greater or lesser degrees of formalised testing. Selection decisions are taken by consensus amongst selectors. In contrast, a 'closed' system is one in which selectors at corporate headquarters nominate 'suitable' candidates to line managers who have the option of accepting or rejecting them. In this situation, there may be only one manager involved in the selection process at head office. The candidate is only informed once agreement about acceptability has been reached between head office personnel and the line manager. The interview in this process consists of a negotiation about the terms and conditions of the assignment.

The second dimension related to the extent to which the process was a 'formal' or an 'informal' process. Within a 'formal' system, selection criteria are made explicit, with objective debate among selectors as to which candidate most closely matches the criteria. An 'informal' system consists of selectors using subjective and often unstated criteria for assessment with minimal systematic evaluation. Four possible variations of selection systems were therefore identified:

- open/formal
- closed/formal
- open/informal
- closed/informal (see Table 25).

	Formal	Informal
Open	Clearly defined criteria Clearly defined measures Training for selectors Open advertising of vacancy (internal/external) Panel discussions	Less defined criteria Less defined measures Limited training for selectors No panel discussions Open advertising of vacancy Recommendations
Closed	Clearly defined criteria Clearly defined measures Training for selectors Panel discussions Nominations only (networking/reputation)	Selectors' individual preferences determine criteria and measures No panel discussions Nominations only (networking/reputation)

Table 25 *A typology of international manager selection systems*

The implications of these variations in selection systems for international assignments in relation to women's participation are:

- *An open/formal system* would see greater clarity and consistency in thinking about international managers and a greater link with formal criteria. This system was seen to provide the greatest opportunities for women to be selected for international manager positions.

- *A closed/formal system* was perceived as similar to an open/formal system. However, the lack of personal contact with the candidate and the fact that the field of potential applicants is determined by the selector/s, with the attendant risk of omission of suitable candidates, may permit individual preferences by selectors to influence nominating individuals.

- *An open/informal system* would decrease clarity and consistency and linkage with formal criteria, and was therefore seen to provide less opportunity for women to enter international management positions, because selection decisions would be more subjective.

- *A closed/informal system* was perceived as the worst situation for equality of opportunity in this area, mixing as it does the potential for subjectivity on the part of the selectors and lack of access on the part of potential candidates.

Case study investigations, carried out as part of the research, indicated that the type of selection system in use for international assignments clearly affected the number of women in international organisations. In organisations with roughly equal numbers of men and women at entry and junior management levels and operating in similar overseas environments, the main differentiating factor in participation rates for male and female expatriates was the type of international selection system in operation.

QUESTIONS

- From your own experience, what do you feel are the key barriers to women gaining international assignments in your organisation?

> ■ What recommendations would you make to increase the number of women on international assignments?

This study highlights the need for organisations to review both their formal and informal processes leading towards the selection of international managers. Harris (1999) recommends the following key actions for organisations wishing to foster diversity in their expatriate management population. It should be noted that although these recommendations refer to women, they are equally valid in relation to other groups (such as geographical representation) that are currently not seen as the norm in the international manager population.

- ■ Organisations need to become more strategic in their planning for international assignments in order to prevent ad hoc and informal placements that may replicate an existing expatriate profile and prevent the adoption of alternative approaches.

- ■ A sophisticated approach to the determination of criteria for effective international managers should be adopted. Competencies should be developed and debated in as wide and diverse a forum as possible.

- ■ Selection processes for international management assignments should be monitored to ensure that access is not unfairly restricted to specific sections of employees. This includes auditing career development systems leading up to international assignments for potential unintended bias.

- ■ Selection skills training for all employees involved in selection for international assignments should be implemented. This training should include raising awareness of the advantages of using diverse groups of employees on international assignments, and should challenge existing stereotypes relating to women and other non-traditional groups.

- ■ Full support should be provided for alternative arrangements for the domestic aspect of international assignments that might influence the perception of accessibility amongst people with non-traditional domestic arrangements.

DUAL-CAREER COUPLES

The issue of dual-career couples is becoming increasingly common and an increasing source of concern to organisations sending individuals on international assignments. Assumptions about the problems associated with sending a woman abroad if she is in a dual-career couple have caused organisations to use this as a reason for not selecting potential female expatriates (Adler, 1984c). There is evidence, however, that male managers may be becoming less 'psychologically immersed' in their work. They are therefore less prepared to make sacrifices that might harm their domestic lifestyles (Forster, 1992; Scase and Goffee 1989). As a result, organisations can no longer expect to supply their expanding global management requirements from male managers alone. The issues surrounding dual-career couples will remain a significant part of the decision whether or not to send an employee on an international assignment – however, organisations will have to look for solutions to the dual-career issue for *both* genders, not just for male employees.

How organisations handle dual-career issues is currently the focus of considerable attention. Surveys indicate a wide divergence of practice among organisations in this area. One survey (GMAC GRS/ Windham International, 2000) reported that 51% of the larger organisations that were surveyed provide education assistance for the partner, and 46% establish partner networks. One company quoted in the report stated, 'We have a $5,000 partner allowance if the spouse [sic] is working prior to the assignment. It is up to $2,500 if the spouse is not working. There is job-search assistance in host and home locations up to $5,000, and a dislocation payment.' In contrast, Cendant International's (1999) survey of international assignment policy and practice showed that 74% of responding organisations did not take into account loss of the partner's income, and 45% provided no assistance for partners at all.

THE IMPLICATIONS OF INTERNATIONAL WORKING ON WORK–LIFE BALANCE

We examined the topic of work–life balance in Chapter 9. In this chapter we have noted that in the context of international working and international assignments, dual-career issues have been used as a key constraint to women's accessing international management positions. An even broader concern for international organisations is the impact of international working on work–life balance.

This book has underlined the importance of international assignments to organisations working across national borders in order to build global competence and integration. It has also shown evidence of failure in some long-term assignments. It is important to realise, however, that success in long-term assignments is not just a function of the individual but also of the partner and family. Research into dual-career couples undertaking long-term assignments highlights the need to take into account both partners' willingness to relocate in order to ensure a successful assignment (Harvey, 1995, 1996, 1997; Linehan and Walsh, 2000). The disruption caused by geographical relocations has also been seen to create tremendous disruption in the lives of all family members (Munton, 1990; Noe and Barbar, 1993; Guzzo et al, 1994). Work–life issues are among the most-cited problems associated with international working patterns for both those in relationships and single employees (CReME, 2000; Fenwick, 2001).

Over the last two decades, the need to acknowledge the influence of work factors on family satisfaction and non-work factors on job satisfaction has become a dominant theme in the organisational behaviour and human resource management literature.

In line with spillover theory (Aldous, 1969; Crouter, 1984; Piotrkowski, 1979), however, most studies are now based on the assumption that there is a reciprocal relationship between the two types of work–family conflict: work-interference-with-family conflict and family-interference-with-work conflict (see Figure 37). The nature of the reciprocal relationship suggests that if one's work interferes with family, family issues may come to the fore as family obligations go unfulfilled, and vice versa.

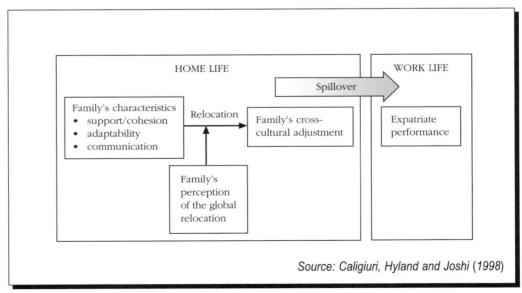

Source: Caligiuri, Hyland and Joshi (1998)

Figure 37 *A theoretical model of family adjustment and expatriate performance*

Although work–family balance has been the focus of a great deal of organisational, governmental and academic interest, it has remained a predominantly domestic-based issue. Work–family conflict is, however, likely to increase in international working scenarios which may involve the physical relocation of the entire family. In such cases, the boundaries between work and home become blurred due to the involvement of the whole family (Harvey, 1985). For dual-career couples, the partner's career may be disrupted and his or her sense of worth and identity may suffer (Harvey, 1997). The children's education may also be interrupted (Fukuda and Chu, 1994) and their social networks destroyed, which may affect their feelings of security and well-being (Harvey, 1985). In short, in international assignments, family life becomes more significant because the whole family is uprooted. Even in the case of short-term assignments and international commuting assignments, where the family may not physically relocate, the additional stressors on the individual living away from home have been seen to exacerbate work–family conflict (CReME, 2000; Fenwick, 2001; Peltonen, 2001).

QUESTION

- What can organisations do to ensure a good work–life balance for employees and their families while on international assignments?

ALTERNATIVE FORMS OF INTERNATIONAL WORKING

In Chapter 6 we explained that the nature of international work is fragmenting – there are many ways in which organisations might now use what can be termed international employees. In part this is because problems with dual-career couples and work–life balance issues for individuals undertaking expatriate or long-term assignments, coupled with an acknowledgement of the increasing costs of such moves, have driven an increase in the use of alternative forms of international working.

Apart from traditional expatriate or long-term assignments, organisations are using a variety of other types of assignment to fulfil international working obligations. Among these the key ones are:

- *short-term assignments* – an assignment with a specified duration, usually less than one year; the family may accompany the employee

- *the 'international commuter'* – an employee who commutes from the home country to a place of work in another country, usually on a weekly or bi-weekly basis, while the family remains at home

- *the 'frequent flyer'* – an employee who undertakes frequent international business trips but does not relocate.

Survey data indicates that there is increasing use of all types of assignment. Surveys by PriceWaterhouseCoopers (1999/2000) and CReME (2000) show the proportion of organisations that anticipate an increase in the use of all four types of assignment – see Figure 38.

271

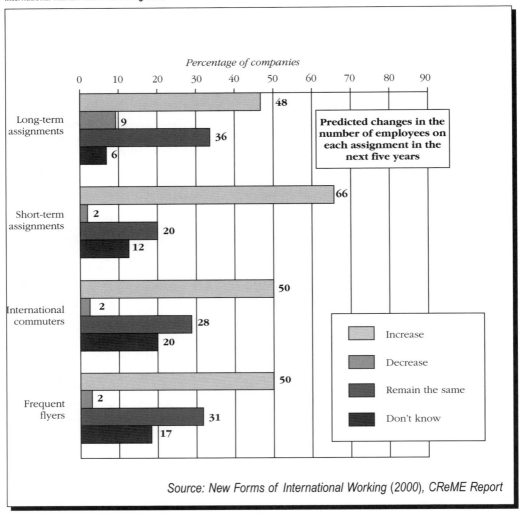

Figure 38 *The proportion of organisations predicting a change in the use of assignments*

One of the main reasons for organisations to adopt alternative methods of international working is to avoid some of the many problems with expatriation outlined in Chapter 12. Alternatives to expatriation are not without problems of their own, however, for both the organisations and the individuals concerned. Statements from respondents to the CReME survey (2000) indicate some of the key issues arising from each type of assignment.

Critical problems for *short-term assignments* are:

- work–life balance issues, which include long hours on a project and social/family separation
- controlling the number of employees
- frequent assignment extensions.

For *international commuter* assignments, the main problems for the individual are:

- burnout
- travel fatigue

- maintaining a balance between work and life

- dealing effectively with cultural issues in a foreign setting (very few organisations provide cross-cultural training for employees on these types of assignments).

Frequent flyers produce more of a problem. Many companies are unable to identify frequent flyers within their workforce owing to the absence of a policy for this type of international assignment (CReME 1999; PWC 1999/2000). Problems here include work–life balance issues.

It can be seen therefore that alternative forms of international working do not provide a complete solution to the problems arising from long-term assignments. Findings from current studies reinforce the need for careful attention to the possible implications of adopting alternative forms of international working.

MEASURING THE VALUE OF INTERNATIONAL ASSIGNMENTS

The need for a more strategic and detailed approach to managing international working from both the organisational and individual perspective has been highlighted in this chapter and previously in Chapter 12. However, despite the importance of international assignments, MNEs are not yet able to fully evaluate the benefits associated with their use. Thus, although some organisations have a clear outline of the international assignments' costs, very few, if any, have anything but a vague or unclear picture of the related return on investment. The need to develop a methodology to measure the value of international assignments is currently the focus of many consultancies operating in the area of IHRM.

Under this approach, the international assignment is seen as a value-generation process, which contributes to the company's business performance improvement (Schiuma, Harris and Bourne, 2003). As already noted in the previous chapter, international assignees are usually sent abroad for one of five main strategic reasons:

- professional development

- knowledge transfer

- transfer of scarce skills

- control

- co-ordination.

Each of these strategic reasons can add value to the organisation in terms of either financial value or knowledge value. Financial value refers to the overall assets of the organisation which can be easily expressed in monetary terms. Knowledge value, on the other hand, includes all the company's intangible assets. This could include stakeholder relationships as well as tacit rules and procedures, corporate culture, etc. In order for managers to be able to measure the value of each assignment, they must be able to identify where each assignment objective will be adding most value. Professional development, for instance, will probably be contributing to increasing the value of the organisation's human capital.

Table 26 points out the direct links that exist between the value driver categories with the value areas of an organisation.

Professional development provides direct value within the human resource area. In fact it is mainly aimed to develop the competence and attitude of the assignee undertaking the assignment.

Knowledge transfer can provide direct value within the stakeholder relationship, human resource, internal business process and intangible infrastructure area. Within the stakeholder area knowledge transfer can generate value, for example, in terms of improvement of relationships with the regulator by transferring to the regulator the organisational cultural approaches to business management – eg in respect of the tax, socio-cultural, and environment regulations. Knowledge transfer provides value within the area of human resource in the form of employee competence. Value in the area of internal business processes can be generated by transferring knowledge in the form of procedures and standards to improve operation process performance. Finally, knowledge transfer can involve disseminating organisational culture and management philosophy, providing value within the intangible infrastructure area.

	Financial value	Stakeholder relationship	Human resources	International business processes	Virtual infrastructure
Professional development			▢		
Knowledge transfer		▢	▢	▢	▢
Fulfilment of scarce skills		▢		▢	
Coordination		▢		▢	▢
Control	▢	▢		▢	▢

Table 26 *A matrix of the direct value-added contribution of an international assignment's value drivers to the value areas of a company*

The *fulfilment of scarce skills* provides direct value within the stakeholder relationship and internal business processes. In fact, an assignment aiming to fill skills gaps can produce value in the area of stakeholder relationships in terms of the improvement of management relationships with the stakeholders of the company, and in the area of internal business process allowing an improvement in process performance by putting in place specialised people.

Co-ordination provides direct value within the stakeholder relationship, internal business processes and intangible infrastructure areas. For example, it contributes to improving the communication processes between the organisation and its stakeholders; it allows better integration of the operations on a global base by sharing information and targets; it supports the organisation in developing a culture on a global base.

Control can generate direct value within the financial value, stakeholder relationship, internal business processes and intangible infrastructure area. In fact, the assignment as a control mechanism can provide value within the financial area by constraining local financial practices; within the stakeholder relationship it can contribute to maintaining good relationships by checking that subsidiaries behave consistently within the local norms and regulations; it can generate value within the internal business area by the definition of standards against which the operation processes have to be executed; finally, within the intangible infrastructure area it can provide value by shaping the local management philosophy.

A key concern with this type of methodology is that the definition of the metrics requires considerable time and effort on the part of managers. A major issue for organisations will be whether these metrics can be operationalised and over what time-scale. If, for example, the organisation is using international working to develop a cadre of knowledgeable and internationally minded executives, at what point are the measures to be applied? It remains to be seen whether organisations will adopt the discipline of developing metrics in an area that is noticeable for its lack of sophistication in planning and measurement.

SUMMARY

This chapter has examined the implications for organisations of diversity in their international workforces. It has addressed the strengths and weaknesses of various forms of diversity initiatives in international organisations. It has then looked at the issue of women in international management and has explored the reasons behind their minimal participation rates. The role of the home-country selection process has been noted as a key variable in terms of women's access to international management positions. It also discussed the implications of international working on work–life balance. Finally, the need for organisations to measure the value of international assignments was discussed in order to develop a more strategic approach to planning for international assignments, which should include diversity considerations. From both a practitioner and an academic standpoint, a good deal of work remains to be done in all these areas in order to harness the full potential of an organisation's international workforce.

LEARNING QUESTIONS

- What are the advantages for international organisations in ensuring a diverse workforce?

- If diversity is seen to be a critical factor of competitive advantage for international organisations, why is the expatriate population still largely white and male?

- Suggest practical steps an organisation can take to alleviate work–family issues for international assignments.

- Is it possible to create metrics to measure the value of international assignments? Suggest critical success factors for implementation.

REFERENCES

Adler, N. J. (1984a) 'Women in international management: where are they?', *California Management Review*, 26 (4): 78–89

Adler, N. J. (1984b) 'Women do not want international careers – and other myths about international management', *Organizational Dynamics*, 19 (3): 79–85

Adler, N. J. (1984c) 'Expecting international success: female managers overseas', *Columbia Journal of World Business*, 19 (3): 79–85

Adler, N. J. (1986) *International Dimensions of Organizational Behavior*. Boston, MA, PWS-Kent

Adler, N. J. (1987) 'Women as androgynous managers: a conceptualisation of the potential for American women in international management', *International Journal of Intercultural Relations*, 407–36

Adler, N. J. (1993) 'Competitive frontiers: women managers in the triad', *International Studies of Management and Organizations*, 23: 3–23

Adler, N. J. and Bartholomew, S. (1992) 'Managing globally competent people', *Academy of Management Executive*, 6: 52–64

Aldous, J. (1969) 'Occupational characteristics and males' role performance in the family', *Journal of Marriage and Family*, 31: 707–12

Brewer, M. B., Dull, V. and and Lui, L. (1981) 'Perceptions of the elderly: stereotypes as prototypes', *Journal of Personality and Social Psychology*, 41: 656–70

Brewster, C. (1991) *The Management of Expatriates*. London, Kogan Page

Caligiuri, P. and Cascio, W. (1998) 'Can we send her there? Maximising the success of western women on global assignments', *Journal of World Business*, 33 (4): 394–416

Caligiuri, P., Hyland, M., Joshi, A., and Bross, A. (1998) 'A theoretical framework for examining the relationship between family adjustment and expatriate adjustment to working in the host country', *Journal of Applied Psychology*, 83: 598–614

Cendant International Assignment Services (1999) *Policies and Practices Survey*. London, CIAS

CReME (2000) *New Forms of International Working*, Executive Report. Cranfield School of Management, UK

Crouter, A. (1984) 'Spillover from family to work: The neglected side of the work-family interface', *Human Relations*, 37: 425–42

Fenwick, M. (2001) 'Emerging forms of international working: evidence from Australia'. Paper at Academy of Management Conference, Washington

Florkowski, G. W. and Fogel, D. S. (1995) 'Perceived host ethnocentrism as a determinant of expatriate adjustment and organizational commitment'. Paper presented at the National Academy of Management Meeting, Vancouver, Canada

Fondas, N. (1997) 'Feminisation unveiled: management qualities in contemporary writings', *Academy of Management Review*, 22 (1): 257–82

Forster, N. (1992) 'International managers and mobile families: the professional and personal dynamics of trans-national career pathing and job mobility in the 1990s', *International Journal of Human Recource Management*, 3 (3): 605–24

Futoran, G. C. Wyer, R. S. (1986) 'The effects of traits and gender stereotypes on occupational suitability judgements and the recall of judgement-relevant information', *Journal of Experimental Social Psychology*, 22: 475–503

Fukuda, J. K. and Chu, P. (1994) 'Wrestling with Expatriate Family Problems: Japanese Experience in East Asia', *International Studies of Management and Organization*, Vol. 24

GMAC Global Relocation Services (2005) *Global Relocation Trends 2005*, Survey Report. Woodridge, IL, GMAC

GMAC Global Relocation Services/Windham (2000) *Global Relocation Trends 2000,* Survey Report. New York, GMAC

Guzzo, R. A., Noonan, K. A. and Elron, E. (1994) 'Expatriate managers and the psychological contract', *Journal of Applied Psychology*, 79: 617–26

Harris. H. (1999) 'Women in international management: why are they not selected?', in C. Brewster and H. Harris (eds) *International HRM: Contemporary issues in Europe*. London, Routledge

Harvey, M. (1985) 'The expat family: an overloaded variable in international assignments', *Columbia Journal of World Business*, Spring 84–92

Harvey, M. (1995) 'The impact of dual-career families on international relocations', *Human Resources Management Review*, 5 (3): 223–44

Harvey, M. (1996) 'Addressing the dual-career expatriation dilemma in international relocation', *Human Resource Planning*, 19 (4): 18–40

Harvey, M. (1997) 'Dual-career expatriates: expectations, adjustment and satisfaction with international relocation', *Journal of International Business Studies*, 28 (3): 627–57

Heilman, M. (1983) 'Sex bias in work settings: the lack of fit model', *Research in Organizational Behaviour*, 5: 269–98

Jelinek, M. and Adler, N. J. (1988) 'Women: world-class managers for global competition', *Academy of Mangement Executive*, 2 (1): 11–19

Jewson, N. and Mason, D. (1986) 'Modes of discrimination in the recruitment process: formalisation, fairness and efficiency', *Sociology*, 20 (1): 43–63

Kunda, Z. and Thagard, P. F. (1996) 'Forming impressions from stereotypes, traits and behaviors: a parallel-constraint-satisfaction theory', *Psychological Review*, 103: 284–308

Labour Force Survey 1989, 1995. London, HMSO

Linehan, M. and Walsh, J. S. (2000) 'Work–family conflict and the senior female international manager', *British Journal of Management*, 11, Special issue: 49–58

Lowe, K., Downes, M. and Kroek, K. (1999) 'The impact of gender and location on the willingness to accept overseas assignments', *International Journal of Human Resource Management*, 10 (2): 223–34

Marr, B. and Schiuma, G. (2001) 'Measuring and managing intellectual capital and knowledge assets in new economy organisations', in M. Bourne (ed.) *Handbook of Performance Measurement*. London, Gee

Marshall, J. (1984) *Women Managers: Travellers in a male world*. London, Wiley

Munton, A. G. (1990) 'Job relocation, stress and the family', *Journal of Organizational Behavior*, 11: 401–6

Noe, R. A. and Barbar, A. E. (1993) 'Willingness to accept mobility opportunities: destination makes a difference', *Journal of Organizational Behavior*, 14: 159–75

Organization Resources Counselors Inc. (1998) *North American Survey of International Assignment Policies and Practices*. New York, ORC

Peltonen, T. (2001) 'New forms of international work: an international survey study: results of the Finnish survey', University of Oulu, Finland

Piotrkowski, C. (1979) *Work and the Family System*. New York, Free Press

PriceWaterhouseCoopers (2000) *International Assignments: European Policy and Practice, 1999/2000*. London, PWC

Reynolds, C. and Bennett, R. (1991) 'The career couple challenge', *Personnel Journal*, 70 (3): 46–50

Roos, J., Roos, G., Dragonetti, N. C. and Edvinsson, L. (1997) *Intellectual Capital: Navigating in the new business landscape*. London, Macmillan

Rosener, J. (1990) 'Ways women lead', *Harvard Business Review*, 68 (6): 119–25

Scase, R. and Goffee, R. (1989) 'Women in management: towards a research agenda'. Paper for Third Annual Meeting of British Academy of Management

Schiuma, G., Harris, H. and Bourne, M. (2003) 'Assessing the value of international assignments', Centre for Business Performance/Centre for Research into the Management of Expatriation, Cranfield School of Management, UK

Sharma, S. (1990) 'Psychology of women in management: a distinct feminine leadership', *Equal Opportunities International*, 9 (2): 13–18

Smith, C. (1992) 'Dual careers, dual loyalties', *Asian Pacific Journal of Human Resources*, 30 (4): 19–30

Society of Human Resource Management (2001) 'How is a diversity initiative different from my affirmative action plan?', 23 July

Suutari, V. and Brewster, C. (2003) 'Repatriation: empirical evidence from a longitudinal study of careers and expectations among Finnish expatriates', *International Journal of Human Resource Management*, 14 (7): 1132–51

The Conference Board (1992) *Recruiting and Selecting International Managers* (Report No 998). New York, The Conference Board

Tung, R. L. (1997) 'Canadian expatriates in Asia-Pacific: an analysis of their attitude toward and experience in international assignments'. Paper presented at the meeting of the Society for Industrial and Organizational Psychology, St Louis, MO

Vinnicombe, S. (1987) 'What exactly are the differences in male and female working styles?', *Women in Management Review*, 3 (1): 13–22

Westwood, R. I. and Leung, S. M. (1994) 'The female expatriate manager experience: coping with gender and culture', *International Studies of Management and Organization*, 24: 64–85

New developments and the role of the HR function

New developments in international HRM

CHAPTER OBJECTIVES

When they have read this chapter, students will:

■ understand why strategists focus so much attention on the issue of organisational capability

■ be able to explain the thinking behind shared process models

■ be familiar with the factors associated with levels of outsourcing and global 'off-shoring' of HR activities

■ be able to explain the role of centres of excellence

■ know how to apply these models to the international HRM context.

This chapter takes a strategic view of some of the new developments in international HRM. A distinction can be made between those developments that are affecting the overall nature of international HRM inside organisations, and the actual role of international HR professionals. In this chapter we explore the first of these issues – new developments in IHRM that are occurring as a result of strategic decisions being made about the function and the scope and scale of its activities. The next chapter considers the second issue, which is the impact of these developments on the role of international HR professionals.

ORGANISATIONAL CAPABILITY

Trends of globalisation, market liberalisation, deregulation and technical evolution are restructuring global markets and challenging traditional approaches to gaining competitive advantage (Hamel, 2000). It is only the possession of specific capabilities and resources that now enables firms to conceive and then implement strategies that can generate what the economists describe as above-average rates of return (Barney, 1997). We introduced Ulrich's model of HR in Chapter 5. The term 'organisational capability' was adopted by Ulrich (1987) for the HR field. Ulrich and Lake (1990) then brought together perspectives from the fields of the management of change, organisational design and leadership, and argued that organisational capability was about competing from the inside out. Organisational capability focuses on the ability of a firm's internal processes, systems and management practices to meet customer needs and to direct both the skills and efforts of employees towards achieving the goals of the organisation.

The idea also has its root in the resource-based view of the firm, as already mentioned in Chapter 11, which argued that in an environment characterised by the globalisation of markets, changing customer demands and increasing competition, it is the people and the way they are managed that are more significant than other sources of competitive advantage (Wright *et al*, 1994; Lado and Wilson, 1994). These newer models of strategy argue that competitive advantage is derived from both internal knowledge resources and the strategic resources or capabilities of the firm. It is 'bundles of resources' rather than any particular product-market strategy that provide an organisation with the capability to compete. These bundles of resources are generally considered to be complex, intangible and dynamic.

ACTIVITY

Ask the main functional leaders in your organisation – or one you know – how they define 'organisational capability'.

Review the skills and competencies that form part of the HR system and assess the extent to which there is any overlap.

In addition to the management of people, developing organisational capability includes the means through which the organisation implements policies and procedures. These means are centred on – and require HR professionals to understand – economic and financial capability, strategic/marketing capability and technological capability. As the HR profession becomes more involved in developing organisational capability, it has chosen to build alliances with – or, depending on your viewpoint, has been forced to work with – the dictates of the last two of these capabilities. Strategic or marketing capability is based around offering uniqueness to customers. This marketing perspective has in fact been a significant driver behind approaches to talent management. The second alliance is based around technological capability. Perceived customer value is considered to result from responsiveness (meeting needs more quickly than competitors), the formation of endearing and enduring relationships, and the pursuit of service quality through guarantees. We shall see later in this chapter that the development of shared service models and the e-enablement of HR systems are but two ways of delivering this organisational capability.

How is organisational capability evidenced?

HR strategy writers find it easier to say what organisational capability looks like than to define exactly what it is. The following formula has become a commonplace explanation of capability in domestic HR strategy:

- *being able to move with speed and agility* into a new market in order to be the firm that sets the rules and then controls the future changes to these rules (in HR terms, removing bureaucratic processes, establishing clarity of governance to enable rapid decision-making, building safe-guarding disciplines into the organisational thought process, and removing vestiges of old ways of doing things)

- *creating a brand for the firm*, such that its reputation draws consumers, and the brand associated with the customer experience of the firm also becomes part of the experience or identity of the firm in the mind of all stakeholders (customers, employees, investors). Employee actions and HR policies are aligned with this identity

- *a customer interface that captures and develops a more intimate relationship*, such that data on customers contains more insight into their actual behaviour and needs, business processes are built around these needs as a priority, and customers also have involvement in or can comment on the design and practice of internal systems (for example, providing feedback for perform-ance management)

- *superior talent*, reflected in high levels of employee competence and commitment, such that there is an employee value proposition that makes the firm an attractive place to work, helps attract people into the right job, entices employees to give their discretionary energy to the firm, and orients them towards effective performance very quickly

- *leveraged innovation and learning*, reflected in new and faster-developed services and products, a culture of inquisitiveness and risk-taking, competencies of inventing and trying, and an ability and willingness to learn from mistakes

- *resources sourced across alliances*, whereby firms can work across boundaries, marshal connections, share information and develop a sense of mutual dependency between a network of partners, which means the best resources can be brought to bear on a situation, to everyone's benefit, without having to formally own or control them

> ■ *assigned accountability*, such that standards exist for employees and that organisational decision-making (who makes them, how they are made and what processes are followed) is carried out with competence, authority and responsibility.
>
> *Source: Ulrich (2000)*

In order to make this diffuse concept of organisational capability more recognisable, Ulrich (2000) described the collection of attributes that it involves in terms of a series of important outcomes that result from their existence. The role of the HR professional is, it is argued, to help clarify these organisational capabilities and to craft the HR investments that are necessary to build them (see box above).

> **QUESTION**
>
> ■ How does your organisation – or one that you know – measure up against Ulrich's criteria?

However, although there is growing consensus about the attributes that represent organisational capability, comparatively little research has been conducted in two important areas:

- how capability-based frameworks relate to multinational firms and their strategies (Tallman and Fladmoe-Lindquist, 2002) – this requires better theoretical insight into the driving factors behind the strategies

- how a firm develops, manages, and deploys capabilities to support its business strategy (Montealegre, 2002) – this tends to require the undertaking of longitudinal studies.

In the next sections of this chapter we explore these two relatively less understood issues.

ORGANISATIONAL CAPABILITY AND GLOBALISATION

Many current models of multinational firms have been described as having a 'capability-recognising' perspective. This means that firms possess some unique knowledge-based resources. However, these resources are typically treated as being home-country-based or somehow belonging to the corporate function and top team. Bartlett and Ghoshal (1989) addressed the possibility that foreign national units could take a major strategic role within the multinational firm. Tallman and Fladmoe-Lindquist (2002) argue that what we need is a 'capability-driven' perspective – an understandable theory of multinational strategy based on how multinational firms attempt to build, protect and exploit a set of unique capabilities and resources.

An important task for international HR managers is to grasp the overall business-level and corporate-level capabilities that are relevant to a particular international strategy. Tallman and Fladmoe-Lindquist (2002) have summarised the key capabilities on three axes:

- strategies of international expansion or global integration

- the necessity to continue generating competitive advantage or to innovate through global learning

- skills and activities operating at the business level or corporate-level routines that integrate these skills across operations.

Their work makes it evident that globalisation can be seen as a strategic effort to treat the world (or a significant part of it) as a single market. This does not, however, imply creating single research and development or production centres, unitary logistic networks or indeed HR systems and processes. Rather, it is the international networking that surrounds these activities and the conduct of these activities in global contexts that provides significant organisational capability: 'The world becomes an important source for new knowledge as well as new markets' (Tallman and Fladmoe-Lindquist, 2002; p.116). Multinational firms can gain sustained competitive advantage by building on and leveraging their unique internal capabilities.

In addition to the understandable focus on transaction costs (and transaction cost economics theory), much of the decision-making on competitive advantage is also based upon the logic of specialisation. Initially, this involves identifying elements of the value chain that can be separated from where the final goods or services are produced. As competitive pressures increase, the next step is to focus on what the organisation is good at (core competencies or capabilities) and consider handing over control of those activities that do not fall into this category. *Offshoring* – the process of sourcing business services from overseas – is defined by Abramovsky, Griffith and Sako (2005; p.6) as 'a type of specialisation where the production of the goods or service is moved overseas'. Offshoring is seen as logical progression from specialisation. It may involve *insourcing* (where the production of the service is still owned and controlled by the firm) or *outsourcing* (where the firm uses a third-party provider to carry out the activity). Outsourcing has been analysed from a resource-based view of the firm (Espino-Rodriguez and Padrón-Robaina, 2006). It is not the capabilities or resources that are the source of competitive advantage, but the exploitation of these resources through the existing business processes.

A more strategic role in this process of capability development comes through process theories. Montealegre (2002) has developed a model of the process skills needed to provide such development of capability. Five key resources were used throughout the process – all things that international HR managers can help build. These are:

- leadership, through the expression and subsequent articulation of strategic intent
- organisation culture, through the mobilisation of supporting routines already embedded in the culture
- information technology, not in the sense of technical investments but more in the way that these investments are leveraged to create unique resources and skills that improve the effectiveness of the organisation
- long-term view – developing a longer-term view of the strategy by developing and nurturing commitment
- social networks, through the cultivation of strong relationships with stakeholders inside and outside the organisation.

However, one of the challenges that faces all of those working with these sorts of decisions has been summarised by De Vita and Wang (2006; p.4):

'The question of the extent to which each (core competence) ... is singularly both necessary and sufficient to justify the outsourcing choice has never been satisfactorily squared ... Ambiguity still reigns on how to establish what, and what not, should be seen as core. Is it what we do best? Is it what creates value? Or is it related to the strategic importance of the activity in relation to changing industry requirements?'

In relation to this last question – changing industry requirements – the HR function has also been subjected to a number of sector-wide developments. In Chapter 11 we introduced the work of Brewster, Sparrow and Harris (2005) which drew attention to three distinct, but linked, enablers of high performance that are creating a new set of pressures on HRM specialists:

- HR affordability – the need to deliver global business strategies in the most cost-efficient manner possible

- central HR philosophy – the need to ensure a common philosophy and coherent practice across disparate countries and workforces

- e-enabled HR knowledge transfer – the use of networks and technology to assist organisational learning.

These issues are in most instances impossible to disentangle from the parallel debates about specialisation, core capability and the technological enablement of service delivery that makes some of these discussions easier (or not, as we shall see) to implement.

We pick up on several of these processes in the next chapter when we focus on managing IHR. However, at this stage the key message is to recognise that the role of IHR managers can be driven by this 'patterned sequence of phases that takes place along the road to capability development' (Montealegre, 2002; p.527). In the context of such globalisation, organisational capability involves managing the conflicting demands of corporate control, global coordination and the standardisation of HR processes. This does not imply building totally standardised HR processes on a global scale but it does entail building a degree of common insight into the nature of shared HR processes and adherence to an overarching philosophy in the design of these processes. The mantra of organisational capability, supported by developments in both the use of technological capability (service centres, e-enablement of HR, and HR process standardisation) and marketing capability (talent management and employee value propositions considered at a global level) has in some firms begun to dominate the activity of international HR professionals (Sparrow, Brewster and Harris, 2004).

STREAMLINING HR SUPPORT FUNCTIONS: HR SERVICE CENTRES

ACTIVITY

Read Reilly, P. (2000) *HR Shared Services and the Realignment of HR* (Institute for Employment Studies, Report 368, Brighton, IES).

What does it tell us about how HR departments can free up enough time and space to take on a more strategic role in order to concentrate on building organisational capability?

We noted in Chapter 5 that, in theory at least, solutions such as outsourcing or developing shared services would be combined with the e-enablement of many HR processes and extension of existing information and communications technology (ICT) systems (CIPD, 2005a, 2005b). We described how:

- the implementation of e-enablement has been fraught with problems, in part because practitioners lack a sound body of theory and evidence on which to proceed, particularly in the area of innovation, absorptive capacity, technology acceptance and change management

- the pursuit of this process across countries is also a relatively under-theorised one, but recent advances in institutional theory have focused on the causes and nature of the diversity in organisational practices, and differing degrees of receptiveness to new technologies (Streeck and Thelen, 2005; Brewster *et al*, 2006)

- the consequences of ICT enablement for HR specialists, line managers and other employees is not well understood, researchers highlighting both significant benefits and problems for these stake-holders (Cooke, 2006).

We now return to some of the theory and practice, in the context of the global pursuit of this strategy.

Ulrich (1995) argues that whereas shared services might look like centralisation, they could turn out to be the opposite. The corporate centre does not need to control the resources or dictate the policies, programmes or procedures. Central structures are balanced by the presence of more HR managers close to the customer, bringing in elements of decentralised service. Central organisation of HR resources comes hand-in-hand with local (or, in an international sense, more probably regional) tailored advice, policy or practice designed around business needs. Administrative functions may be centralised but decision-making remains decentralised. Moreover, a wide range of services can be considered in terms of this need for common provision to recipients – not just administrative work.

Few international HR functions will be able to ignore the continued development of shared service structures. Of course, practice does not always match theory. Central organisation can also imply that a small subset of HR experts hold sway over HR system design and, if they are not internationally minded, then perceptions of customer need may themselves be stereotyped. Lentz (1996) noted that successful organisations walk the tightrope between integrating competitive features of customer focus and flexibility on the one hand and economies of scale on the other.

DEBATE

Discuss the following questions with your fellow-students.

- Are shared service models going to represent a new force for standardisation of HR practices on a global basis, or will they result in more localised and customised policies and practices?

- How easy is it to develop regional shared service centres?

The activities and responsibilities that end up being devolved both to local line managers and to local HR staff vary considerably. Shared service models might in effect offer a 'take it or leave it' option to local management – seen, for example, in Eisenstat's (1996) reporting of a quip made by a manager at Apple that 'My HR representative is not a person – it's a floppy disk.' On the other hand, the models can also be ones in which HR acts as an 'intelligent agent' guiding staff and managers through a maze of complex policy.

Separating out those elements of the HR function concerned with business strategy from those elements of the role concerned with service delivery, it is argued, will have deep implications for the skills and competencies of HR professionals. The radical perspective also links the development of shared service structures to parallel changes in technology that have enabled greater outsourcing of HR activity. Reilly (2000) found that although technology (notably organisational intranets, web-based portals, interactive voice responses, and document and information management systems) has been an important part of the equation, it is a facilitator rather than a driver of change. Technical innovation has enabled organisations to consider a much wider range of HR services on a common basis around the globe. However, the reasons for introducing shared services have been more to do with cost, quality and the general nature of organisational change.

The impact of shared service models on HR functions

Shared services help reduce costs by cutting the number of HR staff needed, by reducing accommodation charges, and by introducing greater efficiency into choices both on what services are provided and on how they are delivered. Cost savings in particular come from:

- falls in HR headcount of between 20 and 40%

- moving operations from high-cost locations to low-cost locations in terms of either office space or employee costs

- the centralisation of focal points used to buy external services (for example, the centralisation of recruitment services in 1999 saved ICL £2 million a year)

- the development of high-volume partnership arrangements with a restricted set of suppliers.

An indirect impact is that the introduction of shared services makes the cost of HR administration far more transparent to the business.

Source: Reilly (2000)

As well as shared services there has been a desire to improve the quality of HR delivery and to enhance levels of customer satisfaction. Improved quality of service is evidenced in a number of ways:

- greater professionalisation of technical skills within the HR function

- more consistency and accuracy in HR transactions, and less reworking

- more awareness of and conformity with both internal and external best practice

- higher specifications of service levels for the internal organisation – and the development of greater trust and transparency – through service-level agreements or through activity-based pricing.

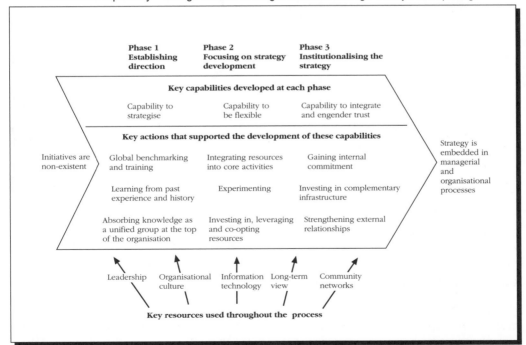

Figure 39 *Key resources used to develop organisational capability*

Issues that invoke cross-national working and interpretation are of course more likely to be escalated upwards to international specialists or centres of HR excellence. Shared services, then, can change the way in which international HR professionals are sourced with their work, and can also bring with them new

Another implication of the move to shared services is that the structures of HR at country level change. By the end of the 1980s most multinational organisations had decided that splitting up the HR function on a country-by-country basis when the rest of the organisation was increasingly aligned behind global lines of business was not helping the function to achieve its objectives. However, concerns about diversity in employment law and the continuance of strong national influences on the employment relationship meant that total alignment of the HR function with other business processes remained problematic. As a compromise, many organisations installed global HR directors as an extra layer in the reporting structure in order to create a position that acted as a strategic business partner (see Figure 39).

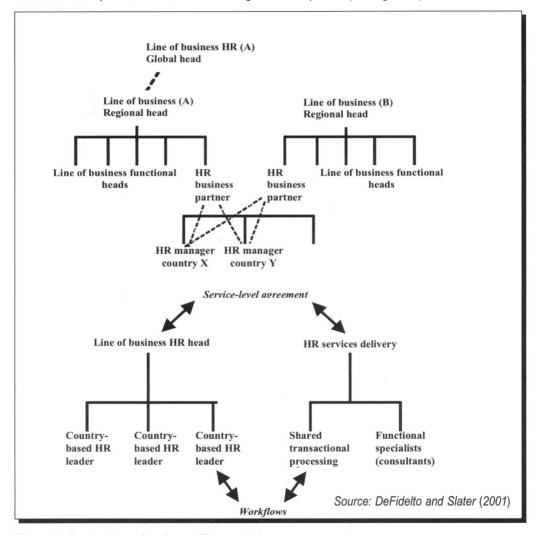

Source: DeFidelto and Slater (2001)

Figure 40 *Regional line-of-business HR organisation*

However, the result was often confusing as HR functions attempted to interweave their day-to-day administration work with the more strategic activities open to them. The advent of shared service thinking in the late 1990s provided the opportunity to transform HR structures towards that shown in Figure 40.

ACTIVITY

Read Ulrich, D. (1995) 'Shared services: from vogue to value', *Human Resource Planning*, 18 (3): 12–23.

Summarise his argument in a paragraph.

GLOBAL HR IMPLICATIONS: RE-CENTRALISATION AND STANDARDISATION OF HR, OR DEVOLVED CUSTOMISATION?

The development of shared service models is having a significant impact on international HR functions. In combination with the other changes discussed in this chapter – e-enablement, centres of excellence, outsourcing and offshoring – it is moving the focus of the IHR function away from managing a global set of managers towards becoming a function that can operate a series of value-adding HR processes within the business internationally. Historically, considerable energy has been spent translating central initiatives into what works within different countries. Now, however, there is a much stronger focus on cross-country and cross-business border implementation issues. HR is moving towards a world where it has to satisfy line-of-business – and not just country – needs, and this is beginning to shift the way that HR professionals think about problems (Sparrow, Brewster and Harris, 2004). The main change is that they now consider whether their organisation has good information systems in place, and whether this gives them the capability of delivering people-related services without their having to pass through the hands of the HR function.

The strategy adopted by the leading MNEs has tended to be one of establishing the principle of e-HR first, and then of reorganising the supporting infrastructure that is needed to enable this, such as the service centres. As with many HR innovations, service centres appear to have followed the 'Gulf Stream ... drifting in from the USA and hitting the UK first, then crossing the Benelux countries ... and Germany and France and proceeding finally to southern Europe' (DeFidelto and Slater, 2001; p.281) – although how widespread it is we do not yet know. Even in terms of international HRM, when looking at country coverage, the overwhelming majority of these HR shared service centres are national – ie they cover a single country. An example of a regional service in IBM is given below.

Case study

IBM's European HR Service Centre and HR issue escalation

IBM's European HR Service Centre is based at the organisation's UK headquarters in Portsmouth. It was established in 1998 and now provides support for over 100,000 employees in more than 20 countries. These 20 countries are serviced by 90 people representing 15 different nationalities. The majority of these people are young and speak several languages. In 2001 the Centre received 252,000 telephone calls, 71,000 emails and over 2 million web hits. Delivering a high-quality service requires enhanced internal control and issue escalation procedures to ensure that people know their area of expertise and do not go beyond their capability. At IBM's *Ask HR*, the average routine phonecall is dealt with in two minutes. The target set is for 80% of calls to result in satisfaction for the customer. These are level-1 issues that can be handled by generalist staff in the Service Centre. A further 19% of issues require more sophisticated responses. These enquiries involve a degree of programme interpretation, issue resolution, training and troubleshooting. They are answered by specialists within the European Service Centre with a target response time of two days. The remaining 1% of enquiries have to be referred to a small number of HR process experts who reside within the general HR function.

Source: Industrial Relations Services (1999), Stevens (2002)

To date there does not appear to be a common path to the internationalisation of shared service models. Many organisations have chosen to create regional centres as part of a single international organisation structure. In contrast to IBM, Hewlett-Packard changed its country-based systems to regional centres but allowed the managers to stay in their original offices. The company sent the work to the people, not the people to the work (Reilly, 2000). Another arrangement has been to use service centres to support global business streams rather than organise them at a regional level on a geographical basis.

The constraints tend to be around those HR services that are affected by employment law, employee relations, works councils, procedures governing dismissal and setting up an employment contract – all more country-focused activities (Industrial Relations Services, 1999). One of the biggest cultural differences affecting shared service models and the e-enablement of HRM concerns data protection. As one example, the holding and processing of personal data in EU countries invokes requirements to gain consent from employees and is associated with different restrictions in different countries (data listing religion and ethnic origin is forbidden for German and Italian companies).

Practice, however, also tends to show that the technological imperative of global service centres can override some of the constraints that exist. A good example of this is France Telecom.

Case study

The Tomorrow Project at France Telecom

As part of its Tomorrow Project, France Telecom is moving its HR community and indeed the whole workforce into more strategic roles. In three years from 1998 to 2001 40,000 people – nearly 33% of the company – changed jobs and moved into re-profiled technical systems. At the same time it started to overhaul its own HR systems. There were 450 intranets in existence and these were collapsed down into 10 service centres covering various global operations. An analysis of the HR community showed that 62% were involved in administrative work. As service centres were introduced, many HR services were e-enabled. The websites offered several services such as TalentLink, PlanetEmploi and e.plan which handled most transactional HR activity as well as vacation scheduling and expense claims. Cost savings were such that the return on investment fell from a planned 18 months to 13 months.

One instructive issue was that in France Telecom a recruitment process required four check-offs by senior managers. As this process was e-enabled, the HR function attempted to get rid of the manual signing-off. Line managers objected and insisted that the webpage had a button inserted to print off hard copies of forms and enable a sign-off by a senior manager. HR acceded to the request reluctantly, but were delighted to find that after a few months the managers realised that this was an unnecessary delay. The practice stopped, and e-enabled HR led to a more decentralised recruitment practice and change in cultural practice.

In summary, then, the impact of shared service models on the international HR function has been to create a number of pressures forcing organisations to:

- consider the cost efficiencies of delivering HR services across different geographical areas

- identify the new HR co-ordination needs as they continue to move away from line-of-country reporting arrangements towards global lines of business

- provide the systems necessary to support strategy on a global basis

- understand which HR processes really have to be different, and which ones are core to all countries

- manage a process of migration towards regional and then global HR service centres

- cope with problems of information deficiency where country-based systems do not provide the information needed to support a global line of business

- manage deficiencies in their own manpower, where headcount savings mean that there is not a good match between HR professionals in each area and the functional data that is needed.

GLOBAL E-ENABLEMENT OF HR PROCESSES

We introduced the importance of e-enablement in Chapter 5. Operational integration in global HR can be achieved through the use of standardised technology. The provision of a common front for employees helps to integrate the HR function around the common employee interests, as discussed earlier. At a practical level the management, through networks and the focus on knowledge management outlined in the previous sections, is putting pressure on company intranets and on the technology needed to support such activity. Consequently, most of the future developments in the shared service models outlined in the last chapter are likely to come about through technological change. Part of the response to the pressure on the international HR function is the pursuit of better ways to do things. A key challenge facing HRM is new information and communication technology. This applies across the board, but the impact on global HRM could be immense. Most organisations feel that they have only just started down this path, but they do realise that technology will dramatically change what HRM can do. The ability to get HRM information to and from, and support on to, line managers' – and even employees' – desks without a formal HRM intervention opens up new and exciting possibilities, enabling HR to focus on its capability and business development roles. Importantly, this e-enablement of HR is being engineered on a global basis. Technical changes are, however, perceived as an enabling factor – not a driving factor – in the move towards more global models of HRM (DeFidelto and Slater, 2001).

The web-enabling of HR activity – both transactional and transformational HR work – is therefore seen as an essential step towards helping HR professionals to advise business leaders on the competitiveness of the firm. As part of this technical evolution, intimately connected with the development of the service centre model, we have also witnessed a process whereby many of the activities in the service centre itself are put online, and an ethos of employee self-service or self-reliance is developed (Ulrich, 2000). Initially, the administrative transactions associated with the HR function (payroll processing, benefits administration, stock purchase plans, regulatory compliance) are made available to employees on intranets. The operations behind the scenes to handle this service may be managed in-house or may be outsourced to firms that have the technological expertise to offer such services at low cost, while also being able to answer employee questions and deliver a sense of employee self-sufficiency. Web-based systems allow employees from anywhere in the world to manage their own requirements. Another example, outlined in the box below, is Ford.

Case study

Moving towards cross-national HR platforms at Ford

Ford reorganised into regional business units, linked through global centres of excellence, in 2000. In response to this, the HR function, which had traditionally focused on delivering services at a national level, changed its emphasis in 2001 to become a pan-European organisation. The aim was to serve its customers more effectively and to strengthen its role as a strategic business partner. To support the new regional focus, Ford of Europe re-engineered the function to help reduce the level of transactional work that HR was involved in. Their approach was to:

- facilitate the development of a global HR platform by launching PeopleSoft across Europe

- use Six Sigma methodology (a quality management system) to identify the HR processes that required re-engineering

- centralise transactional and standardised processes into an internal service centre

- increase the availability of online tools to employees and line managers to enable them to access their personal data and HR tools.

The Ford HR intranet, HR Online, was used to increase employee self-service. This could be accessed by 8,500 employees working for the Ford Motor Company and Ford Credit in the UK, and 13,500 in Germany. As the numbers of self-service facilities increased, the system became increasingly interactive. In July 2001, HR Online was connected to the PeopleSoft system, allowing the implementation of a wider range of self-service applications. This will free administrative staff currently required to manually update previous computer systems, enable HR teams to continue to review existing HR practices, and drive the standardisation of processes across Europe, which was one of the functional objectives for 2002.

Source: Sparrow, Brewster and Harris (2004)

Transformational HR work – not just transactional work – can be e-enabled. This is where more sophisticated HR practices such as parts of the recruitment and selection process, or the appraisal and performance process, are themselves offered in more innovative ways through web-based solutions. Current online access rights and limited update rights are expected to be a stepping-stone to managers' authorising pay changes and performance management data and to employees' providing not only factual data about their preferences but also more dynamic and interactive information around skills and personal aspirations. Computing power is being directed at developing what are called 'proactive pull technologies'. These include modelling systems that allow individuals to see the consequences of their decisions or decision-support mechanisms to assist managers in the areas of discipline, training and selection. Mass customisation of terms and conditions becomes more possible as variations and combinations can be recorded and monitored.

Actual practice of course lags behind the rhetoric – the web-enablement of training programmes, learning communities, compensation system administration, employee relations surveys, communications and grievance procedures is as yet still a rarity. Reilly (2000) argued that speed of progress will be determined by culture, not by technological capability. This comment was made referring to organisational culture and the extent to which this supports the conduct and practice of devolved management. However, as we saw in our discussions of cross-cultural management, this statement is just as applicable to national culture.

Sparrow, Brewster and Harris (2004) found that no organisation had managed to develop a fully effective way of exploiting the possibilities asociated with e-enablement on a global scale. Global organisations are only at the early stages of realising the benefits of this change and are therefore just coming to terms with the implications of the use of information technology in global HRM. Most organisations are still struggling to understand what possibilities the new technology gives them. Nonetheless, initiatives are still being pursued and it remains a significant and developing trend in international organisations with, already, considerable impact on the role and activities of global HR departments, centrally and locally. It will likely affect the credibility and authority of such departments, in turn having significant implications for the roles and activities of line managers. There will also be extensive resourcing implications for global HR functions, given that e-enablement is often associated with shared service structures and adjustments in terms of global outsourcing or insourcing of HR activity.

Significant progress in globalising HR service delivery is being made, then, in three areas (Sparrow and Brewster, 2006):

- technology (commonality of underlying systems and databases)

- process streamlining (optimisation of processes)

- sourcing (making decisions about the possible centralisation or outsourcing of some areas of activity).

Developing a global HR and technology strategy and implementation plan covers everything from the information management of data to global appraisal systems, to compensation and benefits management, to a knowledge-base with a single global Internet feel and look, and to a knowledge management system. However, effective technology-based solutions are to a large extent dependent on the level of process streamlining. Sparrow and Brewster (2006) give the example of developments at BOC in terms of resourcing and recruitment processes. The global HR function aims to have the process in Europe as the process in the South Pacific, unless there are extremely good reasons for a difference. If one area has the best approach and technology for a graduate training programme, it may be asked to carry out the global management of graduates. In the same way, if most of the expatriate managers work in Asia, it may be cheaper and easier to administer them from Asia. With a technology base, time-zones are becoming less important.

OUTSOURCING OR INSOURCING HR

Human resource outsourcing involves 'the purchasing by an organisation of ongoing HR services from a third-party provider that it would otherwise normally provide by itself' (Hesketh, 2006; p.1). Organisations have always outsourced some functions: payroll or management training, for example. As a strategic tool, outsourcing revolves around decisions – about capability (whether to improve or acquire this), scale (providing well-administered services for populations large enough to justify the return on investment), or technology (the benefits of which may be acquired or leveraged through the development of shared services or outsourcing). Hesketh (2006) cites research by the Everest Research group which shows that the spending on HR outsourcing had increased from $75 million in 1998 to $1,562 million by 2004. Research across 28 organisations including Credit Suisse, Deutsche Bank, Royal Bank of Scotland, IBM, Shell and Royal Mail Group shows that the following trends are still evident:

- increased outsourcing of higher-value HR processes such as recruitment

- increasing use of shared service models

- performance issues surrounding HRO deals

- the continued evolution of e-HR activities

- the emergence of new HR roles and competencies

- continuing debates over HR and HRO measurement.

The issue of outsourcing transactional aspects of HRM has been a source of considerable debate in recent years. Advocates for the outsourcing of HR activities (Csoko, 1995; Klaas *et al*, 2001) point to reduced costs, increased service quality produced by greater economies of scale, increased incentives and accountability for service providers, and increased access to experts in specialised areas. The most common targets for outsourcing are those HR activities that can most easily be ring-fenced, and include payroll, training, recruitment, pensions administration and benefits administration.

Vocal too are those who warn of the dangers of outsourcing. There is considerable variation in how firms are responding to this opportunity, and not all of the responses are well thought through (Klaas *et al*, 1999, 2001). The more that practices can be seen to rely on tacit knowledge – the accumulation of experiences that is difficult to communicate to those without similar levels of experience – the more any control of the work process by those without such knowledge results in 'sub-optimal' management (Conner and Prahalad, 1996). It can be argued that if transactional activities can be handled electronically, the benefits of outsourcing shrink considerably (see the Nike case study below). The arguments marshalled against outsourcing tend to emphasise exposure to opportunist behaviour by contractors, limits to the ability of the firm to develop distinctive competencies within its workforce, and inefficiencies because of a lack of contractor insight into the client's strategy and culture (Ulrich, 1996). 2006 saw some significant cases of organisations 're-insourcing' after their outsourcing contracts were seen not to have delivered what had been promised.

Insourcing, outsourcing and offshoring are all seen as different forms of specialisation, by which activities are moved to specialised units. In a global context, one can see local country managers arguing that much of the corporate HR armoury requires deep tacit understanding of the national culture and therefore should not be a candidate either for operation through shared services or, indeed, for any subsequent outsourcing. Organisations must make sensible assessments of this tacit knowledge constraint.

Case study

BBC worldwide international recruitment caught up in outsourcing

The internal international recruitment, selection and assessment function at BBC World Services was caught up in the current drive towards the use of technology and the attractions of a shared service model in this area. BBC People (the HR function) had to make judgements about how best to organise international recruitment activity which were bound up in general changes in HR delivery that had been taking place from 2002 to 2005. As part of its general restructuring the BBC underwent two waves of downsizing. The elimination of 3,780 jobs amounted to 19% of its UK workforce, or nearly 14% of its worldwide staff of 27,000 (Sparrow, 2007). HR was centralised and a business-partner model was introduced into divisions. As part of the process a number of professional services including parts of HR were outsourced. BBC People was reduced from around 1,000 staff to 450 as part of a three-year change programme and 10-year outsourcing deal worth £100 million and saving £50 million. This involved a partial outsourcing process in which about 260 jobs moved to Capita (in Belfast) in 2006, the transfer of posts elsewhere in the BBC, and the loss of 180 jobs. A list of 11 areas for possible outsourcing was drawn up around resourcing, remuneration, contracting, relocation, disability access services, HR advice and occupational health. The conduct of international recruitment comes under this remit. The functions finally outsourced included recruitment, pay and benefits (excluding pensions), assessment, outplacement and some training, HR administration, relocation, occupational health and disability access services. The HR function had to be aligned with strategic objectives, which were to become more creative and audience-focused. Service delivery was split from strategic HR (led by a series of heads of HR and Development in each of the 17 divisions). The focus of these roles was to build capability within divisions. A separate function focused on service delivery to line managers, driven by service-level agreements.

Of the changes at BBC People, the HR director said (Pickard, 2006; p.14):

I subscribe to the view that we will increasingly have quality organisations that can take some of our services and go one better than we can, because they have developed deep expertise in those services in a way most large organisations cannot.

Decisions like that have to be made by all organisations in the context of outsourcing services: can the technical knowledge inside specialised functions be protected, or is sufficient expertise available from an agency? Taking another example related to international recruitment activity, it can be seen that technology now allows organisations to make alternative decisions. As evident in the Nike case study below, advances in technology and e-enablement of recruitment processes have broadened the scope of geographical intake, which in turn has introduced new efficiencies into the process, which in some instances means that firms can actually expand the scope of their internal activities rather than outsource them.

Case study

Nike moves recruitment back in-house in Europe

In 2005 Nike decided to move its recruitment in-house in Europe, the Middle East and Africa to reduce costs and improve the overall quality of the applicants it hires (*People Management*, 2005). This decision followed the successful implementation of a software system at Nike's EMEA headquarters in the Netherlands. The system was introduced in 2002 to automate the recruitment process. It enabled applicants to apply directly for both specific jobs and on a speculative basis via Nike's website. Details are retained on file to create a database of future interest that can be searched for specific competences: 8,500 people are currently listed. Applicants are automatically asked to update their CV every six months for their file to remain active. From June 2003 to May 2004 a total of 556 positions were filled using the new system, 144 of which came from the future-interest database. Nike saved 54% in recruitment costs in the first three years of operation, and reports less reliance on external recruitment and search agencies as a result of the future-interest database. The average time to fill vacancies fell from 62 to 42 days, and the cost per hire was also reduced. Having already established its own databases, Nike is now doing its own research for senior-level headhunting and intends to establish an in-house agency for senior recruitment. This move was intended to allow the organisation's resourcing group to play a more consultative and advisory role.

Hesketh (2006) points out that offshoring is not outsourcing *per se* but rather concerns the completion of the same task in a different location where the costs are significantly cheaper. Decisions about this are driven more by economic theories of labour arbitrage than by the models of organisational capability that drive thinking about shared service, e-enablement and outsourcing. In practice, the decisions by Fortune-500 companies to offshore are driven (in order of importance) by: lower wage costs, reduction of other costs, improved service quality, focus on core competences, speeding up the process cycle, avoiding capacity constraints, extending the scope of services, strengthening an existing affiliate, and access to technology and infrastructure (UNCTAD/Roland Berger Strategy Consultants study, cited in Hunter, 2006). Offshoring can be defined as (Hunter, 2006; p.2):

> 'the act of transferring some of a company's recurring internal activities to outside providers who are located in a different country and market economy, under a formal service contract. As is a matter of common practice in outsourcing generally, both the activities and the factors of production (people, facilities, equipment, technology) and decision rights over how certain processes are performed are often transferred to the new provider.'

In practice, given the distances involved in offshoring, the factors of production are rarely transferred to offshore sites, but the services, processes and decision rights are. Hunter (2006) estimates that a typical offshore deal from the UK to India generates cost savings of between 35 and 45% once offshore overheads (on-site contract management, schedule delays and rework and transition costs) have been accounted for. Not surprisingly, then, Kenney and Florida (2004; p.1) observe:

> 'Globalisation is much more than simply moving employment and activities from developed nations into nations with lower cost forces. Such a simple conclusion obscures the complicated skein of cross-border relationships that have evolved out of firm strategies seeking to balance a kaleidoscope of variables including labour and inventory costs, transportation, quality, concentration of valuable knowledge in clusters and temporal proximity to customers. Understanding firm strategies at a single moment in time is complicated enough, but unfortunately these variables also fluctuate.'

The difficulty faced by IHRM functions is that the calculations of the cost benefits of these sorts of decisions is very difficult *and it varies across countries*. Pyndt and Pedersen (2006) found that the direct benefits of offshoring are easy to understand and are derived from savings in labour costs, foreign suppliers' import of products or services and repatriation of profits. The indirect benefits of offshoring include the value of re-employing the employees in the home country affected by the offshoring. Capital savings can be reinvested in higher-value jobs. Achieving these benefits is dependent upon the home country's ability to train, upgrade and re-employ the home workers. It immediately becomes clear that the institutional context that surrounds the employment relationship both in the country from which work is outsourced and the new location determines the attractiveness (or not) of offshoring. In Denmark the return on every unit of currency invested in offshoring was 1.15, but in Germany the equivalent return was only 0.8. In part this figure also reflects the fact that German firms tend to offshore to East European countries, which have higher labour costs.

Case study

Global HR implications: offshoring

One way in which the development of service centres affects the international HR function is through what has recently been termed a process of 'global HR offshoring'. It has now become feasible to move HR administration overseas. Legal and cultural differences are still considered to inhibit the transfer of more advisory roles. Prime candidates for offshoring include payroll, as well as pensions and benefits administration. According to strategy consultants McKinsey, the amount of offshoring is expected to rise by an average of 71% each year between 2001 and 2008 – twice the rate of most other business activities. Indeed, the global market for HR offshoring should be worth £27 billion by 2008, up from £0.6 billion in 2001. An interesting development is that rather than these activities being outsourced, most tasks are likely to be carried out by direct employees of the firms involved. The USA and the UK together generate almost three-quarters of global offshoring activity.

Source: Crabb (2003)

UNDERSTANDING AND BUILDING CENTRES OF EXCELLENCE

A key question that faces IHRM functions is how to deal with the remaining HR business. What are the most appropriate organisational forms? In practice, multinational organisations have increasingly dispersed activities. They have relied on specialised and often network-based structures to coordinate these activities. The corporate headquarters typically adjusts its level of coordination and control to reflect the role of the subsidiary and the strategic importance of its mandate (Bartlett and Ghoshal, 1989). Organisations are composed of many diverse, interdependent work groups, such as new product development teams and manufacturing planning teams, all of which have unique decision domains, and develop unique perspectives in response to different tasks, goals and environments. Although managers can act autonomously within each of these decision domains, they are affected by each other's actions. Consequently, mechanisms of integration (and the underlying organisational capability to manage these integration mechanisms effectively) are needed, above and beyond the simple summation of the different perspectives that exist within the organisation. The brokering of knowledge inside global organisations through formal structures is one such mechanism (Sparrow, 2006). Can organisations improve knowledge management by design? We focus now on one of the designs that has become an important feature of global organisations – centres of excellence (COE).

> **'A growing body of anecdotal evidence suggests that the COE phenomenon is increasing amongst the world's major MNEs, [and] at the same time this evidence also suggests that many firms are struggling with the managerial issues involved.'**
>
> *Frost, Birkinshaw and Prescott (2000; p.1016)*

The traditional and evolutionary progression of MNEs through international, multinational, global and transnational/network/heterarchy is well understood and generally discussed in the context of the trade-off between global integration and local responsiveness (see Chapter 11). However, as MNEs change their organisation design in response to the need to build more international capability, as part of their natural development they often establish dedicated organisational forms to facilitate this. One such form is the centre of excellence (Ohmae, 1990, 1996). For example, some subsidiaries take on a strategic role in the global organisation that reaches beyond their local undertakings. COEs are organisational units that embody a set of organisational capabilities. These capabilities must be explicitly recognised as an important source of value creation (Frost, Birkinshaw and Prescott, 2002). There must also be a strategic remit, such as the intention to leverage or disseminate these capabilities to other parts of the firm. At the subsidiary level, COEs tend to be established as a consequence of a long and slow internationalisation process within the organisation, or as a deliberate part of organisation design where HQ managers decide to grant autonomy to units that have also been given a specific strategic mandate. Increasingly, small teams or units *within* either subsidiaries or central functions take a lead COE role in one area, other units taking the lead in different areas of capability. Although the leadership of a COE might be vested in a physical location, the centre itself may be virtual, spread across networks of teams in different geographies. Centres of excellence can also be seen in the light of our previous discussion of specialisation – although COEs involve further differentiating the retained business services into those activities in which additional benefits can be obtained if the capability can be leveraged internally.

Current roles for international HR professionals in the development of centres of excellence

There are three particular ways in which the IHR function is being driven by the development of centres of excellence:

- managing the international relocation of staff as organisations – moving these centres of excellence nearer to the global centre of gravity of their core customers; reconfiguring their core competencies on a global scale by moving manufacturing, research and development or logistics operations closer to the best national infrastructures in terms of education or transport facilities; or setting up new centres as part of international ventures or as a result of mergers

- advising on the best HR strategies to coordinate and control such activities

- understanding the centres of excellence that can be created within their own activities, and building networks of HR experts within these areas of competence on a global basis.

Source: Sparrow, Brewster and Harris (2004)

The role of the global HR function has initially been reactive – coping with the need to relocate staff into new countries, considering the special terms and management conditions that should surround such units, and eventually applying the concept of COEs to its own structures (Sparrow, Brewster and Harris, 2004).

QUESTIONS

- What activities, processes and capabilities might constitute a COE, and how should such units be mandated?

- What has to happen in terms of the 'capability-building investments' that are needed? Is it possible to specify capabilities such as decision-making autonomy, requisite levels of connectivity to other sources of competence inside the organisation, leadership, and processes of knowledge management?

- What are the indicators of success, and under what contingencies?

> ■ To what extent do institutional factors preclude or support the long-term survival and contribution of COEs?

In many cases, experts argue that these centres should actually be quite loosely tied into the organisation and coordinated with other units if they are to help search for new knowledge and augment the capability of the MNE (Kuemmerle, 1999). Control typically varies between being direct or indirect and through personal or impersonal mechanisms – what Harzing (1999) calls centralised personal control, formal bureaucratic control, output control or control through socialisation and networks. Recent research suggests that controlling these centres of excellence through socialisation proves dysfunctional (Ambos and Reitsperger, 2002). Understanding and building these more globally distributed centres of excellence into viable operations has therefore become a significant challenge. Holm and Pedersen (2000) found that they must be more than just specialised in their knowledge. They have to be able to maintain one or several critical fields of knowledge that have a long-term impact on the development of activity in the other subsidiaries and units of the MNE. In the longer term, global HR functions that themselves establish their own centres of excellence will begin to learn from the research that has already been conducted into research and development and other technical centres of excellence already established.

It is perhaps worth emphasising as a final point that this chapter has been focusing on new developments: it should not be thought that these are yet common currency among most organisations – even some of the enormous figures of future growth are provided by consultants who have a vested interest in 'talking up' the market. Nevertheless, the kinds of strategic discussions that these developments imply and, indeed, necessitate, will become ever more significant over the next few years.

SUMMARY

The international HR function has come under pressure to evolve in response to a number of drivers, including:

- ■ cost reduction
- ■ contribution to business performance
- ■ quality of service provision
- ■ accelerated internationalisation.

In responding to these pressures we have seen a number of new organisational structures in the international HR function, the most notable of which have been:

- ■ the streamlining and centralisation of HR support functions with the implementation of HR service centres and platforms
- ■ the emergence of e-enabled HR
- ■ the externalisation of certain HR activities
- ■ HR organisations aligned with global business units
- ■ increased devolution of responsibility for HRM to line management.

The transition towards such new organisations is at varying stages of completion within companies. However, the existing level of experience is sufficient to allow some appraisal of the successes and difficulties of these transitions. There has been a powerful confluence of philosophical models of HR, concepts of organisation and technological developments that have begun to change the landscape for international HR managers.

LEARNING QUESTIONS

- What are the implications for international HR departments of the vogue for outsourcing HR activities?

- Identify the effects of thinking about resource capability as the key to competitive success for an international HR department.

- What would be the HR effects of creating a centre of excellence at the British headquarters of an MNE? How might these change if it was decided that the centre should be located in Hong Kong?

- How might the concepts of HR centres of excellence and of outsourcing HRM be connected?

REFERENCES

Abramovsky, L., Griffith, R. and Sako, M. (2005) *Offshoring: Myth and Reality.* London, Advanced Institute of Management Research

Ambos, B. and Reitsperger, W. D. (2002) 'Governing knowledge processes in MNCs: the case of German R&D units abroad', 28th EIBA Conference, Athens, 8–10 December

Barney, J. B. (1997) *Gaining and Sustaining Competitive Advantage.* Reading, MA, Addison-Wesley

Bartlett, C. A. and Ghoshal, S. (1989) *Managing Across Borders: The transnational solution.* Boston, MA, Harvard Business School Press

Brewster, C., Sparrow, P. R. and Harris, H. (2005) 'Towards a new model of globalising human resource management', *International Journal of Human Resource Management*, 16 (6): 953–74

Brewster, C., Wood, G., Brookes, M. and van Ommeren, J. (2006) 'What determines the size of the HR function? A cross-national analysis', *Human Resource Management*, 45 (1): 3–21

CIPD (2005a) *HR Outsourcing: The key decisions.* London, Chartered Institute of Personnel and Development

CIPD (2005b) *People Management and Technology: Progress and potential.* Survey Report. London, Chartered Institute of Personnel and Development

Conner, K. R. and Prahalad, C. K. (1996) 'A resourced-based theory of the firm: knowledge versus opportunism', *Organizational Science*, 7: 477–501

Cooke, F. L. (2006) 'Modelling an HR shared services centre: experience of an MNC in the United Kingdom', *Human Resources Management*, 45 (2): 211–27

Crabb, S. (2003) 'HR facing offshore boom', *People Management*, 9 (4): 7

Csoko, L. S. (1995) *Rethinking Human Resources: A research report.* Report No.1124–95–RR. New York, The Conference Board

DeFidelto, C. and Slater, I. (2001) 'Web-based HR in an international setting', in A. J. Walker (ed.) *Web-based Human Resources: The technologies that are transforming HR.* London, McGraw-Hill

De Vita, G. and Wang, C. L. (2006) 'Development of outsourcing theory and practice: a taxonomy of outsourcing generations', in H. S. Kehal and V. P. Singh (eds) *Outsourcing and Offshoring in the 21st Century: A socio-economic perspective.* London, Idea Group Publishing

Eisenstat, R. A. (1996) 'What corporate human resources brings to the picnic: four models for functional management', *Organizational Dynamics*, 25 (2): 6–14

Espino-Rodriguez, T. F. and Padrón-Robaina, V. (2006) 'A review of outsourcing from the resource-based view of the firm', *International Journal of Management Reviews*, 8 (1): 49–70

Fladmoe-Lindquist, K. and Tallman, S. (1994) 'Resource-based strategy and competitive advantage among multinationals', in P. Shrivastava, A. Huff and J. Dutton (eds) *Advances in Strategic Management*, Volume 10. Greenwich, CT, JAI Press

Frost, A., Birkinshaw, J. M. and Prescott, C. E. (2002) 'Centres of excellence in multinational corporations', *Strategic Management Journal*, 23 (11): 997–1018

Hamel, G. (2000) *Leading the Revolution*. Boston, MA, Harvard Business School Press

Harzing, A.-W. K. (1999) *Managing the Multinationals*. Northampton, Elgar Publishing

Hesketh, A. (2006) *Outsourcing the HR Function: Possibilities and pitfalls*. London, Corporate Research Forum

Holm, U. and Pedersen, T. (eds) (2000) *Managing Centres of Excellence*. Basingstoke, Macmillan

Hunter, I. (2006) *The Indian Offshore Advantage: How offshoring is changing the face of HR*. Aldershot, Gower

Industrial Relations Services (1999) 'IBM delivers international HR', *Employment Trends*, October, No 689. London, IRS

Kenney, M. and Florida, R. (eds) (2004) *Locating Global Advantage: Industry dynamics in the international economy*. Stanford, Stanford University Press

Klaas, B. S., McClendon, J. A. and Gainey, T. W. (1999) 'HR outsourcing and its impact: the role of transaction costs', *Personnel Psychology*, 52: 113–36

Klaas, B. S., McClendon, J. A. and Gainey, T. W. (2001) 'Outsourcing HR: the impact of organisational characteristics', *Human Resource Management*, 40 (2): 125–38

Kuemmerle, W. (1999) 'Building effective R&D capabilities abroad', *Harvard Business Review*, March–April: 61–9

Lado, A. and Wilson, M. (1994) 'Human resource systems and sustained competitive advantage: a competency-based perspective', *Academy of Management Review*, 19: 699–727

Lentz, S. (1996) 'Hybrid organisation structures: a path to cost savings and customer responsiveness', *Human Resource Management*, 35 (4): 453–69

Montealegre, R. (2002) 'A process model of capability development: lessons from the electronic commerce strategy at Bolsa de Valores de Guayaquil', *Organization Science*, 13 (5): 514–31

Nohria, N. and Ghoshal, S. (1997) *The Differentiated Network*. San Francisco, Jossey-Bass

Ohmae, K. (1990) *The Borderless World*. New York, HarperCollins

Ohmae, K. (1996) *The End Of The Nation State*. Cambridge, MA, Free Press

People Management (2005) 'Nike feels benefit of in-house hiring', *People Management*, 11 (3): 11

Pickard, J. (2006) 'Conflicting schedule', *People Management*, 12 (5): 14–15

Pyndt, J. and Pedersen, T. (2006) *Managing Global Offshoring Strategies: A case approach*. Copenhagen, Copenhagen Business School Press

Sparrow, P. R. and Brewster, C. (2006) 'Human resource management in international context', in C. L. Cooper and R. Burke (eds) *The Human Resources Revolution: Research and practice*. London, Elsevier

Sparrow, P. R., Brewster, C. and Harris, H. (2004) *Globalizing HR*. London, Routledge

Stevens, T. (2002) 'The IBM Case Study'. E&P International Seminar on New Organisational Structures of the HR function, Paris, 11–12 April

Streeck, W. and Thelen, K. (eds) (2005) *Beyond Continuity: Institutional change in advanced political economies*. Oxford, Oxford University Press

Tallman, S. and Fladmoe-Lindquist, K. (2002) 'Internationalisation, globalisation and capability-based strategy', *California Management Review*, 45 (1): 116–35

Ulrich, D. (1987) 'Organisational capability as competitive advantage: human resource professionals as strategic partners', *Human Resource Planning*, 10 (4): 169

Ulrich, D. (1995) 'Shared services: from vogue to value', *Human Resource Planning*, 18 (3): 12–23

Ulrich, D. (1996) *Human Resource Champions*. Cambridge, MA, Harvard University Press

Ulrich, D. (2000) 'From eBusiness to eHR', *Human Resource Planning*, 20 (3): 12–21

Ulrich, D. and Lake, D. (1990) *Organization Capability: Competing from the inside out*. New York, Wiley

Wright, P. M., McMahan, G. C. and McWilliams, A. (1994) 'Human resources and sustained competitive advantage: a resource-based perspective', *International Journal of Human Resource Management*, 5: 301–26

Managing international HRM

CHAPTER OBJECTIVES

When they have read this chapter, students will:

- be familiar with the key integration activities engaged in by the international HR function
- be able to determine the key elements of a talent management strategy
- understand the issues involved in building organisational capability through global expertise networks
- appreciate the role of knowledge management and knowledge transfer between international operations
- be able to debate the role of IHR professionals as guardians of national culture.

INTRODUCTION: THE NEW ROLE OF THE IHRM FUNCTION

In this chapter we assess the critical components of effectiveness for HR on a global scale. As we saw in Chapter 5, although around 50% of HR managers across Europe feel that they are proactively engaged in the development of corporate strategy (Brewster, 1994), evidence on the degree of board-level representation shows that the HR function is still relatively weak in corporate headquarters across most European countries. Corporate HR functions – regardless of their international responsibilities – have increasingly ambiguous and uncertain levels of authority, along with ill-defined boundaries and 'muddy' roles (Purcell and Ahlstrand, 1994). Scullion and Starkey (2000) have pointed out that relatively little attention has been paid to the question of the role that should be played by the corporate international HRM function. The dominant view, from the little attention that has been given to the issue (Hunt and Boxall, 1998; p.770), is that:

> 'HR specialists, senior or otherwise, are not typically key players in the development of corporate strategy.'

We begin this last chapter by using two frameworks to help position the IHRM function in its strategic context:

- a model of the integration mechanisms that can be provided by corporate functions (Ghoshal and Gratton, 2002; Gratton, 2003)
- a model of the changing interdependencies between HRM and other corporate functions created as a result of globalisation processes (developed from the work of Sparrow, Brewster and Harris, 2004, and Brewster, Sparrow and Harris, 2005; Sparrow and Brewster, 2006).

THE INTEGRATION MECHANISMS PROVIDED BY THE CORPORATE CENTRE

To take the first issue – the role of the corporate centre – first: as Martin and Beaumont (2001) point out, the corporate centre still generally attempts to shape the strategic direction and strategic change programmes of international subsidiaries by acting either directly as an explicit source of innovation in the pursuit of global cost advantage, local differentiation or knowledge transfer amongst subsidiaries, or indirectly by openly or tacitly structuring an agenda for acceptable HR change strategies or innovations in subsidiaries. These change programmes are often designed to:

- modify the culture of subsidiaries through vision and values programmes (Buller and McEvoy, 1999)

- introduce new or reformed central or normative control over HRM policies (Legge, 1995)

- transfer 'best' organisational practice through international benchmarking exercises (Martin and Beaumont, 1998; Kostova, 1999).

However, such programmes are often criticised for having culture-laden or ethical assumptions (Cray and Mallory, 1998; Woodall and Winstanley, 2000). The problems of cross-border transfer of ideas across multiple countries and layers of management are considerable. We need much better insight into how international HR functions manage the events, activities and emotions in their organisation that usually embed or hinder HR change initiatives (Martin and Beaumont, 2001).

This challenge is all the more pressing, for there is a clear danger that the sorts of pressures outlined in the previous chapter – multiple choices in the HRM model as a result of shared service, offshoring and outsourcing – can lead to a fragmentation of the international HR function. As Gratton (2003; p.18) notes:

'During the past decade we have fragmented the roles and responsibilities of the function. We have outsourced the lower-value operational work, and we are beginning to develop the staff profiling work that will enable us to act as "employee champions". We are also putting the "change agent" roles back into the streams of business to work closely with their line manager partners. Meanwhile the "business partners" are either going into the businesses or clustered around "best practice" centres, which may be located in different places ... This fragmentation of the HR function is causing all sorts of unintended problems. Senior managers look at the fragments and are not clear how the function as a whole adds value.'

Against this view a number of protagonists of the importance of the international HRM function argue that a series of generic international management issues involved in globalisation inevitably create a search for optimal HR practice. Globalisation of itself brings the HR function closer to the strategic core of the business and also leads to considerable changes in the content of HRM (Pucik, 1992). It has been argued that a major determinant of success or failure in international business is the effective management of human resources internationally (Stroh and Caligiuri, 1998). Indeed, many organisations underestimate the complex nature of HRM problems involved in managing increasingly international operations (Dowling, Welch and Schuler, 1999).

The bottom-line question cited by Scullion and Starkey (2000) and originally asked by Foss (1997; p.314) is 'What is it that the corporate HQ can do that cannot be done by financial markets or the business units, acting as independent market contractors?' Ghoshal and Gratton (2002) point to a number of important integration activities at this level (see the Key framework box below).

KEY FRAMEWORK

Mechanisms of integration

The corporate centre has the ability to manage the process of integration. This process has four critical components:

- operational integration through standardised technology – Portals can provide a common front for employees and help integrate the HR function around a common employee brand, as is the case for example in BP

- intellectual integration through the creation of a shared knowledge base – By creating an emphasis on creating, sharing and exchanging knowledge both within and beyond the HR community, corporate HR functions can ensure that the intellectual capital of the function is rapidly codified and shared across constituent HR functions

- social integration through the creation of collective bonds of performance – This is where the function develops a clear sense of what it wants to achieve and how it wants to achieve it

- emotional integration through a sense of shared identity and meaning – This concerns the mobilisation of hearts and minds behind change processes.

Source: Ghoshal and Gratton (2002)

In relation to this framework, we described the role of *operational integration* through shared service centres and e-enablement in the last chapter. In this chapter we examine:

- *intellectual integration* (by looking at the role of knowledge management in the work of international HR managers)

- *social integration* (by looking at the role that working through global networks plays in developing social integration amongst international HRM professionals)

- *emotional integration* (by considering the role of international HRM professionals as guardians of national culture and managers of a negotiated balance between the application of global rule-sets to HR processes and the need for local responsiveness to cultural imperatives).

To these four types of integration we add a fifth important integration role identified by Scullion and Starkey (2000) – the effective management of international management talent. They note that the management of senior managers and high-potential people identified as strategic resources is vital to the future and survival of most international operations. We examine this by considering the role of talent management in an international context. Throughout this chapter we draw most attention to a discussion of how such integration takes place.

CHANGING INTERDEPENDENCIES BETWEEN IHRM AND OTHER CORPORATE FUNCTIONS

As we have seen throughout this book, although there are many differences in HRM across countries and within international organisations of different national origin, many organisations are internationalising their HRM as they endeavour to survive against global competition. Sparrow, Brewster and Harris (2004) examined a number of issues associated with this, including the strategic nature of the HR interventions; the political, process and technical skills that had to be brought to bear to manage these interventions; the contrasting stakeholder expectations of the intervention role; and the link to organisational strategy and effectiveness. They noted four key strategic pressures (see box below)

Four key strategic pressures driving the internationalisation of the HR function

- *maximising shareholder value* – This might take the form of commitments made by large established multinationals to shareholders as to where the organisation will be within a stated time period, or it might be seen in contracts made by new international start-ups with investors in a highly competitive field. International organisations have to keep shareholders with them. The driving force behind most global HR functions' recent restructuring efforts has been the need to deliver global business strategies in the most cost-efficient manner possible. Both people and activities are examined to identify their added value

- *building global presence* – Many organisations realise that as their markets increase globally, the requirement to ensure that they have a presence and be visible in multiple markets also increases. There is often considerable time pressure placed on this need to build global presence

- *forging strategic partnerships* – This is important both for established multinationals and also for not-for-profit organisations. In large multinationals the growth of joint ventures and strategic partnership arrangements has brought with it the need to work with former competitors and collaborators. In not-for-profit organisations a decentralisation of activities to local operations and local staff often involves working closely with other local groups to ensure the delivery of the necessary support

- *creating core business processes* – International HRM responds to the development of core business processes and the movement away from country-based operations towards business-line-driven organisations. However, it does more than just respond. It is often a key part of the reorientation of strategy. HR often has to arrange the staffing, the procedures and the policies to put moves towards core business processes in place and embed them within the organisation. As we saw in the last chapter, the move towards a shared service philosophy has also brought with it the need to standardise or optimise HR processes on a global scale.

Source: Sparrow, Brewster and Harris (2004)

We discussed the concept of organisational capability in the last chapter. In relation to this, Ulrich (2000) has argued that the development of organisational capability – the means through which the firm implements policies and procedures – is now a pressing challenge in several areas of international management. As a result of this challenge, in addition to teaching the topics traditionally associated with the management of people, international HR professionals are required also to understand:

- the basis of the economic and financial capability
- the strategic/marketing capability, and

- the technological capability of their organisations.

This is because, as Malbright (1995; p.119) pointed out, inside firms,

'Globalisation occurs at the level of the function, rather than the firm.'

However, the problem is that the HR function is not one that can currently be considered highly globalised. Indeed, researchers have found that other departments are much more globalised (Hansen, Nohria and Tierney, 1999; Kim *et al*, 2003). If other functional activities are being better connected across geographical borders through flows of information that are intended to enhance levels of innovation and learning, then the HR functions that service them are themselves going to be forced to become more globalised. The future of the global HR function will be both heavily dependent upon and shaped by the globalising activity of two contiguous sets of functions (Sparrow, Brewster and Harris, 2004; Brewster, Sparrow and Harris, 2005):

- information systems and procurement, and
- marketing, corporate communications and strategy.

By implication, the syllabus that we must teach, and the knowledge-base that we must develop, will be influenced by thinking that crosses over the 'borders' between these fields of knowledge.

As a result of the original work and subsequent developments, a new outline of the areas of overlapping interests can be discerned (shown in Figure 41). Again, this model can be used to structure this chapter. In the last chapter we dealt with most of the topics that arise from the interdependence of the HRM function with IS and Procurement functions (shared servive, e-enablement and HR models dependent on IS such as offshoring, outsourcing and centres of excellence). We shall pick up the issue of knowledge management in this chapter – and we shall also pick up the role of the HR function in relation to the activities that have a marketing, corporate communications and strategy dimension.

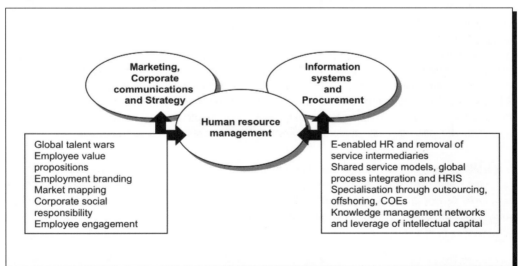

Figure 41 *The positioning of the global HR function against key alliances*

QUESTIONS

- Thinking about the issues covered in this book, what will be the challenges of standardisation, and what will be the challenges of local responsiveness for IHRM?

- What might be done to resolve those issues?

In each of these areas of overlapping activity, organisations still face the challenge, on the one hand, of providing some degree of consistency (through either standardisation or optimisation) of practices around the world so that their operations use the same tools and techniques to obtain candidates who increasingly act as part of a more global community, and on the other hand, of maintaining locally responsive and differentiated approaches:

'There is a great deal of resistance to designing and implementing global systems and policies because "people are different", "laws are different" and "labour markets are different". As the complexity of designing and implementing effective HR systems on an international scale cannot be denied, there are many areas where HR professionals have shied away from going global, preferring instead to implement local or regional solutions. However, ... as more organisations begin to operate on a global (or at least multinational) scale, the need for HR systems that can be used across multiple countries continues to grow.'

Ryan, Wiechmann and Hemingway (2003; p.85)

In practice, global HRM seems to revolve around the ability of the organisation to find a concept that has 'relevance' to managers across several countries – despite the fact that they have different values embedded in different national cultures, and despite the reality that these global themes may end up being operationalised with some local adaptation. The corporate strategy is usually expressed through performance management systems applied globally that measure and manage a balanced series of outcomes that must be achieved. However, organisations also use some superordinate themes to provide a degree of consistency for their people management worldwide and as an attempt to socialise employee behaviour and action. The most common superordinate themes in the process of globalising HR are:

- *talent management* – through which an integrated set of corporate initiatives is aimed at improving the calibre, availability and flexible utilisation of exceptionally capable (high-potential) employees who can have a disproportionate impact on organisational performance (Scullion and Starkey, 2000; Smilanksy, 2004; Scullion and Collings, 2006)

- *corporate and global brands* – whereby organisations think about their external brand image and corporate reputation, and the ways in which their employees identify with and actively support the brand (Harris and de Chernatony, 2001; Davies, Chun, Da Silva and Roper, 2003; Martin and Hetrick, 2006)

- *global capability systems*, built around core strategic competencies that are considered to differentiate the firm and lead to its competitive advantage. These are usually reflected in a series of organisational capabilities or competencies that once specified are integrated into career development and/or performance management systems (Sparrow, 1997).

Each of these brings its own challenges when managed on the global stage, and is considered in turn.

TALENT MANAGEMENT

The first main integration role for international HR professionals that we discuss is the contribution that they can make to the management of talent on an international basis. We considered the issue of expatriate management in Chapter 10 and noted that talent management on a global basis is a far broader concept than plotting a series of international assignments for young high-potentials. Scullion and Starkey (2000; p.1065) concluded:

> '[There is a] growing recognition that the success of international business depends most importantly on the quality of top executive talent and how effectively these critical resources are managed and developed.'

In practice, talent markets still operate in very national ways and even global organisations can find that their relative positioning varies markedly from one country to another. Those organisations that are consistently in the top ten tend to maintain local recruitment strategies, but they mix this local strategy with more global transfer of information and best practices. This is because the talent itself has become more mobile and organisations are therefore having to coordinate the way they manage it on a global basis. Competition also has become more generic – global organisations do not just compete with the best local employers but also with each other. For example, Shell estimates that only 5% of graduates even from the top business schools have the potential for country chairmanship roles (Sparrow, Brewster and Harris, 2004).

Talent management processes can bring a degree of consistency to international resourcing decisions. A strong corporate culture can make the use of talent management approaches and harmonised activities across countries easier. Many talent management systems have an underlying focus on a series of core values that are strongly reflective of the corporate and industry culture, and therefore more easily perceived as being universal (Scullion and Collings, 2006).

The purpose of a successful talent management system is to attract, retain, develop and utilise employees in ways that create (Smilansky, 2004):

- sustainable commercial competitiveness through the alignment of employee competence, behaviours and intellectual energy with business activity
- higher levels of focused innovation
- improved staff engagement and commitment
- lower loss rates of knowledge and experience
- lower external resourcing costs.

When global lines of business are introduced, there is a more immediate relationship between the international HR professional and the global leadership teams within major business functions or markets. Many organisations conduct various 'calibrations' of talent on a global basis in order to plan business development. International organisations want to know who their top people are and what the key roles are within the business that they need these people for. They want to know how they can develop people, get them to key positions, and build succession cover for these key positions. They have to develop a much deeper level of understanding about the links between the business agenda and the capabilities of the most talented people in the organisation, and also understand the potential for mobility around these people (Sparrow, Brewster and Harris, 2004).

Regardless of the ups and downs in the international business cycle, there is then a war for talent taking place (Michaels, Handfield-Jones and Axelrod, 2001). Marketing strategies quickly become outdated and the pecking order of the most desired employers changes quickly. In order to attract and retain the best talent anywhere in the world, an organisation must have a strong and positive employer brand. Many international organisations therefore put considerable effort into developing an 'employee value proposition' (EVP) by identifying the most important features of working for them (Michaels, Handfield-Jones and Axelrod, 2001) – here, HRM policy is influenced by marketing thinking. Employee value propositions are generally used to drive attraction and retention behaviour. The organisation is asking, 'Why should you buy my product or service – why would a highly talented person want to work in my organisation?' The EVP conveys a clear statement of some of the more explicit obligations that the organisation commits to.

In theory, EVPs should be aligned to each major unit within the organisation. However, most international organisations are working hard to create a positive and more global brand for potential recruits. A key challenge for international organisations is therefore the extent to which it is possible to create such global EVPs. This entails offering a compelling value proposition to the employees of the organisation, and to understand and then to market the brand that the organisation represents across global labour markets that all have different values and different perceptions. The challenge for global organisations is to decide what the overriding message is of who they are and what they stand for.

As the world gets smaller, global organisations need to make sure that the way in which they are perceived as a company is similar wherever they go. What do their consumers want from them? What do current employees think? This involves constantly reselling to employees the proposition that their organisation is the place they should work. The challenge is to understand what makes a really good person want to stay with them globally. The answer affects the development of people, which is a key driver of retention, and finally impinges on how the organisation recruits. It affects how the organisation approaches the media, how it conducts its investor relations, how it designs compensation and benefits, and how it designs performance management systems – ie it informs all policies and procedures. These messages cannot be aspirational – they have to be grounded in what the organisation really offers and what potential employees really want. The processes must back up what the organisation says it is. The key messages to potential employees also must make sense in all the organisation's markets worldwide. The organisation has to pick out which messages it can match and where it is able to give out a message that can be fulfilled.

Common responses to talent management in global organisations

Thinking about talent on a global basis is leading organisations towards a series of common responses:

- researching into 'consumer insights' with current and potential employees, sister companies, external agencies, and benchmarking with external companies

- managing the 'talent pipeline' – trying to recruit 'ahead of the curve' instead of the more traditional vacancy-based recruitment

- communicating an awareness in graduate schools and businesses to get the people they are looking for

- developing internal talent pools around the world

- creating skilled and competent teams of assessors in different areas of the world

- managing recruitment suppliers on a global basis, introducing speed, cost and quality controls, establishing master contracts to coordinate the messages conveyed and the use of preferred partners, ensuring audit trails to protect against legal issues associated with global diversity

- e-enabling jobs noticeboards, redesigning websites to convey important messages about the employer brand.

Source: Sparrow, Brewster and Harris (2004)

ACTIVITY

It can often be assumed that many talent management practices are the preserve of large multinationals. However, charities face similar issues of having to compete for a small number of talented people. For example, when a crisis arises, will that expert in dysentery work for Save the Children or for Oxfam? Although of course the financial resources that might be devoted to talent management strategies are more constrained, the practices and experiences of not-for-profit organisations in the international management area are very similar to those of large private sector firms.

Imagine you are the international HR director of an international charity.

- What talent management issues might you have to deal with?

- What would be the key elements of your talent management strategy, and what would you need employees to do to 'make it happen'?

EMPLOYMENT BRANDING

Sparrow, Brewster and Harris (2004) argue that the topics of employment branding and talent management are intimately linked for most global organisations. International organisations are concerned with their 'talent pipeline'. They want to know who their top people are and what the key roles are within the business that they need these people for. They are concerned with how they can develop them to get to those key positions and how they can build succession cover for such key positions. This means that they have to develop a much deeper level of understanding about the links between the business agenda and the capabilities of the most talented people in the organisation, and also understand the potential for mobility around these people. When they conduct such a 'calibration' of talent on a global basis, they have to ask what this suggests for the planned business development. In short, when global lines of business are introduced, there is a more immediate relationship between the international HR professional and the global leadership teams within major business functions or markets.

There has been considerable debate in the profession about the management of employment brands internationally. It is an important challenge for many large international organisations. Employment branding – the image of the organisation as seen through the eyes of *external* stakeholders – represents an extension of brand management and is another development whereby HR thinking has been influenced by that of the marketing function. Building or defending the corporate brand or reputation has become a major concern in many industries. Employment branding requires consistency and uniformity in delivering the brand identity by all *internal* stakeholders, including employees. However, currently, we still know little about the linkages between HR and marketing in the brand management process, despite increasing awareness that the HR function is now becoming involved in this work on an international scale.

Employment branding strategies

A recent study has analysed the aims and strategies of 236 organisations in 11 countries from the financial services, consulting, healthcare, manufacturing, retail and telecommunications sectors. The most common objectives for employer branding work are to enhance the appeal of the employer among potential employees and to secure long-term recruitment of staff. To a lesser extent, the aim is also to create internal pride and commitment and fulfil short-term recruitment needs. It is an externally focused strategy. Most of the information that organisations seek to develop a brand is, however, internal – knowledge and experience of their organisation, internal surveys of employees – with some external analysis of the labour market. Strategies centre on articulating an overall recruitment and retention approach, defining core values for the employer, refining and aligning recruitment processes and planned communication material.

Around a fifth of organisations believe they have a very clear employer value proposition; just as many do not believe so; and around a half feel this can be further developed. Measurement and evaluation is mainly based on levels of employee satisfaction and turnover, and to a lesser extent external employer attraction, total number of applications, employee loyalty and time to fill vacancies. The majority of people involved have HR backgrounds, but the larger the organisation, the more likely that specialists work in marketing and communications, and they are becoming more involved in general. Control still tends to be at an operational level. Some 30% of organisations plan to increase their investments in this area (average investments are €140 per employee per year) and 60% will maintain current investment levels.

Source: Universum (2005)

For global organisations, however, the challenge is how best to create an *authentic and legitimate* brand (Martin and Hetrick, 2006). We can all think of marketing material that serves to put people off, either through its blandness or its rhetoric. The need for authenticity involves constantly re-selling an accurate and sustainable message.

Case study

GlaxoSmithKline post-merger

Immediately after the merger of SmithKline Beecham and Glaxo Wellcome, GlaxoSmithKline (GSK) initiated a global research process to help it define its employment brand and improve its recruitment processes. Opinions as to what the organisation 'meant' varied by location, function and legacy company culture. 70 focus groups were run across 20 locations to reveal common sources of pride and a 'corporate signature' that could subsequently feature on all of the organisation's marketing materials (the 'Together we can make life better' campaign). Guidelines were developed for copy-writing, image usage and layout. The brand was first established in the USA and the UK, and was then marketed across Europe and the Asia-Pacific region.

Source: Ford (2002)

Sparrow (2007) found that as organisations deal with employment branding issues on an international basis, the issues develop through a clear sequence over time. Initially, attention is given to 'stabilising' key people management processes across different geographical operations (making sure that recruitiment, performance management, communication activities and so forth operate to the same levels of professionalisam). Once this has been done, decisions can then be made about the 'look' and 'consistency' of the employment brand. Basic considerations include:

- creating the same physical brand – for example the logo and literature – drawing upon the business strategy and the reasons it provides for why the organisation is now operating in a particular international labour market

- sharing a common mission, vision and set of stated values: attention is given to communicating these consistently through the various programmes and media

- setting minimum HR standards and conditions to shape the nature of employee engagement

- examining how the pay strategy and associated benchmarks define the calibre of applicants

- understanding how this helps bring consistency to the employee experience in terms of competencies and leadership capability.

QUESTIONS

In the light of what you know about international HRM now that you are in the last chapter, how easy do you think it is to manage a global employment brand? What issues would an IHR professional expect to have to manage?

To answer this, analyse the HR activities of an organisation (yours, perhaps) across a series of countries and answer the following questions:

- How important is it that the performance management and development processes are made the same across all the countries as early as possible? What sorts of adjustments to these processes will inevitably have to be made for local cultural and legal reasons?

- How much does the organisation's international operations vary in terms of their adherence to standards and procedures in the area of recruitment? Is there a need to set minimum standards for the conduct of HR before you can create a consistent brand?

- What input is needed from in-country HR partners for a branding strategy to work across countries, and what central oversight is necessary?

- Does pay strategy in different countries define the calibre of applicants that can be attracted? If you attract a different calibre of manager across countries because of this, does it matter? Does it impact on the way that employees will 'experience' the brand?

- Do you have similar 'employee engagement' data across the operations? If scores differ, does this reflect different national values, or different business models being applied, or different levels of professional line management?

It should be clear that managing the employment brand across international operations as a way of bringing some consistency into HRM requires judgements to be made about the capability of the international operations.

GLOBAL CAPABILITY SYSTEMS

Changes in the way that international businesses organise themselves and the desire to harmonise more operations on a pan-national basis has also seen the growth of global competency models. Those organisations using a competency-based approach to recruitment internationally can draw on the comfort that the use of competencies remains in vogue and appears still to be expanding globally. A survey by the World Federation of Personnel Management Associations shows a small increase in the use of competencies from 2000 to 2004 (Wordlink, 2005). Some organisations are integrating their HR around global capabilities. In order to manage talent and foster more international mobility, key HR processes that are intended to help build the organisation's capability are being brought together. This is leading to more coordinated management of external resourcing, talent benchmarking, deployment decision forums, high-potential review processes, a focus on reward and recognition in order to link individual performance, development and reward more closely with performance, and development partnering or coaching. As a consequence, more organisations are using assessment centres for external recruitment, or launching international development centres for internal assessment, benchmarked against single competency models.

DEBATE

Think about an organisation you know. Is it possible or legitimate to define a single set of competencies for use across international borders? Can people from different cultures be accurately assessed against them?

Received wisdom tells us that at a very high level of generalisation single internationally operating sets of competencies are possible – indeed, it is being done by most large organisations. However, experience also shows that there are links between cultural background and people's perceptions of what good performance looks like (and by implication, therefore, the sorts of competencies that will be identified and will be seen as legitimate to assess). Caution must be used when attempting to recruit to a single-competency model derived in one dominant culture but being applied to applicants from another. Case studies of the use of competency models on a global basis also reveal the ways in which they have to be adapted when used for more diverse populations. A recent study by consultants and work psychologists looking at global organisations such as Marconi, Nestlé and the food division of Unilever shows that differences still persist. It concluded:

'Although it should be possible to design competencies that have cross-cultural validity, subtle important differences of perception concerning individual behaviours frequently mean that direct comparisons between candidates from specific countries are subject to systematic bias ... When using the assessment centre technique, systematic differences should be expected between the behaviour of people from different countries as they strive to meet different mental models of what good performance looks like ... [Do not] assume that any competency is universally applicable just because a company has included it in its corporate competency framework.'

Milsom (2004; p.22)

The models of global leadership discussed earlier in this book reaffirm this view. They show that there are scores of different culturally embedded models of effective leadership across cultures. Reflecting all these views, most leading organisations apply a series of pragmatic 'work-arounds' to ensure that the essence of the systems is kept intact across their international operations, but that there is scope for 'reasonable variation' and 'flexibility'. Sparrow, Brewster and Harris (2004) found that the use of specific tools and techniques within talent management systems must come hand in hand with consideration of the issues involving appropriateness across cultures, existence and ease of translation, availability of norms across countries, and the ability of key suppliers and vendors of relevant services themselves to operate on a global basis.

MANAGEMENT THROUGH GLOBAL NETWORKS

We noted at the beginning of the chapter that an important integration mechanism that corporate headquarters can introduce is to create a sense of social integration through the creation of collective bonds of performance. Parkhe *et al* (2006; p.560) recently argued that:

> **'networks are reshaping the global business architecture ... The ubiquity of networks and networking at the industry, firm, group, and individual levels has attracted significant research attention.'**

We examine this now by looking at the role that working through global networks plays in developing social integration amongst international HRM professionals. The HR function has to help the firm develop the capabilities that turn business opportunities (the strategy) into action. Returning to the outline of organisational capability given by Ulrich and Lake (1990) and discussed in the last chapter, it is clear that it is about effective execution of strategy (whatever that strategy might be). What they outline (see the box below) is also essentially a leadership role – a role that is custom-designed for effective HR professionals – but in their prescription one also that is generally conducted through the use of networks and persuasion.

The central tasks of HR professionals in building organisational capability

- to design new organisational structures that meet a strategic charter
- to develop a capacity for change through the management of employee attitudes and the management of organisational culture
- to manage paradoxes by resolving conflicts in order to satisfy multiple and competing demands – this is done by constantly re-balancing each demand and developing practices capable of meeting this flexibility
- to build organisational processes that affect the thinking and behaviour of employees and establish shared operating philosophies
- to build partnerships inside and outside the organisation in order to use HR processes more effectively
- to focus the people management processes around the concept of talent
- to develop and manage forums that allow the expression of competing views but that bring people together when decisions must be made

- to build a 'social architecture' (defined as deliberately constructed groups of independent individuals who are focused on mutually shared goals) to manage the commitment of a coalition of people, then build networks (connected sets of coalitions), and finally use temporary systems (time-bounded systems of people working to a purpose, structure and procedure in order to manage a limited set of inputs) to coordinate their activity

- to rebuild commitment to and from employees by establishing a psychological contract with employees.

Source: Ulrich and Lake (1990)

For international HR professionals, this capability-building agenda is often more concerned with the upskilling of a business function, and with spending more time engaging with the leadership teams of these functions. Global networking is one of the ways that the international HR function can help build this capability across international operations. This has always been important within international HR. However, it is now considered to be critical because of the organisational changes outlined in the previous chapter. Historically, global information, insight into local conditions and best practice have all tended to be shared through the process of international HR professionals' just talking to each other – getting groups of people together within the organisation to facilitate some transfer of learning. Indeed, international HR professionals have to set up informal networks all the time – and this is generally one of their key objectives. It is much easier to have a network in place working on a significant HR issue from the start. With a network, there is more chance of moving quickly, producing higher-quality HR services, and providing a better business focus. There is more chance of success. Networks also suit a more decentralised model of international HR. Global networks are generally not just put in place for the purpose of knowledge transfer. They are used increasingly to cut through bureaucracy and to act as important decision-making groups. They serve several important purposes:

- providing a forum to encourage innovation and growth throughout the business, and a vehicle to get the right people on to the right teams in order to make this happen

- encouraging HR professionals and line managers to think beyond their 'own patch'

- creating a situation whereby membership of the network provides advantages in terms of better-quality implementation for both the line managers and the HR professionals

- getting stakeholders (the senior HR community, presidents in businesses) to buy in to business changes

- forcing the business agenda in forums outside the networks in subtle ways based on shared insight within the network.

However, in very flat and constantly changing organisations, networks tend to break down. Many global organisations are therefore also developing more formal processes to transfer knowledge that capitalise on technology (Sparrow, Brewster and Harris, 2004).

ACTIVITY

Take the example of organisations that you know: consider how you would rate them in terms of their support for global networking.

Compare your conclusions with those of colleagues.

GLOBAL KNOWLEDGE MANAGEMENT STRATEGIES

A third integration activity that international HR functions can pursue is the development of intellectual integration through the creation of shared knowledge-bases. In a competitive marketplace, the act of integrating disparate sources of knowledge within the bounds of the organisation has become a source of advantage (Grant, 1996). Although there has been considerable attention paid to the issue of knowledge management in recent years, 'to date there is yet to be a significant undertaking that looks at issues in managing knowledge across borders' (Desouza and Evaristo, 2003; p.62). Sparrow (2006) outlined five main forms of global knowledge management, or integration mechanisms that are currently dominating the actions of organisations:

- organisational designs, such as the use of centres of excellence

- managing systems and technology-driven approaches to global knowledge management systems

- capitalising on expatriate advice networks

- coordinating international management teams

- developing communities of practice (COPs) or global expertise networks.

We have examined many of these challenges already, so we concentrate here on the role of knowledge management in the work of international HR managers. In the last chapter we discussed the opportunity afforded the international HRM function in helping to build organisational capability. Perhaps the most critical component in terms of international HR positioning lies in its role as knowledge management champion. In a global environment, physical and cultural distance present powerful barriers to successful knowledge transfer amongst HR professionals. Choosing the most effective technological platforms but, most importantly, agreeing the content of the knowledge to be shared and creating knowledge networks is therefore an essential factor in the HR function's globalisation efforts. So far, largely perhaps because much of this debate has been driven by the technical specialists, the possibilities of global HRM as the process which adds to and helps exploit the stock of knowledge, and particularly the powerful intrinsic stock of knowledge, have not been fully developed (Sparrow, Brewster and Harris, 2004).

The HR function also has to grapple with the intrinsic stock of knowledge held in people's heads that is often the key to competitive advantage. Hence international HR departments are taking on responsibility for the conscious development of operating networks, both as practitioners within the HR community and as facilitators elsewhere in the organisation (see the box below).

The role of global HR networks

- to provide and enable value-added and cost-effective global, regional, and local solutions in a series of core HR processes

- to identify customer-driven pan-national issues

- to design solutions to meet specific customer needs and support the corporate people management strategy

- to demonstrate to customers that global connectivity adds value by sharing knowledge and expertise

- to ensure that knowledge and intellectual property that resided within HR silos was made freely available to all of the organisation.

Source: Sparrow, Brewster and Harris (2004)

Many international organisations are experimenting with global expertise networks that also serve a knowledge management role. These global expertise networks provide common HR services for internal customers of the HR function. This might involve the creation and maintenance of a global repository of HR knowledge and expertise or the creation of global communities that enable practitioners in a particular field to 'meet' other practitioners and exchange ideas, problems and best practice. In reality, technology in the form of global intranets and knowledge management systems enables, but does not cause, the required connections and sharing. There is considerable 'social capital' within these communities (ie a lot of importance given to the connections and relationships that each professional can call upon and the resources that he or she can mobilise).

QUESTIONS

- What difficulties might organisations face in building international HR networks?
- How might these be overcome?

Discuss your conclusions with colleagues.

Tregaskis, Glover and Ferner (2005) conducted interviews in six firms and have described the function, structure and process typically associated with international HR networks. These networks can be run through top-down or more collaborative remits and operate through leadership, project or special event team structures. They serve a range of functions including policy development and implementation, information capture, exploitation of knowledge, sharing of best practice, achieving political buy-in and socialisation of members. Face-to-face contact is important in the process of relationship and reputation-building but is often supplemented by virtual working as a way of signalling more global cultures. The level of localisation is generally driven by the politics of acquisition, size, expertise and level of resistance in subsidiaries. HR leadership through networks can facilitate more collaborative solutions, but this depends on the strategic capability of the function, board-level support and strength of international HR networks.

Sparrow and Brewster (2006) note that network and project-based structures have had a significant impact on the conduct and quality of international HR interventions and on the career trajectories of HR professionals. However, there is little clarity about the extent to which these networks can be local as well as global, external as well as internal. The development of (real and/or virtual) shared service centres and centres of excellence – both discussed in the previous chapter – provides global organisations with two distinct models of how these networks might work. From a knowledge management perspective there are also important questions to be resolved as to the location and input of resources necessary for HR centres of excellence. Similarly, the ways in which network- and project-based activity can best be used to build political and social capital within the HR function has to be better understood.

In order to build on this individual social capital, international HR professionals have to build the relationships across the broader HR community. In practice, building strong international relationships still requires considerable face-to-face contact. More importantly, the communities have to work on real business issues. HR professionals from around the world will only work together if it is necessary to solve mutual and pressing business needs. It is clear that network- and project-based structures have had a significant impact on the conduct and quality of international HR interventions and on the career trajectories of HR professionals.

SUMMARY: THE GLOBAL HR ROLE

It will have been evident throughout this book that as organisations operate more internationally, the HR function becomes both the gatekeeper of national institutional and cultural differences, advising on which processes can be standardised and which must remain localised, and also the knowledge agency that transfers ideas across businesses, functions and geographical boundaries within the global firm (Sparrow, Brewster and Harris, 2004). However, it is worth remembering that if you ask any self-respecting international HR professional what the critical determinant of success for his or her function is, you will almost certainly get the response: 'Being a strategic partner for the business.' Some of the processes and capabilities for achieving this are well known to all of us working in international HR: the need for board-level representation, the ability to fully understand the business, the need for excellent analytical and planning skills, the ability to measure the effectiveness of HR interventions, and so forth. Yet being a strategic partner for the business is not the same thing for HR professionals working in domestically based organisations as for their colleagues working in international organisations. A much more strategic role awaits the global HR function, which brings with it the need for additional knowledge and abilities on the part of HR professionals. We have outlined much of this additional knowledge throughout this book. There are two key conclusions that should be drawn about the role of the HR function in international organisations (Sparrow, Brewster and Harris, 2004):

- The added value of the HR function in an international organisation lies in its ability to manage the delicate balance between overall coordinated systems and sensitivity to local needs, including cultural differences, in a way that aligns with both business needs and senior management philosophy.

- Slowly, a distinction is emerging between international HRM and global HRM. Traditionally, international HRM has been about managing an international workforce – the expatriates, frequent commuters, cross-cultural team members and specialists involved in international knowledge transfer. Global HRM is not just simply about covering these staff around the world. It concerns managing international HRM activities through the application of global rule-sets to HRM processes. Most organisations are gradually making this transition from international to global HR.

We have drawn support for these conclusions in the last two chapters by drawing attention to the key challenges that face most international HR functions. Working in a role that is more closely aligned with the creation and building of organisational capability, the international HR function has to make appropriate pledges about the levels of performance that it feels can be delivered to the business. As we saw in the last chapter, the requirement to meet these pledges often exists under conditions of cost control across international operations, or shareholder pressure for the delivery of rapid financial returns in new international operations. Yet the ability of the function to meet these performance pledges is critical.

The international HR function has to help its organisation manage the consequences of several strategic initiatives. This might be global business process redesign, the pursuit of a global centre of excellence strategy or the global re-distribution and re-location of work that this often entails. The HR personnel have to help their organisation absorb acquired businesses from what might previously have been competitor businesses. They become involved in the merging of existing operations on a global scale and the staffing of strategic integration teams. They must manage attempts to develop and harmonise core HR processes within these merged businesses, and also manage growth through the process of acquisition whereby new country operations are often built around the purchase of a series of national teams. The rapid start-up of international operations brings with it the requirement to provide insights into the organisational development needs of new operations as they mature through different stages of the business life cycle. In many international operations the capabilities are changing rapidly as many skills become obsolete very quickly and as changes in the organisational structure and design expose managers to more complex roles. This often requires a general upskilling of local operations.

In order to help free up time for the function to engage in these sorts of activities, it has to capitalise on technology while at the same time ensuring that local social and cultural insights are duly considered when it is imperative to do so – especially when IT is being used to centralise and 'transactionalise' HR processes, or to create shared services, on a global basis. In order to make these sorts of judgements international HR functions have to understand the changes being wrought in the HR service supply chain as the need for several intermediary service providers is being reduced, and as web-based HR provision is leading to greater individualisation of HRM across international operations. Often these international operations have very different levels of 'HR sophistication'. Partly as a consequence, international HR professionals have to learn how to operate through formal or informal global HR networks and how to act as knowledge brokers across international operations.

In truth, there are often quite marked identity issues faced by international HR professionals. Operating through global networks and transferring knowledge across international operations mean that they have to learn how to avoid automatically pursuing a one-best-way philosophy (be it for HR solutions or indeed in terms of general management activity). As knowledge and ideas about best practice flow from both the centre to the operations and vice versa, it is not uncommon for international HR professionals at all levels of the organisation to feel that their ideas are being overridden by those of other nationalities or business systems. This can often be quite challenging because within a domestic HR setting offering advice on best practice might seem to be an appropriate solution and a service that has to be offered by the HR function. Moreover, international HR professionals have to experience and endure frequent changes in the level of decentralisation/centralisation across their constituent international businesses, making it very difficult to establish with authority where their power lies.

A critical aspect of creating effective international HR strategies is therefore the ability to judge the extent to which an organisation should implement similar practices across the world or adapt them to suit local conditions – the 'global versus local' debate. This key challenge requires a high level of strategic thinking on the part of international HR professionals. While scanning the world for best practice, they need to ensure that the policies and practices they implement are appropriate to the unique nature of their international operations. The attributes that are most frequently evident in the work of international HR professionals are outlined below.

International HR competencies

- Being a strategic thinker, articulating the benefits of having an effective HR process and capability, and the risks to both personal and business objectives of not having one.

- Having available strong personal networks inside and outside the organisation and the ability to build some structure into this collection of relationships.

- Being a provider of information and advice within this business network, based on personal expertise and credibility.

- Becoming a broker of appropriate knowledge, learning and ideas across a loose connection of people. Being seen as the owner of important new dialogues within the organisation.

- Displaying capacity for and tolerance of the ambiguities and uncertainties inherent in new business situations, such as working through confused leadership.

- Being a resource negotiator, persuading managers to invest and capturing unassigned resources.

- Being a process facilitator, with diplomatic sensitivity to complex organisational politics and power struggles.

- Mobilising the energy and engagement behind ideas, maintaining pressure on people, managing the impact by under-promising but over-achieving.

- Having respect for the countries and communities being dealt with. Showing insight into their needs both as consumers (as employees) and as clients (as global business functions).

- Showing an appreciation of the ways in which culture influences core organisational behaviours.

- Possessing the capacity to work virtually.

Source: Sparrow, Brewster and Harris (2004)

Although many managers believe that the role of national culture might be overstated and that there is scope for more uniformity of HR process around best practices than country-level HR managers will acknowledge, we end by noting the fifth integration role that international HR functions can provide. This is the development of emotional integration through a sense of shared identity and meaning. We have explored this throughout this text by considering the role of international HRM professionals as guardians of national difference who have to manage a negotiated balance between the application of global rule-sets to HR processes and the need for local responsiveness to cultural imperatives. We have seen that organisations are inventing new global HR systems at different paces and within different parts of their business. We have seen too that there is a new 'line in the sand' being drawn between standardised or optimised global processes and local HR practices. In this context, international HR professionals truly need to act as the 'caretakers' of culture.

LEARNING QUESTIONS

- To what extent is there still a role for the corporate HR function in international human resource management?

- Is it possible to create an employee value proposition on a global scale?

- What types of knowledge do global HR expertise networks need to transfer?

- What will be the impact of working through networks on the careers of international HR professionals?

- Who will act as the guardians of national culture if not the international HR function? Does this role still matter?

- What are the main competencies needed by international HR professionals?

REFERENCES

Brewster, C. (1994) 'The integration of human resource management and corporate strategy', in C. Brewster and A. Hegewisch (eds) *Policy and Practice in European Human Resource Management: The evidence and analysis from the Price Waterhouse Cranfield Survey.* London, Routledge

Brewster, C., Sparrow, P. R. and Harris, H. (2005) 'Towards a new model of globalising human resource management', *International Journal of Human Resource Management,* 16 (6): 953–74

Buller, P. F. and McEvoy, G. M. (1999) 'Creating and sustaining ethical capability in the multinational corporation', in R. S. Schuler and S. E. Jackson (eds) *Strategic Human Resource Management.* Oxford, Blackwell

Cray, D. and Mallory, G. R. (1998) *Making Sense of Managing Culture.* London, Thomson Business Press

Davies, G., Chun, R., Da Silva, R. V. and Roper, S. (2003) *Corporate Reputation and Competitiveness.* London, Routledge

DeFidelto, C. and Slater, I. (2001) 'Web-based HR in an international setting', in A. J. Walker (ed.) *Web-Based Human Resources: The technologies that are transforming HR*. London, McGraw-Hill

Desouza, K. and Evaristo, R. (2003) 'Global knowledge management strategies', *European Management Journal*, 21 (1): 62–7

Dowling, P. J., Welch, D. E. and Schuler, R. S. (1999) *International Human Resource Management: Managing people in an international context*, 3rd edition. Cincinatti, South Western College, ITP

Ford, H. (2002) 'World of difference', *People Management*, 27 June: 38–40

Foss, N. J. (1997) 'On the rationales of corporate headquarters', *Industrial and Corporate Change*, 6 (2): 313–37

Ghoshal, S. and Gratton, L. (2002) 'Integrating the enterprise', *Sloan Management Review*, 44 (1): 31–8

Grant, R. M. (1996) 'Prospering in dynamically-competitive environments: organisational capability as knowledge integration', *Organization Science*, 7 (4): 375–87

Gratton, L. (2003) 'The humpty-dumpty effect: a view of a fragmented HR function', *People Management*, 9 (9): 18

Hansen, M. T., Nohria, N. and Tierney, T. (1999) 'What is your strategy for managing knowledge?', *Harvard Business Review*, 77 (2): 106–16

Harris, F. and de Chernatony, L. (2001) 'Corporate branding and corporate brand performance', *European Marketing Journal*, 35 (3/4): 441–56

Hunt, J. and Boxall, P. (1998) 'Are top human resource specialists strategic partners? Self-perceptions of a corporate elite', *International Journal of Human Resource Management*, 9 (5): 767–81

Kim, K., Park, J.-H. and Prescott, J. E. (2003) 'The global integration of business functions: a study of multinational businesses in integrated global industries', *Journal of International Business Studies*, 34: 327–44

Kostova, T. (1999) 'Transnational transfer of strategic organisational practices: a contextual perspective', *Academy of Management Review*, 24 (2): 308–24

Legge, K. (1995) *Human Resource Management: Rhetoric and realities*. London, Macmillan

Malbright, T. (1995) 'Globalisation of an ethnographic firm', *Strategic Management Journal*, 16: 119–41

Martin, G. and Beaumont, P. B. (1998) 'HRM and the diffusion of best practice', *International Journal of Human Resource Management*, 9 (4): 671–95

Martin, G. and Beaumont, P. (2001) 'Transforming multinational enterprises: towards a process model of strategic human resource management change', *International Journal of Human Resource Management*, 12 (8): 1234–50

Martin, G. and Hetrick, S. (2006) *Corporate Reputations, Branding and People Management*. Oxford, Butterworth-Heinemann

Michaels, E., Handfield-Jones, H. and Axelrod, B. (2001) *The War for Talent*. Boston, MA, Harvard Business School Press

Milsom, J. (2004) 'The growing importance of cross-cultural assessment', *Competency and Emotional Intelligence*, 11 (4): 19–22

Parkhe, A., Wasserman, S. and Ralston, D. A. (2006) 'New frontiers in network theory development', *Academy of Management Review*, 31 (3): 560–8

Pucik, V. (1992) 'Globalisation and human resource management', in V. Pucik, N. Tichy and C. K. Barnett (eds) *Globalizing Management*. New York, Wiley

Purcell, J. and Ahlstrand, B. (1994) *Human Resource Management in the Multi-Divisional Company*. Oxford, Oxford University Press

Ryan, A. M., Wiechmann, D. and Hemingway, M. (2003) 'Designing and implementing global staffing systems: Part II. Best practices', *Human Resource Management*, 42 (1): 85–94

Salancik, G. R. (1995) 'Wanted: a good network theory of the organisation', *Administrative Science Quarterly*, 40: 345–9

Scullion, H. and Collings, D. G. (eds) (2006) *Global Staffing*. Abingdon, Routledge

Scullion, H. and Starkey, K. (2000) 'In search of the changing role of the corporate human resource function in the international firm', *International Journal of Human Resource Management*, 11 (6): 1061–81

Smilansky, J. (2004) *The Systematic Management of Executive Talent*. Wimbledon, CIPD

Sparrow, P. R. (1997) 'Organisational competencies: creating a strategic behavioural framework for selection and assessment', in N. Anderson and P. Herriot (eds) *International Handbook of Selection and Assessment*. Chichester, John Wiley

Sparrow, P. R. (2006) 'Knowledge management in global organisations', in G. Stahl and I. Björkman (eds) *Handbook of Research in International HRM*. London, Edward Elgar

Sparrow, P. R. (2007) 'Globalisation of HR at function level: four case studies of the international recruitment, selection and assessment process', *International Journal of HRM*

Sparrow, P. R. and Brewster, C. (2006) 'Human resource management in international context', in C. L. Cooper and R. Burke (eds) *The Human Resources Revolution: Research and practice*. London, Elsevier

Sparrow, P. R., Brewster, C. and Harris, H. (2004) *Globalizing HR*. London, Routledge

Stroh, L. and Caligiuri, P. M. (1998) 'Increasing global competitiveness through effective people management', *Journal of World Business*, 33 (1): 1–16

Tregaskis, O., Glover, L. and Ferner, A. (2005) *International HR Networks In Multinational Companies*. London, CIPD

Ulrich, D. (2000) 'From eBusiness to eHR', *Human Resource Planning*, 20 (3): 12–21

Ulrich, D. and Lake, D. (1990) *Organisation Capability: Competing from the inside out*. New York, Wiley

Universum (2005) *Employer Branding: Global best practices 2005*. Stockholm, Universum

Woodall, J. and Winstanley, D. (2000) 'Winning hearts and minds: ethical issues in human resource development', in D. Winstanley and J. Woodall (eds) *Ethical Issues in Contemporary Human Resource Management*. Basingstoke, Macmillan

Worldlink (2005) 'Competencies still in vogue, new survey shows', *Worldlink*, 15 (2): 1

INDEX

Diagrams and tables are in italics.

Students

Save 20% when buying direct from the CIPD using the Student Discount Scheme

The Chartered Institute of Personnel and Development (CIPD) is the leading publisher of books and reports for personnel and training professionals, students, and for all those concerned with the effective management and development of people at work.

The CIPD offers ALL students a 20% discount on our textbooks.

To claim your discount, and to see a full list of titles available, visit **www.cipd.co.uk/bookstore** or call **0870 800 3366** quoting '2000'.

Order online at www.cipd.co.uk/bookstore or call us on 0870 800 3366

NB This offer is exclusive of any other offers from the CIPD and applies to CIPD Publishing textbooks only.

The Chartered Institute of Personnel and Development is the leading publisher of books and reports for personnel and training professionals, students and all those concerned with the effective management and development of people at work.

Also from CIPD Publishing . . .

Human Resource Management in an International Context

Rosemary Lucas, Ben Lupton and Hamish Mathieson

This text considers how human resource management, policies and practices manifest themselves in organisations internationally. The text moves beyond the large organisation or multinational corporation by offering discussion about, and providing practical examples from, a wide range of organisations including public and private, small and medium-sized enterprises, and manufacturing or service-based organisations.

Order your copy now online at www.cipd.co.uk/bookstore or call us on 0870 800 3366

Rosemary Lucas is Professor of Employment Relations and Director of the Centre for Hospitality and Employment Research (CHER), Manchester Metropolitan University Business School (MMUBS).

Ben Lupton is Principal Lecturer in Human Resource Management, Manchester Metropolitan University Business School (MMUBS).

Hamish Mathieson is Senior Lecturer in Employment Relations, Manchester Metropolitan University Business School (MMUBS).

Published 2007	1 84398 109 2	Paperback	488 pages

The Chartered Institute of Personnel and Development is the leading publisher of books and reports for personnel and training professionals, students and all those concerned with the effective management and development of people at work.

Also from CIPD Publishing . . .

Cross-Cultural Management

in Work Organisations

Ray French

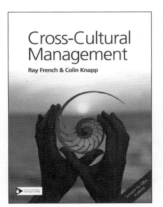

This textbook offers up-to-date and comprehensive coverage of cross-cultural social relations in the work setting. The text provides an evaluation of existing frameworks for understanding cross-cultural differences as they affect workplace behaviour and the management of people. It also examines the inter-cultural competencies needed by managers who deal with employees from different cultural backgrounds, and points to the implications of an awareness of cultural difference for HRM strategies and policies.

Order your copy now online at www.cipd.co.uk/bookstore or call us on 0870 800 3366

Ray French is a Principal Lecturer at the University of Portsmouth Business School, where he teaches in the area of organisational behaviour, managing business relationships, human resource management and cross-cultural awareness for managers. His deep interest in cross-cultural aspects of work and organisation is rooted in his own mixed cultural upbringing and has been reinforced in his career, specifically through close involvement with business courses taught across Europe and in Asia.

Published 2007	1 84398 149 1	Paperback	256 pages

The Chartered Institute of Personnel and Development is the leading publisher of books and reports for personnel and training professionals, students and all those concerned with the effective management and development of people at work.

Also from CIPD Publishing . . .

Managing Diversity

2nd edition
Pearn Kandola

Managing diversity is not just socially desirable, but a driver of organisational competitiveness. This unique and comprehensive set of tools shows you how to ensure that diversity - the vision and policies - gain organisation acceptance and form part of the overall strategic framework that supports long-term business goals.

For those starting from scratch, the tools provide a complete programme for tackling the whole process. For those with more experience of managing a diversity programme an action grid offers a simple diagnostic method to help identify your strengths and weaknesses - with relevant tools to improve performance in specific areas.

All the tools have been thoroughly tried and tested and incorporate best practice and leading-edge approaches. They are designed to be easy to follow and practical so you can achieve measurable results.

Contents list
- Introduction
- Defining Diversity for your Organisation
- Developing Diversity Policies and Strategies

- Gaining Buy-in
- Conducting a Diversity Audit
- Delivering Diversity Training

Order your copy now online at www.cipd.co.uk/bookstore or call us on 0870 800 3366

Founded in 1984, **Pearn Kandola** is a specialist Occupational Psychology practice and the largest group of non test publishing psychologists in the UK and Ireland. They currently employ over 50 staff, 30 of whom are qualified psychologists.

| Published April 2006 | ISBN: 978 184398 130 5 | Pages: 416 |

The Chartered Institute of Personnel and Development is the leading publisher of books and reports for personnel and training professionals, students and all those concerned with the effective management and development of people at work.

LIBRARY, UNIVERSITY OF CHESTER